Rogues

And

Redeemers

ALSO BY GERARD O'NEILL

BLACK MASS
The True Story of an Unholy Alliance Between
the FBI and the Irish Mob
(WITH DICK LEHR)

THE UNDERBOSS
The Rise and Fall of a Mafia Family
(WITH DICK LEHR)

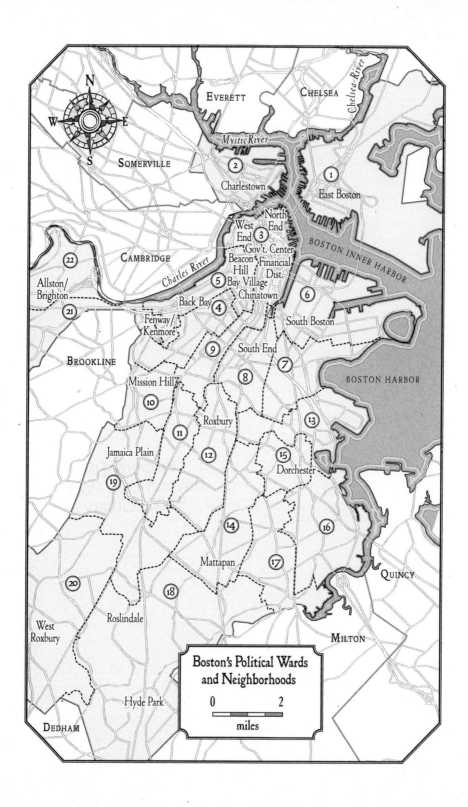

Boston's Political Wards
and Neighborhoods

0   2
miles

ROGUES

AND

REDEEMERS

When Politics Was King in Irish Boston

Gerard O'Neill

CROWN PUBLISHERS / NEW YORK

Published in the United States by Crown Publishers,
an imprint of the Crown Publishing Group,
a division of Random House, Inc., New York.
www.crownpublishing.com

CROWN and the Crown colophon are registered trademarks of Random House, Inc.

Library of Congress Cataloging-in-Publication Data
O'Neill, Gerard.
    Rogues and redeemers / Gerard O'Neill.—1st ed.
        p. cm.
    Includes bibliographical references.
    1. Irish Americans—Massachusetts—Boston—Politics and government.
2. Politicians—Massachusetts—Boston—History. 3. Irish Americans—
Massachusetts—Boston—History. 4. Politicians—Family relationships—
Massachusetts—Boston—History. 5. Political culture—Massachusetts—
Boston—History. 6. Boston (Mass.)—Politics and government. 7. Politicians—
Massachusetts—Boston—Biography. 8. Irish Americans—Massachusetts—
Boston—Biography. 9. Boston (Mass.)—Biography. I. Title.
F73.9.I6O54   2012
974.4'61—dc22   2010053207

ISBN 978-0-307-40536-4
eISBN 978-0-307-95279-0

Printed in the United States of America

Book design by Barbara Sturman
Map by Joe LeMonnier
Jacket design by Dan Rembert
Jacket photographs: skyline image, © Ed Jenner/The Boston Globe via Getty Images;
James M. Curley, © Edison Farrand/The Boston Globe via Getty Images; Kevin White, ©
Charles Dixon/The Boston Globe via Getty Images; John F. Fitzgerald, © The Boston Globe
via Getty Images; John B. Hynes, courtesy of The Boston Globe via Getty Images

10 9 8 7 6 5 4 3 2 1

First Edition

To
Charles Michael O'Neill of the Beara Peninsula in Ireland,
for getting us here

To
my wife Janet, Brian, Shane, Patty, Kylie, and Jack O'Neill

Contents

List of Illustrations

Rogues
And
Redeemers

Famine's Progeny

EARLY ÉMIGRÉS

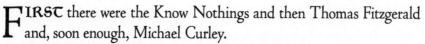

FIRST there were the Know Nothings and then Thomas Fitzgerald and, soon enough, Michael Curley.

The two farmers from the west of Ireland might as well have landed on the far side of the moon as in Boston in the middle of the nineteenth century. Along the dilapidated waterfront, Boston was a hostile and miasmic place where the official government policy was to give Irish immigrants nothing and then keep them down for good measure. They had fled starvation's aftermath when the lifeline potato crop turned foul back home. But they both found only squalor down the pier in an alien world.

Tom Fitzgerald bore the brunt of both ends of the journey, growing up as the oldest son on a potato farm, working the fields from the age of seven and sleeping on a mud floor in a one-room cottage on leased land. Like all Catholics in Ireland under British law, the Fitzgeralds could not vote, hold office, own land, or even go to school. He would face many of the same privations as a young man in Boston as the nativist Know Nothing Party sought to ban the Irish from voting or holding state or city jobs.

And he knew the famine all too well, struggling on his own in the boggy village of Bruff just south of the River Shannon after his mother and sisters and younger brother had emigrated. All alone, he would make a futile last stand against the blight into the 1850s before finally letting go of the exhausting rhythms of an ancient rural life.

Fitzgerald saw the worst of it and stayed until the pernicious blight had burned itself out. He was twenty-three when the fungus struck Ireland's staple crop. The potato wasn't just a steady diet; it was a way of life. It was cheap as dirt, grew like wildfire, and was easy to cook. Houses were surrounded by it—fields of three squares a day for man, woman, and child—boiled or mashed for breakfast, lunch, and dinner, plus leftovers for the livestock. Even in normal times, the interim between the end of the winter's supply and the digging for the new crop was known as "Hungry July." Overlooked by history is the diversity of some Irish farms of the day, which also yielded a variety of grains as well as grazing for cows and sheep. But those crops were part of the English oppression and strictly for the export trade—even as the tenant farmers were starving.

The emigration years unfolded with the fatal forbearance of the stoic Irish patient who endures in the belief that the malady will pass and there's no need to bother the doctor because tomorrow will surely be better. The fungus got a third of the potato crop in 1845, but the feeling was that the next year would be different. And that it was—a wipeout. Then, by 1847, the thinking was, nothing could be worse. Maybe not, but it was just as bad—a vicious replication that battered a moribund populace. The third year of the famine was a biblical scourge, compounded by one of the worst winters on record, with snow starting in November, followed by weeks of hard rain and icy gales. People were dying where they fell in the lanes and alleys and front yards.

An eerie pall beset the west as a gregarious people fell silent in the face of starvation and abandonment. One elderly woman wrote in a memoir about how a clamorous countryside came to a dead stop. "Sport and pastimes disappeared. Poetry, music, and dancing stopped. They lost and forgot them all. The famine killed everything."

Despite several humanitarian efforts in the United States, the prostrate countryside of Ireland left the leaders of Great Britain unmoved. They downplayed the devastation as a passing pestilence and held hard to the quasi-religion of supply and demand. The export trade went on as if tens of thousands weren't dying of starvation where they stood. In June 1847 the British government declared the famine over, even though it was at its zenith, shutting down its limited public works program, ending the only jobs—and hope—for 700,000 Irishmen. Things were so bad that mothers and children died on the roadside after retching the grass that was left to eat. The potato plague would linger for years, and for most of those subsisting along the west coast it was emigrate or die. Tom Fitzgerald's mother and siblings joined the exodus while he stubbornly struggled on.

Even before the famine Irish arrived, Anglo-Saxon Boston was predisposed against all things Catholic and steeped in anti-papacy rhetoric that ran deep into its colonial past, a time when a woman was hanged as a witch on Boston Common for saying the rosary in Gaelic in front of a statue of Mary. After centuries of austere service to a fierce God, the natives recoiled at what they saw as the ostentatious superstition of Catholic rites. Even someone as reflective as John Adams reacted with visceral disdain when he happened upon a Mass, finding it "most awful and affecting, the poor wretches, fingering their beads, chanting Latin, not a word of which they understood; their holy water; their crossing themselves perpetually; their bowing and kneeling and genuflecting."

And yet they came. As early as 1830, there was an uptick in Irish immigration to Boston, mostly tenant farmers from the western counties. Suddenly, while the migration was still manageable, the number of Irish had doubled to eight thousand and the alarm was sounded. An overheated artisan named Samuel F. B. Morse urged his peers to the ramparts against the newcomers: "Awake! To your posts! Place your guards. Shut your gates." And it wasn't just the upper crust that rejected the immigrants. In equal measure, it was the lamplighters, stablemen, and gardeners who feared displacement by job-hungry Irishmen.

Indeed, with the anti-Catholic fervor stoked by Presbyterian firebrands like Lyman Beecher at the Hanover Street Church and sustained by vitriol from Protestant newspapers and journals, protests spilled from the pulpits to the streets. In 1834 a mob invaded the Ursuline Convent in Charlestown and, after harassing nuns to higher ground, burned the building to cinders. Three years later a Yankee fire brigade returning from a call got tangled up with an Irish funeral procession in the city's lower end where the immigrants had congregated. It set off a cascading brawl that, with reinforcements called in by both sides, lasted for two hours. At that, they didn't punch themselves out, but only stopped when the state militia arrived. And it was just a warm-up for the immigration battles that followed famine's ill wind.

A decade later, when things had turned truly dire and desperate families like the Fitzgeralds flocked to Cork or Liverpool, Boston realized that its slowly growing Irish outpost along the waterfront had become a beachhead.

What had been a steady trickle became a tidal wave. There were only about one thousand Irish Catholics in Boston as the nineteenth century began. In 1830, there were eight thousand. But by 1847 the Irish population had surged to about 35,000.

The height of the famine was the year the dam burst in Boston. While not all newcomers stayed within the city limits, with many settling in abutting "Irish" towns, some 37,000 poured ashore. Most were sick, all were unskilled, and none had any place else to go. On just one spring day—April 10, 1847—one thousand swamped the harried port of Boston. The city was forced to build a screening hospital in the harbor on Deer Island and put an immigration station on the Long Wharf entryway. Between 1846 and 1850, 112,664 immigrants passed through the port, nearly four times the number from the first half of the decade.

By the early 1850s, horrified natives realized the Irish constituted one-fourth of the town and had it surrounded. They were the bulk of 64,000 foreign-born residents in the 1860 census, a total that didn't include encircling Irish in Dorchester, Charlestown, and Roxbury, which weren't annexed by the city until the 1870s. One of the outlier Irish families were the Curleys, who lived near the Southampton Street dump in Roxbury Neck.

In the famine decade ending in 1855, most of the 2.1 million people who left Ireland headed for America. From the beginning, East Coast Boston was a logical destination because it had a small Irish population and it was also a mail port for British shipping lines, allowing them to do double duty. The extra profit didn't go into the accommodations. In a city under siege, the harbormaster knew an immigrant ship was offshore by the stench riding the east wind. Usually about forty of six hundred passengers had already succumbed in the petri-dish hellhole belowdecks.

In 1847 two ships were turned away because of diseased passengers. Port officials banished the *Seraph* out of Cork to St. John, New Brunswick. And even the British brig *Mary*, also from Cork, had so many diseased steerage passengers that newspapers reported port officials would not "suffer them to be landed." It led to a brief scuffle between emaciated passengers and sailors who had new orders to set sail for Halifax, Nova Scotia. Yet Boston stayed the "first parish over" for the simple reason that family was already there.

In stratified Boston, there was a sharp distinction drawn between sending relief ships to Cork and tending to the sick trudging down Long Wharf into the North End. By 1855, when more than 230,000 immigrants had decamped in Boston, the cultural divide was as permanent as the sun and the moon. The historian Oscar Handlin wrote that the lines were drawn so tightly around the North End that the newcomers were nearly invisible. He observed there was "no more contact" between the natives and the Irish "than if 3,000 miles of ocean rather than a wall of ideas stood between them." Either way, it was as if the famine Irish weren't there.

Even the fledgling Catholic newspaper, *The Pilot,* which had helped organize food drives for back home, urged those in Ireland to think twice about coming to Boston. The swelling welfare rolls and the recoiling of Beacon Hill Yankees merged into an exhortation to the desperate queuing up at Cork and Liverpool: land in Boston if you must, but head off immediately to western territories. The homily's bleak conclusion was that it was better to die in Ireland, on native soil, than succumb in a Boston slum.

And still they came.

Tom Fitzgerald was one of the last stragglers to come ashore, in 1853. Half of those who came before him were illiterate, and nearly all lacked a trade. Grown men arriving in the New World had a life expectancy of fourteen more years, owing mostly to industrial accidents. The median age of decedents was forty. And the Fitzgeralds would be staggered by the horrific childhood mortality rate, which took a son and two daughters. Well after the fact, it was found that nearly half of those who died in Boston between 1850 and 1855 were children under five. There was no neighborhood breakdown, but it stands to reason most of them were in the infested North End.

Yet, a generation later, one of Tom Fizgerald's nine surviving sons would become mayor, and the Yankees would cry that a bigoted Irish voting bloc had done them in at the polls. Out of the decrepit waterfront, the once-shanty Fitzgerald clan arose, shaking off decades of discrimination and deprivation to produce an endearing hurdy-gurdy character who made patronage an art form and passed on his genetic affinity for politics to those that followed.

In the second generation after him, the mayor's oldest surviving grandson learned the Boston rules so well that they carried him to the White House. John Fitzgerald Kennedy couldn't have been more unlike Grandpa—a refined Harvard man who captured the country with his élan and eloquence. But he combined lessons about old-time retail politics with an impeccable organization that forged a singular style which is as remembered as much as any of his accomplishments.

The bloodline began with Honey Fitz. He was the first brand name in an era utterly dominated by Michael Curley's youngest son, James. They became the founding families that yielded a long line of Irish pols who dominated Boston for nearly a century.

Fitzgerald and Curley were the vanguard of a story about the making of the most Irish city in America, and one that my own family knew, first at a distance and then firsthand.

In 1849, as the famine was slowly fading, my great-grandfather Charles Michael O'Neill followed his older brother, Denis, over from the devastated South of Ireland. Denis had come in through Boston the year before Charles entered via Quebec.

The traffic of that frantic time had some broad patterns: Three of every four immigrants got themselves to Liverpool's bustling harbor to head off for Australia or North America, and half of those going to the United States went to New York City. But there was still a brisk business from Ireland's small coastal cities, with more than five thousand round trips made during the six years of famine pandemonium, many of them to Canadian ports. From beginning to end, 1845–55, about 1.5 million sailed to the United States while 340,000 embarked for Canada and the rest of the exodus landed in Britain and Australia. In all, about one fourth of Ireland's pre-famine population went overseas. The shipowners were hardly the only profiteers. The mass movement of tenant farmers led to an agrarian upheaval in the old country with the rich getting richer. Wealthy farmers, many of them Catholic, moved quickly to consolidate the suddenly vacant land. By 1851 the number of those holding thirty or more acres had increased 16.5 percent, while those holding between one and five acres had decreased by 52 percent.

With all the ships heading in all the directions, there was no more perilous route than the one to Quebec. It had one particular virtue—it was the cheapest way to North America, costing about ten dollars instead of fifteen.

By far the worst year for transatlantic travel was 1847, when the demand was highest following two years of savage starvation and when the ships were at their most unsanitary. In Ireland, the apex of the immigration became a dilemma known as Black '47—the worst time to stay and the worst time to go.

Reports from Quebec were beyond bleak. The famine ships elsewhere were first-class passage compared to the vessels pulling into Grosse-Île in the St. Lawrence River. They arrived with as many dead as alive, and became known as "the coffin ships." The carnage was ascribed to "ship fever," but it was actually typhoid from contaminated food and water. It was so bad that even in the laissez-faire seafaring world, higher sanitation standards were imposed at both ends of the Canadian route.

It's probable that word of plagued passages prompted Denis O'Neill to wait until 1848 to come in through Boston instead of the quarantine station at Grosse-Île. By the time Charles and his seventy-five-year-old father got the money together a year later, they must have known conditions had improved on the Canadian routes, but had worsened for Irishmen in inhospitable Boston. With limited funds, it's likely they made their way on foot to Cork's deep harbor at Queenstown, which offered a regular route to Quebec.

Throughout the diaspora, Quebec was a way station rather than a destination. Once there, Irish immigrants confronted a foreign language and a flat job market. Nearly everyone moved on, usually through Montreal and then south to the United States. By 1849 Canada had become a favored route for Catholics forced off big estates in the southwest of Ireland, when it became cheaper for English landlords to pay cut-rate fares for the evicted than increase tenant taxes for those who stayed. Charles O'Neill may have had a subsidy to flee a disintegrating country where the British consistently refused to distribute surplus grain stored in warehouses. A character in one of George Bernard Shaw's plays corrected a woman who said her father had died in the famine. "No," Malone told Violet, "The Starvation. When a country is full of food and exporting it, there can be no famine." In Thomas Gallagher's "Paddy Lament," there is this grim tally for one of the worst years: four hundred thousand died of famine or related diseases while the British government had 17 million pounds sterling worth of grain, cattle, pigs, flour, eggs, and poultry shipped home. It was enough to feed the six million tenant-farmer and farm-laborer families in Ireland twice over. Charles O'Neill had little choice but to export himself and his aging father on a journey that landed them on a slow barge to Montreal and ended on a final trek into Vermont.

Father and son hailed from the Beara Peninsula on the Kerry side of the border with County Cork. It seems Charles met his wife on the passage, and they all landed as itinerant immigrants in Barnet, a small town in northern Vermont where they probably slept in barns before Charles and Mary O'Leary had their first son. The young family met up with Denis in Rhode Island before they all moved to a "Kerry" town in bustling Connecticut, settling in Sprague, just north of New London. According to the 1860 census, they lived next door to Denis O'Neill's widow on a street where most of the residents still spoke Gaelic. When Charles signed his naturalization in New York with an X, he surely embraced the necessity of renouncing allegiance to foreign governments, especially that of Queen Victoria, who had presided over the famine and Ireland's bursting warehouses. Charles and Mary's sons had truncated childhoods, all working in cotton mills by their early teens.

Their second son, Dennis, migrated to Boston and married Catherine McGee, a domestic from West Roxbury. They first settled in Jamaica Plain and had five surviving children, my father, Richard, being the youngest. They always had a potato patch in the backyard, storing their spuds in the cellar. Richard married M. Claire Sweeney of Allston, whose parents died in our suburban house. My grandparents on both sides told their children of the lasting hurt of the early era, and were especially mindful of its English roots, both here and in Ireland.

After the Irish deluge in Boston, it took decades for the city to settle wearily into camps where everyone's mind stayed unchanged but their mouths remained shut.

That vague rapprochement was unthinkable when the Fitzgeralds washed ashore at midcentury into a sneering plutocracy that held all the cards—education, jobs, wealth, and refined roots extending back to the Pilgrims. The Irish became Boston's instant proletariat, a boundless source of dirty-faced labor—ditch-diggers and hod carriers and steve-dores. In short order, they would double the population of staid, homo-geneous old Boston. The surge made their reluctant host all the more class-conscious as the Yankees circled the wagons around Beacon Hill and its commercial lifeline along State Street. The chafing wasn't just with the old families. To the Protestant peddler, the flinty and thrifty archetype of that era, hard work and sobriety were the maxims of daily life, and there was a resounding cultural clash with hard-drinking, underemployed Irishmen.

It wasn't long before some Irish began exploiting their own through the "padrone" system, in which Irish agents of Yankee employers tapped into the cheap labor pool with take-it-or-leave-it terms of fifteen hours for fifty cents a day. The workers and their families were herded into sheds and stables and cellars along the waterfront, which were often flooded with backed-up sewage. One cellar was home to thirty-nine immigrants. A survey found fifty working toilets in 118 houses. They were strung to-gether into "reeking paddyvilles" that became America's first mass slum. The Boston census of 1870 found that two of every three day laborers were Irish.

Entertainment for the Irish ranged from the primitive to the ghoul-ish, such as the rat pit in the cellar of Barney's Bar in the North End, where men bet on how many rats a dog could kill in a specified number of seconds. Egress was a trapdoor, and the arena was a small circle enclosed by a four-foot-high wall with spectators seated around it—except for the far end, where Barney presided, standing by a flour barrel full of rats. Bets down, he'd dump twenty rats inside the enclosure and then unleash Flora, the neighborhood champion, who devoured them in twelve seconds.

These early immigrants were much less than an underclass, deep at the bottom of Boston's pecking order. The historian Jack Beatty drew them in broad strokes—they were submerged by the most distinct and entrenched upper class in American annals, populated by heroes of the Revolution like John Adams and by such world-renowned literati as Ralph Waldo Emerson.

The bedraggled newcomers stood on excrement. Most came from the lowest rung in woebegone Ireland—the rural farmers who worked a patch of land owned by absentee landlords and suffered the most when the potatoes rotted in undulating profusion. The farming class was trapped in the cellar of Irish society, and sociological studies show that many took to whiskey as an anesthetized way of life that persisted in Boston. When the diaspora was only four years under way in 1849, liquor licenses in Boston had increased by one third to 1,200. A year later, two thirds of the grog shops were Irish-owned, most of them in and around the North End. Whiskey sold for thirty-eight cents a gallon. Natives made a not-unfounded connection between cheap whiskey and a 1,700-percent jump in assault cases.

In fact, mortified Yankees found themselves stepping over or dodging drunken immigrants in the once safe and sedate streets of Boston. It became the core of the Yankees' overly broad case against the Irish—that they were shiftless drunkards who were dead weight on the tax base, now stretched to pay ever-expanding police and fire and hospital budgets. The discrimination showed itself in a raft of newspaper ads similar to the one for "a good, reliable woman" to care for a two-year-old in Brookline, then a Yankee enclave just outside Boston. The nanny would not have any washing or ironing duty, but the job had a pedigree requirement: "Positively no Irish need apply." Similar signs were strategically placed near some downtown-shop entrances, but the enduring sentiment was most commonly found in newspapers. It became so commonplace that it soon had an acronym: NINA.

The historian Francis Russell described a segregation as stark as that in Selma, Alabama, a century later. "The Yankee epigone, appalled by the Celtic locust-swarm," withdrew to his redoubt of Beacon Hill and locked down political control over a suddenly amorphous city and grasped tight the financial reins.

In a polarized Boston, the clashing views of politics became a bloody demarcation around City Hall. To the White Anglo Saxon Protestants (WASPs), who had ruled with stern hegemony for two centuries, government was to enforce decorum and promote commerce—in short, law and order with low taxes.

But to the famine Irish, who had come from rural anarchy where evictions were commonplace, justice a joke, and education unobtainable, politics became everything—the only way out of poverty. They had a short policy agenda as well: jobs and food.

Despite dim prospects, the resolutely rural people billowed into America's nascent cities on the cusp of the industrial age, digging ditches in Boston, plying the mines in Pennsylvania, and pushing the railroads toward Chicago. In the decade after the potato failed, the Irish population in Boston had exploded from one in fifty to one in four.

Thomas Fitzgerald and Rosanna Cox were at the ledger's forefront, having nine surviving children. A farmer at heart, Thomas had joined some cousins north of Boston, but had failed again to make a go of farming rocky soil, this time at six dollars a month. A broad-shouldered and ruddy man, he reluctantly joined his go-getter younger brother in the hurly-burly of the North End of Boston. The man known as Cocky Tom began slum life as a fish peddler working the waterfront's narrow streets. He also found Rossana there, and they married at the height of the poisonous reign of the American Party and its "Know Nothing" vendetta against Irish Catholics.

Fitzgerald and his brother opened a liquor and grocery store, and Thomas moved his burgeoning family upstairs from it. While Thomas dodged the epidemic of industrial accidents, his family didn't escape the calamities of the waterfront. His first daughter, Ellen, died in a cholera outbreak in 1870, and his wife died at forty-eight after struggling to give birth to a stillborn daughter. But, all things considered, Thomas was one of the lucky ones. He lived a long life for the era, dying at sixty-three of pneumonia after seeing most of his sons into manhood. He left a robust estate for the day: $18,162, nearly all of it from three rental properties in the North End.

By the 1860s, when the Fitzgerald clan dominated their neighborhood along Hanover Street, the North End was already divided into Irish villages along county lines from the old country. There were so many Galway families on Copp's Hill that it was renamed Connemara Hill. Donegal émigrés congregated along the Charles River, and it became known as Donegal Square. The long strip from the Old North Church to Faneuil Hall was a mix of Cork, Kerry, and Limerick. The county lines were as rigid in Boston as in the old country, with the Fitzgerald household aware of it from an early age through the story of Mrs. Donovan of Galway reminding her construction foreman husband every morning not to put any Cork men to work that day.

While the Fitzgerald apartment over the grocery store burst with young boys, all a year apart, the tail end of the Irish onslaught brought fourteen-year-old Michael Curley and his mother to a colony of Galway castaways down by the mud flats of lower Roxbury. Though he had survived the height of the famine as an infant, there was nothing for a teenager in the depressed west of Ireland in 1864. As the Civil War wound down in America and new industry took hold, there was a glimmer of hope in Boston. Within five years Curley had married a Connemara girl, Sarah Clancy. With the help of a ward boss, he found work as a hod carrier.

But there would be no estate left by Michael Curley. There was not even a death notice in any newspaper when he died at age thirty-four. He and his young bride had lived between thin walls in a ramshackle tenement along Roxbury Neck, just off the South Bay and downwind from the Southampton Street dump. Short and wiry, Curley worked construction jobs, but, like so many in the first wave of immigrants, he died on a job that didn't have a death benefit to help bury an employee. His frail wife, like so many others, made the fast transition from "widow woman" to cleaning lady to support two surviving sons, and became a steadfast centrifugal force in a neighborhood served by forty-four saloons. Mike Curley died when a blood vessel burst in his brain from lifting a curbstone from the ground to a tailboard. Later his son, James Michael, would tell his own son that his grandfather was buried with money from a wager he won by lifting the heavy stone that killed him.

But, as the Fitzgeralds and Curleys would be reminded frequently, no one had invited them, and they could make do or move on. The first-wave immigrants were so soundly spurned that their descendants remained unassimilated for a generation, as indigestible as uncooked brussels sprouts. Newcomer and native became locked in a smoldering enmity that molded the Boston Irish in a unique way. They possess a fatalistic certainty that nothing is on the level, leavened a bit by a mordant sense of humor that has both sustained and held them back. The downside to a steady diet of waggish chatter is that even the brightest among them tend to pull up short of a full effort as something unsustainable and perhaps even foolhardy. They bear the double scars of a discriminatory society and later the inequities of patronage.

Around the time that Thomas Fitzgerald joined relatives north of Boston, anti-immigrant fervor was sinking deep roots in Massachusetts. It gained most traction among the working men in the WASP-dominated Whig party. The tradesmen viewed the Irish Catholics as lazy louts, but began to fear them as a rival voting bloc. The nativists became part of a national movement against immigrants that quickly evolved into a paranoid sect steeped in secret handshakes and passwords. They became the "Know Nothing" party because of their pledge to withhold even the slightest of information from any inquiring outsider. The answer to all questions about their purpose named them for good: "I know nothing."

Fueled by anti-papal fervor, the Know Nothing movement swept along the immigrant-heavy East Coast, taking power in Pennsylvania and running the table in Massachusetts. The party was anti-Catholic (if antislavery) to the core, but it was also accelerated by resentment within the Protestant working class against the self-serving Brahmin aristocracy that held profits tightly within bloodlines. The tail began wagging the dog, with labor laws rising from Protestant workers on the factory floor.

Nowhere was the Know Nothing movement's might felt more than in Massachusetts, when its candidates, running under the American Party banner, took all but a handful of legislative seats and all the state-wide offices including the governor's chair and the mayor's seat in Boston. It would be a short-circuited power surge that became a historical footnote to the rapidly ascending Republican Party of Abraham Lincoln. But Know Nothing sentiments held the ever-expanding Irish population in Boston away from political office for three decades.

By the time Thomas Fitzgerald gave up on farming in Acton in 1856 to peddle fish in the streets of the North End, official policy in Massachusetts was to freeze the Irish out of public life. The legislature proposed that immigrants wait twenty-one years before getting the vote, and disbanded Irish militia and armories. It required that the King James Bible and Protestant hymns be used in public school, and impeded diocesan control over its own property. It sought to ban Catholics from public office because of their allegiance to a "foreign prince" in Rome.

The Irishman of the hour was Boston's Roman Catholic bishop John Fitzpatrick, who retreated but then made a stand in a small redoubt. He urged quiet retention of voting and limited political prerogatives, and counseled parishioners to stay low while the sectarian storm passed overhead. Abetted by the respect given an educated man by Brahmin Boston, he used astute footwork during the hostilities to keep the fat out of the fire. Fitzpatrick's hand on the tiller and inexperienced leadership in the American Party led to the sudden collapse of the movement after one searing term in the mid-1850s. The deep estrangement in Boston somehow never reached the boiling point of immigrant riots, as it did in Baltimore and Louisville.

By 1860 the slavery issue had become another flash point between zealous abolitionists in Boston and racially resentful Irish families struggling to survive in the cellars and hovels of the waterfront. With its readership constituting nearly one third of Boston's population of 177,840, the Catholic paper *The Pilot* was soon making acerbic note of how blacks in the South lived better than many families in the North End, and supported the Democrats' plan for a gradual amelioration in the South rather than armed intervention for the slaves. There were also caustic references to the hypocrisy of Know Nothings support of emancipation for slaves and deprivation for the Irish. The Irish ambivalence toward slavery lasted until Southern secession began in 1861. In Boston, the two Irish wards voted in vain against Lincoln while the rest of the city gave him rousing support. But the newcomers ultimately sided with pro-Union policies when it came to a call to arms.

While Know Nothing virulence had faded quickly, the anti-Catholic sentiment remained pervasive. The nativist press carefully chronicled the steady rise in crime in immigrant strongholds, and held the measurable squalor and incidence of disease against the slum dwellers, glancing past the city's open sewer beds and contaminated water. Referenda mandating literacy tests and two-year residency for voting were passed to keep Irish from the polls. It was duly noted in Irish neighborhoods that "fugitive Negroes" could vote after a one-year residency. Catholics were prohibited from burying their dead in public cemeteries. Visits by priests were curtailed at the South Boston Almshouse and the Deer Island House of Correction. Hundreds of destitute Irish in poorhouses and asylums were deported.

While the Know Nothings passed almost as fast as they came, giving way to the broader base of the Republican Party, the scorched earth of nativist "reform" left an indelible mark on the legendary Irish memory for slights. The rank prejudice of laws restricting voting rights and eligibility for public office was out there in broad daylight for all to see. And to remember.

Boston had become the stage for one of the most enduring cultural collisions in American history. Unlike other wistful émigrés, the Irish had nothing to go home to. In permanent exile, they stayed put, and the clash with Yankees of all stripes set the city's agenda for half a century.

The Civil War's aftermath led to gradual change for the Boston Irish. Things "improved" to the point where there could be open combat. Guy Fawkes Day, an English holiday that commemorated the execution of a Catholic caught trying to blow up Parliament, had a Boston counterpart known as Pope Day, which culminated with burning the pope in effigy. The celebration had progressed into a semi-ecumenical gang fight on the Common between young men from the Catholic North End and Protestants from the South End.

The freedom to bash each other in roughhouse fun also translated into an expanded job market. Postwar industrialization brought new jobs for unskilled workers in newly mechanized garment factories and textile mills and shoe shops that had once been reserved for craftsmen. By the end of the war, the Irish had entered some trade unions. There were long-term construction jobs during the two decades spent filling in Back Bay, a project that extended the Yankee bastion beyond Beacon Hill. After the war, some of the egregious voting restrictions were repealed by the Legislature, and Boston City Hospital let priests minister to their own.

But the Irish had been so soundly subjugated and had so few options, it took decades more for them to get organized and use their exponential numbers to put an Irishman in the mayor's chair. After the Know Nothings, the next thirty years saw both sides locked in an idiot's embrace of knee-jerk animosity. Whatever the Protestant farmers, small businessmen, and tradesmen wanted, the Irish were against. And there was simply nothing in the Republican Party for immigrant laborers, who flocked to the Democrats right up to the point of dissolving the Union to support slavery. From the beginning, the Irish were put off by high-minded reformers in both parties who promised to clean up city or state government. In the North End and South Boston, that simply meant fewer jobs for immigrants and more subsidies for factory owners or land grants to railroads or turncoat policemen to break strikes.

The antipathy remained a tough two-way street. Even as late as the end of the nineteenth century, the raw enmity still ran deep. The Boston Brahmin Henry Adams, scion to presidents and a Harvard historian, lamented to a friend that "poor Boston had run up against it in the form of its particular Irish maggot, rather lower than the Jew, but with more or less the same appetite for cheese."

In response, the ward-boss system of politics evolved slowly in Irish neighborhoods as a shadow government to combat the stacked deck at

City Hall—even if everyone knew the machine was dominated by saloon owners and contractors in search of cheap labor or City Hall connections. "Good" government meant one thing only: jobs. And for those with flair and boldness, politics was the way out. It needed no special training or pedigree. You just had to talk the talk better than the next guy. The voluble Irish could always do that.

But even with booming numbers changing the landscape, there was no overnight coup in Boston. For one thing, organized insurrection was not part of the Irish makeup. Back home, the history of rebellion was that the rebels were always outmaneuvered and frequently betrayed. If they were raucous in the North End pubs, they knew how to tiptoe around power, with the first batch of elected officeholders deferential in practice if not oratory. Thoroughly subjugated for nearly fifty years, the Boston Irish were never able to coalesce into a conventional big-city machine like those that took over New York and Chicago. Everyone looked out for number one as new, smaller wounds simply replaced old ones. There was bravado at election time in the Irish wards, but everyone knew who owned the utility companies and their limited supply of low-level jobs. It would take the second generation to find its strength in birth rates.

But the trend was clear, with numbers telling the tale. Between 1860 and 1880, Boston's population had doubled to 363,000, half from continuing immigration and half from annexation of inner communities. When the Know Nothings swept to power at midcentury, there were twelve wards. Two decades later there were twenty-five.

Slowly and surely, a citywide network emerged. In the beginning, the closest thing to a ward boss who could herd bumptious Irish neighborhoods into a cohesive political force was Patrick Maguire. He was an early émigré who first landed in Prince Edward Island in 1838, where he was a printer before moving to Boston at age fourteen. He got into real estate and made enough to buy his own stridently Irish Catholic newspaper, *The Republic*. He personified the sharply drawn divide between all things Irish and all things Republican. He became president of the Democratic City Committee that handpicked candidates with the singular platform of "Jobs for Micks."

In the 1870s, after a Democratic Yankee mayor lost at the ballot box because of Irish hires in the police department, Maguire bided his time to let the rising tide lift the Hibernian boat. He recruited another early Irish immigrant and kindred spirit who had come to Boston at age five, about the same time as Maguire. Hugh O'Brien was also an apprentice printer before buying his own publication. As a young man, O'Brien acquired a dry financial publication called *The Shipping and Commercial List* that nevertheless became an important resource in a seaport city. He was known for competent efficiency, and was first elected to public office as an alderman in 1875, where his conscientious work ethic made its mark. Maguire saw him as a comer, and his committee endorsed O'Brien for mayor in the early 1880s; this was quickly followed by an endorsement in *The Republic*. In turn, O'Brien was opposed in the Yankee paper of record, the *Transcript*, and denounced from Protestant pulpits. He was narrowly defeated, but rebounded to succeed a lackluster Republican in 1884. He had out-Yankeed his opponent by running on tax cuts and balanced budgets.

It would take another decade of consolidation before another Irishman became mayor. Patrick Collins had to be cajoled into taking the job after serving as a Democratic congressman and diplomat in the Grover Cleveland administration as consul general in London. He arrived in Boston as a four-year-old with his widowed mother after his father had died of pneumonia in Cork County in 1848. Collins had a Horatio Alger climb to the top of his profession, rising from grade-school dropout and upholstery apprentice to a place in the Harvard Law School. His fatherless family was so commonplace that one Bostonian of the time viewed Irishmen as the "perishing class" and noted how rare it was to encounter any Irishmen old enough to have gray hair.

Collins's hair was a distinguished slate by the time he was mayor. In his two terms from 1901 to 1905, he received Republican support and business coterie approval. He would die in office and be damned by faint praise for fighting extravagance in city government.

It took sixty years after the first famine boats arrived off Long Wharf before a Boston-born ghetto Irishman—running overtly as an Irishman and not a wannabe Yankee—was elected mayor. Remarkably enough, it was two full decades after the Irish population had exceeded that of the natives. But numbers weren't enough. A genuine candidate needed money and organization. The first one with the goods was John "Honey" Fitzgerald in 1906—Tom's third son, the smart one, who went to Boston Latin School and then Harvard Medical School for a while until his father died and he had to man the family business and oversee younger brothers. The new patriarch came out of the waterfront with his own agenda and not that of Brahmin businessmen.

Johnny Fitz's first real job as a boy in the 1870s was selling newspapers. After a while he earned his own spot on the corner of Park and Beacon Streets. He didn't know it, but he arrived there at the tail end of an extraordinary, even dazzling, era.

From the beginning of the nineteenth century through the Civil War, Boston was the center of trade in America, mostly from its fleet of sleek clipper ships that could get the goods back from the Far East faster than competitors. And then it moved into the industrial age, with Massachusetts the first state to develop the factory system.

The old families took wealth from the Asian trade and put it into manufacturing that put the cloth-making process under one roof, raw cotton to finished product. As well, Boston banks underwrote the pulsating spread of railroads, mills, and mines across the emerging country. But the Civil War, which brought such vindication to Boston's abolitionists, also marked the end of the city's primacy. The industrial age had raced away from the Puritans' city on a hill and galloped west. Boston became the auditor rather than the leader of the new prosperity. By 1880, export trade was 30 percent of what it had been before the war. The waterfront warehouses were falling apart, and the harbor was no longer a thoroughfare.

One measure of the retreat from the legendary verve of the Yankees was the rise of the family trust, through which scions could live off interest to maintain inherited households and keep up with Harvard tuitions. Over time, a tepid guardianship took hold of a once-vibrant center of commerce. The story of a cloistered complacency was famously captured when one Beacon Hill dowager exclaimed to another, "Why should I travel when I'm already here?"

Fitzgerald's contemporaneous cultural counterpart, albeit fictitious, was the eponymous protagonist of *The Late George Apley,* by John Marquand. Apley represented the apogee of all things Brahmin. He was "born" in a town house on Beacon Street and raised at arm's length in a repressed world of evening sherry and flinty commerce. George and Little Fitz were of the same time but different worlds. They lived two miles apart, but with vastly different lifestyles. Apley was born to a family that made its fortune in the China trade and later from the Lawrence mills and, finally, with worldly adventure and vitality lost for good, from staid banking.

While Fitzgerald struggled daily to make ends meet and hold a family of nine brothers together, the fictional Apley was in a more subtle ordeal, trapped in a programmed life of Harvard Yard and country houses in the suburbs and on the Maine coast. Fitzgerald married the love of his life, but Apley was forced into an arranged marriage within his own ranks. Fitzgerald was a fun-loving extrovert who was always losing things but always finding what he needed and forging his own way. In Apley's gilded world, everything was always in its correct place in the dining room and checkbook. He let himself be funneled into a leaden marriage and fell into the same kind of sterile and strained relationship with his son that he had with his father. Fitzgerald's children sat in his lap and lit up his life.

Apley's one defiant breakout was a brief love affair with an effusive Irish girl from South Boston who teased him as her "Back Bay dude." Her background included a farmer grandfather from Galway and a contractor father. Apley's parents were horrified by Mary Monahan, and sent George off with an aunt to visit the museums of Europe for the summer so he would forget her. The affair petered out when George returned to Harvard, but even his father wondered at the end of his life if his son would have been better off with Mary. In his dotage, George fell prey to an Irish blackmailer's scheme that was strikingly similar to the traps set expertly by real-life Boston rogue Daniel Coakley. Set up, Apley was "discovered" with a prostitute in a downtown hotel. The blackmailer was a distant cousin of the Monahans, and Mary helped George negotiate his way out of utter disgrace.

With no little irony, the same fate befell John Francis Fitzgerald.

Little Fitz was an exuberant campaigner whose signature stage number was leading rallies in a spirited rendition of "Sweet Adeline." High-energy chaos was his trademark. At the end of his first term, one tally of the peripatetic mayor's two years in office was 1,200 dinners, two hundred picnics, one thousand meetings, three thousand speeches, and five thousand girls danced with. But it was more than high spirits that kept him too long at one dance with one particular lady.

Toward the end of his second term in 1913, Tom Fitzgerald's third son was done in by Mike Curley's second son, with some help from the disreputable Dan Coakley. A black-bordered letter was delivered to the Fitzgerald home in Dorchester. It referred to a cigarette girl and warned of embarrassment to come.

When the Boston Irish came of age in politics they found two polar opposites pitted against each other. One was a short man and ambitious glad-hander with the high-pitched voice, who had five nicknames and pumped up crowds with sing-alongs. The other was a broad-shouldered man with a voice as sonorous as that of a Shakespearean actor, the *magna vox* of Ward 17, who mesmerized with golden oratory, a regal loner known as James Michael Curley. Never Jim.

Little Fitz, Fitzy, the Little General, Napoleon of the North End, Honey Fitz. He started many of his speeches by telling his county-conscious audience how he loved County Mayo because his dear dead mother came from Mayo. Or he loved County Cork for the same reason. Or was it Sligo? Fitzgerald's idea of a conversation was to buttonhole someone on the street for ten minutes of machine-gun chatter before dashing off with a parting salutation about how much he enjoyed their conversation. He was the master of shaking hands with one man while talking to another and smiling at a third.

But James Michael Curley thought Fitzgerald was an insipid stage Irishman, and that he and his mawkish supporters should be put on a fast boat back home to dear old Eire. Among other things, Fitzgerald was in his way and the combative Curley didn't mind saying so. He relished confronting hecklers. "You swine," he once challenged a crowd at a county fair. Another boisterous gathering in Southie got his jutted jaw and rolled-up sleeves; he called them pickpockets and crapshooters and milk-bottle thieves from the podium as he loosened his tie and took off his suit jacket.

One charmed with refrains of "Sweet Adeline," while the other would knee you in the groin. When the votes were finally there to control City Hall, it was a free-for-all in America's first city. Politics was not for the faint of heart. The rough-and-tumble was such that one candidate bragged about throwing a punch at the governor at Fenway Park while his opponent's rejoinder was that he swung and missed. And there was "Cyclone" Boneilli's campaign platform that bragged of his having the longest criminal record of anyone in the race. His challenge: "Go down to the Roxbury District Court and see for yourself." His opponent returned fire by taunting that they were only misdemeanors.

But Curley and Fitzgerald towered over all. Each would have his day in a new city shaped equally by America's original intelligentsia and by illiterate greenhorns from the West of Ireland.

The first full-dress battle was Little Fitz against a Harvard banker, each the product of a bifurcated place where class enmity became a staple of life. The playwright Eugene O'Neill could have been talking about Boston when he said that Ireland is a place where there's no present or future, but only the past happening over and over.

CHAPTER 2

Shawn A Boo

JOHN F. FITZGERALD

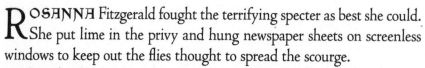

ROSANNA Fitzgerald fought the terrifying specter as best she could. She put lime in the privy and hung newspaper sheets on screenless windows to keep out the flies thought to spread the scourge.

But the disease's steady progress down Hanover Street that August was a medieval curse to the old-country Irish steeped in superstition and barricaded inside frail tenement walls. Rosanna was frantic to save her infant daughter in a time and place where babies died in less than a week from typhus or diphtheria. But in the North End of 1870, cholera was the fastest killer of all once its virulence seeped from untreated sewage into the water supply.

Like the plague in Europe's Dark Ages, the disease's progress was marked by black ribbons on the doors of stricken families. Despite Rosanna's primitive precautions, the dreaded insignia appeared at 435 Hanover Street after taking the most vulnerable in the household, Ellen Rosanna, named for her grandmother and mother. She died within hours after overwhelming diarrhea became shock. She was one of eighty deaths in twelve days.

The epidemic had followed a lethal heat wave that had evaporated the water cover of the nearby sewer beds of the Roxbury Canal and abetted the deadly bacterial transfer into the water supply. Boiling water was the answer, but nobody knew. Instead, city leaders blamed cholera in the slums on the people who lived there rather than on the open cesspools.

Six months earlier, after a string of eight boys, the Fitzgeralds had joyously welcomed a blue-eyed girl to the family. Rosanna hovered over the new baby with concern borne out by city statistics. The grim records for the early 1870s show that for every five children born, two would die before their fifth birthday, making Boston's childhood mortality rate the highest in the United States. But the Boston board of health put politics before epidemiology. In 1875 it did a study that blamed the high rate of childhood mortality on the immigrants' inherent susceptibility to certain deadly diseases, and noted that two thirds of the city's foreign-born population were Irish, also the highest rate in the country. The official pronouncement was breathtaking—the high death rate was in the Irish genes.

Samuel Adams Drake, who chronicled Boston landmarks and historical figures, passed over the North End for his walking-tour guidebook after finding himself there at the tail end of a rainy day. "The air was filled with the stench arising under the warm sun from the mud and garbage of the gutter, and from every door and window of the overcrowded tenements peered forth a swarm of dirty humanity." Onward to the White Horse Tavern and Trinity Church.

The relative prosperity of the Fitzgeralds was no protection against contaminated water. The family had taken root in the once-grand North End when Tom Fitzgerald met Rosanna Cox there in 1857 when he was a thirty-five-year-old fish peddler, long after the Yankees had withdrawn to their stronghold on higher ground. The Fitzgeralds had nine surviving children, with the third son, John, bursting with enough energy to carry them all. They started out in two rooms in a packed tenement near the Old North Church that overflowed with the unskilled and downtrodden. They were in the "mixed" neighborhood of refugees from Cork and Kerry Counties and the woebegone city of Limerick. Neighbors included Tom Fitzgerald's sisters and mother. But the family's driving force was Tom's entrepreneurial younger brother, James, who started a combination grocery and liquor store in the tenement's first floor. Tom manned the grog shop, a move up from fishmongering on the streets of the North End.

Again he stayed put, never taking to the open road where the gumption money was in the days before retail stores. For his era, he was an old Irish bachelor when he married Rosanna, but made up for lost time with four sons in five years, and he eventually had nine sons in all. Three of them followed him into the liquor trade, but two drank heavily and died young. Rosanna called it "the curse of the liquor money." But then there was John Francis.

Not that their small markets put the Fitzgeralds high off the hog. They lived above the saloon in a bare-bones tenement with one toilet for nine families on four floors. The entrances had no doors, and beds were piles of straw. Yet the sprawling family had begun a slow ascendancy. Owning a saloon and grocery store made them high society in such an unforgiving place. They were in a house without doors, but they had food on the table. Within ten years, Thomas was able to move "up" to the thoroughfare of Hanover Street, a gone-to-seed place where Cotton Mather and Ben Franklin had once lived. He bought a three-story brick building there and, with the money from tenants, eventually bought two more buildings around the corner.

But Tom Fitzgerald, failed farmer, discouraged peddler, and reluctant shopkeeper, became a good businessman despite himself. His operation got a favorable business rating report from what later became Dun & Bradstreet. Yet Hanover Street had its heartbreak as well. It was where cholera found them and where Rosanna would die at age forty-five, struggling to deliver her twelfth child.

From the beginning, there was a special energy about Tom and Rosanna's third surviving boy. Even though Johnny grew up in a society within a society bounded by the dilapidated waterfront and the menacing incline of Beacon Hill, he never felt trapped there like his father, who pined for the turf fires and open spaces of back home.

John held a strong, lifelong fondness for the thronged North End streets of pushcarts and urchins and horse-drawn wagons. As a boy, he loved how the neighborhood got smothered in winter fog and scalded by steamy summer days. When the bustling waterfront finally got quiet at night, he and his brothers fell asleep to the distant sounds of mournful ship horns and the closer clanging of ferry bells.

Young Johnny Fitz first distinguished himself as a fourteen-year-old crack-of-dawn newsboy. Always drawn to the hubbub of politics and sports that dominated the talk in his father's store, he had a head start for touting his papers by following events of the day and calling out their headlines as he hustled about the city's financial district, a short walk from the North End. He was first in line to get his papers at three a.m., and first to sell out. He liked everything about newspaper offices, with their organized chaos and rumbling press runs and cast of nocturnal characters. When he started out, he lacked the seniority to claim his own corner to hawk his papers, and he had to roam up and down the alien streets of downtown, ranging along Washington Street and then up to Tremont Street and then deep into the Yankee territory of Beacon Street that was lined with brownstone town houses.

It was as a newsboy that he first glimpsed the rarefied life at the epicenter of the Brahmin world. On a cold afternoon in 1879, as he called out headlines from the *Boston Globe* across from the State House, he saw a lumbering Irish cook with bundles for dinner making her way gingerly along frozen Beacon Street. He offered to help, and as a reward, she sneaked him into the kitchen of 31 Beacon Street to warm up. He asked to poke around and, with the master of the house out for the rest of the day, she agreed. Fitzgerald came upon an enchanting play room that filled his imagination. It was awash with elaborate wooden toys— miniature soldiers and horses, hand-painted boats, and bright red fire engines. It was a distinct world designed for childhood, a discreet protection he never knew existed. He held the thought that one day his own children would have such toys in such a welcoming room of their own.

It was indeed a fateful visit. The manor house belonged to Henry Cabot Lodge, a Harvard professor who would soon be elected to the state senate and go on to hold a US senate seat as his own fiefdom. He would become a national figure when his isolationist policies after World War I stopped President Woodrow Wilson's effort to form an international League of Nations. It was unimaginable to young Johnny Fitzgerald as he had tea with a charwoman on a winter's day, but the august Lodge family and the striving Fitzgerald clan would one day have a famously intertwined history.

By the time Fitzgerald came of age in the 1880s, the baby steps toward Irish political power in Boston had broken into a sprint. First there were barroom associations that ran the street politics, and then the sheer power of numbers took over and surged from precinct to precinct and finally from ward to ward.

When Fitzgerald was twenty-one, Boston elected its first mayor of Irish descent. After serving as chairman of the Board of Aldermen, Hugh O'Brien was elected in 1884 to the first of four one-year terms. He had been sanctioned by Yankee overseers as almost one of them, down to his dour demeanor. O'Brien held close to the standard agenda of low taxes and tight budgets.

Running on a contemporaneous track was Patrick Collins, a famine immigrant who had arrived with his widowed mother. His first job as a young boy was as an upholsterer, but his quick mind and some friendships got him into Harvard Law School. In 1880 he caught the first waves of Democratic power in Massachusetts by winning a congressional seat from expanding immigrant voters in the city's North and West Ends as well as in East and South Boston. He served three terms and tried vainly to force the square peg of Irish Catholicism into the round hole of Episcopalian rectitude. He preached accommodation as the road to assimilation, but was ultimately rebuffed for me-tooism. After decades of grief and prejudice, there was simply too much blood in the eye for the Irish to make nice. The second-generation Irish wanted nothing less than the challenging rhetoric of Johnny Fitz and then the roundhouse punches of James Michael Curley.

Yet after a congressional stint and time as a diplomatic envoy to England, Collins still thought he could turn the corner on assimilation and calm the rambunctious factions in Boston. Though he was mayor for two terms from 1901 to 1905, he did neither. His exhortations about caution and patience were ignored and he died in office after taking to drink, sadly out of step with his times.

Johnny Fitz burst into City Hall in a special election after Collins's death, arriving at the same place but from a far different direction.

Fitzgerald also did some time at Harvard, but was much more slum kid than ivory tower. He was smarter than most and always on the move, an almost comic whirlwind. When Fitzgerald was growing up in the North End, only one out of twenty went beyond grammar school, let alone graduated from high school. Yet he graduated from Boston Latin, the elite preparatory school, and was not about to join his brothers behind the counter of the family grocery and liquor store. After poor medical care and the appalling sanitation of the era had brought such grief to their home on Hanover Street, Thomas Fitzgerald pushed his quick-minded son John toward Harvard Medical School on pooled family money, with everyone pitching in for the one with the brainpower and the best chance to make his mark. He would become a doctor to fight back.

But, once again, the cold hand of death reached into 435 Hanover when Thomas died suddenly of pneumonia. The father's death not only stopped John's stint at medical school, but made him the de facto head of the sprawling family. His first big decision was to ignore an entreaty from the local priest to distribute the younger siblings among relatives. They would stay put, with John pushing them out the door in the morning, either to school or to work in the corner store. To center the family, he not only had to quit school but he also needed a job. Second to the parish priest, the neighborhood luminary was ward boss Matthew Keany.

Keany took a shine to Johnny Fitz and enlisted him as a right-hand man because of his easy way with the customers. Keany eventually helped Fitzgerald get a prized job as a clerk at the then powerful Custom House at the handsome pay grade of $1,500 a year. Fitzgerald folded himself seamlessly into the shadow government of ward politics by embracing its one simple but inviolate rule—votes for jobs. No ingrates allowed. He became a "heeler" known for his peppery oratory, falling back on his newsboy energy to be the first guy at the right corner for setting up his soapbox. After three years at the Custom House, he stepped down to open a fire insurance business in the North End, an outgrowth of his winning ways with neighbors and small businessmen. He had a nodding acquaintance with everyone, and knew all voters by name. He shamelessly extolled the "dear old North End" in so many forums that his supporters became known as "dearos."

Other pols derided him as maudlin, but the dearos carried Honey Fitzgerald a long way. He was an affable bantam rooster with the gift of gab who was easy to underestimate. The glad hand had some steel in it. When push came to shove, he went with the ward ethos. Working the polls early on, he saw a family friend vote the wrong way and turned on him as a breaker of the code. It cost the man his job.

The income from the Custom House job and the family insurance firm put Fitzgerald in a position to pursue his heart's desire, the quiet and attractive Mary Josephine Hannon. She was in the broader Fitzgerald clan and had stayed behind on the family farm in Acton that Tom Fitzgerald had to abandon thirty years earlier. She and Fitzgerald shared the same great-grandfather and had known each other as teenagers. John fell for his second cousin at first sight. Josie was the sixth of nine children, with two siblings having died at young ages. She and Fitzgerald knew repeated bereavements, but the deep shadows never completely lifted for the lugubrious Hannons. They owned a house and ran a productive farm, but were keenly aware they were at the bottom of the social ladder in a "swamp Yankee" agrarian town.

The exhilarating visits of their high-energy cousin from Boston, when Fitzgerald imposed his contagious good cheer on a hard-faced household, were rare social events. His exuberant excursions along back-country roads in borrowed North End cars were adventures that had everyone gasping and laughing and talking about another memorable afternoon with Johnny Fitz.

But a marriage gave the Hannons pause. While dispensations for marriage of second cousins were routinely granted by the Catholic Church, Josie's parents resisted it for years out of fear that the union would produce mentally deficient children. Fitzgerald's persistence wore them down, and Josie and John were wed in Concord in September 1889. They were almost old-timers for those days, he twenty-six and she twenty-four.

Josie had to give up her pastoral roots and begin married life in the clutter and clamor of the Fitzgerald family's homestead on Hanover Street. She got her own space in time for their first of six children, a radiantly healthy girl named Rose. With his family under way, Fitzgerald made his first move in elective politics, standing successfully for Common Council. His sole agenda was a park to spruce up the decrepit North End at a time when amenities for the poor were not deemed governmental matters. His single-minded pursuit resulted in a small shimmer in public life, and the park on Commercial Street was a hard-fought victory he savored throughout his life. The council paid next to nothing, but the benefits were enough to allow Fitzgerald's youngest brother, Henry, to run the insurance business and John to plot his course in politics.

Fitzgerald had found his calling and was securely in place when his mentor and second father, Matt Keany, died of pneumonia. In making the elaborate funeral arrangements, Fitzgerald demonstrated the take-charge leadership needed to succeed the bushy-haired Keany. He used the ward boss's secret lists of the beholden to seal support for his ascension in a district that was turning over. The waterfront was shifting by whole streets to Italian and Jewish immigrants as the second-generation Irish left the North End for the open spaces of Dorchester and Charlestown and South Boston. Those who departed were reminded that they were leaving with a lifelong obligation. Like homing pigeons, they were expected to return home on election days to vote in their precinct of origin, where old neighborhood names never fell off the rolls.

New and old immigrants coalesced around Fitzgerald in 1892 as he audaciously vaulted from the din of the seventy-five-member Common Council to the thirty-five-member state senate, leapfrogging the Board of Alderman and House of Representatives. It was a rise that needed a boost from someone outside the North End, as the senatorial district spilled over into the adjacent West End and into the strong hands of taciturn Ward 8 boss Martin Lomasney. Fitzgerald visited Lomasney at his modest Hendricks Club in the West End as an eager supplicant, and was given a measured audience by a rock of a man who was in politics for more than just the power of it. Lomasney brought some genuine loyalty to the equation, taking care of "his" people's basic needs as he went about his unchanging daily routine in his customary frayed straw hat.

Fitzgerald impressed the boss with sheer personality, and won the Ward 8 endorsement oblivious of his ace in the hole—Lomasney loathed Fitzgerald's senatorial opponent. With Lomasney's imprimatur, Fitzgerald became one of the senate's youngest and most progressive members, voting in vain for a minimum wage of two dollars a day and limitations on workdays for women and children. His other priority was getting friends and relatives state jobs.

When Fitzgerald set out for the senate, Lomasney was the first among equals of the ward bosses. As Boston's Irish began moving from servile slums to City Hall, power remained diffuse. There was no Tammany Hall consolidation as in New York. While each district had its man to see, no one was in charge overall. But Martin Lomasney came the closest. While other bosses had more flamboyant styles, Lomasney's gruff strength was unwavering loyalty to those who gave the same. He became known reverentially as the Mahatma, a Far East title for the wise and good that fit an even-handed man.

Fitzgerald took over the North End with a bluster that disguised a driving ambition. Patrick Joseph Kennedy, the paternal grandfather of a president, ran East Boston out of his pub and liquor store with hard looks. By the turn of the century, the South End and Roxbury became the subjugated territory of James Michael Curley, who collaborated with no man. While the boundaries were clear, power remained diffuse.

In an unsettled period, Fitzgerald jumped the line once again to land in Congress in 1894. It was a race he barely won in a thoroughly Irish district, beating an incumbent with Lomasney's help in Ward 8. He held the seat for three undistinguished terms, but made enough money to buy a house in the sticks of Concord and move his wife closer to her rural roots. As politics dictated, he maintained a legal residence among his "dearos." His biggest issue in Congress was one that served him well— opposing literacy tests for immigrants which could prevent them from voting and becoming a nettlesome political force. Fitzgerald squared off against another Massachusetts legislator, the frigid Henry Cabot Lodge, the curator of the magical toy haven at 31 Beacon Street that had so entranced the teenaged Fitzgerald when he was taking trespassing tea by the kitchen fire.

Lodge was just getting under way as a dominant force in the US Senate.

Taking due measure of the burgeoning Irish in Boston, he decided they could stay in his country, but Italians and Jews had to go. They were the new indigestibles, and Lodge began his first push for the literacy testing that Fitzgerald opposed for his new dearos. In a stirring speech that he always remembered, Little Fitz praised the gumption of those leaving faraway homes for hardship and struggle in a new land. Fitzgerald also claimed a suspiciously pat exchange with Lodge when the two bumped into each near the Senate chamber after Fitzgerald's snappy rejoinder speech.

> LODGE: You are an impudent young man. Do you think the Jews or the Italians have any right in this country?
>
> FITZGERALD: As much as your father or mine. It was only a difference of a few ships.

The bill was vetoed by President Cleveland but Lodge kept going, finally prevailing two decades later at the jingoistic run-up to World War I.

After one term in Congress, Fitzgerald's ambition turned to the mayor's office. To get there, he decided it was better to get the support of the bosses that Lomasney was always fighting with. Despite the Mahatma's crucial backing for his early career, Fitzgerald broke with him, joining the "mayor makers"—three other bosses set on freezing out Lomasney and picking future mayors. They had previously selected a Yankee Democrat, Josiah Quincy, a good mayor but half a loaf for the Irish bosses. They finally got one of their own back in the mayor's seat in 1901, the brittle and efficient Patrick Collins, who, among other things, found Fitzgerald a buffoon.

After Collins's election, Fitzgerald bowed out of Congress to get in line for the mayor's chair. His stint in Washington had been hard on his family, with him in a boardinghouse in D.C. and they in Concord Junction. His daughter Rose found his absences interminable, and recalled fondly how thrilling it was when her father bounded from the train, swept her up, and made her close her eyes while he pulled a present from his bag. "To my mind, there was no one in the world like my father," she recalled. "Wherever he was, there was magic in the air."

Fitzgerald's first move was to get a bona fide Boston address. In 1903 Josie gave up her country estate and relocated to a big, ornate house on a Dorchester hill, with a mansard roof and attached solarium. A stained-glass window guarded the entrance. Beside it was the Fitzgerald coat of arms and a Gaelic inscription that informed visitors they were calling on Shawn A Boo (John the Bold). Part of the down payment came from Fitzgerald's purchase of a small newspaper, *The Republic*, a remnant of what the first Irish boss, Patrick Maguire, had launched decades before. It had a tiny circulation and little content, but businesses supported it with large ads to stay on the good side of a prospective mayor. The new publisher soon took in the small fortune of $25,000 a year.

At the outset of the twentieth century, the Irish had stopped performing the traditional supplications that had them kneading their scally caps in their hands and hopping from foot to foot at the service entrance of city life. Honey Fitz was the perfect transitional figure, the right blend of hard charger and Irish vaudevillian. His trademark may have been singing "Sweet Adeline," but he could cut a deal and keep a careful list of friends and foes. Francis Russell, the elegant Boston historian, has written that Fitzgerald's emergence as a "political buccaneer was as decisive a date in the history of Boston as General Howe's evacuation of the town."

While Fitzgerald treaded water, Mayor Collins caught pneumonia on vacation and suddenly died in September 1905. Wasting little time, Fitzgerald broke loose from his cabal of the bosses, knowing they would conspire against him anyway. After a ten-year hiatus, he turned to his original patron for higher office—Martin Lomasney. Fitzgerald would have received his support were it not for one of Lomasney's closest friends getting into the race first and asking for help. "Don't say another word, old sport," was his answer to city clerk Ned Donovan. Even though he had the Mahatma, Donovan didn't know what hit him when the Honey Fitz blitz got rolling.

It was a nonstop foray through all twenty-five wards. Fitzgerald introduced the first prowling motorcade, with the candidate bouncing around in the backseat of a big red car to greet his dearos who spilled out into the streets. He was leading the baleful "outs" who were clamoring to ransack Collins's buttoned-down City Hall. It would be a simple equation. A big gang to replace a small one. But the Mahatma's Ward 8 was a fierce battleground that reached the point of drawn guns. Old allies were asunder. And enemies sought mutual advantage. It was a fleeting thing, but Fitzgerald's most enduring enemy, James Michael Curley, was with him this one time, it being in both their interests to break the hold of the bosses. On primary eve, Fitz gave a speech in each of the twenty-five wards, ending his touring pageant at his favorite old haunt, the Jefferson Club on Hanover Street. His voters rolled through every precinct until Ward 8, but eked out a slim, satisfying four-thousand-vote victory in the Democratic primary. Again, with the Ward 8 exception, Fitzgerald rolled to victory over the Republicans in the final.

A half century after Thomas Fitzgerald arrived in Boston to sell fish in the Irish slum, his third son was mayor. The Boston of Louis Frothingham, his Republican opponent for mayor, was done, an obituary written from the ballot returns. While there were battles to come, the numbers were stark. The Yankees accounted for only 11 percent of their city on a hill, while Irish were now about 40 percent of the populace in an expanding landscape.

There was another sea change of political style. The aloof Collins was no workhorse, frequently starting his day at 10:00 a.m. and leaving by 3:00 p.m. Little Fitz brought the chaotic bustle of his campaign to the staid mayor's office, arriving early and staying late, thriving on the inefficiency of dealing directly with constituent appeals for benefits or jobs. In one brief window, recorded by a *Boston Post* reporter, Fitzgerald sat with twenty-six petitioners over thirty-two minutes in a brisk procession of mostly happy customers. Constituents came first, and official duties about contracts and departmental decisions were relegated to the evening shift. The mayor had dinner at home only on Sundays and holidays.

But his first term was an unfocused flea market, with the City Hall turnstile whirring and no one quite in charge. With a budget of $33 million, the city outspent the state by four to one, with a seat-of-the-pants mayor running forty-four departments employing twelve thousand people to serve a city of nearly 600,000.

While Fitzgerald thrived on the hectic pace, he was never able to see the forest of policy for the trees of patronage. His fevered pace precluded a more thoughtful approach to the spoils system that had become second nature to him. Jobs for votes and effective government were as incompatible as ornate Bulfinch columns on either side of a shanty stoop. Fitzgerald kicked open the vault door and, making no bones about it, went on a spending spree to reward supporters with jobs and city services. He framed the political dynamic for a generation—City Hall as a spill-over cornucopia for constituents funded by real estate taxes on commercial property. It turned the old Yankee equation on its head.

The first Fitzgerald administration was the old North End patronage machine writ large. No holdover city job was safe. By the end, one of every forty-two residents in Boston held a city job that kept them inside when it rained and finally out of the construction trench. Bartenders and construction foremen were suddenly running the show. The provisional appointment to get around civil service became an art form. There was such a profusion of deputy sealers in the weights and measures department that even an obscure, out-of-the-way agency managed to have its own featherbedding scandal. There were ludicrous new jobs for tea warmers and tree climbers and a new tier of watchmen to better watch those warming tea or climbing trees. The mayor's youngest brother, Henry, was patronage chief, and "See Henry" resounded along the halls for those in line for a real job or for those being jollied along to the exit. Government became a family affair, with Little Fitz's brothers forming a kitchen cabinet that met after hours to hash things out among John, Jim, Eddie, George, Mike, Joe, and Henry.

James Fitzgerald, the oldest brother and a well-to-do tavern and hotel owner, had his own cachet. Self-possessed and focused, he was a counterpoint to the impetuous mayor, ideally suited to the role of behind-the-scenes power broker. But long days and a brotherly brain trust still did not bring order to the proceedings. Amid the anarchy at City Hall, it became hard to say whether graft or incompetence was the core problem. One chapter heading in a history of the era laid it bare about the Fitzgerald patronage stampede and the phalanx of favored contractors—"Burglars in the House."

And it all left Fitzgerald vulnerable. He had lasting Democratic opposition in the 1907 primary that converted into votes in the final election for the thrifty and bland Republican George Hibbard, who ran on a one-sentence platform of "cleaning up the mess." The former postmaster ousted Fitzgerald and delivered on campaign promises by cutting debt, payrolls, and maintenance costs. The Yankees moved in for the kill in 1909 with their "strong mayor" city charter reform that was aimed at locking in gains and paving the way to restored hegemony. It gave the mayor a four-year term, banned the party primaries that had become a Democratic advantage, and replaced the thirteen aldermen and the over-populated Common Council with a nine-member City Council. Despite the machinations, the "strong mayor" plan backfired badly.

But before Fitzgerald could tip over charter reform by becoming the strong mayor no one on Beacon Street envisioned, he had to survive a vintage bribery scandal from his first term that revealed the graft behind Fitzgerald's public face of blustery good cheer. And it also introduced a venal Boston character who later became the architect of Fitzgerald's downfall.

The scandal erupted just before election day in Fitzgerald's unsuc-cessful bid for reelection. Arising from a carefully timed report by the highly partisan Boston Finance Commission that nevertheless produced the goods, it focused on just one of many instances of the city paying exorbitant prices in no-bid contracts designed for kickbacks. But this one was different for one reason: it came with a cooperating witness. It concerned a mundane contract for flagstones for city streets. Fitzgerald's purchasing department had dumped a long-standing contractor to give the job to a favored competitor at twice the cost.

In a hospital-bed interview with investigators, the department's second-in-command admitted taking money from the new contractor, but repeatedly resisted implicating the mayor. After Fitzgerald was defeated for reelection, he threw the department head under the horse-drawn trolley. He told a grand jury that Michael Mitchell, an overmatched undertaker who was seldom at City Hall, was the sole decision-maker on awarding the contract. Mitchell was indicted, but the scandal also focused attention on Fitzgerald's extravagance and the disparity between his income and his mounting assets. In addition to the Dorchester estate, there were frequent trips down south in the winter and to Maine in the summer, as well as jaunts to Europe.

The district attorney cut the mayor slack and confined the case to

Mitchell and the contractor in a conspiracy-to-defraud case. But the fly
in everyone's ointment was Mitchell's scrappy lawyer, a warts-and-all
Irishman whose blue-collar career covered the waterfront. Daniel Coakley, who had moved from streetcar conductor to newsman to lawyer, had
once been a Fitzgerald supporter who served on his Parks Commission.
But he was affronted by how quickly Fitzgerald had hung Mitchell out
to dry. Even though the mayor moved toward Coakley's side as a "don't
recall" defense witness, Coakley held the grudge tight. There it lay as a
tripwire going forward.

The white-hot bribery story cooled with Mitchell's conviction. He
did his time quietly if not well. Fitzgerald stayed low during the colorless
reign of a Yankee reformer that left the electorate hungry for the enter-
taining disarray of Johnny Fitz. In 1909 his renewed quest for a second
term stirred the Good Government Association to settle on the bluest
of blue, a quintessential Beacon Hill Brahmin named James Jackson
Storrow. The Irish could dismiss the association in caustic shorthand as
sanctimonious "goo-goos," but not Storrow's impeccable credentials. He
was preordained Harvard. Captain of crew. Wealthiest banker in New
England. Briefly president of General Motors. In-laws with descendants
of Commodore Oliver Hazard Perry of the War of 1812. But Storrow
was a rare Yankee Democrat in a Democratic town. Rarer still was a
genuine civic altruism, which had him serving as chairman of the school
committee and at the helm of the Boy Scouts and community groups.
Despite his squared shoulders and chiseled good looks, he couldn't give a
speech, and hemmed and hawed at the public podium. In a town where
politics had become the new entertainment, Storrow couldn't juke and
jive with a crowd.

Against the backdrop of charter reform, the election was seen as
a winner-take-all moment in which everyone in divided Boston understood the stakes. To win against a well-heeled Yankee, Fitzgerald needed
every single Irish vote in town. He especially needed his new rival, James
Michael Curley, in the South End, and his old enemy, Martin Lomasney, in the West End. The solution: Curley was given Fitzgerald's old

congressional seat to bide his time for mayor, and Lomasney eventually sold some property to the city at a premium.

Honey Fitz also needed to change the subject from bribery and a convicted department head. So he railed against the rich Yankees who only cared about the tax rate and nothing for the people. If put to music, the campaign theme was a lilting, familiar refrain:

"Begorrah, but I'm just a poor Irish Catholic boyo from the slums."

Second beat: "And I'm fighting a Harvard blueblood who's trying to buy the election."

Third: "And jest look at the starchy man who's anti-everything that matters, like labor laws and parochial schools."

Storrow's response was a gravely measured cascade of legalese newspaper ads on the evils of "Fitzgeraldism." Nonetheless, the briefs documented corrupt dealings at City Hall.

The final gun from Fitzgerald was the race card—the attacks were just more prejudice against Irish Catholics.

The stage was set for a down-to-the-wire donnybrook about who was going to run Boston for good.

Storrow was a stiff and earnest man whose lineage went back to the Tories in the Revolutionary War. He prided himself on having a grand sweep and being a big-task thinker who mulled weighty matters as he looked over the Public Garden from his Beacon Street perch.

But his to-do list was more eclectic than insightful as he pondered what was best for the region. While immigration and housing, with no elaboration, were on his list of nineteen important things to straighten out, so was, at number two, the question of why New England hillsides were not producing more "high class apples." Such musings were not the usual stuff of Boston politics.

Storrow's broad agenda was nothing less than righting the ship of state. He rhapsodized about the rare opportunity of charter reform in a letter to one of his government professors at Harvard, noting that Fitzgerald had been tainted by scandal, and he detected that Irish dissent was in the air. But he misread the usual Irish caviling as defection.

He would be dismayed when the Irish refused, as he put it, "to array themselves" under his banner. And Storrow's biographer rued "new cleavages" between the Irish and natives, ignoring that the deep divide was more than a half century old.

For his part, Fitzgerald took to the road again in a roaming caravan that included song-and-dance routines, a fast-moving vaudeville show. Headed by the now-familiar red car, he traveled thousands of miles, crisscrossing a city locked in winter.

The last Fitzgerald rally at Faneuil Hall, on the outskirts of the North End, was a show-stopper that produced a fortuitous signature event. As Fitzgerald worked the crowd on the way to the platform, the brass band moved from "The Star-Spangled Banner" to "The Wearing of the Green." When Fitzgerald approached the stage, the band killed some time with a tune of the day, "Sweet Adeline." It caught the crowd, who joined in the chorus. By the second verse, Fitzgerald's eyes were dancing and he sang it solo at the foot of the stage.

Fitzgerald was peaking at the perfect time, and historian Russell recorded it as epochal. "In that bellowing moment of beaming fair faces, the Honey Fitz legend was born." The song became a staple that Fitzgerald never tired of. For starters, he sang it thirty-five more times at events through the final election weekend, the last one while standing on the roof of a taxi. Honey Fitz won by fewer than two thousand votes out of about 95,000 cast.

Beacon Hill went into mourning that such a discredited man could beat one of their exemplars. Storrow had lost despite outspending Fitzgerald two to one, with his $100,000 an unprecedented amount at the time. Storrow fell back on his renowned self-control after the narrow defeat of January 11, 1910. In the last week, charges had filled the air, libel suits had been filed, campaign workers had gestured wildly across the "cleavages." In one postmortem letter to a supporter, Storrow was a study in self-conscious understatement. "I seem to be just as fresh today as on the day the racket began." To his friend A. Lincoln Filene, he confirmed the obvious—that it was "a racial and class feeling" that did him in. Irish with unforgiving memories had indeed made a racket. Storrow stayed involved in sundry public issues, and nearly saved the day before the 1919 police strike, when he headed an ad-hoc citizens' committee that recommended cops be allowed to unionize but not be affiliated with the much-feared American Federation of Labor. The advice was rejected with calamitous results.

But Fitzgerald's victory over Storrow had a shelf-life problem. To gain the uniform support required in such a tough fight in a polarized town, he had to promise the bosses and especially Curley that his reelection would be his mayoral swan song. But after Fitzy broke in his new spats, the commitment began to dissipate as being mayor became a comfortable pair of old shoes.

Indeed, his second administration was smooth sailing, or at least much less bumpy than the first. He didn't seem as overrun by the job and its handsome rewards the second time around. And he exulted in the irony of being the first beneficiary of charter reform—a four-year term that, as his oldest daughter, Rose, said, "relaxed us all." The second term was coming to an end on a high note. Rose had married a Harvard man who was no blueblood. He was Joseph Patrick Kennedy, the out-of-my-way son of ward boss P. J. Kennedy of East Boston. And "Fitzgeraldism" produced some genuine accomplishment and popularity. The city and the harbor had picked up business and vitality, and residents watched amenities sprout through construction of playgrounds and a new high school and another hospital, along with the Franklin Park Zoo.

But to run again meant a brawl with Curley, the street fighter who stopped at nothing. Even worse, Curley's style had caught hold—the more brassy and insulting he became, the better the Irish voters liked it. Curley had been waiting his turn impatiently as a junior congressman, and longed for the big stage of Boston. He began pounding his table in Washington over a broken promise of one final term for Johnny Fitz. As usual, Curley pulled no punches in a face-to-face showdown with the fifty-year-old Fitzgerald. "You're an old man," Curley told the mayor. "Get your slippers and pipe and stretch out in your hammock and read the *Ladies' Home Journal.*"

A heavyweight title fight was in the works for November 1913. Each announced for mayor, with Curley taking preemptive aim by announcing first. By then, he had an ace in the hole, given to him by Fitzgerald's enemy from the Mitchell trial—Daniel Coakley, a seasoned blackmailer representing a woman named Elizabeth Toodles Ryan. She was a cigarette girl who helped run a gambling emporium in middle Massachusetts, where she shared at least a dance with Fitzgerald late on a summer night.

In short order, a black-bordered letter was received at Fitzgerald's Dorchester home by his ashen-faced Josie and deeply aggrieved daughter, Rose—who, at twenty-three, was the same age as Toodles. Get out, the letter said, or face family disgrace. Fitzgerald vacillated, but quickly bowed to his insistent wife when Curley began joking with reporters about some upcoming lectures he was planning, including "great lovers from Cleopatra to Toodles." Josie ordered Shawn A Boo to withdraw, and so he did, citing ill health.

The tale of Toodles and Johnny Fitz was never told as an exposé. Indeed it was not even mentioned in a biography published ten years after Fitzgerald's death. But it shadowed Fitzgerald in later campaigns as an insider's smirk that did damage to his standing in the game. He got taken by a cigarette girl and cornered by Curley. Before Toodles receded from her day in the sun, there would be testimony in a court case cooked up by Coakley from a man who swore he saw the mayor stealing kisses with Toodles under a September moon in 1912. Fitzgerald would be followed by a ditty that stuck: "A whiskey glass and Toodles's ass made a horse's ass of Honey Fitz."

Forced out of a race he would have likely won, Fitzgerald soon joined with the ward bosses in a failed effort to stop the Curley juggernaut. Honey Fitz began a gradual decline that stripped the spring from his lively step. He ran for high office in 1916, 1918, 1922, and 1930, but always under a vague cloud of opprobrium. In the end, he was unfairly pegged as an affable sort with wobbly knees who was no good in the clinches. The family member who came out the stronger for the year of shame was his daughter Rose, who, while losing some respect for her father, knew her future when she saw it. Finally free of the nimbus of her irrepressible father, she had gained the self-assurance to marry Joe Kennedy, a fast-rising young man. Fitzgerald's three sons did not fare nearly as well: one died of drink, another stayed in a low-level job with the "Edison" electricity company, and the third worked as a toll collector on the Mystic River Bridge. As his father had done before him, Honey Fitz buried three of his children.

The sunshine in Fitzgerald's later years came from working with his grandson Jack Kennedy in plotting a campaign for Congress in which the stars aligned to bring the Honey Fitz story full circle. More than thirty years after Toodles had chilled his marriage and dimmed his future, one of Rose's sons navigated his way to win the 1946 primary in a crowded congressional field. It was a special election to succeed Fitzgerald's archenemy, James Michael Curley, who had been convicted of fraud for being a front man in a flim-flam company hawking World War II munitions contracts that never materialized.

The congressional district was a proprietary issue in the Fitzgerald clan. It had been Honey Fitz's a half century earlier, and he lectured his grandson at Jack's suite at the Bellevue Hotel near the State House about the strategy behind rounding up ethnic voters. The torch was passed as the dearo talked stagecraft and crowd appeal with the *PT-109* war hero and Harvard grad who was developing an engaging presence with a special cachet.

The war profiteer was replaced by a war hero who launched a storied political career while settling a family score. Jack Kennedy's victory meant that there would be one lone holdout in the Massachusetts delegation against signing a commutation petition for the jailed James Michael Curley. Young Jack said no and meant it. The next generation adopted a new maxim from an old sentiment: Don't get mad; get even.

But if Jack was the hard-charging grandchild who indulged an obsolete chatterbox before he got down to business with no-nonsense aides, it was the scion of the Kennedy clan, Teddy, who bonded with Grandpa. Edward was the ninth child, and he occasionally fell through the cracks in his nomadic years of boarding schools and living in the heavy shadow of sibling attainment. But he was never an afterthought with Grandpa.

In turn, Ted was spellbound by the energy and joie de vivre he witnessed as he watched Honey Fitz regale the world at large wherever he found it. Every time they had dinner at the Hotel Bellevue, Ted would meet the entire staff all over again, and anyone else who wandered by. When his grandfather was in his mid-eighties and Ted a teenager, the Kennedys brought Fitzy to their Palm Beach estate to escape the Boston winter. But they could never just put him on the beach under an um-brella. He had to be around people. So one of Ted's Florida jobs was to drop him off at the lobby of The Breakers, where he would ease himself into a comfortable chair. For the day. The hotel clerk was tipped to alert the beaming former mayor that one of his countrymen had landed. One ring from the front-desk bell meant the guests were from Massachusetts. But two rapid rings announced the jackpot—former constituents. Up he bounded—why, you folks must be from Boston. Say hello to John F. Fitzgerald, mayor of Boston. Lunch and dinner usually followed. Ted would pick up Grandpa at ten p.m., after a good day of remembrance with well-heeled dearos.

CHAPTER 3

The Good Shepherd

MARTIN LOMASNEY

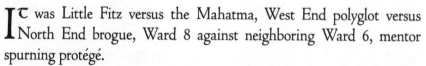

IT was Little Fitz versus the Mahatma, West End polyglot versus North End brogue, Ward 8 against neighboring Ward 6, mentor spurning protégé.

It was a turn-of-the-century mayoral donnybrook and then some. Before it was over, it was as bad as it had ever been in the Boston trenches. Guns were drawn at one of the West End polling places and the mayhem led to a long-term breach between mayoral front-runner John Fitzgerald and Ward 8's protective boss, Martin Lomasney.

In 1905, after the sudden death of incumbent Patrick Collins, Fitzgerald virtually ran from the cemetery services to the election department to take out papers for mayor. The ward bosses were not well pleased with such independent alacrity. Until then, Lomasney had been in Fitzgerald's corner, giving his peppery pal from the North End the monolithic Ward 8 voting bloc for his earlier runs for state senator and congressman. But this time Fitzgerald ignored all the bosses, and even though Lomasney was frequently at odds with his peers, he became part of the Stop Fitzy conspiracy. Martin never liked a fast-moving ingrate.

The other bosses knew the best way to get Lomasney on board against Fitzgerald had a name—Ned Donovan. He was a close friend of Lomasney's and a former colleague in the legislature and the current city clerk. Donovan was ambivalent about running for mayor and taking on the indefatigable Fitzy until he talked it over with the boss. Game plan forged, he was in, and the election went down to its rabid end. Fitzgerald won the Democratic primary by a small margin, using thugs at rival polling stations.

In the bitter aftermath, the only question in Irish Democratic Boston was what would the man known as Mahatma do in the final? Could the West End's good shepherd abide Louis Frothingham, a Republican Yankee, over turncoat Fitzgerald, newly ruthless but still one of our own?

In his traditional election-eve gathering of the faithful in his West End political club, Lomasney laid it out straight from the shoulder: Fitzgerald is going to win, but I can't be with him. And in case there was any doubt: "I am not going to lie down or be with the gang that has done such a job on us."

He said he had not taken attendance and was going to shut off the lights in the Hendricks Club room for two minutes. He then said that anyone who didn't want to support a Republican could slip out and there would be no hard feelings. All would be welcomed back to the big tent of his political office as West Enders in good standing.

In the dark silence that followed, no one stirred and the crowd held the same faces when the lights came on. Ward 8 voted Republican for the first time, but, that astounding development aside, Fitzgerald became mayor.

It was a trademark event for Lomasney, who dominated Ward 8 as benign dictator for a half century. He was a rare Irish pol—laconic at the podium and careful not to over-promise like James Michael Curley and Honey Fitzgerald. His word was as solid as his ribcage. But he didn't hand it out often. His style was captured in his famous maxim for survival in Boston politics: never write it down if you can talk, and never talk if you can nod.

He came up through the ranks and knew the patronage the way a tax lawyer knew the IRS code. He could horse-trade jobs with the best of them, but he had some basic standards in a hard business, sticking close to the idea that there was a way to do it—and not to do it. His marching orders to his troops were to play hard but "keep it legal." In political combat, his view was that the ends always justified the means as long as the means are arguably aboveboard.

As the Irish came into their own, he was everything his contemporary Daniel Coakley was not: an ascetic who neither smoked nor drank. A gruff loner who cared deeply about his "family" of up-against-it West

End constituents. For Martin Lomasney, there were no neutrals in a political fight. You were with him or against him, and he kept careful score. But he was seldom gratuitous in his retaliations, and his hard measures usually served a broader purpose.

He was a West End street urchin who became a one-man employment agency, spending the bulk of his long days finding jobs for sons and husbands, and doling out cash for overdue rent or food bills. He matched the sick with a doctor, and dealt softly with the troubled boy. He not only had his eye out for political comers, but also ran for office himself, serving on the Boston Board of Aldermen and then in the house and senate. He once came close to being elected as Speaker of the House in the days of waning Republican rule. His dominance was built on two interwoven tenets: political clout came from delivering voting blocs, and strong allegiance came from voters who owed their jobs. Yet even the foremost muckraker of the day, Lincoln Steffens, who came to Boston to tip over bandwagons with exposés, went away with lasting admiration for the man known for dedicated stewardship.

As a member of the large Hibernian club whose families had suffered under the Brahmin plutocracy, Lomasney was more than vigilant about settling old scores and righting historical wrongs. But, unlike many of his peers, he always worked with facts. As a legislator at a state constitutional convention, he seized on the issue of the wildly disproportionate state aid to favored private charities and educational institutions. His research found that $49,000 went to Catholic institutions while Protestant ones received $18 million. He led the successful fight to get language into the state constitution that banned such gifts.

His political strength was anchored by his disciplined lifestyle. He was a pathological creature of habit, adhering to a daily regimen that underscored why he never forgot where he came from. He lived simply among his immigrant neighbors who always came first.

But Lomasney wasn't so monastic and selfless that he ignored his own best interests. While politics consumed his life, his avocation was real estate. He did not object to selling parcels for a premium to developers doing business with the city, or even to the city itself. Inside the Hendricks Club, there were two doors with equal billing. One said MARTIN LOMASNEY REAL ESTATE. He would leave an estate, sizable for the day, of $200,000.

Yet his clear priority was getting his West End slates into office. Lomasney never lost on his home turf for City Council or the legislature. But the mayoral elections were the rub. He opposed Fitzgerald's unsanctioned grab for power in 1905, and the steamroller corruption of Curley's intermittent reign. Lomasney first fell out with Curley even before Curley was mayor and backed the odious Joseph Pelletier for governor. And Martin's strong bond with his brother soured for a while when Joseph backed Curley in the hard-fought mayoral election in 1921. Time took the sting out of his wars with Fitzgerald, but he fought Curley until he was a sick old man living alone in the Hotel Bellevue that overlooked the West End.

Martin Lomasney was a muscular man with hard, clear, blue-gray eyes that squarely regarded visitors and carefully recorded body language. His lantern jaw above a fifty-cent black bow tie became his visage in newspaper cartoons. A high-end bow tie as a gift from the Mahatma was his sure signal of lasting approval. Nothing was ever said.

His speaking style evolved from halting to vigorous, matching his pugilistic gestures. He punched out fact after fact, a torrent of information, before he came up for air. He lacked Curley's melodrama and Fitzgerald's song and dance, but he could marshal an argument and get men to do what he wanted.

He always wore a loose-fitting suit so he could thump points home in debate. The style never changed—a mortician's outfit of black bow ties and dark suits and, in winter, a black overcoat. Another constant was a battered straw hat that he wore indoors and hung on a hook next to his rolltop desk. It became his talisman much like the shopworn baseball caps favored by superstitious players as a sign of dues paid in combat. He always had an umbrella tucked tightly under his arm for all weather when he went on brisk, five-mile walks every nightfall.

He was fanatically punctual. His meals were clockwork events, with breakfast at 7:45 sharp and lunch at one and dinner at six. He started his day with a pot of tea, three eggs, and a side of applesauce. Lunch was always soup with crackers and yet more applesauce—and oysters, only from Cape Cod, when they were in season. He abhorred the banquet circuit, seeing it as the purveyor of bad food and worse oratory. He abided one banquet for himself in 1892 when he left the city health department to take his place on the Boston Board of Aldermen.

He started his day with the same barber in the same shop giving him a shave. Both were men of few words, with Lomasney reducing the daily exchange to "good morning" when he sat down and "good day" when he left. When the barber, Louis Comfort, tired of the work after two decades, Lomasney got him a job as a court officer on the proviso that he give Mahatma a special shave every Sunday morning at the Hendricks Club.

As a ward boss, he decided early on to deliver his votes on the basis of respect and not fear. His view was simple and steadfast: "A man without sympathy for the masses never gets far in politics." And his Hendricks Club reflected his low-key compassion, devoid of what he called "the inquisitorial terrors of organized charity." But he had no use for the self-righteous "reformer." "The uplifter," he said, "is never liked." *Reform* was a Yankee word for "unemployment."

And consistent with his self-effacing style, he didn't wear his Catholicism on his sleeve like Fitzgerald and Curley, who turned Mass into political pageant. On Sundays he'd slip into St. Mary's in the North End, sit at the back, and leave quickly to avoid the glad-handing at the back of the church and on the sidewalk.

In his early career in politics, Lomasney had to beat back charges that he was really a "novey," an impostor Irishman from Nova Scotia. It was so persistent that he finally put it to rest by giving a speech entirely in Gaelic, the dying language he had learned from his grandmother. His parents' marriage records revealed the usual immigrant lineage. Although his father had in fact passed through Nova Scotia on his way to the West End, both of his parents were famine Irish. Maurice Lomasney was a thirty-four-year-old tailor from Fermoy, County Cork, who married Mary Murray, thirty, of Lismore, Waterford, in 1853 at St. Mary's.

They started out on South Margin Street in the West End. As in most Irish homes in the early diaspora years in Boston, there was the searing grief for a dead child. Two sons died before Martin was born in 1859. His younger brother, Joseph, followed him into politics and was a sure and trusted hand despite a short-lived falling-out about the merits of James Michael Curley. Martin attended the Mayhew School and always remembered celebrating the fall of Richmond there in 1865 to mark the end of the Civil War.

Tragedy found him firsthand at age ten. He was walking with his father on a steamy August day when Maurice suddenly fell dead to the sidewalk of sunstroke. Martin took away a permanent fear of sunlight from his father's shocking demise. He always carried an umbrella for the sun, and never vacationed in the summer. He stayed inside most of the day, emerging at nightfall to walk his neighborhood, sticking to the shady side of the streets.

His mother died shortly after his father, and Martin and his brother moved in with their maternal grandmother and an aunt. The ladies reared the boys. His grandmother spoke only Gaelic, and Martin acquired the great skill of being able to talk to new Irish immigrants in their native tongue.

For all his native intelligence, Martin had a rudimentary education at best, barely able to write and leaving school for good in the sixth grade when arithmetic moved into fractions. He could just about handle a checkbook. But he became self-taught and a voracious reader. His speeches were concise and clear, with a strong structure. All his stories had a beginning, middle, and end.

As a street scamp, his playground was North Station, where he sold newspapers, shined shoes, lugged bags, and held the reins of carriage horses. He had a brush with the law at twelve, when a truant officer hauled him to court and only his Aunt Joanna was there to speak on his behalf. He feared juvenile jail, but Joanna convinced the judge that he would go back to school. He did, but only for a year, quitting for good when he was thirteen. His truancy trauma made him a lifelong advocate of second chances.

Martin Lomasney got started in politics at fourteen with a job for City Councilor John Duggan, who also worked for a Catholic temperance society. It was an early and abiding framework for life and politics. Duggan preached that a politician "should be like a clergyman or doctor: somebody who worked to benefit people and make their lives happier and easier." While Lomasney took no prisoners to get political power, his main purpose was to watch over his neighborhood's interests from the Hendricks Club.

An early mentor, Michael Wells, who served at different times as a state representative and on the Common Council, put the seventeen-year-old Lomasney to work as a laborer in the Boston Street Department. He got the job only after proving himself in the ward work of getting voters to polls in the presidential election of 1876, when the popular vote was eventually overturned in Congress in favor of Rutherford Hayes.

Lomasney saw the connection between politics and employment when his work at the polls got him a job digging ditches for $1.75 a day. He helped shape the new streets of Commonwealth and Massachusetts avenues in the emerging Back Bay. He put the shovel aside to become one of 130 lamplighters who tended to more than ten thousand gas lamps in the city each night. Lomasney's territory was the West End, where he turned the lights on at dusk and off at dawn and fixed them when needed for one and a half cents for each tended lamp.

It was good money, but he began his real education by spending a good part of his downtime each day at the Common Council chamber, listening to the arguments and issues as the city started its inexorable shift from Yankee to Irish. He got to know both sides of every issue, and especially the ins and outs of parliamentary procedure, which later became his forte. Early on, he became a prodigious factotum in the political world, encyclopedic and much sought after about who said what about this or that.

He also got his first lesson in political infighting when he pushed back against a baseless complaint about his work as a lamplighter. A city councilor overreacted to a constituent, but had to back down when Lomasney presented him with some hard facts about an erroneous grievance of laxity. A short while later, when Lomasney's mentor, Michael Wells, died suddenly in an accident, the spiteful city councilor moved against Lomasney, who lost his job and discovered the bleak inequities of the spoils system.

Lomasney immediately set out to become his own protector by building his own political network. He put up a candidate to succeed Wells, who was on the bad side of a dominant Ward 8 figure, state senator Owen Galvin, who caustically dismissed Lomasney's pick. Until then, Martin was more a doer than a talker. Not this time. He not only told the senator he was in a dogfight but made it clear to Galvin that he was going to beat his candidate. Lomasney's man bolted the caucus nominating process and ran as a long-odds independent against a sanctioned rival. But win they did when William Taylor took his seat on the Common Council in 1884. More important, the defiant lamplighter had caught the fancy of the caucus audience, and word spread throughout the ward of a young comer named Martin Lomasney.

The unexpected victory paid immediate dividends in Lomasney's appointment as an inspector at the city Board of Health, an agency run by Taylor's father.

Within a year of the upset by the upstarts, Lomasney institutionalized his agenda by forming the Hendricks Club. Now twenty-five, he was a good distance from Duggan's "clergyman" prototype. In fact, his platform was to oppose anyone vaguely sympathetic to Galvin, an internecine war that went on for ten years, reaching its zenith when Lomasney was charged with attempted murder of Galvin in a political case that was soon dismissed. Lomasney's high ground was his club, and he ran a tight ship. He banned alcohol in the club, and would send those in disarray from drink home with escorts. There would be no pitching of Irish drunks into the street, but there was zero tolerance once inside.

His right hand at the club was Edward Donovan, a legislator and crony whom Lomasney viewed as his second brother. Donovan was the club's titular president, but it was Lomasney's show. The club was named after Grover Cleveland's vice president, Thomas Hendricks, who favored the Irish when few on the national scene did.

The club continued to resist the city's Democratic Party, and put together an Independent slate in 1887, a big consolidation year for Lomasney-backed candidates. He placed Donovan and another man in the House and two on the Common Council. Within two election cycles, the Lomasney slate was in charge and embarked on a twenty-year roll until charter reform reduced the size of the council in 1909.

One of Lomasney's early conquests came when he threw his support to another upstart, John Fitzgerald of the North End, who wanted to vault to the state senate after only one term on the Common Council. Lomasney's defection came as a shock to incumbent George Mcgahey, who had earlier challenged one of Lomasney's candidates in a different election. Martin had not forgotten. It was a lasting lesson for Lomasney as he saw how bloc voting in Ward 8 could have impact in races centered in adjoining wards. Martin became king of the swing vote.

But after backing Fitzgerald for Congress, they had their Waterloo in the mayoral race in 1905. Lomasney wanted the mayor's chair for his close friend Ned Donovan, but Fitzgerald beat them both. The tone was set in the early going, when Fitzgerald derided Donovan for not making a speech for the Democratic Party in fifteen years, and Donovan noted for the record that Fitzgerald had not shut up for the same time period. Fitzy attacked Lomasney as well by casting Donovan as a puppet in an elaborate spectacle that would give Lomasney control over City Hall. Lomasney's army stumped hard for Donovan, and Ward 8 gave him a two-thousand vote cushion, but Fitzgerald still carried the city by 3,743 votes on primary day.

It was a rare defeat for the Mahatma. But in the epic showdown between old Boston and the Irish insurgency, he had little choice but to stand with Honey Fitz against James Jackson Storrow in 1910. And he would have supported Fitzgerald against Curley, before Toodles changed everything. One version of Boston political history from the end of Fitzgerald to the Depression was Lomasney fighting off Curley's effort to dilute Ward 8 as a power bloc by expanding its boundaries to get Curley voters inside.

Shortly after Fitzgerald beat Storrow and the Goo-Goos, distress flares reached the famous urban muckracker Lincoln Steffens about charter reform's disastrous demise and Boston's disturbing demographics.

Steffens was well known as a left-wing journalist who had written about "the shame of the cities" wrought by corrupt ward heelers. He sought out Lomasney, who greeted him coolly, making him wait until some paperwork was done at his rolltop desk. He then turned the tables on the urban dragon slayer. Lomasney brought him up short, growling, "What's your graft?"

Steffens demurred. Lomasney elaborated: "You understand all right. . . . Lay your cards on the table. . . . What portion of your regular fee do you intend to give me?"

The real question was—how do you like it when someone assumes you're corrupt on hearsay? Steffens understood immediately and was amused by the bold tactic, even if he had been drawn to Boston because the forces of regal rectitude had just been beaten by a stage Irishman. Although he spent a year in Boston and had leveled broadsides at corruption in other immigrant cities such as New York and Chicago, he never produced his "plan" for reforming Boston.

Lomasney became a cynical supporter of civil service, which imposed some qualifications on government service. Martin liked its continuity. He got his people in the door, and civil service kept them there as foot soldiers in the permanent West End army. Over time, it allowed the inmates to occasionally run the asylum. But Lomasney liked its element of fairness and the way it kept his appointees safe from purges. His end of the deal was to provide a modicum of suitability—pick-and-shovel men with the strength to do it and accountants who could add and subtract better than he could. His first-in-line Irish had to be at least functional.

As Lomasney moved from ward heeler to public personality, he began paying closer attention to public relations. He never had the stagecraft of Fitzgerald or Curley or even Coakley. But he knew he had to do more than be an employment agency if he was to be a political force. So he did the best an introvert could do. His signature event was an annual burst of exuberance at his famous Sunday-before-election-day

meeting at the club, when he would announce his slate. The ritual provided some theater for his followers and even for the general public. Press
photographers were given rare and carefully prescribed access. He got
quite lathered about his candidates' exaggerated virtues, pulling off his
suit jacket and then his collar and bow tie in animated appreciation. It
wasn't Fitzgerald's "Sweet Adeline" or Curley's Shakespeare, but it was a
crowd-pleaser that Lomasney came to enjoy.

But counting the votes was an all-business affair. Each neighborhood
had a leader, and each street a lieutenant, who had to make sure all the
identified voters did their duty. No rounding off. If sixty voters were
identified, sixty had to show up. The precinct director's job was to iden-
tify all Democratic voters from the police census list and enlist them
short of outright threats. Lomasney's ethical stretch was the "mattress
voters," expatriates who listed boardinghouses as residences. Six rooms
were good for sixty votes as the Ward 8 homing pigeons flocked in to
vote from other sections of the city or communities around Boston.

His political philosophy came from street credibility and not from
John Locke and Adam Smith. His mantra was food, clothing, and shelter. "A politician in a district such as mine sees to it that his people get
these things. If he does, he hasn't got to worry about their loyalty and
support."

Lomasney may have started backstage to fight off Owen Galvin,
but, despite his introspective nature, he knew he had to put his money
where his mouth was. After taking the measure of the public figures in
his orbit, he said "why not" and jumped into electoral politics. He ran
for alderman in 1892, and it became the first in a nearly uninterrupted
string of elected offices he held over four decades. Most of his time was in
the state legislature, where constituent service was less demanding and he
could run his Ward 8 empire and real-estate business from a respectable
perch with a good view of the city.

His first stint as alderman was more than Politics 101. The learning
curve included an assassination attempt by a deranged constituent who
got off three shots at him outside City Hall. A West End man, still
angry over a citation from Lomasney's days as a health inspector, carried his grudge to extremes. He opened fire on the new alderman as he

walked into City Hall, grazing him with one shot, missing with another, but getting him in the hip with the third. Lomasney was drolly stoic in his recuperation: "The people didn't think an awful lot of aldermen, but they didn't think we ought to be shot without a fair trial."

After four years on the board, he moved "up" to the senate and then "down" to the house, where he served off and on for decades.

Even though he had just arrived at the State House in 1896, the *Boston Post* pushed him as the kind of shrewd and seasoned leader to succeed the recently deceased Patrick Maguire as the boss of the ward heelers. But the other ward bosses rebelled and formed the secretive Board of Strategy to head off Lomasney and hold close the prerogative of picking mayors. Its charter members were Joseph Corbett of Charlestown, James Donovan of the South End, and Patrick Kennedy of East Boston. The political dynamic in Boston for years to come was the Mahatma against the Big Three.

While Lomasney's toughest loss was Fitzgerald over Donovan in 1905, it was a passing summer storm compared with his enduring winter with James Michael Curley. The former faded with slow-healing bruises from a hard-fought campaign, but Curley's stranglehold on patronage and his jut-jawed effrontery in not "keeping it legal" at City Hall left permanent scars.

The breach lasted nearly twenty years, no surprise given the iron will and score-keeping of both men. Lomasney had held his nose about Curley in his first mayoral run, seeing him as the lesser of two evils, with the alternative being a tepid man backed by the Yankee Goo-Goos. His reward was Curley trying to dilute Ward 8 by expanding it, and getting stiff-armed on jobs.

It moved to open hostilities when Lomasney supported the quirky Yankee Democrat Andrew J. Peters, who beat Curley in his reelection bid in 1917. Curley began bad-mouthing Lomasney at every turn. As a state representative, Lomasney fashioned a simple rebuttal: he took to the House floor with an order that the Boston Finance Commission's report on Curley's profligate first term be forwarded to the attorney general's office for prosecution. The motion was adopted with eager Republican votes, but died in an office whose inhabitants had no stomach for a fight with Curley.

The discord peaked after Curley's narrow comeback win in 1921 over Thomas Murphy, an old warhorse from the early Irish ascendancy who was greatly favored by Lomasney for his seconding speech for Hugh O'Brien decades earlier. The next year Lomansey filed a vague, retributive bill that provided a format for removing a mayor for improper conduct. It was billed as a good government generality, but everyone knew the target. It was presented in tandem with yet another order to get the Finance Commission (FinCom) report to the attorney general again so that prosecutors could take a hard look at the financing of Curley's Jamaicaway mansion, along with kickback projects for roadbuilding and city property insurance and contractor bonding.

Once again, there were no takers. But it was beside the point. Lomasney was just making it clear where he stood on the dominant political force in his city. His final plea was that "no man in public office, no matter who he may be, is greater than the law of this commonwealth."

The response was vintage Curley, dismissing Lomasney as a has-been crank: "Why bother to enter into a controversy with a man who is politically dead?" And Curley's trump card in all disputes: I'm in and you're out. "The old fellow can't seem to stomach the fact the city held an election last December and that the people elected Curley."

Toward the end, the Mahatma softened, even on Curley, with peacemaking patronage and time combining to assuage if not heal old wounds. But his heart was in his last campaign, for it was for a true-blue protégé. Lomasney shed his collar and bow tie in an election-eve stem-winder for a second-generation Hendricks Club member named Bill Prendible. As a young man, Prendible had sensed that Lomasney could use some company on his nightly strolls around the West End, and he fell into one of Lomasney's permanent routines. Rain or shine, the pair walked the perimeter every day for fourteen years. Martin lived to see Prendible elected to the below-the-radar but powerful job as clerk of Suffolk County's criminal court.

But shortly after Prendible's election in 1932, Lomasney fell ill with respiratory and heart problems. His doctor, who had ordered rest and quiet, found just the opposite was going on. They had a showdown, with the doctor saying Lomasney could live ten more years if he stayed away from the tumult of the Hendricks Club and politics. "How long if I don't?" Lomasney asked. Perhaps a year, the doctor said. And it was almost to the day. Lomasney told his followers on his seventy-third birthday that it was too hard for him to stay away from politics, and so he wouldn't. His big concession was to recuperate in Florida that winter, and he was seen off at South Station by a group headed by Bill Prendible and Honey Fitzgerald. He was back in the spring, but in worse health, his heart problems compounded by influenza.

Finally he did have to give up the Hendricks Club. Each day he walked slowly from his room at the Hotel Bellevue to sit on a folding chair near the statue of General Charles Devens at the State House, where he could look over the West End that lay at the bottom of the hill. After a lifetime of solitude, with scores of acquaintances but only a few close friends, one of them sat with him as he lay gravely ill in his small room on an August day. They were talking about West End matters, with Lomasney regretting his prolonged absence, when he abruptly changed the subject and lamented about his lonely life. "Here I am, after all these years, going out within the four walls of a hotel room, with no home of my own and no family to shed a tear." His somber rumination passed quickly and he turned stoic once again, saying his way precluded family, that no one could have pursued politics the way he did and be married with children. "I guess it wouldn't have been fair to a woman," he said with a wan shrug. He died on August 13, 1933.

Curley and Fitzgerald dominated the obituary tributes, one more heartfelt than the other.

Fitzgerald said, "Martin M. Lomasney leaves no successor. His dynamic force, his uncompromising stand for things that he thought were right, his burning love and devotion to Ireland, his loyalty to the poor and unfortunate, had no match."

And the ultimate compliment: "When I was mayor, he never asked me to do one single thing that meant money in his pocket."

And the muckraker Steffens, who had been warned that Lomasney was the worst of Boston's sinister bosses, reported that he found just the opposite. "He had strength, rough kindness, tribal loyalty, and, rarest of all—intellectual integrity. He could think straight in whatever he did. He put his kind on the map."

The Hendricks Club, with its rolltop desk and lonely straw hat in place but sadly bereft, folded quickly. It had been a one-man show, and it was suddenly as cobwebbed as vaudeville.

The building would survive, but Lomasney's cherished helter-skelter neighborhood would not. The view from General Devens's statue was dramatically altered by urban renewal's wrecking ball in the late 1950s to make way for a cluster of luxury apartments owned by one of the leading "reformers" of the "new" Boston. When the demolition was over, it was as if Cossacks had leveled a village in the Crimea. Only two churches and a hospital were left standing. It was hailed as vital progress in a tawdry part of town. But the new day was a bad turn for a good shepherd's legacy.

CHAPTER 4

Himself

JAMES MICHAEL CURLEY

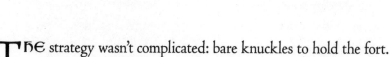

T ɦ e strategy wasn't complicated: bare knuckles to hold the fort.
    James Michael Curley had fallen to chicanery in Ward 17 twice before when he stood for the Boston Common Council. But this time he was after a sure thing. He wanted the huge advantage of being atop the ballot of 1899. He and his brother John and several able-bodied brethren set out to assure primacy by laying siege to the city's election department entrance the night before filing day. While they got there first, they barely held on, withstanding several flying wedges of brawny competitors with the same agenda. His brother suffered a broken jaw, and Curley and his gang were left black and blue.

    But as Curley remembered it, when the clerks arrived that morning, "we still held the fort and my name topped the ballot." He coasted to victory, launched with a warrior's baptism in rawboned ethnic politics. His bloodied knuckles would keep him on top of the ballot for most of the next fifty years.

    It was an opportune beginning, Curley being the right man at the right time. His constituents were on the slightly better side of a half century of squalor and deprivation, but the shards of that era, the dilapidated housing and subsistence pay, needed his raised sonorous voice. He spoke for the belt of Irish discontent that ran deeply through Roxbury, South Boston, Charlestown, East Boston, and Dorchester. Its center was his home turf—the disaster zone known as Ward 17.

    Curley bulled his way to power, and from the first scrum forward, opponents knew they were in for a no-punches-pulled brawl, or a dialectic that left no stone unturned. It became his pugnacious calling card, and his hot temper flared for good and ill throughout his storied career.

He railed at opponents in public forums and, even as an older man, called the bluff of hecklers by rolling up his sleeves and beckoning them to the podium. While he became known for his golden oratory at political rallies, quick fists and cutting ripostes anchored his success. And his truculence chilled the passive press of the day, keeping it away from his barely concealed "where's mine" graft, which could have sullied his standing before his legend took hold.

One dustup seems to have given him a permanent leg up on the media. In 1926, a quarter century after he barricaded his way to victory, he had an astounding encounter with a critical publisher on a city street. Once allies, they had been fighting over money for months, and when Curley spotted him near State Street at lunchtime, he blocked the publisher's way and then decked him with an uppercut.

From that point on even as the evidence piled up, the hint of a critical report brought an arched eyebrow and, if pursued, the threat or fact of libel action. The glare froze later efforts by the *Herald* and the *Post* to get at Curley's white-envelope dealings with city contractors and, worse still, the "dishonest" graft with blackmailer Daniel Coakely.

The more entrenched his power became, the less tolerance he had for the usual give-and-take of politics. In his third term as mayor, Curley veered out of control at times. In one incident, with arms waving and eyes popping, he chased a school committee woman out of a radio studio for mild criticism. And even that seemed restrained when, a few months later, he dove across a table at the chairman of the State Democratic Committee for suggesting Curley had pocketed $15,000 intended for presidential candidate and Irish favorite Al Smith. And some fast remarks from Curley to the governor he was succeeding in 1934 led to an unseemly scuffle between them at inauguration day ceremonies.

How did a crook and brawler attain such primacy and become a Boston institution? For starters, many Irish love a crook and a brawler, at least one who can stay "one of us" without going too far, which is usually defined as getting caught. He had become "our" rogue and he knew it. A masterful salesman who knew his customers well, Curley used the "us versus them" refrain to perfection. His lifestyle excesses were dismissed as righteous payback for decades of collective grief. Who cared about petty graft when he was standing up to incestuous Yankee bankers and taking on all comers with fearless bravado? Even as an old man, fresh from a federal penitentiary for fraud, he was welcomed home with brass bands and cheering crowds. The historian William Shannon attributed the Curley allure and longevity to his status as the "spokesman for a state of mind."

Curley would last five decades in politics because he had no quit in him and no shame. He would be in and out of office in equal measure. A most reluctant banker when on a restless sabbatical from politics by defeat or term limit, he simply ran for the next available high office. All the time. Governor. Mayor. Senator. Congressman. He never evolved into a lovable old man of politics like Honey Fitzgerald. On the contrary, he stayed a defiant provocateur from start to finish. When he was through excoriating Yankee overlords, he even turned on Southern Baptists for sinking Al Smith in 1928 because he was Catholic. He fought with Boston's cardinal and several governors and Henry Cabot Lodge and President Roosevelt. But with all the ups and downs, Curley compiled a unique scorecard: four times a mayor and four times a congressman. Governor for one infamous term. The list of defeats is almost as impressive: state house of representatives, state senate, governor, and US Senate. He even lost six times for the job he loved best—mayor of Boston. His durability was not rooted in a party machine he controlled. His strength surpassed that of a mere ward boss. He was his own machine. He was James Michael Curley.

The street-urchin son of a charwoman and a hod carrier became an inimitable American character. He was known for florid oratory and brio on the stump. But it was his brass and humor that made him an indelible original. James Cagney for real.

He burst onto the national scene in 1932 as a crafty clown at the Democratic convention that nominated Franklin Roosevelt. Unlike many Irish Catholics in Massachusetts, Curley decided that Al Smith, the former New York governor who had been trounced four years earlier by Herbert Hoover, had had his chance. But the diehards controlled the state delegation and froze Curley out. Or so they thought. He insinuated himself into the Puerto Rico contingent and cast the island's six

votes for FDR in the fourth and deciding ballot in Chicago. He introduced himself to the floor as Alcaide Jaime Miguel Curleo and did a jig
as he passed the baleful Massachusetts delegation.

Even in his dotage, he had no trouble looking a gift horse in the
mouth. Edwin O'Connor's novel *The Last Hurrah*, loosely based on Curley's career, depicted him as a noble rogue who had more principle about
him than the shallow whippersnapper who beat him with TV ads. Curley, of course, threatened to sue before realizing the book would assure
his place in history. The Curley-based protagonist became even more
benign in the movie starring Spencer Tracy.

Ðe was born poor in an Irish slum in 1874. Both of his parents, Michael Curley from Galway and Sarah Clancy from nearby Connemara,
had come to Boston a decade earlier. They landed as young teenagers,
and it would be a hard life. With the help of a ward boss, Michael was
hired as a hod carrier. The pair married young and moved into a rickety
three-decker, one of scores of tenement houses built around that time
expressly for the disdained shanty Irish who flooded Roxbury Neck, a
remote place that had only recently been annexed by the city of Boston.

The flat was just off the fetid North Bay and the Southampton
Street dump that blew across the slum with a malodorous breeze of
low-tide ferment and refuse's tinny stench. The only refined structures
in the area were the stately symbol of St. Patrick's Church, which was
built in the 1830s amid raids from hostile Protestant mobs, and Boston
City Hospital, which opened its doors in the 1860s to combat cholera
among the poor. One of Michael Curley's sons would expand the hospital so much that Irish Boston thought James Curley built it brick by
brick.

But, those refinements aside, day-to-day life in Roxbury Neck was
permeated by hard drink to ward off hard times. Each block had its
"growler"—an overrun and usually out-of-work father who groused his
way from one bar to the next. A settlement-house worker took a sociological snapshot on a Saturday night in the 1870s that found 391 men
imbibing in twenty-seven saloons.

Michael Curley did not succumb to the pervasive alcohol of the neighborhood, but fell to the other scourge of the era—the unsafe work-place. He was interned in the Irish immigrant burial ground—the Old Calvary Cemetery—next to his youngest son and namesake. Like so many others in the first wave of immigrants, he died on a job that had no benefits save a paltry paycheck. There was no help from ward boss P. James "Pea Jacket" Maguire this time. Dead was dead. It would be Sarah and the two boys against the world.

The historian Francis Russell recorded that Ward 17 children came into the world with clenched fists. So arrived James Michael Curley less than a decade after the end of the Civil War. He would run with street gangs before he was five, and stay within the prescribed turf just a few miles but a world away from where the new neighborhood of Back Bay was taking shape.

By his teens, James Michael Curley knew the only road out of Lower Roxbury was politics. He had long been enthralled by the pageantry of it all—the parades, fireworks, marching bands, and streetcorner oratory. At fifteen, he took full-time work driving a wagon for C. S. Johnson Grocers, hauling barrels of flour up and down three-decker tenements. He got to know the byways of his time and place, and was soon driven by an unfocused ambition for something better than lugging goods around Lower Roxbury. He was promoted to a sales job at Johnson's, but his salary was only eleven dollars a week. He realized a city job wouldn't do it for him either. He easily passed the civil-service test for fireman, but looked past the stationhouse ennui toward a more challenging career.

In his early twenties, he zeroed in on elected office. As a garrulous and feisty young man in and out of Irish tenements every day, he came to know firsthand the abject dependence of most households on politi-cal figures for food and shelter. One of his favorite delivery stops was the political hangout inside "One Arm" Peter Whalen's tobacco store, though it didn't take long for him to get on the wrong side of One Arm by supporting the wrong candidate. No matter. He reviewed his rivals and concluded he could do it better. He knew he had what it took—a strong, rugged face, a sturdy frame, and, while no backslapper, an engag-ing way. Instinctively he moved toward a run for the seventy-five-member Common Council. He passed the plate at church, went to night school, read the classics at the local library, and joined the Ancient Order of Hibernians.

By the time Curley got started in politics, he was hardly a pioneer. He benefited from Irish inroads established long before his initial forays. The first Irishman was elected to the populous Common Council in 1857, to the Board of Aldermen in 1870, the Congress in 1880, and to the office of mayor in 1884. But it was a fits-and-starts progression, with one Yankee mayor ousted as late as 1878 for appointing Irishmen to the police force.

By Curley's time, the biggest challenge was intramural ghetto politics rather than the slowly fading discrimination of the ruling elite. It was a tough league where he became equally adept at trading punches and verbal jibes, honing his skill at the slashing invective that became his trademark. He had to run more than once for the Common Council. But once in at the age of twenty-five, he began his longest continuous stint in public office, a two-decade run in which he moved briefly to the state legislature and then back to the higher tier of Boston's layered government—the Board of Aldermen. He next moved to a reconfigured city council as a charter member of a scaled-back nine-member body that was the brain child of "reformers" in 1909 who thought eliminating district seats in favor of a citywide chamber would keep the Irish in check. Instead, the Yankee-dominated Good Government Association got overrun by an Irish population that had seeped into every neighborhood except Back Bay and Beacon Hill. Curley then took a two-term hiatus from city government to sit in Congress before busting into the mayor's office, which was his holy grail.

After his first victory at the turn of the century, he formed his own club in Roxbury, the Tammany Club, which took its name from the infamous New York City political machine. Though politics would be his full-time job, he needed what he called "an anchor toward windward," a backstop for defeat at the polls. In his first term, he and his brother John opened an insurance agency for New York Life.

As a member of the Common Council, he unveiled the staple of his public life—a one-man employment agency for constituents. He placed seven hundred men and women in his first two years in office. Patronage jobs became the sine qua non of his realm. There was little he wouldn't do to keep a family of voters beholden, even becoming a domestic mediator or character witness in court to keep a constituent on the job. The idea was to keep breadwinners out of bread lines and, above all, in the voting booths.

But with influence-peddling becoming his stock in trade, it did not take long before he was in court as a defendant rather than as an advocate. Shortly after his first term in office, he and another man were convicted in federal court of fraud because they posed as constituents taking a civil service test for the post office. Curley had researched the law beforehand and thought the only penalty for impersonation would be banishment from taking other tests. He had overlooked the fraud part. Not so a federal judge who sentenced him to sixty days in the Charles Street Jail. It was the first—but not the last—time he survived and even prospered politically after a criminal conviction. In fact, the first time around, he spun it as the ultimate constituent service. Crime? Could such a selfless act be a crime? Curley later said that the County Meath man he took the test for "couldn't spell Constantinople but he had wonderful feet for a letter carrier." A new Curley slogan was born: "He did it for a friend."

Curley was elected to the Board of Aldermen from jail, returning with his usual flair, at least by his memoir's chapter and verse. The day he was released, he got a heads-up that the board president was planning to declare his seat vacant, what with its occupant barely out of prison. After a change of clothes, Curley was whisked to the second-floor chamber and took a seat next to Daniel J. Whelton. He leaned over to the president and said, "I understand that you propose to move that my seat be declared vacant."

"Yes," said Whelton, "I do."

"Well," said Curley, "I just want to inform you that if you present such a motion, you will go through that window." Whelton nodded, and in the silence that followed, the motion remained motionless and the president remained on the second floor.

Curley never eased up after that combative start. His first political tempest came at the Board of Aldermen, and it reeked of kickback. He had led the fight to allow an East Boston shipping firm to lay track along the waterfront to transport boxcars between loading docks. The proposal was packaged as vital to keep Boston from slipping further in national rankings as a seaport. After the mayor vetoed the measure and the board declined to override, Curley went into orbit, demanding a new vote and hotly refusing to yield the floor. Another alderman then alleged that most of the board had taken bribes, telling each of them one by one that they had been bought, and bought cheap. He changed the refrain slightly when he came to Curley: "The gentleman from Ward 17 was also bought, but not so cheap. You received twice as much because you handled the matter." The accusation caused a press firestorm that slowly declined to cinders. A grand jury was impaneled with fanfare, but issued no indictments.

The loading-dock flap introduced another standard Curley tactic when he faced criticism over pungent deals. After a backstage accommodation was struck, his jut-jawed advocacy was usually followed by wild-armed indignation at the very mention of impropriety. In 1905 Curley quoted *Othello* in the aftermath of the East Boston shipping dispute. And not for the last time: "Who steals my purse steals trash. . . . But he that filches from me my good name robs me of that which not enriches him and makes me poor indeed." It was part of a white-lipped rant about what were accurate stories about who said what. In his continuing lather, Curley foolishly wrote an extortionate letter to the *Boston Traveler,* which had criticized his tirade. The newspaper held a city contract to print the minutes of City Hall meetings, and Curley intimated that he might strike the annual $8,500 publication appropriation "in the interest of economy." The die was cast with the media, and a stratagem was born: Don't explain—attack.

As Boston skittered into the twentieth century, Curley's unapologetic rise closely paralleled that of the Roman Catholic Church, which was changing from the submissive accommodation required by the Know Nothing era to boldly assertive. Just as Curley was no Hugh O'Brien, Cardinal William O'Connell was no Bishop John Fitzpatrick. The mayor and the cardinal both rode the same political wind, with Curley taking control of an Irish electorate and O'Connell using the numbers to forge an alternate universe with his parochial school system. In 1915 O'Connell put it on the line, urging Catholic manhood to square its shoulders and "look the world in the eye and say 'I am a Roman Catholic citizen. What about it?'"

But O'Connell and Curley were too similar to get along or share center stage. While the cardinal was the youngest of eleven children from an immigrant household in Lowell, he nonetheless acted to the manor born. He studied in Rome for many years and wore his erudition heavily on his robed sleeve, and his pretensions earned him the sobriquet of "His Pomposity." His domestic staff outnumbered anything to be found on Beacon Hill. Yet he could throw a hard, nimble jab, wondering at one point how it was that there were any children at all born in repressed Puritan homes. He was no less autocratic than Curley, telling the faithful, "When I ask you to do anything, trust me and do it." The cardinal and the mayor fed off each other as the Irish machine and flock matured simultaneously. Curley's swagger and the cardinal's hauteur melded into an energized hegemony, and the decline of the Yankee became inexorable. But before it was over, the town wasn't big enough for two prelates.

As Curley closed in on the mayor's office, he would always personify the paradox of many singular public men—a loner who could engage a crowd far more easily than the man met on the street. He was widely acquainted, but had few close friends, an aloof egotist who always wanted to do a job himself rather than delegate it. For who could do it better? Whose better hands?

Shortly after Curley became mayor in 1914, he moved into a grandiose mansion far beyond his means. To the question of how he could afford a $60,000 mansion on a $10,000 salary, Curley said he owed it to a stock tip. But everyone knew the source of the money was city vendors. The manse on the Jamaicaway was clearly the house that Boston contractors built. And the household they supported. With surprising ease, the graft quickly became beside the point. Curley's neo-Georgian retreat and his lavish lifestyle became a neat trick. He turned them into a get-even symbol for the struggling Irish who saw his opulence as everyone's gain and a delicious effrontery to the waning plutocracy. His house became his persona, an imperial outpost on the outskirts of town that stood for the Irish ascendancy. The more he flaunted its splendor, the better his voters liked it. The redbrick Valhalla was built on land and materials from contractors Curley had cultivated as an alderman and a city councilor, but its upkeep made graft a way of life dependent on the cash cow of public contracts. The care and feeding of the house made Curley a perennial candidate who could not afford to be out of office.

The manor had few equals even in Back Bay. The bitter taste of poverty still in his mouth, Curley's status and elixir became money. He wasted little time before cashing in, with construction beginning, fittingly, on Saint Patrick's Day in 1915. Curley built a twenty-one-room, 10,000-square-foot mansion on a two-acre site that was four miles from Ward 17, where Curley had been a delivery boy. Inside, it had an oval dining room off a cavernous front hall with a massive chandelier and a three-story spiral stairway. There were five bathrooms, twenty-eight mahogany doors, and countless gold-plated light fixtures. The one plebeian touch was provided by cookie-cutter shamrocks dotting the white shutters framing its many windows.

Broke no more, Curley became an obsessive spender. Over the decades, hundreds of thousands in graft came in the door, albeit with a goodly portion going out a side door to uphold his coveted title as "mayor of the poor." He presided over a personal dole system for constituents while tending to his personal extravagance.

Fifteen years out of Ward 17, Mayor Curley went first class on all matters. He became Boston's guest at the finest hotels around the world, with long stays in Palm Beach, on Sea Island, Georgia, and in Bermuda and Cuba, as well as regular trips to Europe. He summered by the sea in large, rambling houses and traveled with servants and drivers. His estate wanted for little: a cook, an upstairs maid, a gardener, a cleaning woman, and a governess for his children. He had oriental rugs, a wine cellar, and a yacht. There would be Havana cigars and fresh-cut flowers every day. And private schools for his children. Despite the extravagance, he never lost his rapport with the down and out. His Robin

Hood welfare office, where the poor lined up at the side entrance to the grand house, gave him an unflagging constituency who were with him through thick and thin. In jail and out.

Not so on Beacon Hill. The Boston Finance Commission, which was controlled and stoked by Yankees at the State House, chased Curley almost from the moment the cornerstone of the house was laid. It found contractors who did city business carrying work for Curley on their books with the notation NC—"no charge." At the end of his first term, the mayor testified before the commission that he got the money to buy the land from a stake he had in a plumbing and heating company. But he could never show what he did for the company in return. It was just one of several convolutions devised with his lawyer, the cantankerous and creative Daniel Coakley. The probe came to naught when the troubling evidence was handed off to the compromised hands of District Attorney Joseph Pelletier, who was in Coakley's hip pocket.

The refined digs on the Jamaicaway got their finishing touch from Curley's strong wife and sole adviser, the former Mary Herlihy, who kept the mayor on an even keel and safely enveloped in a solid family life. Curley had married late for the day, at thirty-two, but the union produced nine children, though only two would survive him. When Curley was a congressman biding his time for mayor, the pair took etiquette lessons that Mary treated seriously while James Michael lampooned the teacups and trays when he got back home with the boys in Ward 17. Mary made friends with President William Howard Taft's wife while Curley alienated a young undersecretary of the navy named Franklin Delano Roosevelt. But the social graces she acquired made her a good fit for matron of a manor with a large staff and some more or less distinguished guests. In addition to running the house, she kept Curley away from his worst instincts and home for supper. There would be no dalliance with a Toodles Ryan. At least in his marriage, Curley stayed above reproach.

Curley's first venture beyond the tight Ward 17 turf was two terms in Congress that were undertaken, he always insisted, on the promise from Honey Fitz that he would bow out in 1914 to gear up for a US Senate race. While in Congress, Curley seized on the same issue with the same antagonist with whom Fitzgerald had clashed more than a decade earlier—Henry Cabot Lodge and his unremitting war on immigrants.

It was the old story: Curley saw new voters where the priggish Lodge saw uncouth tax burdens. Lodge had come around some on the Irish, bowing to their growing numbers more than to a change of heart, though his unvarnished nineteenth-century assessment was the Beacon Hill norm—the Irish were "a hard drinking, idle, quarrelsome and disorderly class always at odds with the government." But Lodge's softened stance on the Irish in Curley's first congressional term did not extend to the new wave of Italians, Poles, Hungarians, and Russian Jews. He saw them as coarse threats to the survival of America, and said so. If they couldn't read or write, they should be sent packing. Curley, on the other hand, saw them as fellow travelers who bustled around the streets of the North and West Ends doing jobs nobody else wanted. A Lodge literacy test failed, but passed five years later during the xenophobia surrounding America's late entry into World War I in 1917.

Immigration was one of Curley's staple campaign themes as he began training for the main event, the battle royal with the incumbent mayor John Fitzgerald. Honey Fitz was in his prime at fifty years of age, and, despite his agreement to vacate City Hall, he was clearly making plans for reelection in 1914. He may have been the first Irishman born in America to be elected mayor of Boston, but in Curley's view, Fitzgerald had commandeered his job.

Fitzgerald was much more the go-along-to-get-along pol. He took the system for what it was—a loosely structured, nothing-for-nothing road out of the slum. He had cultivated a ward boss and then succeeded him. When he ran for mayor, he ran as a machine candidate who had formed alliances with most of the bosses. Curley would always run against the bosses because he couldn't bear to share power with any of them.

After Fitzgerald was forced out, Curley's job was half done. He still had to face the ward bosses' candidate, Thomas J. Kenny, a City Council member and successful lawyer from South Boston. He was a tentative campaigner with a flock of endorsements, most prominently the

Yankee-dominated Good Government Association, which cut him little slack with Irish voters outside his home precinct. But Kenny got support from arch-rivals from opposing camps. With Curley in the race, Tom Kenny was the one thing James J. Storrow and Honey Fitzgerald could agree on.

Curley trounced Kenny, deriding his mediocrity and currying favor with new voters in Boston by trumpeting his opposition to literacy tests. The city's forty foreign-language newspapers endorsed Curley in a polyglot chorus as the conventional press lined up behind the less threatening and business-friendly Kenny.

Curley lived and succeeded by sheer moxie. He ran against the machine and most newspapers, and ended the campaign in Kenny's home base in Southie with memorable stridency on hostile ground. His voice rising against catcalls, he denounced them all. "I'll be elected mayor of Boston and you don't like it. Here I am. Does any one of you bums want to step up here and make anything of it?"

In addition to his hard-nosed drive to succeed, Curley's main asset was his booming voice with its singular inflexion—a baroque mix of high Oxford and raspy Ward 17. He honed it into a weapon that was usually delivered with a hard glare or exaggerated forbearance. The refined intonations disappeared entirely when he got into a real argument. But when giving a speech, his grandiloquent phrasing became the old-time religion. He dressed up the mundane with ornate flourishes about "Wednesday last," or slowly enunciated dates as "nine-teen hundred and seven-teen"; vital civic matters were serious "obleegations" taking place in the city of "Boss-tun."

But Curley reverted to Ward 17 brawling even in victory, a sore winner in the spikes-high tradition of contemporary baseball legend Ty Cobb. After his triumph in 1914, he had a particularly ungracious handoff with the vanquished Fitzgerald. They had nearly come to blows the night before Curley's inauguration, when the new mayor turned his back on Fitzgerald's congratulatory hand. At the formal swearing-in the next day, Curley greeted everyone in sight but Fitzgerald. Finally there was a cold exchange. Curley, wearing a half-smile and bearing a grudge for Fitzgerald's clandestine support of Kenny, finally said, "How are you, Mr. Mayor?" "Good morning." croaked a crestfallen Fitzgerald, looking close to tears.

Frigid formalities over, Curley was finally ensconced in the mayor's office, having promised to clean up City Hall and wipe out ward bosses and introduce massive public-works programs for parks and schools and playgrounds. He was true to his word. In his own fashion. He removed hundreds of Fitzgerald workers and rolled up the ward-boss system into one preeminent personage—Superboss Curley. But the workforce soon surpassed Fitzgerald's, as did city expenditures.

He set a ruthless tone right away when it became clear that Fitzgerald's supporters, along with the business community, were pushing for a recall election, an early referendum on a new mayor that nearly succeeded. (Curley lost the vote badly, but the winning margin failed to meet the requirement of being 50 percent of the registered voters.) Inside City Hall, the recall issue came to a boil with Curley's appointment of a new commissioner of public works, who oversaw a patronage army of three thousand employees and two thousand more through favored contractors.

The mandate in April 1915 to the new commissioner: any city employee who even talked about a recall election was to be discharged for high treason. Lest there be any confusion of his intent, the mayor issued the "forty-second-cousin" rule: "If anyone heads a recall movement I will remove him and every relative of his in the city service down to the forty-second cousin, and every friend, and every friend of a friend I'll cut to the bone."

But Curley was equally vigilant on his promise to give a hearing to any constituent without an appointment. Petitioners were screened by a phalanx of secretaries, and then a dozen would be brought into his office, waiting to be pointed to a chair next to the mayor. He would regard each squarely and ask, "What do *you* want?" He would do what he could immediately, or explain why nothing could be done. When he stood up, it was time for a different dozen, until he reached his claimed daily limit of two hundred supplicants.

Like Fitzgerald's before him, Curley's administration was a profligate system of kiting checks—the jobs and parks and schools were added without a second thought about cost. He simply raised taxes on commercial buildings and ran a Ponzi scheme to finance benefits for lower-income voters. He was changing the face of Boston while making enemies who couldn't wait for the next election.

In his reelection fight in 1917, he was outfoxed by an alliance of the one ward boss left standing—Martin Lomasney—and vengeful Yankee businessmen tired of paying for playgrounds for Irish kids. He was beaten by an old trick he knew well and had used himself—tilt the race with a spoiler who cut into the leader's vote. He was narrowly defeated by Andrew Peters, a bizarre if heavily credentialed Yankee Democrat with a yen for young girls. Curley was crippled by James Gallivan of South Boston, a congressman with a safe seat not up for reelection, who finished a strong third with a flock of sure Curley votes. Glum and out of office as the titular and restless president of the Hibernia National Bank, Curley vengefully challenged Gallivan in his congressional district the next year, but was defeated again.

But in 1921, undaunted as usual, he narrowly won another four-year term as mayor. From then on, he was able to consolidate power, and the next decade and a half were his glory years. He was mayor from 1921 to 1925 and again from 1929 to 1933, and then governor from 1934 to 1936. He could have stayed mayor the whole time were it not for a new Yankee law from the State House aimed at him that banned successive terms. In his forced interregnums, Curley did not sit idly. He worked backstage to keep the mayor's chair in inept hands and away from someone who could capture the public's imagination as he had.

When in power, Curley embraced the bitter enmity of the bankers and lawyers who ran downtown, and strategically placed playgrounds and stadiums around the city neighborhoods where his voters lived. Much of it was built by the unemployed and grateful soldiers back from World War I. In addition, he replaced mudflats in Southie with a mile-long beach that came with its own L Street Bath House. Firemen got better work schedules. Unions were reconvened. Pensions for city workers were arranged. Beacon Hill and Back Bay got ice water.

His legend was assured with the close election in 1921. His opponent was an old-school waffler whose career went all the way back to the first tame Irish mayor in the 1880s, who stuck closely to the Yankee agenda of low taxes and minimal services. While he had all the bosses and the Goo-Goos, the aging John R. Murphy was the perfect foil for Curley. He had been a minor official in Hugh O'Brien's first administration and then a lackluster legislator and, most recently, the fire commissioner for a screw-loose Yankee mayor.

At a joint appearance, the ponderous Murphy, pince-nez nearly perpendicular to his face, recapped his long résumé with a restless crowd. When it was Curley's turn at the podium, he appeared theatrically feeble and squinted out at the crowd and frogged, "I don't see anybody here that I welcomed back from the Civil War." With a trademark riposte, Curley defined Murphy as an over-the-hill relic.

His puckish cracks were just the overt strategy. Curley also directed down-and-dirty whispering campaigns, with his followers spreading rumors that Murphy was seen eating steak on a fasting day or attending an Episcopalian service. While Murphy had been in and out of politics his entire career, he had never experienced the Curley treatment. There were men in black with Catholic prayer books bearing bad news in Charlestown that, regrettably, it had come to their attention that Mr. Murphy was weak of faith and morals. Did you happen to know he was a Mason and about to marry a sixteen-year-old? And South Boston voters were beseeched by earnest impostors claiming to be from the Hawes Baptist Club seeking votes for Mr. Murphy. They were rewarded with slammed doors from the lower end to City Point.

Another, more subtle factor in the 1921 election was that it marked the first time Boston women had the right to vote. And an open-letter appeal on election eve by Mary Curley was thought to have given heft to Curley's 2,698-vote edge of the 145,000 cast. But the true differential was Curley's connection with workaday Boston. He was their desperado, taking operating revenue from downtown commercial property owners and landlords around the city. It was a simple formula in a city where seven out of ten Bostonians leased the roof over their head. The landlords pay the freight and Curley's contractors build the parks with commissions to the mayor.

Curley's second term was another sustained assault on the city treasury, spurred in part by his fiery reaction to the retaliatory Republican legislation barring Boston mayors from succeeding themselves. So, in 1924, Curley ran for governor instead and gave the Yankees a good statewide race, with Alvan T. Fuller beating back the Boston rabble-rouser in a Republican year.

The next year, hamstrung by the succession law, Curley was a backstage force in a mayor's race that saw him undermine his own brother's candidacy—John being one Curley too many for center stage—and throw his support to his hack protégé fire commissioner Theodore Glynn. The objective was clear—whoever came next was not to leave a heavy footprint. In fact, Curley wanted neither Democrat to win. In a diffuse field, he ended up with a Republican who held the office loosely while Curley voters waited for his return. To say nothing of the sixteen thousand municipal workers either on unpaid leave or supervised by a Republican who expected a full day's work.

Getting the right empty suit as a stand-in for "Himself," as his singular person came to be known, was not the only Curley coup during his reluctant sabbatical. Toward the end of 1926 he won a memorable encounter with a Boston publisher that gave Curley the upper hand with the press the rest of his days. Among other things, it would keep the rare enterprising reporter away from kickbacks and blackmail, most of it waiting within careful reports prepared by his archenemy, the Yankee-dominated Boston Finance Commission, which unearthed gamey deals several times—to no avail.

Curley's clash with the publisher stemmed from a dispute about who owed whom. Frederick Enwright's *Boston Telegraph*, a tabloid once in Curley's corner, had become a major critic during his unsuccessful 1924 gubernatorial race. For about a year, the pair had squabbled about a debt. On an Indian summer day in October, as the lunchtime crowd was building, Curley spotted the publisher at the corner of Devonshire and State Streets in the financial district. Curley blocked Enwright's way. They argued briefly before the mayor decked him with an uppercut and then danced around him, demanding that the publisher get up. Enwright thought better of it and stayed down.

A former reporter in Boston and New York, Enwright became a publisher in the 1910s in Lynn, a port city north of Boston. He launched his Boston tabloid in 1921. It was known first as the *Telegram* and finally, for its epitaph, as the *Telegraph*. The publisher and the mayor saw mutual advantages in each other when Curley ran for reelection in the year that Enwright's paper got under way along with the roaring twenties. But the strong-willed pair soon had a mud fight over money. In the beginning, Curley had given Enwright some seed money and then ads from beholden contractors to help get the paper off the ground. In turn, Enwright's paper was the only one of the city's six dailies to endorse Curley. But it wasn't long before each was calling the other a deadbeat. Enwright said that once Curley was out of office, he was cut off from his usual income from contractors and sought money from Enwright on the dubious claim that he was flat broke.

Each thought the other an ingrate, with Curley contending he kept the paper afloat in the early days and Enwright taking credit for making the difference in Curley's close victory in 1921. The bad blood simmered until the fisticuffs at high noon on October 4, 1926, near the old State House. Curley's version was that they had been feuding about Curley's failure to get another candidate to pay Enwright $50,000 for editorial support, and Enwright, in retribution, had been criticizing Curley in his news pages. The unspoken subtext of the loud argument was editorial support for sale. No one denied that.

A recent spate of *Telegraph* criticism was hot under Curley's collar when he spotted the hulking Enwright in a lunchtime crowd. Enwright claimed that Curley was drunk and sucker-punched him in the back of the head, knocking the burly, six-foot-four-inch publisher to the ground. But witnesses said there was a face-to-face confrontation and that Curley floored Enwright with a lightning punch to the jaw.

Between public jobs, Curley was hanging his fedora in exile at the Hibernian Bank a few blocks away on Court Street. In the fight's stop-the-presses aftermath, reporters inundated Curley's office. "We hear you were assaulted today," one ventured. Curley smiled and became pro-lix: "Well, yes. I was assaulted but I hope you will not accuse me of an overwhelming conceit if I say that James Michael Curley defended him-self creditably."

Two days later the *Telegraph*, harking back two decades to Curley's stay at the Charles Street Jail for civil service fraud, printed a cartoon of a man in a jail cell. It portrayed Curley in a prisoner's striped uni-form anchored by a ball and chain above the cut line, "Curley the thug." An accompanying editorial said that Curley had learned to hit from behind as a street fighter, and urged him to get off the booze and out of town.

Within a few days, Curley obtained a warrant for Enwright's arrest for criminal libel. In the days before the US Supreme Court changed the burden of proof in libel cases, Enwright was faced with the legal burden of proving the literal truth of his generally accurate portrait. Under the centuries-old common law, he was tight in the grasp of the topsy-turvy libel jurisprudence of the day—guilty until proven innocent. Even in a criminal case.

Curley had indeed done a two-month stretch in jail for fraud, but he hadn't worn a striped suit and ball and chain. He was known to take a nightly bracer, but was hardly a drunk. And he had been in a barroom brawl or two in Ward 17, but there were no witnesses who would say so in 1927. The trial judge decreed that "thug" meant conviction for a vio-lent robbery; Curley had gone to jail for taking a civil service exam for a constituent.

The stacked deck had Enwright struggling to prove every assertion exhaustively. The prosecutor's sole burden was to establish that Curley was intentionally ridiculed by a malicious defendant. The jury agreed, issuing a guilty verdict in three and half hours.

Curley connected with the electorate through soaring oration and a rascal's charm. But his standing within his profession may have been secured on that October day in the financial district. Not only did he knock a publisher on his backside, he put him in jail and then into bankruptcy.

What's more, a decade later, when Curley's tragicomic reign as governor was coming unglued with corruption charges, he held the Fourth Estate at bay with threats of defamation suits. Even if reporters were game, there was little appetite for a fight in the publishers' suites. The convincing evidence of kickbacks that kept tumbling out of the Boston Finance Commission was spun as just more anti-Irish partisan politics. Charges were never prosecuted in court or pulled together in print. The *Post* and the *Herald* sniffed around some of the storylines, but were stifled by either a suit filed or threatened.

All the broad protection afforded publishers by the US Supreme Court in libel issues and editorial commentary were decades away from the prostrate publisher on State Street. It took nearly a half century—and never did Enwright any good—for his brand of rough commentary to become suit-proof. Ultimately the Supreme Court ruled that opinion pages were not subject to the same libel standards of truth and falsehood as news stories. As opinions, they were neither right nor wrong. They were just one guy's view that readers could take or leave. But in 1926 Enwright's opinion got him run out of town, all the way back to Lynn.

Curly biographer Jack Beatty reflected on the Enwright case and the pass Curley got from the press. He said that as time went on, it evolved into an unspoken immunity conveyed by an era's ethos. "It was partly because of the conventions of the day, partly because of the ethnic inhibition, partly because of his property tax leverage with publishers, and finally a sense of futility, that Curley was the tide coming in and what the hell do you do about that? Over time, Curley's graft stopped being news."

After sitting out the middle of the Roaring Twenties, Curley was reelected mayor as the country—and especially Boston—collapsed into the decade-long Great Depression. His third term started with the usual flourish, but also with Curley's private life in turmoil. His wife had been slowly dying of cancer for three years, and friends saw him staggered by the emotional load and then anchorless when she died at forty-five in 1930. One day he would stoically say it was God's will, and the next he would suddenly smash a bottle to the floor in a restaurant. Francis Russell wrote of Curley during this period that "he drank too much, he coarsened physically, he grew bombastic and careless, he had less control over his quick temper."

The "careless" part nearly tipped him over in his third term, always said to be the most dangerous for long-running mayoralties with incumbents prone to complacency and greed. Curley had appointed a businessman friend as city treasurer. Among Edmund L. Dolan's credentials was that he was the straw owner of Curley's ninety-three-foot yacht *Maicaway,* an allusion to Curley's famous house with shamrock shutters on the Jamaicaway. While cash kickbacks from contractors had been the coin of his realm for decades, Curley had moved into more elaborate conflict-of-interest conspiracies. Dolan had formed two companies to do veiled business with the city. The first was a meat-packing firm that charged city institutions such as the jail and the hospital one third above the going rate. The second was the Legal Securities Corporation, which both sold and bought bonds from the city, with Dolan taking commissions on both ends and doubtlessly splitting them with the boss.

The WASP-laden Boston Finance Commission dug into Dolan's firms, and the treasurer was eventually charged with stealing $170,000 from the city. In desperation, Dolan tried to bribe a juror, but was sentenced to two and a half years in jail after taking the fall for the mayor.

In another case, while it took years to play out, Curley paid dearly for commandeering about half of an $85,000 damage payment the city owed to an equipment company. When approached by a lawyer looking to get payment from the city, Curley put first things first: "How much is in it for me?" The answer was $40,000 for Curley when the company got its payment. In effect, they split the city payment. The incident underscored Curley's tight grasp on the city's purse strings. Little moved without his imprint. He could take a cut of services coming in and even payments going out. He had 'em coming and going.

But this one was sloppily handled late in his third term, and the kickback arrangement became known by the next mayor, Frederick

Mansfield, an old Curley enemy who still bore the scars from the 1929 race when Curley beat him. Mansfield nurtured a civil suit for repayment while Curley tried to run out the clock with thirty-four continuances. But the contest ended as one of a kind—the only court action in Boston history in which the mayor was successfully sued for profiting from the city's payment to a contractor. The court order of restitution would bring rare public opprobrium that couldn't be fobbed off as Yankee vindictiveness. But the mayor muted the disclosure by suing the *Herald* for libel when it raised questions, freezing further press coverage.

In the end, Curly escaped conviction on what could well have been extortion charges. But there was rare public shame in the humiliating edict that he repay the city $42,629 in weekly installments. It was probably the first financial obligation he had to take seriously in his adult life.

If the third term ended badly, it only seemed an extension of the bad omens that had surrounded the campaign against Mansfield at the outset—ranging from his wife's deteriorating health to the stock market crash to the mayor's distemper. What should have been a cakewalk against a candidate with a Yankee name and financial background in an overwhelmingly Catholic city, became another barely won cliffhanger.

A preoccupied Curley had taken his eye off the ball. He was distraught over Mary's illness, for she was his true love and anchor. As best she could, Mary Curley had kept his temper in check and rhetoric restrained. But with her taken to a sickbed in the upstairs bedroom, Curley roamed loose and brooked no criticism. He may have been secure politically, but he was unraveling personally. He summed up his problem with typical hubris: No one can defeat me except myself.

Indeed, he almost did just that with a wild show of disdain over what was small bore in Boston politics. Curley was losing the sense of give-and-take that was the hallmark of city campaigns. He always gave better than he got, but as the Depression took hold and his wife failed, he had no tolerance for even the mildest reproach. Toward the end of the 1929 campaign, while waiting his turn in a radio studio anteroom, he heard Jennie Loitman Barron, a member of the school committee and a Mansfield supporter, claim that Curley's school building program was more for favored contractors than students. When it came Curley's time to speak, he veered quickly from a defense of the program into an intemperate personal attack. He claimed that Barron had offered to work for his campaign for a price and had then received a better offer from the Good Government Association. His radio tirade over, he burst out of the studio into the waiting room where Barron sat with her husband. "Where's Jennie?" he shouted. Barron turned away in tears as her husband sputtered in her defense. Curley slammed on his derby and stormed off. It turned out that, rather than offering to work for Curley, she had declined a Curley intermediary's request to join his campaign. The contretemps with a woman helped turn a projected five-to-one rout into another close Curley victory, winning by 19,000 out of 216,000 cast. Mary was too ill to attend the inauguration, and died six months into his third term.

As the hard times calcified into economic paralysis and Franklin Roosevelt routed the overmatched Herbert Hoover halfway through Curley's term, the mayor tried vainly to exploit his early support of Roosevelt into largesse for Boston. But Roosevelt and his top New Deal aides never trusted Curley, having watched him disengage Boston from local bankers and state planners while plundering the city treasury. Curley tried to cash in on the national "work and wages" programs, but got less than his fair share because federal administrators knew most of it would go to pet contractors who would loop some of it back to Curley. The mayor not only demanded New Deal money, but he also had conditions: no auditors, and public jobs only to Curley contractors.

Curley clashed as well with a man who should have been another natural ally—a Democratic Yankee governor named Joseph Ely. But Ely knew that Curley wanted his job and had tried to undermine his recent election. Curley chafed with Ely's administrators on joint federal/state construction projects on the same "my guys only" basis. One searing result was that while Boston was entitled to 22,800 jobs under the Public Works Administration, it got 12,500.

Curley's self-serving obstinacy penalized not only the city, but, in the long run, also hurt his career. For all his obsequious courting of Roosevelt, including his high-risk role in ditching Irish Catholic Al Smith at the

1932 convention that nominated Roosevelt, he never got the high-profile national post he dearly wanted. Roosevelt simply never trusted him. After several false starts and trial balloons, the only concrete job offer he ever got was ambassador to Poland. In his heart of sinking hearts, Curley had to know that for all his crowd-pleasing oratory and magical footwork on the public stage, he was barely in the second tier. Poland wasn't worth much then, even in Ward 17.

His slim prospects were part of his continuing personal grief over his wife's death. With Mary gone, the marriage of his daughter, and his older sons away at school, the once-boisterous supper table had fallen sadly silent. Curley became erratic and even oblivious to the consequences of his actions. While lean-to shanties sprung up along the road to the city dump, he planned a six-week trip to Europe. It was a distraction to mitigate his bereavement that was tone deaf to the travail in his political terrain.

At the end of his third term, Curley needed a new challenge to deal with his angst and his empty nest, and a power base to fight off the hot pursuit of the Boston Finance Commission as scandal encircled the city treasury. Investigators had joined forces with Mayor Mansfield to pore over the city ledger in a hunt for waylaid money.

Curley had to watch his successor over his shoulder as he set out after the highest office he would ever hold—governor of Massachusetts. In a sense, he ran for governor to stay out of jail. He sold himself as a mini-Roosevelt who would duplicate the pump-priming programs being rapidly established in Washington. Indeed, historian Charles Trout gives him high marks for efforts in battling unemployment and pushing public-works programs, and Trout quotes a labor leader as extolling him for passing more progressive laws in two years as governor than any previous administration had done in ten. The scandal swirling around city treasurer Dolan stayed below the radar, submerged in part by another Curley threat of a libel suit. He was able to roll over his Democratic opponent in the primary by 150,000 votes. His Republican opponent, straight out of central casting, was Gaspar Griswold Bacon, who was genetically opposed to the New Deal, which was already revered as a panacea by the voting public. Curley worked his specious Roosevelt connection hard, overpromising on what he could extract from Washington. Still he won by 109,000 votes.

But his reputation would suffer for the winning. He tried to run the state as he had run the city, and it didn't work. He reputation was rooted in being a flamboyant, can-do mayor who built things for his core voters. But he had no such easily pleased constituency as governor. Instead he faced an ambivalent electorate, skeptical of his intentions and honesty, which bought him only because the alternative was a bland Yank who hated the New Deal. His two years as governor were both the pinnacle and nadir of his public life. His term was marked by constant battles with the legislature and sporadic news stories about his past and present stewardship. One trenchant assessment was that Curley had made state government "ludicrous part of the time, shocking most of the time, and tawdry all of the time."

In truth, he had become flagrant in his corruption and boorish in his behavior. His time as governor was nearly nonstop turmoil from the opening gun, when he got in a shoving match with his arch-foe, departing governor Joseph Ely. The low-brow beginning continued when the pushcart market chaos of his City Hall style moved up Beacon Hill to the State House. State agencies were immediately overrun with idle hacks while the governor's anterooms teemed with his motley petitioners. The open door was Curley's fabled common touch, but it kept him away from his new, broader responsibilities.

And it wasn't just the old-school parade to his office that frittered away his day. At the top of his agenda was stopping the Boston Finance Commission from nipping at his heels. The commission was amassing a devastating criminal case against him, and Curley took fast, drastic action that cared not for public perception: He orchestrated a turnover in the Governor's Council with job trades, and, once reconfigured with Curley lackeys, it began impeaching FinCom members as deficient state appointees. Curley stopped official inquiries in the manner of a tinhorn despot—he purged the investigators. It wasn't pretty, but, from his perspective, it was the best of two bad options—appear the heavy-handed autocrat or sit in the dock for fraud and extortion. While his actions were seen as survival tactics in much of Boston, the putsch ruined him as a statewide figure and made reelection impossible. Robin Hood had become Al Capone.

So Curley did what he always did in a crisis. He exulted in the furor and went on the offensive. His arrogance was literally on parade as he toured Massachusetts like a visiting dictator from Panama in his limousine with the license plate "S1" followed by state police motorcycle escorts, with military aides in blue-and-gold uniforms bringing up the rear. A series of much-publicized accidents that included a fatality brought the madcap tours to an end. But he was back in form when he arrived loudly at Harvard Yard to celebrate the university's tercentenary, escorted by drummers and trumpeters in outlandish regalia. He was greeted by a frozen smile from President Roosevelt and a smattering of boos.

In the throes of the worst years of the Depression, Curley's top priority was to emasculate the Finance Commission. He joined forces with that relic of colonial days, the Governor's Council, which could up or down many gubernatorial appointments. Curley ceded some of his patronage prerogatives to forge a crucial alliance with the ever-pragmatic antihero and dominant force on the council, Daniel Coakley. The disbarred blackmailer had settled into the perfect landing place for a rogue—the nothing-for-nothing hock shop formally known as the Executive Council. Although Coakley had denounced Curley as a bully, coward, and jailbird just four years earlier, the two birds of a feather became fast allies and Curley, as he had in a bribery scheme in his first term as mayor, stooped to Coakley's level. They made the council their star chamber.

Curley's first move was to seek abolition of the FinCom through legislation. When that failed, he tried to bribe members with plum jobs in return for resignations. Falling short again, he began bare-knuckled power plays that left a public stain on his name. The skeptical voters who took a chance on him were now appalled. He went to the council, where he demanded the removal of two FinCom members for cause. He convened a kangaroo court at the council with state troopers at his side. When a lawyer protested the lack of due process, the governor had a ready answer from Ward 17: "You sit down or I'll throw you out."

Before it was over, he had reconstituted a more pliant council by swapping judgeships for resignations, but he finally got what he was after—a realigned council that gave him a subservient FinCom. His first replacement on the FinCom was beyond self-serving. With boundless brass, he appointed the lawyer for his former city treasurer Edmund Dolan—to the board that was investigating Dolan and Curley. He was forced to withdraw that appointment, but soon enough the new lineup delayed the extradition of Dolan from Florida, where he had been hiding out. It bought time, and, in the end, Dolan took the fall.

Next, Curley used the new appointees on the Finance Commission to stalk Mayor Mansfield, who had pushed the Dolan scams hard. Among other things, the governor appointed his brother John to the State Tax Board to harass Boston landlords and office-building owners. And he fired the state Registrar of Motor Vehicles after one of Curley's sons lost his license for drunken driving. There were also giddy purges along the breadth of government in banking, insurance, education, and law enforcement. And he and Coakley were at their worst in manhandling the Parole Board. During the Christmas season of 1935, the Council pardoned 254 convicts.

Despite the bread lines and makeshift slums popping up around Boston, Curley continued to spare no expense for his family and staff. When his daughter Mary married the reprobate son of an advertising mogul, Cardinal O'Connell officiated at the wedding and her father held a reception for 2,300 guests at the Copley Plaza. One winter in his reign, he took the entire gubernatorial staff with him on a Florida vacation.

Although Curley thrived on conflict, he had never been in battle gear for this long and on so many fronts. His public agenda of jobs for the middle class never got fully off the ground, and was underscored by chronic unemployment. His saving grace was genuine dedication to progressive labor legislation. He fought a losing battle with distrustful New Deal bureaucrats that resulted in the governor announcing major initiatives that never crossed the finish line.

Disrobed as an unprincipled Boston pol, a pejorative that stuck, Curley faced certain defeat if he sought reelection. So he gathered himself, claimed the governor's job was beyond any one man, and promptly announced his candidacy for US Senate.

But he got trounced by that scion and namesake of Yankee Boston, the heavily credentialed Henry Cabot Lodge Jr. Curley may have been in a tough fight in 1936, but at least he had a more stable home life. The widower was dating a warm woman who brought some zest back into the Jamaicaway home. Curley took some time away from the State House warfare and found some fun in campaigning against his favorite target—overweening Yankee rectitude. "Little Boy Blue," he called Lodge, deriding him further as a wet-behind-the-ears poseur trading on his name, a young man who was wearing diapers when Curley was first in Congress a quarter century earlier. In a tart exchange of zingers, the return volley was that when Lodge was in diapers, Curley was serving time in the Charles Street Jail.

Despite a record landslide Democratic year, with Roosevelt winning forty-six of forty-eight states, Curley lost by 140,000 votes to a newcomer Republican. He had paid the price for his crude performance as governor, for the endless squabbles of his petty brand of politics, and, most of all, for the downright venality of his axis with Coakley on the FinCom purge.

The coup de grâce was the awarding of construction contracts for the massive Quabbin Reservoir project in central Massachusetts, newly designed to supply the Boston area with drinking water by flooding several sparsely populated towns and then building an aqueduct system. By the end of his administration, Curley was knocking the doors of state government to grab building contracts for his favored few. In a secret meeting that excluded the chairman, Curley surrogates on the Metropolitan District Water Supply Commission shifted a large contract to negociant firms for three times the amount awarded to the original builder, creating a $300,000 slush fund above the reasonable cost of the work. It was too rank for the new state attorney general, Paul Dever, who overturned the deal.

Dever, the youngest person ever elected attorney general, was an ambitious, moon-faced man who took office with Curley in 1934 and would go on to be governor himself. He was unbeholden, and Curley instinctively distrusted a man half his age who could conduct criminal investigations. The tone for their dealing was set in a tart exchange as both settled into new jobs. Curley paid a "courtesy" call, planting his foot heavily on Dever's office radiator during a short visit. "Listen, you little pisspot," the new governor said to the new attorney general. "What do you want?"

Outside of the Quabbin project, Dever kept a respectful distance and Curley ran wild in his final days as governor. It was Katie-bar-the-door. The governor created income for himself by paying contractors unwarranted bonuses for work already completed or yet undone, easy money from safe players used to the backroads of state government. And there was the usual Christmas frenzy for pardons and paroles pushed by the highest bidders during "clemency" auctions at the Governor's Council.

Despite the uniformly bad reviews, Curley ran for governor again two years later, in 1938, but fell to a Yank who loved the New Deal, Leverett Saltonstall, a craggy-faced WASP who could pass for a native in South Boston. For Curley, the governor's office was a pinnacle with a sharp decline that left him sprawling and nearly unelectable. In quick succession, the perennial candidate lost for senator, governor, even mayor. But he still didn't smell the hay in the barn. On the contrary, he took stock and announced with gusto, "Nobody is through with politics who has ever tasted it."

Yet the defections were evident in the hallowed home turf, and culminated in the mayoral election of 1937. His voters sensed that maybe all the problems of the day were not caused by Yankee "pirates" from Back Bay, and realized the New Deal benefits far surpassed Curley's one-man dole system. It was increasingly clear that Washington bureaucrats could care better for Curley's constituents than he could. For starters, there was the dramatic rise of unions and the expanding safety net of unemployment compensation and minimum wages. Instead of righting himself back home, Curley was decisively beaten in the city he once owned, losing by more than 25,000 votes to Maurice J. Tobin.

Tobin was the protégé Curley had always feared, the acolyte who learned too well. Young, handsome, and bland, at thirty-six, Tobin was nearly half Curley's age, and he used the difference discreetly against the titan who had begun to show his years. Tobin's tone was understated for a Boston campaign, but he was unmistakable about the age issue: "My opponent first ran for mayor in 1913. I was twelve years old that year." His attack was muted yet clear: "I will not mention my opponent's record. You all know it too well." And Tobin also had the support of the usually neutral *Boston Post*, which hit Curley below the belt, waiting for election day so there could be no rebuttal. Its standard page-one format included a daily quotation box, and on the day the polls opened, it featured Cardinal O'Connell. "Voters of Boston: Cardinal O'Connell, in speaking to the Catholic Alumni Association, said 'the walls are raised against honest men in civil life.' You can break down these walls by voting for an honest, clean, competent young man, Maurice Tobin, today. He will redeem the city and take it out of the hands of those who have been responsible for graft and corruption." While the cardinal was not making a direct endorsement, and his quoted remarks did not refer to Tobin, the prelate remained unavailable to a frantic emissary from Curley seeking clarification. There would be no correction from the massive rectory as the clock ran out.

Curley lost again to Tobin in 1941, but it was a tough, down-to-the-wire race as World War II loomed. Tobin went on to become governor and then part of Harry Truman's cabinet as labor secretary, but the ornery Curley outlived him when Tobin died young, at age fifty-two. With several enemies dying off in 1953, Curley's reaction was "Well, that only leaves Mansfield." Curley was a fast-moving guest at the Tobin wake, arriving not to praise but to bury.

But he was sixty-seven when he lost to Tobin for the second time in 1941, and it seemed it might be the end of the line. Yet he still had fire in his now-ample belly. Within months he returned to his hard-core voters in the monolithic Irish wards of Roxbury and South Boston and Charlestown, which dominated a newly gerrymandered congressional district. They sent him back to wartime Washington after a three-decade absence. At this stage of the game, Curley wasn't in it for glory. He needed the money. Among other things, he was in a loan-shark situation with the city he had once ruled, because of the $500 weekly payments he owed for swiping half of a settled bill uncovered by Fred Mansfield. The $40,000 plus interest had become serious money. Shameless as ever, Curley went on the radio and appealed to the loyal cadre of his personal welfare system. The message: Robin Hood was broke and it was time to step up. Curley pulled off the unimaginable—openly begging for money to repay the city because he got caught taking a bribe. It produced a traffic jam in front of his mansion, with countless beneficiaries leaving coins and bills strewn across the lawn or piled at the front door.

Not long after he returned to Washington as a congressman yet again, dire straits propelled him toward James G. Fuller. They met through an intermediary before Curley had even been sworn in and within weeks of the attack on Pearl Harbor. War was in the air when Curley had run into the open arms and quick-buck hustle of a con man just out of jail for kiting checks. The former encyclopedia salesman had landed in D.C. and sniffed out money possibilities in willy-nilly munitions contracts needed to support a two-front war. Fuller needed a front man to beguile clients about the company's conjured connections with federal bureaucrats, and Curley needed a sinecure to augment his income. Himself agreed to become the figurehead president of the Engineers' Group, Inc., not knowing—and perhaps not caring—that his partner was a veteran swindler and an ex-convict. How much Curley knew about the plan to take the money and run is unclear. He resigned from the firm before taking office in 1942, but within two years, Senator Harry Truman's implacable committee on war profiteering was investigating the group's defrauding vendors seeking Air Force contracts.

Curley was indicted in September 1943 for the least of his flim-flams, and one that yielded him next to nothing. He had put his name on a letterhead and lost track of it when it didn't produce much. He thought it was something piddling he could talk his way out of, but this was no-nonsense Washington and not pliant Boston. It was Truman and the Department of Justice, and not Joe Pelletier and Dan Coakley. No one had his back. His defense was the same as always: self-righteous reformers were after him again. He simply substituted New Deal zealots for heartless WASPs and, in his safe Irish seat, indictment notwithstanding, was reelected to Congress in 1944.

Curley still thought he could breeze by the minor munitions matter when he decided to bolt from the capital in 1945 to run for mayor again in a crowded field. It was a wide-open race in a down-on-its-heels Boston that was trying to get its bearings in war's aftermath. Boston was becoming a backwater place facing massive institutional problems. If some of the city's dingy contours were Curley's doing, he still knew how to change the subject and move into a political vacuum. In a city struggling with returning veterans and deteriorating housing, his theme was perfectly pitched to a town needing a kick-start: "Curley gets things done." So what if he was under indictment in Washington for stuff everybody does down there? He won by a two-to-one margin for the fourth time against a field of nonentities that included—best of all—a Tobin protégé.

But it wasn't long before the Engineers' Group case brought him— and delusional Boston—down hard. Two months after his election, he was convicted of mail fraud. Subdued by what lay ahead, he returned to South Station while out on appeal. It may have been his greatest curtain call, with a welcoming mob so raucous that it took him a half hour to get to his car. The reception bucked up the shaken if felonious mayor. He would run the city in a dilatory way for another year and a half until he was sentenced. Despite his preoccupations, he still had his playful spark. One day, as he was driven away from City Hall, he spotted his old rival John Fitzgerald walking along Washington Street with his youngest grandson, Ted, who had just handed Grandpa a bulky school bag. Curley had the driver pull over and, sticking his head out of the window, gravely intoned, "I see that you are still carrying your burglar tools, John."

Even with the weight of prison on his mind, Curley retained his succession-game acumen. He needed a caretaker rather than a comer in the mayor's chair while he was away, someone who would warm the seat and then go away quietly. Curley didn't like what he saw in the city charter succession lineup concerning an absent mayor. It required that he be replaced by the president of the City Council—John B. Kelly, a man who might want to stay too long. To get around that would need special legislation and the help of the governor to get it. He didn't like what he saw there, either—Maurice Tobin.

So Curley devised another Machiavellian bit of magic. He would help the Republican lieutenant governor, Robert Fiske Bradford, unseat Tobin in 1946. Curley's biographer, Jack Beatty, recorded the irony: "The great Brahmin baiter set out to make this *Mayflower* descendant governor of Massachusetts." Curley assailed Tobin and endorsed Bradford, and it worked with much of Curley's old guard. Bradford took enough Boston votes away from Tobin to win statewide. Curley had scored another first—a Republican friend in the governor's office. Who owed. Maybe Kelly was not inevitable.

But a few months later, in June 1947, there were no more rabbits to be pulled out of a hat in federal court. He had strung out the appeals for two years and nearly died shortly before his sentencing. But after getting the Last Rites, he rallied, arriving in court in a wheelchair and underweight. His lawyer listed his ailments, but the obdurate judge gave him at least six months at the federal prison in Danbury, Connecticut. "You're sentencing me to die," Curley rasped. But the unmoved judge did not hear the great orator out; he promptly left the bench. Curley grabbed feebly at the railing to pull himself up, and began to speak as the court was cleared, suddenly alone quoting Shakespeare to court officers waiting to pack him off on the first leg to prison.

Yet by the time Curley got to Danbury, where his prized Havana cigars were promptly confiscated, Governor Bradford and the Republican legislature gave him unexpected succor. In less than two hours a bill was enacted to depose Kelly as acting mayor and put the Boston city clerk, John B. Hynes—and his lack of political ambitions—in his place.

Efforts to get Curley an early release foundered despite a petition signed by 100,000 Boston residents and another signed by more than one hundred fellow congressmen. The only member of the Massachusetts delegation to resist the entreaty from majority leader John McCormack of South Boston was the delegation's newest member and holder of Curley's former seat—John Fitzgerald Kennedy. Even though Kennedy's father had secretly bankrolled Curley's most recent mayoral victory—in exchange for Curley vacating his congressional seat for shiny new Jack— there was an old score to be settled. The Kennedy matriarch, Rose, remembered well the family heartache in 1913 when Curley blackmailed Honey Fitzgerald out of public office. Despite the surge of political entreaties, President Truman let Curley serve five months—a month short of the minimum and a slight that Curley never forgave or forgot.

The mayor struggled mightily behind bars. Danbury Prison was hardly the leisurely lark he had as a young man at Charles Street Jail when he poked his way through bookshelves in the jailhouse library. His trademark resilience was damaged, and, with release in sight, his daughter reported that he was strangely tentative about facing the lusty Boston crowds again. He had aged and seemed permanently forlorn. But, once paroled, he found more sympathy than disgrace in his return as an ex-convict. He was still the mayor, and a loyalist crowd greeted him as he got off the train at Back Bay Station. While there was a brass band playing "Hail to the Chief" when he arrived home at the shamrock house, it was a head-down Curley who made his way unsteadily to the front door with a policeman on each elbow. Yet he seemed to draw strength from the comforts of home along the pastoral Jamaicaway. It wasn't long before the familiar surroundings put him on his feet. Ever adaptable, he was soon at City Hall getting his groove back.

But the familiar landscape had begun to shift under his feet. The old ad-hoc ways were not enough for the Irish moving into the middle class. Meager jobs shoveling snow or pushing a broom were now outdated by GI Bill education and Social Security. The parks and beaches were all built, but badly in need of repair. The tax rate was tapped out. Boston was lurching toward bankruptcy.

Even so, Curley looked forward to easy reelection to a fifth term, sporting a license plate on his car that said as much, with the single numeral 5, the first advertisement of yet another campaign. His stand-in, City Clerk Hynes, had kept on all Curley appointees and had dutifully put aside all the contracts that underwrote Curley's home upkeep and lifestyle. The contracts were the mayor's top priority on his first day on the job, and when he finished several hours of review and signing, he announced, "I have accomplished more in one day than has been done in the five months of my absence." Hynes was more than hurt by the dismissive remark. In the Boston Irish tradition, he decided to get even.

In the 1949 election campaign, Hynes refused to get out of the way. Affronted by Curley's cavalier treatment, he set out to reclaim the office he had fallen into. While Curley denegrated Hynes as a "little city clerk," the mayor found himself in a real fight. With his hard-core supporters shrinking almost by the day, he came up short by fifteen thousand votes of Hynes's tally. Curley was out of Lazarus acts. He was done.

After the loss to Hynes, Curley's last days in office were not pretty. Just as he had vacated the governor's office more than a decade earlier, he dragged away anything not bolted down. He grabbed rapaciously for a final time, awarding a garbage contract for twice the low bid and reaching a surprising accord with one of his oldest enemies—downtown commercial property owners. He agreed to millions in tax abatements that, among other things, left the Hynes administration in a deep financial hole. On his last day, Curley stuck out his chin and said "lump it" a final time, creating so many litigants that he had to be surrounded by aides as he darted into a waiting car to avoid a pursuing deputy sheriff bearing a summons. It was an unlovely sight: the seventy-five-year-old mayor as a thief in the night one step ahead of the law.

The shamrock house had become too pain-filled and empty to be a home anymore. Out of the cash flow of public office, Curley could no longer pay for the upkeep and staff. He and Gertrude were making do with a dead-of-night pension whisked through the legislature by Thomas "Tip" O'Neill, then speaker of the Massachusetts House. Curley sold the house to the Catholic Church, which sold it to the city of Boston thirty years later. It was a final double billing, with the city paying twice for Curley's grand house. A last laugh for the last great rogue of Boston.

William Shannon, who chronicled the Irish in America, viewed Curley as a seminal figure whose legacy was his unique ability "to define, dramatize and play upon the discrimination, resentments and frustrations suffered by the Irish community in its long passage" from detested minority to fractious majority. As the Irish crested as a political force, Curley became passé.

But never forgotten. Nearly ten years after his last hurrah—and two perfunctory sorties for mayor that were fund-raisers more than campaigns—he took ill and expired quickly at "his" hospital, Boston City, a stone's throw from his boyhood tenement in Ward 17. He was waked in the State House under battle flags while 100,000 paid their respects. The city came to a halt for two days, until he was buried from the cardinal's church, Holy Cross Cathedral, in the largest funeral procession in Boston's history.

Tip O'Neill surely had Curley in mind when he said that old politics were show business while the new are just advertising.

Neil Nolan, an accomplished musician and resigned city employee who came to Boston from Prince Edward Island, had a succinct explanation for his son Martin about the pragmatic larceny of James Michael Curley. Martin, a reporter and editor at the *Globe* who wrote a lyrical and astute column for decades, said his father offered him an early Irish perspective one summer day after Neil had strolled by the L Street Bath House on his way to fish off the Castle Island Pier. "They all steal," the father told the son. "At least he built stuff."

CHAPTER 5

The Badger Game

DANIEL COAKLEY

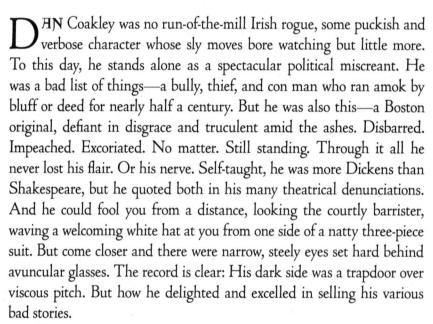

DⱯN Coakley was no run-of-the-mill Irish rogue, some puckish and verbose character whose sly moves bore watching but little more. To this day, he stands alone as a spectacular political miscreant. He was a bad list of things—a bully, thief, and con man who ran amok by bluff or deed for nearly half a century. But he was also this—a Boston original, defiant in disgrace and truculent amid the ashes. Disbarred. Impeached. Excoriated. No matter. Still standing. Through it all he never lost his flair. Or his nerve. Self-taught, he was more Dickens than Shakespeare, but he quoted both in his many theatrical denunciations. And he could fool you from a distance, looking the courtly barrister, waving a welcoming white hat at you from one side of a natty three-piece suit. But come closer and there were narrow, steely eyes set hard behind avuncular glasses. The record is clear: His dark side was a trapdoor over viscous pitch. But how he delighted and excelled in selling his various bad stories.

This artful dodger's career began when he quit school at fourteen in 1879 to join his teamster father behind a horse-drawn wagon. He had recently graduated from the Harvard grammar school in South Boston and delighted in presenting himself in later years as a Hah-vahd man. In truth, he went to Boston College until the money ran out and he had to take a job as a fare collector with the Cambridge Street Railway Company, which ran horse trolleys between the polarities of Boston life—tawdry Scollay Square to recondite Harvard Yard. More at home at the scruffy end of the line with its card sharks and whores, Coakley was dismissed from the railway company for stealing fares.

So he took a night-school class in shorthand and landed a job at age twenty-three as a reporter for the *New York Sun.* He returned in short order to Boston as a sportswriter for the *Herald,* and worked a second job as a boxing referee. His coup as a journalist was crashing through a Mississippi swamp on a donkey to scoop other boxing writers with a telegram that carried first word of the victory of Boston's hometown favorite John L. Sullivan over Jake Kilrain in the city of Hattiesburg.

But, feeling mired and restless in the sports department after five years, he followed his older brother's path to jurisprudence, reading law on his own in Timothy Coakley's office and passing the bar on the fourth try. In those days, being a lawyer didn't even require a high school diploma. His specialty became slip-and-slide injury cases, exercising special zeal in suits against the railway company that had cashiered him.

After admission to the bar, Coakley first ventured into politics as a state representative from East Cambridge when the legislature was still top-heavy with WASPs, with one of the few other Irish interlopers being John Fitzgerald in the Senate. Coakley attached himself to Fitzgerald's rising star and was named a member of the Boston Parks Commission in Fitzgerald's first term as mayor.

A couple of election cycles later, Coakley jumped ship to join James Michael Curley and begin yet another love-hate relationship with yet another mayor. In the beginning, they were conspirators in a gamey blackmail scheme, and Coakley was the mayor's disputatious lawyer before the Boston Finance Commission in their investigation of how Curley was able to afford his fabled mansion on the Jamaicaway on a public servant's salary. At the end of Curley's first term, Coakley maneuvered all the carefully amassed FinCom evidence against the mayor to his compromised ally in law enforcement, Suffolk District Attorney Joseph Pelletier, who flushed it.

Curley had no trouble supporting Pelletier for unsuccessful gubernatorial runs, but blared bombast when Pelletier talked apostasy about running for mayor. That desecration led to a decade-long breach between Curley and Coakley, made worse when Coakley twice ran for mayor as a spoiler to take votes away from Curley or his appointed stand-in. They did not reconcile until Curley's single term as governor in the mid-1930s. It was a business decision, as Coakley had become the dominant force on the Governor's Council, which specialized in taking bribes to pardon hardened criminals.

As a lawyer, Coakley had moved briskly from small tort cases to criminal law and then larger civil suits, nearly all malodorous affairs. But he became a wealthy man and a political force when he moved from backstage at City Hall to manage the 1909 election of Pelletier as district attorney in Boston. It was an insidious axis that ended in suicide for Pelletier, but with the resilient if disbarred Coakley landing on his feet.

While it all ended badly, the First World War years and the Roaring Twenties were astounding periods in Boston's legal circles. For a decade, disreputable Dan had three district attorneys in his vest pocket while he preyed on those with the money—sometimes with loans arranged by Coakley—who faced bogus charges that Coakley could make go away. The marks were usually either his own clients who, after talking openly with Coakley about their problems, suddenly found prosecutors zeroing in on those problems. Others came as referrals from the district attorneys who knew a job for Dan Coakley when they saw one.

Prosecutors in tow, Coakley fixed cases with a phone call or short courthouse conferences. In tight chronologies, a charge appeared and then fell from docket books with the coda notation of *nolle prosequi,* a Latin phrase loaded with discretion for prosecutors to end cases without explanation. The postmortem of the era found that a gamut of criminal charges had slipped softly from dockets to the courthouse floor. Larceny. Theft. Abortion. Fraud. Receiving stolen goods.

But sexual entrapment was where the money was.

It turned out that Coakley's true calling was the scurrilous badger game, in which ardent suitors of loose women found themselves in over-the-barrel mortification—especially hypocritical Brahmins.

Coakley had set himself up as the Merlin of the defense bar, waving magical wands over indictments cherry-picked from prosecutorial files or from Coakley's own exploited clientele. For mutual benefit, Coakley and Pelletier staged dog-and-pony shows for terrified clients to demonstrate Coakley's clout. In one routine case, documented by investigators long after the fact, an impatient Pelletier told an anxious defendant to go "fix it up" with Coakley in his law office. The fix-up charge from Coakley was $15,000. He then gave the district attorney the short end—$2,500, which also happened to be twice the average annual salary of the day. Investigators found that Coakley regularly showed off for clients in his office, leaning back in his chair and no doubt winking reassurances as he chatted amiably on the telephone with the district attorney. "I'll be right over, Joe," he'd say. Or with the ominous bravado in front of the client: "Joe, don't indict until you hear from me."

The buzzards swarmed most ruthlessly around doddering old men with money and not-so-sweet young things. The climatic moment usually involved doors knocked down by allegedly aggrieved husbands or ostensible police detectives and all-too-real photographers. The terms: your money or your reputation. It was lucrative, and it was ethnic payback. Many of the victims came off the social register with names such as Bigelow, Fiske, and Searles.

But it was more than vaudeville bathos with a socialite caught with his fancy pants around his ankles. It could be coldly tragic. Like when Mae Daly began sitting on Edmund Barbour's lap. Barbour was an aging Beacon Hill bachelor and financier when he first struck up a relationship with the sixteen-year-old Mae in 1906. But it was hardly sex on a tabletop. It was never consummated, and began when Barbour was sixty-five. Edmund would give Mae presents now and again, and she would visit him in his State Street office or Beacon Street home, where she would sit on his lap and they would spoon. Until Mae brought it Coakley's way when Barbour was seventy-seven and losing his vision. On an afternoon in 1918, as they sat in Barbour's office's swivel chair, two men purporting to be investigators from the district attorney's office burst in, shouting, "Now we've got you!" Mae urged the befuddled Barbour to see a lawyer named Coakley, who explained it would require several payments to obtain a quiet end to Barbour's unseemly predicament. Over the next few years the virtually blind Barbour paid Coakley $300,000 to keep secret a nearly chaste affair with a consenting adult.

A year earlier, in 1917, a more elaborate and sordid incident proved only slightly less lucrative because Coakley had to share his "fee" with a more extensive conspiracy that eventually unraveled. His collaborators included the current and former district attorneys of Middlesex County, the most populous county in Massachusetts and adjacent to Boston. And, with fleeting reference deep within later court records, the mayor of Boston.

Coakley drew Curley into the extortion ring when the mayor was flying high near the end of his first term and willing to veer away from his "honest" graft with city contractors for a big score. The mayor shared in the proceeds, but paid a long-term price when he and Coakley had their inevitable scorched-earth falling-out. The piquant Coakley took to taunting the mayor publicly about his role with an oblique reference: "Oh, shades of Mishawum."

Mishawum Manor was an old fashioned bawdy house, and some of its prominent patrons fell into Coakley's maw through his connections with former Middlesex County district attorney William Corcoran. The ex-prosecutor had been hired to represent the Mishawum madam when a night of noisy debauchery became a local police matter the next morning.

It all began in Boston when three Hollywood moguls threw a party at the Copley Plaza for the silent film star Fatty Arbuckle. But the real party followed at midnight in the manor in the nearby city of Woburn. The event planner was known by the alias of Brownie Kennedy, and among her ten guests that evening were Paramount Studio executives Adolph Zukor, Jesse Lasky, and Hiram Abrams. This was far more than petting in a swivel chair. Most of the young women were casually nude when the moguls and friends arrived, and there was much foot traffic to upstairs rooms. The Hollywood hotshots thought that a check at daybreak for $1,000 was the end of their boys' night out.

But two months later, Abrams got a call out of the blue from the mayor of Boston, telling him of unfinished business at Mishawum Manor. Curley told Abrams that a return trip to the East Coast was urgently in order if he was to avoid indictments on sundry morals charges. But fear not: Curley happened to know a renowned lion of the defense bar named Coakley, a man you could talk to and, what's more, who was on excellent terms with the district attorney of Middlesex County.

Abrams met with the stern-faced team of Curley and Coakley at a Boston hotel. Cutting to the chase, they told him some of the party girls were underage and others came with irate husbands contemplating alienation-of-affection suits against Paramount. The solution—get Coakley started with a fast $10,000 retainer.

The other Paramount executives, later referred to as "moving picture men" in court records, were summoned to Boston to be bit players in a tightly staged production featuring Coakley and another wind-blown district attorney, Nathan Tufts. Coakley presented the chastened hat-in-hand moguls in person to make clear that they were no West Coast rowdies, but rather businessmen of character. But the meeting was really to display Coakley's clout with the prosecutor. The dubious Tufts, a burly former football player at Brown University and a Republican acolyte of Calvin Coolidge in the state senate, played hard to get. He wondered rhetorically what he was supposed to do with complaints from distraught husbands. But Coakley had a proposal: What if he rounded up retractions from the aggrieved husbands and ascertained that the alleged innocents were no longer in the jurisdiction? Tufts said he would consider it.

Indeed he would. A matter of days before he took a payoff, Tufts castigated the trio from Paramount as "licentious Jews." Ethnic slurs announced, he told Coakley he would drop charges when the promised releases were delivered. Coakley said "done deal" and charged the moving-picture men $100,000 for the last roundup.

For a decade, the real untouchables in Boston weren't the social elite in the symphony-and-sherry world of Beacon Hill. It was a small club headed by a former boxing referee and trolley-fare thief and his corrupt cabal of top prosecutors. They held all the cards, and those in legal circles who even suspected the pungent collusion scurried away without a backward glance. Too much firepower.

Except for Godfrey Lowell Cabot, a king of the Brahmins bred for tribal war, who boasted blood ties to two of the richest familes in town and was a pillar of the reproachful Watch and Ward Society that reigned for decades over the moral suitability of theater and literature in Boston. Son of a doctor and first cousin to the president of Harvard College and to Oliver Wendell Holmes, he lived to be 101. In addition to holding vast tracts of land, he was a pioneering industrialist who specialized in producing tons of black carbon needed for tires for the burgeoning automobile market. But even with his unlimited resources and legendary single-mindedness, he met his match in the street-smart Daniel Coakley.

Cabot had learned of the badger game after Barbour's downfall, and added the new issue of blackmail to the Watch and Ward's usual agenda of banning books deemed obscene. Word of his interest brought tips to his moral high ground on Beacon Hill. There were victims aplenty, but no lawyers willing to bring a case for fear of career-ending exile by law enforcement if allegations misfired in court. It had come to this: Godfrey Lowell Cabot was having a problem finding a lawyer in Boston. Years later, Cabot reflected that it was one thing to get help to kill a lion, "but when you go out to kill a skunk you've got to do it yourself." The infighting and intrigue between the warring camps was something out of the Russian Revolution, which also was just getting under way. Cabot set aside his own vaunted scruples to fight fire with fire. He had a bug placed in Suffolk County district attorney Pelletier's office and an employee planted in Coakley's office to steal documents.

Cabot's secret war backfired for a while when the detective he hired to pose as a Coakley employee turned out to be a double agent more of Coakley's world than of Cabot's. The counter-thrust was Pelletier's unsuccessful attempt to set up the wrathful Watch and Ward man with a prostitute. But by the end of 1918, Cabot's unyielding crusade finally got the timorous Boston Bar Association to begin an investigation into the Coakley coterie. But the first legal repercussion from the pat hand of power was Pelletier's indictment of Cabot and two of his lawyers for possessing stolen goods—documents taken from Coakley's office. After that case fell quickly by the wayside on a technicality, the state attorney general filed petitions at the Supreme Judicial Court in 1921 for the removal of Pelletier and Tufts from office, as well as for the disbarment of Coakley and former district attorney William Corcoran.

The fat was in the fire. After extensive hearings before the Supreme Judicial Court, the overwhelming pattern of collusion in diverse cases between Coakley and the district attorneys was summarily judged enough for removal and disbarment.

What started with the hand-to-hand combat of the Barbour case rippled through the legal landscape. Former prosecutor Corcoran started the cascade by admitting guilt for which he was disbarred. The rest of the dominoes fell down the courthouse steps. All hands were disbarred. Pelletier, despite losing his law license, defiantly mounted a losing reelection campaign for district attorney. The disgrace was so severe that a Republican was elected as the new Boston Suffolk County prosecutor. Tufts relocated to New York to live out his life quietly as a businessman.

But the disbarred Dan Coakley denied all and fought on.

The last step in the Cabot jihad was separated out from those that led to everyone's disbarment. It was a stand-alone charge of criminal conspiracy against Coakley and Corcoran, but it failed with banner headlines in 1924. At the end of the trial, Coakley shook hands with all the jurors as they filed out of the courtroom after they had affirmed his acquittal. Coakley then received a hero's greeting by milling supporters outside the courthouse. The nimble ex-barrister hardly missed a legal fee, running his thriving practice as a "manager" while lawyers in his firm were in and out of court every day. He even announced for mayor, but didn't muster a real campaign until four years later. In 1928 he finished fourth out of ten, cornering just enough votes to stop Curley's seat-warmer for the job, Teddy Glynn.

But the 1930 race for governor was as rawboned and hate-filled as it gets, even for the Boston zeitgeist. It brought out the melodramatic worst in the bitterly estranged Coakley and Curley. While neither man was on the ballot, both loomed large backstage, each angling for future benefits. Curley wanted to head off the Yankee Democrat Joseph Ely, who could lay lasting claim to the office that Curley fancied for himself. Perhaps for that reason alone, Coakley allied himself with Ely. It started out with the odd coalition of a barefaced Irishman and a swamp Yank from the Berkshire Mountains. And it ended in the tumult of unmatched calumny.

The vituperative Coakley used the race to foil Curley's scheming and to sully his archfoe in a series of diatribes delivered on the growing medium of the day—radio. Much of it played out in a single day at one radio station, and was a family affair that involved not only Curley and Coakley, but also a son from each camp.

The studio of WNAC turned into a scene of brawling bedlam when Curley, waiting in an anteroom for his turn at the mike, overheard

Frank Donahue, chairman of the Democratic State Committee, level name-and-number corruption charges against him on the air. Donahue alleged the mayor had pocketed $15,000 that was supposed to go to Al Smith, a favorite of the Boston Irish who had been swamped by anti-Catholic sentiment in the presidential election of 1928.

A red-faced Curley charged around the station, shouting, "I'll get him!" Telling his son James junior and another aide to stay out of it, he burst in the studio door and denounced a startled Donahue: "You are the damnedest liar I ever knew." Curley lunged but missed as his son jumped on his back. After Curley shook him off, another young man tried to intervene, but the enraged Curley stopped his mad pursuit of Donahue long enough to knee the peacemaker in the groin. It turned out to be Coakley's son Gael, who was there as part of Donahue's retinue. The portly, bespectacled Donahue fled through a back door with Curley and his entourage in hot pursuit. A house detective from a nearby hotel finally stopped the rampage.

Not long after the incident, Coakley counterattacked with "equal time" over the same studio airwaves. Around midnight, dripping venom, Coakley called Curley a "guttersnipe" and "jailbird" and several kinds of coward while nervous technicians, prepared to pull the plug, monitored his soliloquy for profanity. His account of Curley's assault on his son had the flair of an old sportswriter. He claimed Curley held his son close, kneed him hard, and then, over his shoulder, urged his henchmen to "give it to him again."

It was another in a series of Coakley's grandiloquent radio speeches, his vitriolic version of fireside chats. They were usually overdrawn portraits of shimmering good versus darkest evil, almost all revolving around Curley. Even before the assault, he had rebuked Curley as an "unscrupulous mountebank" and, what's more, a "blatant, shallow humbug." But his earlier diatribes were pattycake affairs compared to his midnight ramble on behalf of Gael Coakley.

"Since I last talked to you, two hours ago, my young son, a boy of 130 pounds, has been brutally assaulted by that masquerading thug, who, God save the mark, is mayor of Boston." He also scored Curley's gang as a "band of blackguards" whom he later promoted to "gunmen." He lamented that television was not advanced enough to show the public "the demonic expression on that wolf face." And after saying it would slander a yellow dog to liken one to Curley, he could not help himself. "He is a yellow cur."

Yet, weeks later, when Ely was on the verge of a narrow victory, the bitter Coakley-Curley contretemps bowed with surprising ease to pragmatic politics. At an election-eve rally, Curley hailed Ely as "the clean, able, brilliant leader of democracy from Western Massachusetts." Leading the applause in the first row was Coakley, who, asked about Curley's change of heart, winked that they were all just good Democrats out to win. Ely served two terms, and Coakley was a frequent and smiling visitor to the governor's office.

Approaching sixty, Coakley settled into his second career as savvy sphinx at the anachronistic Governor's Council, beginning with his election in 1932. It became his perfect resting place before, God save the mark, he reached too far. But for a decade the nine-member artifact was hog heaven for Coakley, who eventually held veto power over all judicial appointments and pardons and some sway over patronage jobs.

His new stature emboldened Coakley to seek reinstatement as a lawyer, and his petition included signatory support from a governor and a US senator, to say nothing of sixty-five district court judges looking for raises and the 3,740 lawyers eager to join them on the bench. But the power play ended up in the cold hands of the unbending president of the Boston Bar Association, who adjured to the Supreme Judicial Court that it should view Coakley's contrition as a crock. It was so noted.

With the Governor's Council job in hand, Coakley ran for mayor one last time in 1933, again more to settle scores with Curley, who wasn't even in the race. Sixteen years after the fact, he gleefully jabbed Curley about Mishawum Manor, skipping around the stage as he disingenuously begged the mayor to release him from a long-ago lawyer's confidence on a subject that had as much toad in it for him as for Curley. But this was no dance with Toodles, and Curley was no Honey Fitz. The mayor was a litigious gutter fighter who had thoroughly intimidated an already docile press with a succession of threatened or filed libel suits. He knew Mishawum would stay offstage and out of the papers. And so it did.

After a decade of steady warfare, it turned out that the pair of wizened adversaries needed each other. Their long entanglement was put aside in 1934 when Curley became governor for his scandal-plagued term. The bile was stanched with an inaugural-day summit meeting. Curley desperately needed to stymie the Boston Finance Commission, whose ardent Yankee investigators were once again breathing down his neck about mayoral kickbacks. What's a knee in the groin between family friends? Could it be that Curley wasn't such a yellow cur after all?

Coakley's overture: "What will it be—war or peace?"

"Have I the choice?" Curley asked.

Coakley smiled. "Then it will be peace."

After Curley ran his course as governor and headed toward Congress, Coakley was left behind to crank up his pardon machine on his own. It finally crashed when Coakley went too far—even for a Governor's Council member—in 1938. He personally wrote the petition for rising Mafia star Raymond Patriarca of Providence, Rhode Island, who had served but eighty-four days of a three-to-five-year sentence for armed robbery. It put Patriarca's mug shot with his curled upper lip on page one for all to see the sullen face of rehabilitation in the Commonwealth of Massachusetts.

Coakley had put himself in the crosshairs of the state's two preeminent Republicans, Leverett Saltonstall, who had just become governor, and his successor as speaker of the House, Christian Herter. A committee was convened that recommended Coakley be impeached. The House endorsed it and the case wended its way slowly to trial in the Senate in 1941. With Coakley representing himself, it was another eight-column-headline sideshow that ran the month of September. Exhibit A was the Patriarca petition that extolled the gangster as a changed man intent on going home to Mother. It included hosannas from three priests—one never consulted, the second deceived, and the last contrived and signed devilishly as "Father Fagin," a sardonic allusion to the Dickens character who lured young men into lives of crime.

Toward the end of the trial, the state attorney general and the seventy-one-year-old Coakley nearly came to blows. During the prosecutor's two-hour summation, Coakley blithely twiddled his thumbs. Along with evidence that he took $1,000 from a convicted murderer, the bogus blessing from Father Fagin did him in. Despite his tearful and forceful plea, Coakley was the first official impeached in three centuries of state and colonial history and banned forever from public office. As his daughter wept, he sat impassively while the 26–10 vote was announced against him. He stood at the Senate door to glare at those who had voted in the affirmative and to double-clasp the hands of the urban Irishmen who stuck with him.

Disbarred and stripped of office, Coakley remained as chipper and brash as ever. But as time went on he knocked a little less frequently on the usual doors at City Hall and the State House and was rarely seen at his favorite haunt, the bar at the Parker House. After five years in exile, he grimaced about being broke and fed at his children's sufferance. Yet he still kept a Parker House suite along with a town house in Brighton and a snug cottage on Cape Cod. He threatened a tell-all memoir, but it never appeared. When it came down to it, what could he really say about Curley and Mishawum that didn't bite him back? He also talked about seeking reinstatement to the bar, but nothing came of that, either. After spanning the old and new of Irish politics, he stayed sedately by the windswept and aptly named Buzzards Bay for his final five years. He was buried at eighty-six at St. Margaret's, just past midcentury in the same year, 1952, that John Francis Fitzgerald's grandson narrowly won Henry Cabot Lodge Jr.'s US Senate seat.

CHAPTER 6

Whispering Johnny

JOHN HYNES

ALL John Hynes wanted was a simple thank-you. Instead he got blown off in the morning and denigrated in the afternoon in time to make the evening papers. It put a mild man into a cold rage that would unravel an era. James Michael Curley was undone by a wisecrack.

It was easy to miss at the time. Indeed, it was seen as a sign that Curley was back to his old jaunty self after his supporters, just days earlier, were shaken to see policemen assist a pallid and pained mayor up his front walk, the finish line of an ignominious return from prison. He was halfway through his fourth term as mayor, but would have to finish it as a paroled felon who did five months at Danbury Prison.

And yet he rallied again, remarkably revived by a combination Thanksgiving and seventy-third birthday celebration at his Shamrock mansion. He took inventory—still kicking and, yes, still mayor. He headed off to City Hall the first Monday he was home, assured that little had changed. His loyal stand-in, city clerk John Hynes, had agreed with Curley's daughter that all appointees would stay in place and, more important, that building contracts—Curley's lifeblood—would be carefully set aside.

Himself breezed into his office and gave Hynes a hearty if dismissive greeting. "Good morning, Johnny. I'll see you later." Hynes took his leave back to the city clerk's office while the mayor spent the rest of the day computing his share of $39 million in contracts.

But Curley made a fateful error at day's end. He took the unassuming John Hynes for granted in public. He held a press conference that got off to an awkward start until a reporter asked about the eight-hundred-pound gorilla in the room. How was prison, Mr. Mayor?

"Well," Curley said off the record, "they gave us spaghetti in the morning for breakfast, and we had spaghetti in the afternoon for lunch, and we had spaghetti at night for dinner." And then he got guffaws with one of Boston's casual ethnic slights: "You'd think I was a goddamned guinea."

But that was the least of it. Full of himself, he blundered far more on the record than off. "I have accomplished more in one day than has been done in the five months of my absence." The offhand snub became a banner headline an hour later.

Hynes fumed to a friend on the street outside City Hall when he saw the papers, and then had an out-of-character explosion once he got home. His son, Jack, then a teenager in high school, was taken aback by his usually mild-mannered but clearly unhinged father, the first and only time he saw him so angry. Hynes stormed from room to room, slamming his palms on tabletops and yelling "I'll kill him! I'll bury him!" His wife tried to settle him down with "this too shall pass" entreaties. But Jack remembered his father cutting her off by saying, "I'm gonna run against that son of a bitch and I'm gonna beat that son of a bitch."

When John Hynes calmed down, he got on the phone and laid plans for a stunning apostasy—the disparaged caretaker would challenge the legend in the next election. His first call was to Curley enemy and former mayor Maurice Tobin, and the second was to Andy Dazzi, the head of classified advertising at the *Boston Globe*. One had a political organization, and the other business contacts and media clout.

To cast aside the unpretentious Hynes as a timid bureaucrat was to misjudge a determined man who came up the hard way and from the same neck of the woods as Curley. His parents were Irish émigrés, and his mother had died when he was a boy. While he had none of Curley's brawny charisma, he knew one sure thing as he set sail against a strong wind—he would have an aging tiger by the tail. So be it.

It was good he had his anger to sustain him. As he began his audacious rebellion, he seemed utterly overmatched even by an infirm Curley.

Hynes was a short, slight man who was always impeccably dressed in a banker's suit. He wore rimless glasses under wavy hair that made him look like a kindly country doctor. Once in a while he would mix in a splashy tie. While people were drawn to his down-to-earth manner and straightforward honesty, he had no core accomplishment to talk about other than keeping the trains on time when he served in the clerk's office. Starting out, his glaring deficiency in facing off with Curley was mediocre oratory. Soft-spoken, he seldom moved his audience and would be up against a man who, in full voice, could both challenge and caress a crowd. Hynes may have been a smiling everyman in plain-rimmed glasses. But he was easy to misread and would not be denied.

Like Curley, he left school at fourteen, but he avoided the roughneck adolescence of the mayor by heading downtown to work as an office boy at the American Telegraph Company, tending to inkpots and chattering machines.

Hynes was twenty-three years younger than Curley, born in 1897 on East Lenox Street in the South End. It was a hardscrabble upbringing. His lugubrious father, Bernard, was a car inspector for the Boston & Albany Railroad, and his mother, Anna, died when he was seven. His teenage years had him and his older brother, Thomas, alone against the world, somewhat set apart from his three half sisters from his father's second marriage. Barney Hynes was a forbidding man of the old Irish school where children were to be seen and not heard, especially if there were a bunch of them. He rocked glumly in his corner chair after work and left the family to fend for itself.

But John had his mother's brightness and ability to plunge straight ahead. His family became part of a small Irish migration within Boston that moved into Dorchester after the turn of the century, when trolley cars pushed their way into what had been rural farmland. The Hyneses moved into one of its rows of single-family homes.

A grammar school dropout, John started at the telegraph company for fourteen dollars a week. He took business courses at night school and then did a brief tour in the Army Air Corps in World War I. He began his City Hall career when he returned, working as a stenographer in the health department before moving to the auditing department. His ascendency—and real education in Boston politics—began when he became the chief clerk for Curley in the mayor's second term in office.

He went to law school at night and passed the bar in 1927, a year after he married Marion Barry from South Boston. They had five children: Jack, Barry, Richard, Marie, and Nancy.

Hynes would impress his peers as a gentle and even erudite man who knew literature at least as well as Curley and had some of the poet in him, writing first as an avocation and then as his business required. But his flair was more for writing his speeches than for delivering them in a soft monotone.

In 1929 he entered the permanent bureaucracy by becoming an assistant city clerk under the straight-shooting Wilfred Doyle. He joined the army in World War II, but his service was cut short by illness. He became *the* city clerk in 1945 as part of an elaborate succession scheme set up by Curley to make sure he would be greeted home from jail by a caretaker and not a challenger.

Hynes's daughter Marie remembered the early years as an idyllic time, with her father a warm family man who indulged his children to make up for his own distant father. Everyday he'd come home from work and follow the same routine, which ended with a carefully divided candy bar that had been stashed in his overcoat. He'd have some inviolate "alone" time with the afternoon papers in his den as the children listened outside for the telltale rustle of newsprint that signaled a move from his chair to his coat for the biggest chocolate bar in Dorchester. He'd be swarmed by children in search of a one-fifth share. Marie told the Boston historian Thomas O'Connor that she thought her father "was trying to make up for the lack of warmth and enjoyment he himself never had as a child." The years before he became mayor made for a simple life anchored by family, daily mass, and a midday chat with his wife to see how things were on the home front.

Despite his five children, Hynes looked past a deferment for an officer's appointment in the army after the Japanese attacked Pearl Harbor. An ear infection resulted in an early discharge and again he saw no combat action. Earnest as ever, he later told a reporter, "But I tried. Enlisted both times."

When the time came, it would not be enough for the Veterans for

Curley, with bellicose bookie Edward "Knocko" McCormack painting Hynes as a wimp just short of a traitor—even though his own man stayed home from the first war and conspired with a war profiteer in the second.

Even though Hynes was an accountant with a law degree, he somehow escaped the craft's curse of leaden legalese and developed a flair for political rhetoric, with some poetry on the side. With some irony, he wrote a short biography called *That Man Curley* during the mayor's unsuccessful senatorial race in 1936. He got to know the candidates on the stump and backstage, writing speeches for Curley and Maurice Tobin along the way. But he went straight home from City Hall, bypassing the nightly exodus to nearby watering holes like the Parker House bar. He joined the Holy Name Society and not much else. His only vices were a weekly poker game and an occasional round of billiards or golf.

But he had strong convictions and was aggressive enough to mobilize quickly in the wake of a headline announcing CURLEY TAKES SLAP AT HYNES. After a quarter century at City Hall, he saw the landscape clearly. Curley voters were dying off, and the new, younger ones were weary of his standard harangues about Yankee perfidy while the city's tax base flatlined and the housing stock in the old neighborhoods fell apart. Hynes saw a tired town ready for a fresh start.

Curley still had his blindly loyal army of City Hall workers out to their second cousins in the old, disintegrating neighborhoods. The public payroll quotient in Boston was off the charts, 50 percent above the average for the eight largest cities in America. Another beholden group were the 55,000 vulnerable voters in public housing. They were the incumbent's diehards.

Hynes and his emerging advisers knew well the price of Curley's go-it-alone machine. The paucity of state and federal aid required the highest real estate taxes in the country, which, perversely, was funding featherbedding in police and fire departments and underwriting the nation's highest per capita expenditures for welfare and hospitals.

It would require careful footwork to attack Curley's tax rate, which favored homeowners over downtown business, without appearing critical of the average voter who benefited from Curley's unraveling municipal Ponzi scheme.

Hynes bet his election on the new returning veterans and their young families who were moving to the city's outer wards. The wager was that they would connect the dots between a bloated workforce and sky-high tax rates. He had some leaders in the wary business community from the get-go, and didn't waste any time courting city workers who would never be with him.

Candidate John Hynes had a compelling backdrop. In 1947 the calls for reform resonated even in jaded, cynical Boston. The mayor was in jail and the council so overrun by endemic corruption that it was talked about openly in its deliberations. Around the time that Curley matriculated into Danbury Prison for fraud, a license for a water taxi in the harbor was trapped in legislative limbo when a council member from Mattapan charged that the holdup was pending payoffs to his colleagues. That got a "so what?" retort from East Boston council member James Coffey, who seemed irritated that bribery was even an issue. "I will take a buck and who the hell does not know it? I would like to know the guy who does not take a buck."

Reformers were dismayed that Curley the jailbird still had such a strong hold on the electorate. Behind bars or not, it appeared he could be mayor for life. As he headed off to jail, polls found that a sizable majority thought he was doing a good job. A convicted felon had an astonishing approval rating of 62 percent.

The prospect of a perennial Curley mayoralty sent business community leaders into orbit. Their first move was an extreme measure that would have phased out an elected mayor in favor of a tax-cutting city manager system adopted by neighboring Cambridge. But at the end of months of pushing and shoving, the only government change still standing was a stealthy victory for Curley. Reformers replaced the disgraced twenty-two district City Council members for nine at-large members— an echo of the charter reform of 1909. But the only item that adversely affected Curley in that 1947 referendum vote was losing the advantage of a crowded final election that he stacked with spoilers to make him the plurality winner.

The new election format, which took effect in 1951, required a run-off preliminary election in September to be followed by a two-person final. Stripped of a cluttered ballot, Curley would have to stand alone at the end, as icon but also as target.

But what the change meant for John Hynes was that he would have to defeat a titan twice—the old way in 1949, and the new way in 1951. Curley grumbled, but, in truth, he felt he could live with the blandly titled "Plan A" form of government.

Curley may have outfoxed the reformers yet again, but he didn't fully grasp voter dissatisfaction. Curley's biographer Jack Beatty set the scene for Boston voters in 1949: "A corrupt mayor, a corrupt City Council, a corrupt press, a swollen city payroll, a dying city economy, and the highest taxes beneath the wandering moon."

Even with the usual spoilers making their last appearance in 1949, it was clear early on that it was a two-man race, with Hynes as the man to beat. He had most of the Tobin coalition rooted in the business community behind him, and the ear of unaligned veterans. Curley had the fossilized but fervent city workers.

Sitting yards apart in adjoining offices in City Hall, they prepared for battle. Hynes predicted doomsday in Boston unless the city turned the page on the Curley machine. Curley's answer was his standard ad hominem—that Hynes was an over-his-head waif, "a little city clerk who has never been out of the city except to attend a convention." But Hynes pounded on the theme that Curley was a harmful relic of yesterday and that "the day of that kind of man is gone forever. We can't afford the city bosses anymore."

Of all the colorful characters who made up Curley's army of aging foot soldiers, the epitome was Edward "Knocko" McCormack, a World War I combat veteran and roustabout straight out of the pages of *The Last Hurrah*, the novel about Curley and his motley liege men. Knocko was an open-shirted, cigar-chomping, red-faced, pot-bellied behemoth who, on a steamy summer night, could be found at his Southie bar-cum-bookie joint serving up draft beer wearing a jockstrap under an apron and sometimes topped by a tam-o'-shanter. He was his own bouncer as well, scrawling the names of the banished and their offense on a large chalkboard. One entry was "Brought a Guinea to the bar."

As his accomplished brother John moved into the leadership in the US Congress, he was still just the "Congi" to Knocko, whose profane outbursts at campaign meetings made him a Curley favorite who played his straight man—what do you have to report, Knocko?—to get the latest tirade against the turncoat ingrate Johnny Hynes.

For a brief while, Knocko was the face of the Curley campaign at his headquarters on Bromfield Street, with his messy desk just inside the front door. But his crass talk and garish demeanor scared away some incongruous supporters from Beacon Hill, a gaggle of refined old ladies charmed by Curley but appalled by Knocko. There was a motion to ban Knocko entirely from headquarters, but Curley nixed it, needing Knocko's gusto and linkage with their vivid pasts. Curley's solution was to shift Knocko's disarray to the back of the shop, but under a proud sign that said it all: VETERANS SIGN UP HERE WITH KNOCKO. It kept the office's entrance safe for WASP dowagers and put Knocko back into his old Yankee Division uniform and out of harm's way.

And Knocko, who had dodged German machine guns in the Argonne, got into the fray at the end after hearing Hynes take credit for being a veteran in a radio interview as well as intimating that the veteran clique around Curley harbored a gangster element. Knocko took that personally and took to the airwaves in his booming last-call voice. "I want to say to you, Johnny Hynes, that the closest you ever came to a foxhole was in the back of a movie house, watching John Wayne win the war. . . . You marched into the army a private and marched out as a captain. Now, Mister Johnny without a gun, who was the political gangster that bribed Santa Claus and got you your commission? Think about that one, voters, when you go to vote next Tuesday."

It was called "Knocko's Socko" in the newspapers, but it was shrill vaudeville to newer voters, who viewed McCormack as an artifact from a bygone era. While some returning World War II veterans had supported the Curley-gets-it-done campaign in 1945, four years later they saw Curley's legacy for what it was—a moribund city swimming in red ink. "Johnny without a gun" was the last thing on their minds at the polls that November. The "think about that one" that resounded most was a succession of double-digit rent increases from neglectful landlords struggling with Curley's confiscatory tax rate. The bad thought for voters at the lever was *Why am I paying more for less?*

As strongly as the winds of change were whipping across the city, Curley would surely have had another term but for the lack of a simple thank-you to his stand-in. Hynes told his son that a "good job" salutation instead of a gibe would have enlisted one more experienced hand to Curley's 1949 reelection team—city clerk John Hynes.

In the late 1940s, Boston was a bottomed-out place. Its textile plants had already moved south, and its shoe and leather businesses were not far behind. The mainstay shipping industry was long gone. Railroad cars no longer disgorged produce at warehouses along Summer Street. Machine shops were laying off. Inflation was spiraling. The suburban migration of fast-growing electronics firms to the encircling Route 128 was under way. Even shabby housing was in short supply. Old, narrow downtown streets were falling apart under increased traffic.

Yet this was the grim setting for a triumphal return home from prison by James Michael Curley. As thousands cheered him at Back Bay Station, few associated their dim prospects with his self-absorbed stewardship. This was more than just style over substance that captured the crowd. It was a willful disconnect that gave a pass to the captain of the *Titanic.*

So it was almost a biblical retribution when the context for Curley's fateful remark about him getting more done in one day than John Hynes did in five months was his figuring his take on construction projects. His throwaway line to reporters did more than stacks of FinCom reports had ever done—it galvanized an opponent with an alternative agenda that had more than just business support.

Hynes's upset election wasn't just the end of James Michael Curley. It marked the first thaw in a century of intense Irish-Yankee enmity and the beginning of an uneasy partnership to save the commercial center of New England.

It had become clear to long-disengaged bankers and merchants that downtown was dying, and that this time, the collapsing walls would surely fall on their insular way of life. They moved tentatively toward Hynes as the only game in town, but the budding alliance was clear enough for Curley to begin calling Hynes a stooge for State Street.

In his autobiography, Curley argued that it was the New Deal's Social Security and unemployment compensation that ended his cachet as "the best friend of the poor." But those benefits had been around for nearly two decades when he was finally turned out for good. By then, it was civil service jobs in federal offices and an array of veteran services that began putting Curley and other city bosses out of business. The new courthouses and post offices and VA outposts were just the beginning in a shift away from the Curley system.

As his patronage power ebbed, so did his renowned physical strength. While he remained unflappable and still could summon the booming voice and grand gesture, he no longer looked the part. He had revived after a half year in prison, but he could not hide the sallow skin and rheumy eyes and shaky gait of a man in his mid-seventies.

Along with business support against an infirm candidate, Hynes benefited from a subtle but distinct change within the Irish community. For decades Curley had happily exploited the petty warfare in his disorderly electorate that could never agree on a premise long enough to spell it out. But Curley's downward spiral was not due to a rebellion by a suddenly unified opposition. It wasn't even from a crumbling political machine. It was not having an A-team at all. There were no bright comers around him because he didn't trust them, especially after what he viewed as backstabbing young acolytes like Maurice Tobin. Instead he surrounded himself with the Knockos of his world. True blue but ham-handed.

In addition, Curley's stemwinder speech at streetcorner rallies with warmups by Irish dancers and banjo players had become the political equivalent of minstrel shows. Curley recognized the shift away from his forte, but had trouble adjusting to radio's need for short, snappy statements. His idea of a sound bite usually involved Othello.

Johnny Hynes may have been a "little clerk," but he was quicker to his point in radio interviews and succinct in his Holy Name Society breakfast speeches. And his audience was now third-generation families who had shaken off the hurt of Yankee tyranny as they moved into single-family homes in Dorchester and West Roxbury, and away from the three-deckers closer to downtown. The only uniformly ethnic neighborhood left as the last-hurrah election campaign began was the Italian North End.

Once Hynes committed to running against a legend, he brought his own cast of appropriately named characters to the jamboree. There was self-proclaimed senator Elmer Foote, double-talking Sammy Goodwin, "Jabber" Burke, who always made it known he once pitched for Holy Cross, and Barney Levenson, who had boxed under the name of Spider Murphy. Levenson told Hynes's oldest son, Jack, about his nom de guerre. "Jackie, let me tell ya. I'd get booked for a fight and the kid would be Irish and the referee would be Irish. And I was losing. Well, I finally figured it out and just made the name up and made myself Irish And I started winning fights."

Hynes attracted returning veterans who wanted more from and for their city, and realized neither would happen with yet more Curley. While some businessmen saw just more of the same from Hynes, others began taking him at his word—that it was in everyone's interest to reinvigorate a declining city. As the tight campaign wound down, there was a late surge of Yankee supporters such as Robert Cutler, Henry Shattuck, Stuart Rand, and Henry Parkman into the Hynes camp. The smattering of WASPs joined a time-for-change middle-class coalition of Irish, Jews, Italians, and, to a lesser extent, blacks from the South End and Roxbury who had never felt welcome in Curley's City Hall.

The Hynes campaign boiled down to a hunt for new voters who wanted a more responsive city government. The managers brought in young bright lights led by a recent Harvard Law School graduate, Jerome L. Rappaport. He initially took charge of recruiting students from colleges in and around Boston. But Rappaport soon became a whirlwind within the campaign, dominating the advertising and voter canvassing effort. One of his power points was to turn a perceived Hynes weakness—that he was no match for invincible Curley—into a strength by showing

Curley's vaunted political machine was a myth. He also worked on exposing the related fable that Curley had a lock on the Irish vote.

Rappaport helped reveal Curley's machine as a Wizard of Oz operation with few capable ground troops. Hynes's strategy was a careful blend of high and low roads. Signs went up around the city to get rid of "Curley Gangsters," while the avuncular Hynes never mentioned Curley by name in his stump call for clean and honest government. The most forceful he got were allusions to Curley's age, branding the "present" administration as "tired and forlorn." The final days of the campaign came down to dueling slogans, with the recycled "Curley Gets Things Done" trumped by Hynes's "Restore Boston's Good Name."

The gulf between the disaffected ranks of younger families in the outer wards and the steadfast old guard left Boston a house divided in the final days. It made for the highest turnout in Boston history and the most votes James Michael Curley ever got—126,000. It just happened to be fifteen thousand fewer than John Hynes's tally. What was more remarkable than Hynes winning was the hold a worn-out ex-convict with tired theatrics retained on nearly half of voting Boston. While the pair split the city's twenty-two wards evenly, the streetcar suburbs finally had more voters in them. The diehard Irish of the inner city—the original immigrant strongholds of Charlestown, South Boston, East Boston, and the North and West Ends—stuck by Curley. But the "two toilet" Irish wanted a new day. They bought Hynes's simple, last-straw message: "The day of that kind of man is gone forever."

Hynes's youngest son, Richard, a retired lawyer who teaches Boston history at Boston University, is still struck by his father's gumption in taking on Goliath. "Geez, you have a fifty-two-year-old guy with five kids in a small house in Dorchester who loved a job that had just been made a lifetime appointment. And yet he goes for it. When you measure the span of the risk against the circumstances, it's quite something. He told me many times that anyone could have beaten Curley in 1949, that everyone was tired of him. But not anyone did it. He did. Son of a gun."

By the time Hynes was sworn in at Symphony Hall in January of 1950, there were clear-cut promises to keep on tax reform, but what even ardent supporters misunderstood was the magnitude of the new mayor's quandary: change things or the city goes broke.

While Hynes was a low-key figure for a Boston pol, he worked hard on the public relations of his new status. From the start, he looked for ways to set himself apart from backslapping peers so he could connect not just with the emerging middle class but with downtown businessmen as well. He dressed the part and was disparaged for it at times by some who saw him as a "hoper"—a Yankee wannabe. But his subdued if natty attire got him the image he was after: a mayor on equal footing with the movers and shakers.

He eschewed Curley's confrontational style, which had taken him such a long way while slamming the door for everyone else. Hynes sought a new coalition that did not depend on a rabid base fired up incessantly by the old Irish resentments. It was a softer new way that signaled genuine interest in mutual solutions from a man who had a foot in one camp and a toe in the other. He ran a campaign that held out the prospect of partnership with downtown businessmen on the premise that the city's perilous financial situation was bad for everyone.

In some ways, Hynes's new tact was a page taken from the playbook of John F. Kennedy, who had used advertising and precise polling to target his voters as he supplanted old-school politics with just the right mix of Irish and Harvard. Young Jack moved seamlessly from Curley's old congressional district to Henry Cabot Lodge's Senate seat in 1952 as Johnny Hynes was well under way at City Hall. Kennedy's sophisticated approach was light-years away from the buffoonery of the ward-heeler days that treated politics as a game with a sole objective—have a drink and get a job. The new Irish came to appreciate Kennedy's lighter, quicker humor as well as his ruthless pragmatism, which took no prisoners. Elections were no game; they were to get power to change things.

At midcentury, Kennedy was unveiling his manifest destiny while the mundane business of saving his family's native city fell to the "little clerk." But Hynes's new frontier was nearly as daunting as Kennedy's spirited assault on the national complacency of the Eisenhower years: Could an Irish mayor get businessmen to trust City Hall, to move from nascent rapport into a coalition to save a city?

It was a tentative start at best. But Hynes began not only to meet with business leaders but also actually to listen to them. He sought their ideas, solicited their support, and began appointing them on advisory panels with one main goal—renewal based on an infusion of state and federal money and rooted in the understanding that Boston was in a tax crisis.

Hynes's epochal victory turned brittle in the cold light of day. After Curley's spending spree, Boston's tax rate was out of control. Downtown development was an oxymoron in a city whose commercial center featured strip joints and tattoo parlors. The port was in disarray, no new buildings were even in the planning stage, no housing was being built, and the infrastructure was in shambles.

Hynes's campaign hailed the dawn of a "new" Boston, but the gut question when the shouting stopped was, given a century of class warfare, could any mayor forge a partnership with business and still hold his constituency?

It was more than a tall order. It was the cow over the moon. Many thought it was so quixotic that Hynes would fall flat and get beaten two years hence in the inaugural Plan A election of 1951 by the ever-resilient Curley.

Yet that thinking underestimated the man and the tenor of the times. Even the old Curley haunts were losing their numbers and clout, and the tribal chants about ancient wounds were falling on deaf ears. Curley fatigue had sent some young Irish families past the outer wards to the suburbs in a search of better housing value. The city's population was on its way down from 800,000 to 700,000.

In the aftermath, there was daunting opportunity. Curley was finally done, but now what? Could John Hynes really shove off in such a dramatically different direction?

His inaugural speech was similar to those that went before it. Promises for new housing and expansion of streets to unclog traffic, and a garage under Boston Common to further relieve congestion. But his real plan for the future was tucked away toward the end with a short reference to slum clearance. His plan forward included a new map for old Boston.

Hynes's goals were so steeply uphill as to be perpendicular. Even with change in the air and some healing of old wounds in the outer wards, the latent hostility between Irish Catholic and Yankee Protestant was just an insult away, a conditional response to decades of Curley's rhetoric that was matched quietly on the other side by redlining of Irish neighborhoods by banks and insurance companies. As Ephron Catlin Jr. of the First National Bank said in a rare burst of candor: "God, how the business community hated Curley."

The city's financial situation was the same as it had been since Honey Fitzgerald took City Hall for the Irish. The establishment had pushed itself away from the table and decreed aridly, "Run the place into the ground if you must, but do so without a dime of state aid or bank investment."

After Fitzgerald became the city's first four-year Irish mayor, the legislature erected a maze of restrictions that made it just about impossible for a Boston mayor to run his own affairs. All expenses had to be paid from one source—real estate taxes. Irish mayors reacted by shifting the burden disproportionately to downtown office buildings. But the steady exodus of voters from inner-ward apartments to outlying homes in the 1940s changed the political calculation. The unfair burden became all the more egregious, and abatement payments to businesses escalated. The tax burden had to be spread around more, and there was no place for John Hynes to hide.

By the time he took control, Boston's tax rate was the highest of twenty comparably sized cities, and even the steady shift in the legislature from Republican to Democrat didn't work in Boston's favor. The new Democratic majority comprised mostly suburbanites with traditional disdain for the mess Boston pols had gotten themselves into.

Given the expectations, Hynes had to prove he wasn't just more of the same. The trick of it was to stay true to his roots without alienating supporters with his overtures to business leaders. Make nice, but stay Irish. The context was set with more blunt buckshot from banker Ephron Catlin: "Nobody had ever seen an honest Irishman around here."

John Hynes was so soft-spoken he became known as "whispering Johnny." Yet he had a temper waiting for those who sought old-school advantage. Like the car dealer who, shortly after Hynes's election, left a black convertible in his driveway with a Christmas bow on it. His daughter Marie recalled that he had some brisk instructions for the dealer looking for City Hall business: "Get that car out of my driveway right now or I'm calling the police." Curley would have called the dealer only if he didn't like convertibles.

Hynes set a new tone, starting with first things first: Get the house in order. As city clerk, he was intimately familiar with how City Hall had become overrun by overlapping departments and boards, many to nudge around make-work projects that went nowhere while the patchwork quilt of government just grew larger. It fell to his wunderkind chief of staff from Harvard Law, Jerome Rappaport, to cut the hydra-headed monster down to size. It also gave a self-aggrandizing man a bird's-eye view of City Hall's inner terrain. It took a while, but departments were reduced from thirty-eight to twenty-six, and some progress was made in bringing order to the messy and corrupt stable of inspectors in the building, fire, and health departments.

One of Rappaport's findings was self-serving for his own long-range ambitions, but also an undeniable necessity for planning a new Boston: an agency to launch renewal projects and devise a master plan for coordinated development.

But after recognizing the planning needs for a new landscape and updating zoning regulations and traffic routes, Hynes soon faced another election with Curley. Under the new election format, a two-person final was in place just two years later.

Predictably, Curley lashed out at Hynes's early efforts at rapprochement by citing failures to get state funding for housing projects because Hynes didn't want to offend "Henry Shattuck and his Republican friends."

Hynes's rejoinder was equally predictable—no turning back now. He was making progress that would be stopped the day after his defeat. He had some moxie to go with the new agenda this time around, finally acclimated to standing toe-to-toe with Curley on the same stage. In one joint appearance, Curley criticized the incumbent for not finding the money for an oil painting of George Washington at Dorchester

Heights during the British evacuation of Boston. "Why, when I was mayor," Curley intoned, "there was always sufficient money for such worthy purposes." With a small smile, Hynes countered, "If there was any money left in the treasury when I succeeded you, I have never been able to locate it." Even Curley had to laugh at that.

In September 1951, the city's first preliminary election drew more than 200,000 voters to the polls. Hynes along with a new slate of council and school committee candidates proposed by the New Boston Committee, an amalgam of progressives organized by Rappaport, rolled to victory. Hynes received 108,009 votes to Curley's 77,000—about 50,000 less than the latter had received just two years earlier. Even with the writing on the wall, Curley still stunned his diehard supporters by announcing he would make "no contest" of the runoff in November. The final election was a big day for the New Boston lineup. Hynes won by the largest margin ever—78,000 votes. In a clean sweep for Hynes supporters, five of nine new council members and four of five school committee members had been endorsed by the New Boston forces.

Ever so slowly, momentous change was under way, initially just as urban blueprints from academics, mostly from Boston College and MIT.

By the time Hynes had beaten Curley twice in two years, change was a mandate, especially when it became clear that significant federal funding would finally be available to pockets-inside-out Boston. Title I of the Housing Act of 1949 brought both money and muscle to the table. Within a year of passage, the low-wattage Boston Housing Authority was suddenly given the added clout of being the city's primary planning agency. It could designate residential areas as "blighted" districts for development as business offices or housing. With the feds picking up two thirds of the tab, the authority could take slum property through eminent domain and clear it for sale to a private developer at reduced rates. The housing agency's stated goal was to convert much of 2,700 acres of blight into middle-class housing.

But the first and easiest priority was transportation. New routes had to be found to move the area's bursting population though a downtown

Boston, which had become a maze of ancient and narrow streets. New roadways along the edges of neighborhoods also had the advantage of not taking on powerful political constituencies. There were few protests to worry about, and hefty state and federal subsidies would pay the freight.

Two vital transit projects got off the drawing boards in the Hynes years: the Central Artery, which would run along the waterfront to bring commuters in and through town, took shape (Hynes stood by it even though it cut off a slice of Chinatown and an edge of the North End); and a major downtown parking facility, which was designated for the hallowed ground below the venerable Boston Common.

Hynes also began spadework on five downtown renovations that would need final pushes from his successors. Three of them had no natural constituencies to spark neighborhood protests. Nevertheless, all proved elusive and long-running.

Given federal money newly available for blighted urban areas, the most achievable seemed the leveling of gaudy Scollay Square to make way for a Government Center anchored by a new City Hall. But finding tenants and sorting out eminent-domain takings of scores of businesses got bogged down in red tape.

The second renovation also seemed overdue and more doable— converting an abandoned railroad yard in Back Bay for office buildings. But it got mired in legal technicalities after the city tried to give a special tax break to the Prudential Insurance Company to help it build a signature office tower. Things moved fitfully and, after tax deals were twice ruled unconstitutional, were finished by others. But Hynes saw it first and pushed it hard for a decade.

The third downtown revival was to rescue the disarray that had replaced an early-nineteenth-century produce center named after the take-charge early-nineteenth-century mayor Josiah Quincy. That proved to be the longest-running "sure thing," and had to wait nearly two decades before rows of smart shops and restaurants were assembled into Boston's top tourist attraction.

But real urban renewal in Boston did not start with downtown office towers sprouting up on abandoned railway yards; it began where poor people lived. It was all high-minded and part of a sensible effort to lure upscale workers back to the city with luxury housing. But it gave renewal a bad name in a city with contentious ethnic neighborhoods. The first takings ended in infamy—not so much for the results as for the process.

Hynes's administration used a time-honored strategy employed a century earlier against the Irish: boot the poor out of downtown neighborhoods in the name of progress. The first of two cleared tracts was a thirteen-acre section in the South End known as New York Streets, a small minority residential district for 850 families that eventually gave way to light industry.

It was the first significant use of Title I of the US Housing Act of 1949, and an ominous omen for all older neighborhoods. The new statute underwrote eminent-domain takings of dilapidated housing by local authorities to clear land for new development. It focused on blighted areas, a designation that resided squarely in the eye of the beholder. The Chamber of Commerce saw vital advancement while the residents saw basic shelter. The bulldozed area in the South End lay fallow for a decade, and the "light" industry came to include the *Boston Herald*, landing heavily on the "skid row" it had castigated in earlier editorials favoring the project.

But the big flap that reverberated for decades—and nearly stopped neighborhood renewal in its tracks with permanent damage to Hynes's legacy—was the decimation of one of the city's oldest waterfront sections. The West End's narrow streets with their ramshackle five-story tenements near the Charles River were a logical site for a huge upgrade. And that's basically what happened. But there was some betrayal in the fleet of sleek apartment buildings that sprung up in place of 2,700 homes for mostly Jewish and Italian immigrants. Despite repeated promises of relocation assistance from city planners and reassurances from politicians that residents could choose to resettle there in low- and moderate-income housing, seven thousand old West End inhabitants were evicted by the city and left to fend for themselves.

To further complicate matters, the early downtown projects were out of sequence, with the residential makeovers in place before downtown was fixed. The units went up before the jobs were in place. But at least all the projects started around the same time. The thinking was that the new West End would kick-start Boston's commercial center and revive its middle class. While this put the cart before the horse, it was so new and novel that it worked despite itself, drawing professionals back to the city, many of them working at the Massachusetts General Hospital, located in the middle of the ongoing construction site. The media endorsed this project in lockstep, looking past the wholesale evictions as a necessary evil to get to a new day. The endeavor launched a new axis of Catholic bishop, Yankee banker, and Irish mayor, and created a permanent power base in town, greeted with howls and hosannas as the Boston Redevelopment Authority.

But the other side of the easy storyline of progress was a permanent subtext of deep distrust of City Hall in the blue-collar neighborhoods. The mood would simmer for fifteen years after Hynes left office before exploding over forced busing that was supposed to fix racial imbalance in neighborhood schools.

By the end of his first full term in 1955, Hynes's vision for a new Boston had jelled. He had made progress in getting government and business leaders to agree on an agenda—clearing slums to revitalize downtown. But all the balls were at various altitudes as the mayor juggled madly to keep them aloft. Could Whispering Johnny get across the goal line or just run around willy-nilly behind the line of scrimmage?

It was very much an issue when Hynes stood for reelection for his second four-year term against the Democratic minority leader in the Senate, John Powers of South Boston. Powers came from an impoverished family with the typical immigrant background—his father was killed on the job while working as a streetcar motorman.

The rotund, cigar-chomping Powers was decidedly old-school and legendary for his fervent and rather mindless constituent service. He had close ties to organized labor and, like Martin Lomasney of an earlier era, made astute use of parliamentary procedure to manhandle the legislative process. He was first elected to the House of Representatives in 1938 and was undefeated in two-year intervals until he squared off against Hynes nearly two decades later. Even with an eighty-one-year-old Curley making a cameo appearance in the preliminary election, there was a low turnout. At that, Hynes got but 39 percent of the vote, an edge over Powers but hardly a rousing endorsement.

As Curley had in the Last Hurrah election of 1949, Powers tried to make the toxic connection between Hynes and Republican Yankee businessmen. He worked to put Hynes between a rock and a hard place: to get the financial wherewithal to revive Boston and somehow not deal with the money boys.

Powers sought to maneuver the election into a false choice of two "philosophies"—one subservient to State Street and tax giveaways and his better way of taking nebulous care of the little guy. Hynes tried to stay above the fray, but he had to get into the nitty-gritty before it was over, painting Powers as a Curley hack and then, in the final days of a tightening race, as beholden to a loose federation of Southie bookmakers. In the end, the campaign overheated into a reprise of the Last Hurrah, with the same result based on the same allegiances. The old fault lines prevailed, with Hynes winning by about thirteen thousand votes on the strength of the outer-circle neighborhoods and Powers taking all but one of Curley's inner wards.

The mayor's oldest son, Jack, remembers it as "a tough fight. My father didn't like John Powers. He thought he was a South Boston wise guy. He didn't consider him very honest and that went for his whole crew. The night before the election he went on television and said Powers was 'the darling of the mob.' So, there were hard feelings that stayed that way."

The last term for John Hynes slipped quickly into lame-duck territory. He had been an unlikely catalyst for pushing a stubborn status quo city toward a full-service metropolis. But even as this courtly gentleman with a kindly mien got everything under way, he also unleashed a brutal process aimed at saving the village by burning some of it. The shift in thinking was accompanied by an abdication to the interests of real estate developers and urban planners who cared not a whit for neighborhood camaraderie or traditions.

The price of progress would be seen by most as worth it—but barely. Doing something about woebegone Scollay Square and the bedraggled

West End and a rundown slice of Back Bay also meant obliteration by eminent domain—a formal policy of pushing the poor out of their homes and shuttering long-standing if marginal businesses. It was a precarious equation at best.

The reverberations from an overdue facelift damaged race relations and revived dormant class enmity in the old Irish neighborhoods of Charlestown and South Boston. The Yankee overlords were replaced by bow-tied urban planners who pored over maps without seeing any of the people.

Ironically, the estrangement arose from high hopes and good intentions. The New Boston Committee had been formed in 1950 by key Hynes supporters after Curley was dispatched for good. Its prime mover was Jerome Rappaport, who oversaw the administration's outreach to neighborhood leaders. The objective was to centralize power to achieve coherent political leadership that would replace ad-hoc Curleyism.

The committee stepped into a void left by the somnolent newspapers of the day and the demise of the bumbling and corrupt twenty-two-member City Council. While the timing was right, the question became whether it had the right leadership. Rappaport wore two hats, as overseer of the committee and as mayoral chief of staff. But Hynes gave him a wide berth and appeared to view conflict of interest as a necessary evil.

Rappaport's New Boston Committee had an unexpectedly short run. It collapsed in Hynes's first full term and its demise was a severe setback in the effort to get the legislature to authorize flexibility in the city's tax system. Hynes needed maneuverability to attract new business with lower rates on one hand and not soak established enterprises to make up the difference on the other. Without that authority, the mayor was painted into a corner, where he was left to float listless trial balloons for alternatives like payroll and sales taxes that needed State House approval.

Jerome Rappaport departed shortly after his brainchild dissolved in 1952. With some irony, he gave up on the committee's effectiveness when it was unable to stop private business from obtaining city park land in the Fenway neighborhood. The successful action by Sears, Roebuck paled in comparison to Rappaport's later acquisition of an entire neighborhood.

Said to be disillusioned, he left city service to specialize in tax abatement work for private commercial clients, disappointing some of his New Boston colleagues. But they hadn't seen anything yet.

Che mega-project that Hynes had pushed valiantly and well was to entice the Prudential Insurance Company to build an office tower in the Back Bay over a railroad yard. But the planning was stuck on the two-yard line for years and came to symbolize the tax dilemma of trying to give a tax break to one company on the backs of others. Among other complicated things, the unequal treatment raised constitutional issues.

Throughout the decade, sleepy Boston lagged badly behind other major cities, barely a caboose on the fast-moving renewal train then roaring through New York and Chicago. They had key ingredients that America's first city lacked—state and federal funding and ruthless dynamos at the helm. In fact, New York's legendary power broker, Robert Moses, was pretty much done by 1959, when Boston was barely under way. He had 28,000 apartment units in mostly high-rises, and ribbons of roads crisscrossing low-income neighborhoods. As well, Chicago was in the hands of a brick-and-mortar man, Mayor Richard Daley, who also favored highways over poor people. In both places, if there was massive displacement of the destitute with business support, there was the will and the way that Boston lacked.

Indeed, the myopic Boston business community was one of the biggest hurdles facing Hynes—followed closely by the courts and the legislature. While Hynes had none of Curley's hubris, he still loathed the idea of hat-in-hand appearance before legislative taxation committees. The down-to-earth Hynes viewed such supplication as beneath the dignity of his office. His reticence became another potential checkmate.

The gleam of a soaring tower first glinted in John Hynes's eyes at a mayors' conference in Washington in 1951. A Florida official told him that Prudential was going to build a regional center in Jacksonville and was looking to locate another one in the Northeast. Hynes had an immediate vision of it over the rundown railroad yard between Back Bay and the South End. He returned home to the fortuitous news that Boston

& Albany Railroad executives were selling the land in question for $4.5 million.

But two years later there was more political will than business support to do a Prudential deal. Lukewarm lunches were held with business leaders, and the proposition drifted to the back burner even as Hynes made it clear that the city's tax assessment would stay at the rock-bottom $4.5-million price the railroad was asking. But Prudential wanted a long-range tax break that was strongly opposed by downtown business executives who worried that the "Pru" Center would be harmful competition. The upshot was that a business-is-back beacon in Back Bay remained stymied in a city where the total property valuation was $400 million less than it had been in the Great Depression a quarter century earlier. The effort seemed permanently sidetracked in 1955 when a proposed tax break was deemed unconstitutional by the state Supreme Judicial Court.

Nevertheless, the project mostly gyrated forward as an idea whose time had come. In 1957 Prudential agreed to buy the 28.5-acre site from the railroad on a wing and a prayer that was greeted by Hynes as a rescue mission from "the encircling gloom." The insurance company was still insisting on a sliding value assessment for the site during a seven-year construction period. Then a new player was added to the mix, the political carnivore known as the Massachusetts Turnpike Authority, which agreed to take over the site to plow through an extension of its roadway into Boston, build a convention center on air rights above the roadway, and set aside land for a $150-million Prudential Center.

There was even a fatuous groundbreaking ceremony featuring a ninety-foot-high wrecking ball and pols in suits and soft hats staring at the levers of heavy equipment. Not many shovels were turned before the Supreme Judicial Court once again ruled the latest tax arrangement unconstitutional.

The hole in the ground looked to be the burial site of Hynes's best hope for a turnaround. It would take a new administration to figure out that a way around the fatal tax flaw was to convert the Pru project into a unique urban renewal site with special public-use requirements.

Even the easiest target of all—the Government Center to replace forlorn Scollay Square—was trapped in red tape. To older Bostonians, the square still had the nostalgic allure of the Prohibition era, but newer residents saw it as a dreary anachronism that had once featured vaudeville acts like the man who played the violin with his teeth and then danced with his bulldog. But its new incarnation needed a federal office building that had proved as elusive as getting a consensus on the design of a new City Hall.

At the end of his term in January 1960, all Hynes had to show for a decade of nudging and nurturing was a hole in the ground in Back Bay, a solid plan in need of commitments for the Government Center, and acres of cleared land in the West and South Ends.

The New Boston banner of John Hynes drooped. In his decade, more than 100,000 residents had left town for better suburban housing and the Boston tax rate rose skyward, doubling in his tenure. The city's bond rating was the lowest of any American city with a population over a half million. A stooped Hynes became a little like Harry Truman, a straight-from-the-shoulder everyman who people liked but concluded unfairly was in over his head. History would be kinder to both, but as Hynes left office, the lack of progress was a letdown that had political scientists poring over electorate behavior to explain "the alienated voter."

Hynes's son Richard remembered that his father had an instinctive sense of timing, never more evident than at the beginning and at the end. He was fully aware he had to seize the moment against Curley, and then just as sure that it was time to go when he had done all he could. After departing City Hall, Hynes opened up a small law office in a tired building on Tremont Street overpopulated with other lawyers. "No one was knocking the doors off," said Richard. "He was a little lonely up there. He didn't land on his feet until [governor] Chub Peabody made him head of the banking commission. He enjoyed that, a much better end note."

But, given the city's relentless financial bind, John Hynes remained trapped in a perception that he was a man with plans that seldom happened. The high promise of getting the city out of Curley's shadow faded into second thoughts about what exactly had been wrought. If he turned the ship of state around some, did he also get taken for a ride by opportunists like Rappaport?

It took a can-do successor to salvage Hynes's template. But, as Hynes's old slogan once said about the city itself, it restored a good name.

Not that ascribing due credit was a priority with his successor, John Francis Collins. He was especially niggardly about the Prudential Center, which had been pushed through so many twists and turns by Hynes. After Collins sorted out the tax-break dilemma, the building of the era shot up like a strong tree. But Collins oversaw a dedication ceremony in 1962 to which Hynes was not invited.

Jack Hynes recalled how that oversight was resolved with his father taking his proper place. He said that Carroll Shanks, the president of Prudential during all the 1950s gyrations, ended a conversation with his father the night before the ceremony by saying he'd see him in the morning. "My father said, 'Well, I won't be going.'" A shocked Shanks asked why not. " 'Well, I'm sorry to tell you I haven't been invited.' Shanks said, 'We'll see about that.' He called back to say John Hynes would be sitting right beside him at the ceremony."

The Collins slight stuck in the craw of a proud man who was just looking to give a little wave to smattering applause. While he was stoic about it publicly, his son said, he remembered it well in private. "Sure, it rankled him when proper credit was withheld, but he kept quiet, knowing that if he complained it would look like sour grapes. That was never the old man's style."

CHAPTER 7

All or Nothing

WEST END DEMOLITION SITE

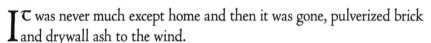

I*T* was never much except home and then it was gone, pulverized brick and drywall ash to the wind.

Then it became something else entirely, something Boston needed more than a romanticized run-down neighborhood: a stake in the future.

In demolition's bitter aftermath, the West End has become the rare case when going to extremes finds truth of nearly equal weight in both places.

Its rehabilitation was a desperate measure in what was a moribund city in dire need of a middle-class neighborhood for professionals. And it got one.

But it was also the original sweetheart deal of the urban renewal era in America, with developers buying an entire neighborhood on the cheap on a twenty-year installment plan. In the end, three partners netted at least $370 million over the life of the project, according to a Boston real estate specialist.

And, on a human level, it was a tragedy that tossed immigrant families into abandoned streets while giving a connected former city official control over fifty downtown acres for decades. After a rocky start, the West End's sleek replacement became the crown jewel in a family real estate empire that raked in money from rents, condo conversions, and (finally) outright sales. The breathtaking fact is that the well-intentioned mayor of Boston ceded a neighborhood where seven thousand residents had lived to a top aide who made a fortune.

What happened was so drastic that the main developer—Jerome Rappaport—has conceded he'll probably never live it down even as he stoutly defends himself and the end result of his endeavor. "Let me just say," Rappaport said, "I didn't decide to take the West End. This was a program of the city, state and federal governments. . . . If I were older, I probably wouldn't have done it. But I was young and foolish and idealistic. Back then, other investors were looking to invest in Route 128 and Texas. I assure you—not the West End of Boston."

Rappaport has argued that such radical action was Boston's only chance to infuse middle-class money into a city whose tax base was stagnant, trapped between expanding exempt institutions and deteriorating low-income neighborhoods. He rightly presents Charles River Park as an emblematic effort that lured young professionals to live by the river and helped revive the city's center.

Sitting in his massive State Street corner office with Boston sprawling at his feet, the dapper octogenarian said in his resonant baritone that the West End project has to be understood in the context of the economic calamity in down-and-out Boston of sixty years past.

But his cornucopia also has to be measured by how it came to be an indelible paradox of midcentury urban life—a triumphant travesty that permanently alienated blue-collar Boston.

The devastation was there for everyone to see. At the end of the 1950s, a sagging but proud old neighborhood was reduced to a moonscape, with the forty-eight acres between Beacon Hill and the North End obliterated over eighteen months. All that was left standing were a hospital, two churches, and the historic Harrison Gray Otis House, which was always more Beacon Hill than West End, and had dominated the thin strip of Yankee homes that ran to Bowdoin Square. It was cold comfort to the evicted that the only house to survive once belonged to an early-nineteenth-century mayor known for his careful planning.

After the city took the property by eminent domain, it left thousands of evicted residents high and dry, urging them coldly toward public housing projects. Even with few prospects, only 10 percent took the stigmatized option of living in welfare tenements. The stark fate of its residents made the West End another bloody demarcation point in how workaday Boston viewed city leaders from then on—more them than us.

The endgame was an apocalyptic urban landscape that became the final refuge for elderly widows holding out in barricaded apartments on deserted streets. The dingy avenues were overrun at night by roaming bands of teenagers using vacant buildings for drinking parties. The final evacuation became a panicky pell-mell with villagers fleeing a bulldozer blitzkrieg. The city later used the scrambling exodus as justification for why there was so little relocation help—hey, everybody left on their own.

And yet there is no denying the dispassionate core argument for downtown renewal: Imagine the city without a revived West End. The old neighborhood would have been a lingering hobo sleeping it off in the doorway of a newly resplendent downtown.

While that disconcerting prospect remains persuasive, its corollary— that the West End made possible all that followed—is not. In fact, the West End project sputtered along in fits and starts for twenty years while the adjoining Government Center project supplanted Scollay Square in a third of that time during the 1960s. The gathering of government buildings became the real impetus for reviving the waterfront and sprouting a succession of new office towers in the financial district.

The West End simply took too long to unfold to be a pile-driving catalyst. The developers did it piecemeal at their own self-interested pace while the city actually lost revenue throughout most of the building period. In 1959 the city's costs totaled $7.7 million from property acquisition and clearance and the loss of tax revenue from the neighborhood. Even with three new apartment complexes in place, Charles River Park tax payments didn't exceed the annual $546,000 tax yield from a slum until 1968. In the first decade of building, from 1961 to 1971, the city recouped about $5.5 million in taxes, 30 percent short of its upfront money.

A review of the city tax records bears out what MIT researcher Martin Anderson claimed in an early-1960s urban renewal study—that advocates were misleading when they pushed the tax benefits of rehab. Anderson estimated that the city wouldn't hit the break-even mark until 1980.

Development advocates deflect the cost analysis to note simply that renewal projects were never meant to make money for the city. Rappaport's bottom-line assessment is that the renewal program was not for the city to sell land for a profit, but to get attractive buildings in the ground. "When you balance it all out, I think the pluses, including the discomfort, are justifiable. It is one of the better urban renewal projects for quality and livability. Would the city have been better off if we had done nothing? I don't think so."

But the terms given the mayor's man by the city, even measured by the depressed market at the time, rank somewhere between a fire sale and a stickup.

Rappaport's partnership didn't have to pay real estate taxes until construction began, or even buy the land until buildings were occupied. While most of Boston assumed the partners had bought the land, they merely controlled it indefinitely under leases at 1950s prices.

One of the side effects of the little-known arrangement was delay. The partnership could hold off building until conditions were optimal and the market was right. The new incarnation of an old neighborhood so easily razed took shape in slow motion, with each discrete complex taking its place at its own tempo from 1962 to 1976.

And while the city's deal with Charles River Park sent the right signals to an estranged business community, there was no getting around the human toll, with mostly Italian immigrants tossed into the street. The newly created Boston Redevelopment Authority (BRA) stumbled badly out of the gate. Its planners provided little of the promised relocation money and city politicians delivered on none of the pledged low- and moderate-income replacement housing.

While the neighborhood was disparaged by planners and developers, it retained a strong hold on those who lived—and survived—there. To them, it was a proud old European neighborhood suffused in authentic aromas from Italian cooking and the bustle of Jewish commerce.

One of the observers was Herbert Gans, a sociologist who moved there for a while to study the project. He has long contended there was a social agenda in favor of demolition, and that planners used overstated crime rates as yet another reason to start over, part of a policy stampede to be rid of dark and dingy streets and the people who lived on them. He argued in his book about Boston's "urban villagers" that while urban renewal was never pretty, the West End failed particularly by not giving the displaced the relocation assistance needed to get to comparable housing.

Asked to take a long look back over five decades to his "field lab" days, Gans stuck to his guns. "I haven't changed my mind about any of it," he said. "The city was swayed by the easy federal money and didn't take very good care of the people who deserved better. Relocation was lacking and there was misinformation about alternative low-income housing."

Rappaport takes careful exception to Gans as his argument, stripped clean, was that Gans didn't see the West End for what it was—an over-rated slum. He shifts slowly from Gans not being accurate about the quality of life and the idea that residents had meaningful lives there. "I'm not here to denigrate," he advises, but adds, "They were all five-story walk-ups with one bathroom. Buildings that had outhouses out back. No light. No egresses." His account glosses over long-running resistance to his project that got little press coverage at the time but today makes Charles River Park one of the bitter benchmarks of urban politics in America.

It is not so much that it was done. But how it rolled out. Even some community activists concede the West End was decrepit, but they still ask, did everyone have to be evicted en masse after being promised some low-income housing where they lived? And what about forty-eight acres being handed over to Mayor Hynes's chief of staff, who made mega-millions while developing it in fits and starts? The politics of it were enough to make Curley blush.

But Mayor Hynes's oldest son, Jack, a longtime Boston television newscaster, hasn't changed his mind any more than Herb Gans. "I get a kick out of these guys who rewrite history on it," he said. "Total nonsense—that it was a quaint neighborhood, a slice of old Boston where everyone pulled together and looked out for each other. It was an abandoned, boarded-up place, a derelict village." Recalling stagnant Boston, he lauded Rappaport as the one developer able to do such a big job in a flat-broke city.

In his book, Gans understood well how determined Jack Hynes's father was to make a game-changer out of the West End. Where Gans saw the need for more street protests in front of City Hall, instead Hynes saw neighborhood leaders clinging to the naïve hope that a good and decent man would see the light and change his mind. But on this one, Hynes was as obdurate as a stony Yankee banker dealing with a two-day overdraft.

Che West End of yore was a layover location, a catch basin, following the same settlement patterns as the original home for immigrants, the promontory waterfront of the North End. It, too, moved from Irish to Jewish to Italian—but just a few decades later than the first waves. The Jews dominated through the 1920s but moved on as Italians became the largest ethnic group. In the first half of the twentieth century, the West End lost half of its 23,000 residents. By 1957 it had seven thousand residents, about half of them Italian.

The neighborhood had settled into two distinct parts, with some decent streets in the "upper end" closest to its none-too-happy neighbors at the Massachusetts General Hospital. Nonetheless they were briefly exempted by bureaucrats as not "blighted" enough for the sledgehammer. But eventually the bankers insisted on all or nothing for renewal. All the streets were placed within the obliteration lines in 1956, especially the "lower end" that was targeted on everyone's map from the beginning. It was a bad patch for the poorest and oldest that morphed into Scollay Square's skid row.

Renewal began as a nebulous notion in 1950 when the Boston Housing Authority received federal funds for preliminary planning on what to do about rundown sections in the worst of the worst neighborhoods—the West End, South End, and Roxbury. When Mayor Hynes first took office, one neighborhood was quickly and firmly put out of bounds—the North End. With full-throated politicos like Frederick Langone and Gabriel Piemonte on the attack, trial balloons for renewal in the cohesive North End were shot down with such resounding thuds that no one dared float them up again.

Not so with the disorganized West End. The idea of redevelopment there was broached in the spring of 1953, but took four years to take hold and then it spread like wildfire. When it was too late, a small group of young families formed a Save the West End Committee that fought City Hall gamely from then on.

A review of news accounts found that, despite its radical scope, the large-scale displacement remained mostly on the back pages of Boston newspapers for the first few years amid promises that the end result would include low-income housing for residents. But the news clips didn't mean there weren't anxious protests; it meant they weren't covered.

A 1953 story in the *Boston Globe* carried an announcement by the Boston Housing Authority that a proposed $20-million project would level much of the West End, but be mitigated by low-income housing for 1,175 families. Officials also reassured residents in other accounts that there was "no need to worry" about relocation and that there would be room for those wanting to stay in the new neighborhood.

But as demolition neared in 1958, the planning explanation from city officials shifted to include high-rise apartments for middle-income tenants. And finally, shortly before the wrecking ball smashed into its first brick wall, the public explanation changed dramatically. It was to be *all* high-end rental units that would cost five to ten times more than the typical West End rent of twenty-five dollars per month. Residents could stay—if they could pay $125 a month and fit families into a single-bedroom high-rise.

Indeed, there had been ominous portents of a heavy-handed project run by insiders two years earlier. The 1956 "sale" revealed a pat hand from a stacked deck. The transfer of twenty city streets to private hands got off to the kind of start that would mark nearly all West End–City Hall transactions—an opaque process clouded by last-minute confusion, with observers left asking, "What just happened?"

The sale of the land was to be a two-step sales procedure—sealed bids to be followed by a public auction to up the ante further. But on decision day, it was suddenly announced that the high bidder had withdrawn and the auction was canceled. In a cloud of West End dust, the Rappaport group had the only viable offer and was declared the "owner" of a new neighborhood. Rappaport, the young prodigy from the Bronx, who graduated at age twenty from Harvard Law School and led the chorus for change at City Hall, was suddenly fending off cries of "fix" that echo to this day.

Looking back, Jack Hynes is unblinking about what happened. Was the fix in? "I don't know, but I tend to think that the old man did [Rappaport] a favor. He was impressed with him and had confidence that he could carry off a project like that. But it was part of the fabric of politics then. 'He helped me so I'll help him.' [Rappaport] was a capable guy and his earlier work was a consideration. Sure."

In the run-up to the sale agreement, there had been small protests as things unfolded, but no public clamor until the bidding fiasco made it unmistakably clear that the process was rigged. The contretemps also pushed the truculent director of the Housing Authority, Kane Simonian, to center stage. He oversaw the process that gave the Rappaport partnership a downtown neighborhood for a lease agreement rather than a purchase price.

In the aftermath of the bungled bidding, Simonian turned brusquely imperious. Asked by a reporter what had happened to the auction, he said peremptorily, "We decided not to have one." Later he said a higher "price" for the property would only have meant higher rents down the road. He refused to provide the basis for the city's contention that the Rappaport group had a "superior" credit rating.

In fact, the partnership had never done a project like the West End. The *Christian Science Monitor* reported that the youthful team's inexperience was a major problem when it sought construction financing from Boston lenders—even with federal mortgage guarantees in place. Ultimately it got financing from the John Hancock Insurance Company, and the group went on to do rehabilitation jobs in New Haven, Philadelphia, and New York.

As the controversy receded, things moved toward demolition. First the city and federal governments signed a contract for the feds to pay two thirds of acquiring the buildings and clearing the land. Then surveyors set up shop on the outskirts. Finally came D-Day, in April 1958, when the city took title to the property via eminent domain. When school ended in June, the migration began in earnest. Demolition began on some streets while others were still occupied. By year's end, half of 2,700 households were gone.

Even with heavy machinery gathering on the periphery, there were more empty promises from the Boston Redevelopment Authority. Board chairman and leading city Realtor Joseph Lund said, "Every family will be treated fairly and in a sympathetic manner and no one will have his home taken from under him." He vowed the agency would "find new homes for every family" required to move. Nothing of the kind happened.

Instead, three years later, pioneering upscale residents moved into a new neighborhood known as Charles River Park in the first of four complexes named after Boston literary lions. Emerson Place took its spot on the landscape and on the tax rolls for about $31,000 in the first year. Hawthorne next. Then Whittier. Finally, Longfellow.

The deal was even better than indicated in the cozy bidding arrangement that provoked ebbing outrage in the mid-1950s. While it was billed as a sale, it was really a leasehold contract with option to buy that kept start-up money at a minimum. Rappaport confirmed the leasehold arrangement.

In a closely held agreement, the developer team paid pennies a square foot while construction was under way. The developer only paid for the land after each one of four separate complexes was built and occupied. For example, at Emerson Place, the first two towers cost only $13,500 a year to carry as it was being built in 1961 and 1962. When it was fully rented, the developers paid the city about $303,750 for the property. The rock-bottom terms were six cents a square foot to rent, and then $1.35 per square foot to buy about five acres.

The terms were never updated over the long history of an evolving upscale neighborhood. The bottom line for eight towers, a complex for elderly housing, and a shopping plaza was $1,711,000 for 28.7 acres—or about $60,000 an acre for prime land. The rest of the site was for roadways and sidewalks and parking. In contrast, in the mid-1960s, a vacant acre in downtown Boston was worth about $2 million, according to a Boston market specialist.

Today, Rappaport takes a "mistakes were made" stance while insisting it all had little to do with him. The city asked him to build something, and he did it. "I don't want to be the person who defends Kane Simonian and the authority during the initial taking. It was a learning experience for government." It's as if he was a bystander. He said it was a "rough start" for cities across the country before eminent domain and relocation assistance got more defined and empathetic.

Yet sources inside the BRA say that Rappaport forged close ties with Simonian, who was the first director of the soon-to-be omnipotent Boston Redevelopment Authority, and with James Colbert, a political columnist and irascible force on the board of directors. The pair were classmates at Harvard and came to dominate the inner workings of the BRA for decades.

While they had diverse interests and different responsibilities, Simonian and Colbert advanced a secondary agenda at the agency far below the radar of major new projects like the Prudential Center and the Government Center. Colbert paid obsessive attention to the mundane aftermath of West End development—the final cleared quadrant that became a cash-cow parking lot. It was nurtured as attentively as any apartment complex or office building ever put in the ground.

The view inside the BRA was that Simonian was a true believer in the new West End housing, but had little choice other than to carry water on the parking lot because he owed Colbert for his job and pay grade. In the transition to the administration of John Collins, a new top gun for the BRA came in from New Haven, Connecticut. The vainglorious Edward Logue brought his rave reviews with him to take Simonian's job as executive director. But, working behind the scenes, Colbert saved the title if not the function and allowed Simonian to keep all that he had in place while the Master Builder took on new vistas in the 1960s.

Burly and blustery, Simonian was a bull in a china shop, given to loud and profane remonstrations that regularly rumbled out of his oversized office. He rode his staff hard, and was notoriously impatient with those who did not perform to his standards. Yet he was steadfastly loyal to his minions and, almost despite himself, retained a strong following among them.

Simonian's diminished purview was primarily the West End and New York Streets projects that never had meaningful residential input. He was the single-minded operations manager who got the property in shape, from relocations, such as they were, to site preparation. Known for his attention to detail, he frequently got lost in the weeds without the bigger picture coming into focus.

With one thing or another, the West End kept Simonian busy for nearly forty years. The project dogged him, even following him into the headline on his obituary. To his outspoken chagrin, he never quite outran the razing of a free-standing neighborhood and was defensive about it in much the way that police commanders can be when pressed about citizens' charges of brutality.

He was eclipsed early but stayed late, permanently battle-scarred from a losing fight for primacy with Logue. All the new initiatives—and ribbon cuttings—went to Logue and his expanding staff of Ivy League planners. For the next decade, the BRA was a bifurcated workplace that regularly put two agendas before boards of directors—nuts and bolts with Kane and big ideas from Ed. Logue ceded Simonian this much: he could be lord high commissioner of the West End protectorate while the director fried bigger fish.

But if the outspoken Simonian was easy to keep track of, Colbert clung to the shadows. He was seen as a quietly malevolent figure, abrasive with the staff and viewed with fear and loathing by all City Hall politicos. As board treasurer, he was an exacting martinet not above demanding proof that phone bills were for BRA business. He was given free rein by councilors and even the mayor's office because of his kingmaker days as political editor of the old *Boston Post* and as a weekly columnist for a chain of small papers with big readership in the outer wards such as West Roxbury and Roslindale. He became one of the profession's malignant mentioners who fussed over the compliant and sullied the less so.

He was remotely inscrutable at the board meetings, a loner sitting to one side, looking like a drowsy Buddha in owl glasses until he sprang to life the second an adversary was done talking, striking hard and fast, especially if the issue concerned the West End parking lot. When Colbert dropped dead one morning in his shower, the 1980 services were sparsely attended. No board members or political figures were there. One longtime BRA staffer observed how different it would have been if the deceased had been a close relative of Colbert's. In that case, attendance would have been mandatory, with absences noted indirectly and tartly in columns to come. The church, the staffer said, would have been overflowing with dry-eyed mourners checking their watches.

Cbe final indignity to the dispossessed of Martin Lomasney's old neighborhood was the shameful game within a game played backstage at the BRA over a grubby if lucrative place for commuters to park their cars.

In the second half of the 1960s, Colbert and Simonian pushed an antithetical agenda: to stop completion of Charles River Park on a site ripped from immigrants in the name of progress. Colbert was a field marshal fighting a rearguard action to keep one fourth of the old West End as a parking lot pumping out cash under the ostensible control of a local family who leased the property from the authority. Colbert even dispatched young BRA staffers there to count cars coming and going. The assignment left some of the staff—but not all—confused by what keeping tabs on cars in the lot had to do with anything.

In 1970 the second West End scandal unfolded. As Logue had looked past someone else's project to his own, he had left the parking-lot issue to be played out in a murky parallel universe. The same Colbert-Simonian alliance that expedited three apartment complexes in the 1960s did an about-face on phase four, obstructing final completion with equal fervor. The reason? It appeared that Colbert had his own horse in the race and different plans for the last ten acres of the West End.

Like the original conveyance of the West End to Rappaport, the parking-lot terms were ludicrous—an open-ended, no-bid monopoly for minimal rent. The lot moved from one vacant vista to another as apartment towers rose one by one elsewhere on the cleared site. And from the first days of demolition, the management stayed under the tight control of the Mantia family, which started out with a florist shop off Cambridge Street before adding "Gus's Parking" lot for forty-five cars under a BRA lease in 1958.

The rent-to-income ratio for the lot never made sense. It was off the charts from the beginning, zooming far beyond the norm for other nearby parking operations leased from the city. The typical proportion in five other comparable locations was one part rent to 1.5 parts income. But the massive lot run by Gus Mantia and his brothers had the staggering ratio of one part rent to ten parts income, according to projections based on car counts made at the lot by a team of *Globe* reporters in 1970. An investigative report found the Mantias had paid $132,200 in rent for income of $1.4 million during the previous decade. The last year was the biggest, with income of $191,000, a figure worth more than $1 million in today's dollars.

After five o'clock, the day's cash was carried by one of the Mantia brothers in a green money bag to an apartment the family leased on the sixteenth floor of Emerson Place.

As the third apartment complex was completed in 1968 and the final construction phase appeared imminent, the Harvard classmates at the BRA strategized to keep the parking lot in place for as long as possible.

But after a *Globe* exposé about the parking lot that refused to die, there was simply too much adverse publicity in it for Mayor Kevin White to stick with the gamey status quo. The face-saver all around was to shut the lot down as unneeded with the opening of a new city-built parking garage up the street at the foot of Beacon Hill.

Despite a long-cleared battleground on the far corner of the West End, with new and old blood on it, it took five more years for two oversized thirty-five-floor towers to take their positions as Longfellow Place. The last pieces were not finished until 1976. Or until the rental market was to Rappaport's liking.

In fact, it would take thirty years for Jerome Rappaport to see his first bad cards from the City Hall deck, and he fought the threat in the highest courts and to the bitter end. He finally met his match in populist mayor Raymond L. Flynn, who picked a righteous fight in 1985 to put mixed-income housing on at least one tiny scrap of the West End. Flynn turned the issue over to a BRA director who had the intellectual firepower—and the political autonomy—to go toe-to-toe with Rappaport and his army of lawyers. Although it turned into something of a good deed going punished, Stephen Coyle insisted that some units on the 1.5-acre site known as Lowell Square be reserved for residents who had lost their homes way back when.

It was a five-year court battle before the city wrested a parcel back from the Charles River Park satrapy. At the outset, the parties had a slight difference of opinion about the value when Rappaport tried to claim the last morsel for 1956 prices under the yellowed parchment of his original option to buy. He offered $95,000 while the city's low-end appraisals put the price between $5 and $7 million.

It was late in 1990 when the BRA's right to name a new developer was sanctioned by the state appeals court and let stand by the Supreme Judicial Court. About half of the 183 units were deemed "affordable" for lower-income families but, in turn, only half of them were set aside exclusively for West Enders. The nostalgia factor faded when it became clear there were not enough takers who could afford the move back home, even with subsidized rents. The once-rigorous screening process was reduced to anyone who could produce an old post office box address.

It took nearly seven years, until 1997, for Lowell Place to open its doors. By then, Coyle had left the BRA to become CEO of the AFL-CIO Housing Investment Trust. But, as one measure of his commitment to the mixed-income corner off Lomasney Way, Coyle's trust underwrote $12 million of Lowell Square's $32-million tab. He was front and center at the dedication ceremony.

After a half century, no one ever beat Rappaport except Steve Coyle. His Bronx was Waltham, a gritty city near Boston. He went to the "local" college there, which happened to be Brandeis University, where he studied urban affairs. He could match Rappaport's academic achievement and political acumen, even earning a degree from the Kennedy School before there was a Rappaport Institute. He also brought a Stanford law degree to his job at the BRA.

He knew politics from the ground up, and was a rare city planner who had a rich background in both elective politics and local housing issues. He was a Waltham city councilor for seven years and director of the housing authority there as well. After working briefly in the federal housing bureaucracy and at an architectural firm in San Francisco, he became one of the brightest lights in the Flynn administration. He had a long reign as head of the BRA in a job known for its high turnover, working there from 1984 to 1991 before leaving to run the AFL-CIO trust in Washington.

Coyle is the tenth of fourteen children, and his mother was a Southie lifer until she was put on the street in the 1940s to make way for the infamous D Street housing project. She was an early urban-renewal refugee. Like many of the Irish who arrived in Boston, her family was from Galway. Coyle's father was a Kerryman, and, like many from there, he landed in New York City. The family got under way in Boston, and they moved several times around Southie before the father found work in Waltham. His maternal grandmother became part of the family's lore—and Coyle's memory bank—for trying to stick it out alone on a dreary street near the D Street project. She didn't make the move north until she was evicted as the last holdout. "In the forties," Coyle said, "there was no discussion. The city talked to the landlord and the landlord posted a 'vacate forthwith' notice on the door. That was it. I used eminent domain twice to clear title on abandoned property. But I never evicted people. 'That could be my grandmother' was my thinking."

His lasting memory of the many family gatherings in his adolescence is of the women in the kitchen reminiscing about good old Southie and the men talking politics from the same era, all fraught with nostalgia that made things seem better than they were. But one sour note always crept in—the trauma of displacement. "There was a deep sense of community and culture that was damaged by those disruptions. It affected me greatly and shaped my thinking about urban renewal. I go back to its beginning in Boston. As a Brandeis student, I went to some of Ed Logue's great, convincing talks about what was needed. But I remembered the women in my mother's kitchen as well."

Coyle studied social justice and urban renewal in tandem, and sees them as two sides of the same coin. If he lays it on a little thick about Southie roots, he has walked the walk. Nearly every time he returns to Boston on business, he heads over to Lowell Square, where he is heartened not to see what he calls Jerry Rappaport's New York apartments. "It's always stirring to see what got done there."

CHAPTER 8

Baby-faced Assassin

JOHN COLLINS

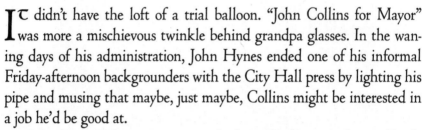

I⊤ didn't have the loft of a trial balloon. "John Collins for Mayor" was more a mischievous twinkle behind grandpa glasses. In the waning days of his administration, John Hynes ended one of his informal Friday-afternoon backgrounders with the City Hall press by lighting his pipe and musing that maybe, just maybe, Collins might be interested in a job he'd be good at.

Like Curley's dismissive wisecrack about Hynes more than a decade earlier, the mayor's lighting a little candle for Collins with a handful of reporters was another small thing that made for big history, a ripple to sustain a sea change. Reporters found Collins cagey but clearly interested.

Hynes had been casting about for a successor shortly after his bruising reelection contest with John Powers ended in 1955. He knew in his gut he wasn't running for mayor again, or anything else. He was done. But as he pushed his New Boston agenda uphill, he was haunted by the likely prospect that the man known in his house as the "little rat" would be running the show one day soon. The mayor had even had a secret recruiting meeting with Endicott Peabody, but "Chub" wanted to be governor. So Hynes's offhand remark about Collins was hardly a playful moment. It was the unmistakable first step in certifying Collins as a dark horse in a race that seemed over before it began, held in the tight grasp of a prohibitive favorite, state senate president John Powers of South Boston.

While Hynes and Collins were not close, especially by temperament, Hynes had long been impressed by Collins's strong performance in the legislature and in his statewide race for attorney general. He liked Collins's no-nonsense intelligence and stand-your-ground oratory. He also remembered well that Collins had been one of his early, brave supporters, giving Hynes the prized endorsement of an "intown" state rep as the city clerk plotted against James Michael Curley in 1949. Collins wasn't coy like Maurice Tobin, who held back so long with his finger to the wind that his tepid imprimatur almost didn't count for much when it finally arrived.

Having grown up in the titan's home precinct, Collins made a gutsy, prescient calculation for a rookie that Curley's day had passed and he was best served by falling in behind a new-breed politician like Hynes. He would be part of a group that wanted to change things in dire times, and not just paper over problems and line their pockets.

His Hynes endorsement had quick repercussions. In an early stump speech in his 1948 campaign for state representative in Curley's old ward, Collins was greeted by a barrage of rotten tomatoes. Eyes flaring, he challenged his attackers, telling them Curley was done and vowing that none of them would ever be welcome in Johnny Hynes's City Hall. And left unsaid: or in mine.

After a series of public defections, he was summoned to Curley's mansion for a chiding chat in 1951. Curley, direct as ever, asked why a Ward 17 kid went with Hynes. Collins, just as direct, talked about how his father had gone to see Curley for a job in the hard times of the Great Depression, and came away without an audience. So there's a reason for you, Mister Mayor: Why should I be with someone who wouldn't even talk to Skeets Collins?

In 1959, Collins was a tough guy in tough circumstances. His political star had crashed when he nearly died in the 1955 polio epidemic and he found himself lucky to be in a wheelchair for life. On the strength of plucky campaigning by his wife, Mary, and two brothers, he was elected to the City Council, but soon withdrew to the musty sinecure of Suffolk County Registrar of Probate. It was so far off the political map that the registrar might as well have been a commissar in Uzbekistan before it was a country. It made no news and had no profile.

But it was a clean, well-lit place to plan an insurgency. Floating just above sea level, Collins had three things going for him—brainpower, the determination of the afflicted, and the resonant fact that many people in town didn't trust the blustery John Powers one bit.

Collins was a baby-faced assassin. He had a quick smile, the tousled hair and demeanor of the boy next door. But hard blue eyes. When he got to scheming, he slowly rolled a small cigar in his mouth.

While the cherubic Collins seldom showed his hardball disposition, he always felt he made an uncharacteristic mistake when he let up toward the end in his first statewide race—a 1954 defeat by the Republican incumbent attorney general, George Fingold. Five years later, when he set his sights on Johnny Powers, rule number one was to pull out all the stops against the much better financed and higher-profile candidate.

In a remarkable role reversal, Powers's aura of inevitability attracted academics and government reformers who plied him with white papers on urban policy as well as early support from the business community. And it was the angelic Collins who went down and dirty in the stretch run.

In 1959 it was finally "next time" for Powers. It was supposed to be a cakewalk when he no longer had to run against nice guy John Hynes, whose avuncular style made Powers look like a walking political cartoon, a brash, cigar-chomping caricature no matter what he said or did. But now he was revved up, with an open field ahead of him. The newly crowned senate president had the Kennedys; an overstuffed war chest; most of the statewide Democratic office-holders; a montage of pictures with his friend Cardinal Richard Cushing; endorsements from most of the newspapers, even the Republican *Herald*; and city workers looking for a new home.

And he had the pragmatic if not wholly compatible support of a forward-thinking brain trust that included a new state representative from Brookline named Michael Dukakis.

Another member was Beacon Hill Brahmin Herbert Gleason, who plied the candidate with urban-renewal backgrounders to save a still-stymied city and, well, to be with a winner. "I thought he was going to be mayor," Gleason said. "I wonder at my arrogance, but I thought he needed to be educated. I gathered like-minded people and we'd have lunches at a club on Beacon Street. Powers was genuinely flattered by the attention. But he was not intellectually engaged. I don't think he thought we were going to help him win the election. He never asked, 'What are people doing?' or 'Why is this important?'"

As Powers set out, it looked like a cinch, with the only opponents being unknowns from the bottom of the ballot. But Collins brought his shrewd grit to a flaccid primary field. It was nip-and-tuck, but Collins's first upset was in the September preliminary when he bested eccentric city councilor Gabriel Piemonte by 2,500 votes to face Powers in the November final. He became the candidate nobody knew but wanted to find out about.

In fact, Collins had paid his dues and was buttressed by a small but fiercely loyal following. While he could be coldly patrician, he came from the usual meager roots of Boston mayors—a blue-collar neighborhood redlined by banks and spurned by downtown society. He was born in 1919 in the Irish Catholic section of Roxbury, the oldest of three sons of Frederick "Skeets" Collins, a mechanic for the Boston Elevated Railway, and Margaret Mellyn. He graduated first in his law-school class, just in time to enter the army after Pearl Harbor, rising from private to a captain in counterintelligence. Once discharged, he was elected to the Massachusetts house of representatives for two terms and then the same in the state senate.

After marrying Mary Cunniff from Jamaica Plain, he charted his course as his own man in 1948 when he turned his back on his old Roxbury neighborhood and cast his lot with upstart Hynes against the neighborhood's favorite son.

After he gathered himself up from the Fingold defeat, Collins needed to get back in the game. The City Council was something of a step down, but he saw it as a way station to the mayor's chair. He surmised that Hynes had one more term in him, and announced for the City Council in 1955. Then tragedy struck. That summer, with the polio scare at its height, the virus felled Collins and three of his four children. As he tended his children while they lay in hospital beds, he used his pocket handkerchief to absorb their tears and sweat, and then wiped his own brow, not knowing how easily the damp cloth could transfer the virus. He picked up the virus from them, and although they recovered fully, his polio became a life-and-death matter.

The dire prognosis was that, if he survived, it would be as a bedridden paraplegic. But he slowly recovered, though he was permanently paralyzed from the waist down. Advised to withdraw from the council race, he said no way, we'll just work harder.

Like Curley, he had a remarkable wife named Mary who took over the day-to-day management of her husband's stagnating campaign. Along with Collins's two brothers and a kitchen cabinet of advisers, she managed the door-to-door retail politics, and Collins made the runoff for nine at-large council seats. While bedridden in a hospital, Collins began to read deeply about Boston's history, and studied urban planning. He also resumed his daydreaming about what he would do if he was ever elected mayor, devising a practical agenda of what could get done quickly to revive the city. His dreams sustained him, as did the Boston voters who rewarded his moxie by placing him third in the final tally for council.

As always, Collins saw things as they were. Boston was in the doldrums, treading water with plans in the works, but nothing to show for it. It was in the grasp of a bad mind-set—that nothing works out for the best. There was chronic despondency that needed federal money first and dynamic leadership second.

The future mayor looked out at a sad old town. "The blight and decay was overwhelming," he wrote. "Seventy percent of the housing stock was substandard. The waterfront was literally falling into the Atlantic Ocean. Scollay Square had half a dozen burlesque houses, honky-tonk places and tattoo parlors.... But the people who worked on State Street sat at their rolltop desks and thought everything was all right because it was the same today as it was yesterday."

When he left the hospital just before Christmas, it was to a new home with the living space on one floor. Struggling with a devastating disability, he fulfilled a hospital-bed pledge to be on the council floor for the first day of business in January 1956.

But after a year of juggling the council work with his handicap, Collins appeared to withdraw from the fray for good by agreeing to take a caretaker job as registrar of probate, a low-level post usually reserved for high-achieving hacks focused on long lunches and extended weekends.

But not John Collins. It would be a perch overlooking City Hall, where he could quietly plot a stunning succession. Like Hynes, he had the drive to look past a lifetime appointment for the grief and glory of running the show.

He took the body politic by surprise in 1959 when he edged Piemonte to get Powers alone in the final. Much as Hynes had used low-key humility to combat Curley's flamboyance, Collins turned his disability into a strength. He used his FDR-like struggle with polio in his first television speech as a mayoral candidate, having the camera pan up from his wheelchair to a shoulder-and-face frame. From that day forward, he answered questions about his infirmity with a stock reply: "You run a city with your head, not your feet."

And he parlayed his pluck into a calm persona, with him playing the Bing Crosby priest to Powers's gruff Victor McLaglen. He crafted an image as an upbeat newcomer in a wheelchair against a disheveled power broker who always needed a shave. Collins also sensed political hay in Powers's motley retinue. "Johnny Powers would come into a room with six guys in big hats," he'd say later with a smile. "I would come in alone."

The first reading of the electorate's disposition favored Collins. In the preliminary, the heavily favored Powers received only 34 percent of the vote, enough to easily get him in the final runoff, but the margin was a little better than half of what was expected.

Collins also took tough, clear-cut stances on controversial issues, presenting a more forceful bearing than the tentative Hynes, who had tiptoed around supporting a state sales tax to ameliorate the city's crushing property taxes. Powers was against it, and fought it successfully in the senate when Governor Foster Furcolo first proposed a limited 3-percent levy. Collins embraced it without reservation.

The bold stroke brought Collins incremental defections from the Boston business community, which had been backing Powers tepidly as the odds-on favorite, even with the strong likelihood of him adopting the standard Curley tactic of overloading commercial property taxation to curry favor with voters in small bungalows.

One of Collins's public business supporters was the most notable—the estimable Henry Shattuck, the personification of a Back Bay Brahmin with tight linkages to financial institutions, Harvard, prestigious clubs, and law firms. Collins brought him on board with a simple overture: Will you help me? Collins related his coup to Boston historian Thomas O'Connor as the serendipity in plain sight. No need for a hard sell, the blunt Shattuck told him, "I'll support you . . . what would you like me to do?" Sign a newspaper ad, kind sir. Done.

Later, Collins said his building rapport with business leaders, who had been supporting Powers, was a matter of simple expediency. "I owed them nothing and they owed me nothing, so we could get right down to business."

As always, issues like the sales tax gave way to attack ads, a shift that favored Collins toward the end. It was Outsider against Old School. Uphill gallant versus Insider rogue. Little people struggling with fat cats. The motifs came together as one in a potent final ad campaign reduced to a play on words: Stop Power Politics.

And as always, it turned dirty in the home stretch, with Collins completing his metamorphosis from boy-next-door to hitman-in-a-wheelchair. His attack theme shifted from Powers the ward boss to Powers the crook. Not a cent of bookmaker money in my coffers, he stipulated to a question not asked. Then Sal Bartolo fell out of the sky.

Sal was a sudden game changer who burst on the scene four days before the election. On the way home from Logan Airport, one of Collins's foot soldiers from the deeply layered Suffolk County bureaucracy, a staffer in the district attorney's office, was attracted by flashing cruiser lights in East Boston's Maverick Square. Connie Fitzpatrick had stumbled upon an IRS raid of several bookie joints, including one belonging to former featherweight boxer Salvatore Bartolo, whose Ringside Café sported a prominent POWERS FOR MAYOR sign. The quick-thinking Fitzpatrick snapped several photographs at two in the afternoon. Nine hours later, Collins was on the eleven-o'clock news announcing Powers's close association with Bartolo. His advisers also turned it into a lampooning cartoon, heavy on boxing imagery. In front-page ads on election day, a loutish Powers was shown taking one on the chin from the big gloved fist of a Treasury agent. As well, they came up with a 1958 photograph of Bartolo together with a beaming Powers that cropped out young US Senator John F. Kennedy.

The accumulation of images formed a fatal final impression for outer-ward voters already inclined to protect the New Boston strides made by John Hynes. Powers would only carry his home wards in South Boston, with Collins taking a solid citywide victory in one of the city's biggest upsets.

Even before the Bartolo raid, there were echoes of the earlier Hynes criticisms of Powers's excessive spending on billboards and signpost ads, along with sound trucks running all over town. It was tough to do in avid Boston, but Powers got overexposed and people once again began asking, "Where's all this money coming from?" Collins's final answer was "Ask Sal."

Bartolo was the final installment in the role reversal that had Collins hurling the kitchen sink at Powers while the Southie tough guy was issuing white papers on urban policy from a brain trust of Brahmins and progressives. After the battlefield was cleared, the pragmatic new mayor met with Powers's think-tank advisers. He would adopt many of their initiatives.

On election night, John Hynes's son, Jack, well under way in his career as a television reporter and anchor, was working for Channel 5, a station then owned by the *Boston Herald-Traveler*. He had set up a broadcasting booth in a corner of the city room, and after the polls closed, he ducked out to join his father and a group of old-timers for supper. His father had early election results from key Irish precincts that had always gone big for Curley. When he looked up from the papers, he smiled and said Collins had won. The old pro saw that Powers was not winning by enough in old strongholds. The three-time mayor forecast Collins the winner by fifteen thousand votes, but was short by nine thousand. Back in the newsroom, Jack told the imperious *Herald-Traveler* editor Harold Clancy that he was hearing that Collins was rolling to victory. Not a chance, Clancy scoffed. "I guess we'll see," said the rookie with inside information. It still does not displease Jack Hynes that he was right that night.

In the final analysis, the political scientists saw the vote as more anti-Powers than pro-Collins. The Bartolo raid was a big factor in the two-to-one advantage Collins received from voters who did not participate in the preliminary. In a study of the election called "The Alienated Voter," Boston University professor Murray Levin measured it eight ways to Sunday with charts and tables and surveys. But Levin's copious work boiled down to two reasons why voters switched from leaning toward Powers to voting for Collins: the "power politics" advertising campaign and the Bartolo raid.

Henry Spagnoli, a true-blue loyalist and trusted aide who went back with Collins to his campaigns for state representative, downplayed the Bartolo angle, pushing back against any historical judgment that would have his man riding into office on the strength of a late sucker-punch. He gives two reasons for the stunning upset—television and women. "The biggest thing that happened for John Collins was television," he said. "It was the first time that television played a really big part in a local election. John Collins came through as a guy you could trust and Powers as the guy you couldn't. The mayor had a natural way about him. Women were drawn to him. Johnny Powers was this short guy who surrounded himself with tall people. He wore these great big hats that made him look like a gangster. Hey, that's his problem."

Herbert Gleason, an earnest lawyer from an old Massachusetts Yankee family who looks on the sunny side, said that when the roof fell in on election day, Collins moved quickly to acquire the position papers—if not the authors. Gleason recalled that when the transfer issue came up, Powers said, "Sure, give them to him." Asked if the race ended with no love lost between candidates or camps, Gleason averred that "nobody loved John Collins. He was ruthless."

Collins may have been the lesser of two evils to a dispirited electorate. But he took his sudden surge as a mandate to push home all the tentative inroads and grandiose ideas advanced by John Hynes. The supremely self-assured man from Curley's old neighborhood saw Boston entering a new phase where the political will was combining with business support to finally get things done.

The road ahead was clear if difficult. Curley had been dead a year, and was already a romanticized relic. John Hynes had limped to the finish line with a dignified stoop. He was soon an anonymous lawyer in an office building around the corner from City Hall and then state banking commissioner. A new day was nigh. In his pleasant, ruthless way, Collins had no compunction about using his opponent's ideas to implement his predecessor's plans. And call it all his own.

He got off to a brisk start in his inaugural speech, zeroing in on what he saw as the dual problem facing the city: increased governmental spending, and rising taxes to underwrite it. As countermeasures, he would cap salaries, reduce the workforce, and push hard for a state sales tax as a new revenue source for Boston.

It was all prudent and proactive and precisely what Boston business leaders wanted to hear. But the fiscal straits were also slightly overstated. Although the bankers saw bankruptcy looming behind the city's lowered bond rating, Hynes had left Collins with a $4-million surplus. It wasn't a clean bill of health, but extra cash was a fine calling card when the new mayor sought help from the recently formed Boston Coordinating Committee. It was quickly nicknamed "the Vault" by *Boston Globe* political editor Robert Healy because its leaders met each week in the basement of Ralph Lowell's bank.

The first request from Collins was up the Vault's alley—could he get some short-term data-processing experts to put the Assessing Department on its feet? In other words, get some efficiency and fairness into City Hall's war room in the assault on business interests. Charles Coolidge and Carl Gilbert thought this was a capital idea. In later years, Collins would be hypersensitive to any inference that the Vault was a shadow government that set the table for City Hall. Somewhat defensively, Collins later said that he met with the small group every two weeks at four p.m. sharp, but he set the agenda and shaped the decisions. That said, there was no getting around that he met business leaders on their turf and on their terms. He had to give them something of mutual benefit, and remaking downtown into office towers for commerce and government while reclaiming the waterfront was not a bad start.

But despite his budding bond with business leaders and his stature as a former legislator, the Collins administration got off to a rocky start at the State House. The Powers-dominated legislature gave him a fast "no" on getting basic budgetary control over the police budget, one of the anti-Curley remnants passed decades earlier to curtail spendthrift Hibernian Boston. Collins wasn't even allowed to testify about it. And "no" again on requiring the other three communities in Suffolk County to pay their fair share of municipal expenses along with Boston.

But the most resounding defeat was a double blow to both Collins and Governor Foster Furcolo. Their strong advocacy for a 3-percent state sales tax to help reduce the intractable property tax burden ran splat into the senate president's door. Powers misled Furcolo about supporting the levy, but Collins wasn't as surprised when Powers engineered the bill's demise. Where Hynes stayed above the distasteful fray of sniper attacks by State House committee hearings, Collins liked the contact sport. He soon partnered with Furcolo's successor as governor, John Volpe, by promising not to run against him, but to work with him. Collins finally got control over the law-enforcement budget and the police commissioner appointment.

After the sales tax went down, Collins regrouped by hiring lobbyists, wining and dining legislators at corned-beef lunches, working the phones, and testifying in person in the kind of hands-on forceful advocacy that Hynes avoided and wasn't much good at.

He made inroads in the house of representatives with the legislature's other power locus, roguish and hard-drinking house speaker John F. Thompson. He also used the Boston delegation to outflank Powers. The senator from South Boston, Joseph Moakley, who went on to be a legendary congressman, told Collins how pleased he was to be invited into the mayor's office—for the first time.

As Collins built up support with legislative leaders, he impressed the rank and file and the business community with no-nonsense cost-cutting. He collected overdue taxes, adopted a "no hire" policy that cut $13 million from the budget, and reduced the workforce by three hundred. Such economies went a long way with suburban legislators who usually saw the city as an undisciplined bounder that was always forced to pass the hat. There was clearly a new dynamic at work at City Hall—coolly efficient

John Collins pushing an urgent agenda instead of pipe-smoking John Hynes hoping for the best.

Henry Spagnoli, who served most of Collins's two terms as deputy mayor, was the rare campaign manager who could also handle the day-to-day administrative work. He acknowledged that Collins was tough-minded and brusquely decisive, but stressed his humanity to the point of using a word that has never appeared in the same sentence as John Collins. "He was a pussycat . . . he could be a soft touch. People are surprised by that, but I saw it all the time."

Spagnoli recalled that his first job with Collins was as city fire commissioner, and he remembered being summoned to Collins's home on a weekend after a desperate fireman had crashed a Collins family barbecue in the backyard to complain about having been frozen on the civil service list for a lieutenant's job. Spagnoli: "Most other mayors would have said—if they'd even talk to him at all—'Not now, friend, make an appointment.' But John called me about it. I said, 'This guy went to your house? I'll deal with this.' He said, 'Henry—do you know what kind of courage it took to come to my house? He's great. You gotta make [promote] him.' We took care of it."

Spagnoli said the inner circle came up with a way to determine which side of the mayor they were dealing with on a given day. "We had a rule about how long to stay in his office. If he was chewing on his cigar—get out and get out fast. But if he was rolling it in his mouth, he was playing with you, testing out something. You could stay for a while."

Of all the tough decisions made in his first year, the most momentous one for Collins was to bring in an accomplished outsider to run the city's redevelopment agency. Edward Logue had moved from World War II to Yale Law School and found his niche in New Haven. He became one of the master planners of the "new" urban landscape. Starting in 1954, he was *the* expert in how to mesh smaller cities and federal dollars.

Logue had built up such a head of steam in New Haven that several of Collins's advisers, including the kinetic Joseph Slavets, head of the business-leaning Municipal Research Bureau, urged the mayor to check him out. It took a while to convince him, but Collins came to like everything about Logue: his efficiency; his broad outsider perspective to shake up narrow-minded Boston; his mastery of the new federal programs; and his single-mindedness, which he would need in a hard-nosed town that fought anything new with tooth and claw.

Logue would blithely collect enemies as he and Collins became the synergistic yin and yang of the New Boston. Both were indispensable for the tough decisions to extricate a city from old blueprints. One without the other would have been far less than half as good. Collins gave Logue his head and had his back. Logue was loyal and adhered to the "no surprises" rule by running major things by the mayor first.

Not that the imperious Logue was overly solicitous. He would run his own shop, thank you. His first tough negotiation was for himself: He demanded an outlandish salary for the day, $30,000. It was one third higher than the mayor's pay, but, typically, Logue figured out a way to get the Feds to pay 80 percent of it. And he demanded that the Boston Redevelopment Authority be the repository of both design planning and execution. He began with a significant staffing upgrade and centralization of all major decisions under his aegis.

His first big procedural decision was to finish the two pending Hynes projects—Government Center and the Prudential building—to kick-start downtown renewal. But Ed Logue wasn't about finishing other people's work. From the beginning he saw his imprint as being residential rehabilitation in old neighborhoods around a new downtown. With West End wounds still visible in strafed ground, he stressed that his renewal would be kinder and gentler to a skeptical populace.

To mollify the skeptical neighborhoods, Logue adopted a catchphrase reassurance: This time there would be "planning with people" to avoid much-feared disenfranchisement. The storyline from both the mayor and Logue always included grace notes about preservation over destruction, and coordination rather than edicts. The sales pitch stressed Logue's strong sentiment that the BRA was finally in a position to oversee the vital interplay of fiefdoms like the state department of public works and the quasi-independent Turnpike and Port authorities into something approaching synergy with Boston. Mayor Collins devised a community meeting coda about the city's cost for the renewal that had a Kennedy cadence to it—the question was not whether Boston could afford to do this; rather it was whether it could afford not to.

But the real sales pitch wasn't at VFW posts in the neighborhoods. It was in the boardroom of the Boston Safe Deposit and Trust Company. Twice a month Collins met with Yankee Boston to make sure Ralph Lowell and Charles Coolidge and the rest of the Coordinating Committee were on board. While Collins remained defensive about who set the agenda, a formal memorandum of understanding left little doubt who had the upper hand. Signed by Collins, Logue, and Coolidge, it stated that no downtown building would be constructed without approval from the business leaders.

One of the first coordinated moves with strong formal business support was the big job given the Greater Boston Chamber of Commerce in 1962 to resuscitate the woeful waterfront. Indeed, Collins would become known as a Chamber of Commerce Irishman, only slightly less derogatory than Harvard Irishman.

When the waterfront project began, there was much talk about getting a first-class aquarium in place, but the main targets were sprucing up dilapidated Atlantic Avenue and putting apartments and condominiums along the nearby wharf area that ringed the North End. Plus a redo for Faneuil Hall and the teetering warehouses around it. The plan was to have pedestrian malls to supplant the haphazard fish and produce markets along the waterfront. Logue signed on, and opened a federal fund pipeline. But the project was an intermittent thing, especially concerning the final design and theme for Faneuil Hall, which did not get resolved until well after Logue's tenure.

Logue set his course with an early flourish, however. His first priority was to outflank his entrenched board of directors at the BRA. While ceding the title of director and two projects under way in the West End and the New York Streets to Kane Simonian, Logue cared not about Simonian's bleating and wounded feelings. He grabbed hold of everything else. Collins tried to keep the peace between the two strong-willed men at the top of the BRA by using a World War II reference—Simonian would remain a four-star general in a new headquarters that now included a newly commissioned five-star general.

It didn't take long before Logue had a take-it-or-leave-it ultimatum for the meddlesome board—they could up or down his projects, but not modify the contents. It was already clear that Logue was both show horse and workhorse. He and his staff habitually burned the midnight oil on a blitzkrieg pursuit of federal dollars for his master plan. (When Logue signed out of City Hall one morning at 2:14, the night watchman played the number in the street lottery for a jackpot.)

His first priority was to develop downtown and to connect with business leaders, who became eager collaborators. Logue's opening challenge was to solve the endless tax-break quandary that was stopping the Prudential Center.

But as Collins took office in 1960, the state's highest court once again ruled that the special tax arrangement for the Pru was unconstitutional. And, once again, the fed-up insurance company was threatening to pull out of Boston entirely.

As Collins urged the public not to hit the panic button, the body politic coalesced in a rare unifying moment to find a remedy. The governor, mayor, attorney general, state legislature, and city council—almost always at cross-purposes—came together for this one exigent time. The key was finding a way around the constitutional impediment of having the Pru pay taxes under a lease rather than be buffeted by the fluctuating property valuations. The solution was to compute the Pru "tax" as an urban renewal project on a "blighted" site with a public purpose and community benefit. Technically, that meant it was no longer a private commercial venture getting a special tax deal that other businesses could not get. It got a long-term lease arrangement to insulate it from the vagaries of Boston's gyrating tax rate.

By the end, even Cardinal Cushing was endorsing a private development in the name of rejuvenation. In May 1960, the legislature approved a plan that tied the Pru project together with the Massachusetts Turnpike Authority in a $300-million package. The Pike would do a $100-million extension of its toll road into downtown Boston through the old railroad yard. It would also build a 2,500-car garage over its roadway, and the Pru Center would rise above that foundation on "air rights" granted by the Pike. The Pike would grant a long-term lease to the Pru, and the city would get the "pass through" rent of at least $3 million a year.

While the "blighted site" rationale was first proposed by Attorney General Edward McCormack, Logue pounced on it as his own—just as Collins would nudge Hynes out of the way to lay claim to the Pru Center.

The scene was perfectly set for the sharp-elbowed Logue. He used the momentum for change to get additional amendments to Chapter 121A to make the BRA the only game in town. The new provisions became the linchpin to not only clearing the way for the Pru Center but also to removing state oversight for city eminent-domain takings and to give the BRA total design control by eliminating a rival city planning board.

With all the ducks in a row, enhanced BRA power, and a new taxation rationale for the Pru, the state's supreme court gave preliminary approval to the arrangement in August 1960 and issued a more formal decision in late 1961. Off-and-on construction resumed for good in early 1962, doors opened in 1965, and a new era of downtown renewal was under way.

After the tormented Pru Center was finally set on a clear path, the next big carry-over project was the Government Center.

Like nearly everything in hard-luck Boston, the project was so fragile that one man could hold it up. In his last year, Mayor Hynes began courting the head of the US General Services Administration in Washington, D.C., to put an "anchor" building in the soon-to-be-cleared Scollay Square. But Franklin Floete wasn't buying.

At the outset, it came down to one bureaucrat with a fleeting history with Scollay Square and, at last, some overdue serendipity.

For a while, Harvard grad Floete had it in the palm of his hand. A GSA building for federal agencies was the indispensable first piece for reviving the garish and mean streets of old Scollay. While he had some slumming nostalgia from his college days for the square's Old Howard burlesque house, he was dubious about the city getting its act together for such a large project and feared "his" building would be stranded along skid row.*

But the Old Howard was barely on Floete's screen. All things considered, he favored a "sure thing" Back Bay location for the GSA regional headquarters. He stayed noncommittal throughout lame-duck arm twisting by Hynes and several visits from the New England congressional delegation.

But Collins and Logue saw the catalytic power of expunging Scollay Square and putting downtown offices in its place to serve as the daily cog of governmental life. Collins even turned to one of John Powers's strong backers from South Boston—John W. McCormack. He had the added weight of a leadership position in the house of representatives and made clear his support to Floete for reshaping downtown Boston.

But despite all the political pressure, the tipping point for Floete may have come from Hynes disciple and then fledgling West End developer Jerome Rappaport, who had a tangential relationship with Floete that he didn't know about until a fortuitous conversation with his mother-in-law. One night, after Rappaport came home grousing about what an obstructionist idiot Floete was and how needless delays were killing the Government Center project, he was brought up short by Edith Vahey, who asked if by any chance he was referring to Franklin Floete. Yes indeed, he said. You know him? Well, he was my first husband, she announced.

Tell me more, Rappaport said. In short order, he was on the phone with a social calling card for a bureaucrat he had just been denouncing. "All the GSA administrators," Rappaport recalled, "view new buildings as their own, built in their own image. I spent some time convincing

---

* Aptly, the bawdy Old Howard had a subterranean connection with the local Mafia. At the same time the renewal bulldozers were moving into place, the FBI, under orders from Attorney General Robert Kennedy to finally catch up with mob activity, put an illegal bug in the Providence headquarters of the New England Mafia. It picked up a call from Boston underboss Gennaro Angiulo claiming he had paid a City Hall official $25,000 to assure the transfer of the Old Howard's license to one of his "combat zone" joints. Only the sustained opposition of the Catholic Church stopped the relocation.

him that 'his' building would be the centerpiece of an entirely revived area." And brimming with prospective tenants for the new Charles River Park.

Whether it was the son-in-law of his first wife or the collective weight of congressional entreaties, Franklin Floete came around in the summer of 1960, telling Collins he was in, a decision that set the rest of the dominoes falling into place. After the GSA decision, the state legislature overwhelmingly authorized a $26-million state office building.

As fortune finally smiled, Ed Logue was alacrity itself, seizing on the transformative prospect of ditching old Scollay for the gravitas of government. The tattered square—the symbol of Boston's too-long stay in the Great Depression subsistence economy—finally succumbed. Logue launched a coordinated attack, taking property by eminent domain after getting buy-ins from the governmental agencies involved. His federal connections paid quick dividends by giving Logue, for the first time, the right to make "early" acquisitions before the Feds accepted the overall plan. Logue was not one to tarry with a head start.

He got the Feds to sign off on early land takings, and since there were few residents in the honky-tonk square, he didn't have to go through the motions of "planning with people." Even without formal City Council approval, bulldozers moved into place in February 1962.

But it wouldn't have qualified as a renewal project in Boston without a monkey wrench being thrown in at some point. The Government Center's bomb thrower was the white-bearded and plain-speaking Walter Muir Whitehill, a historian and keeper of the flame for ancient Boston's old guard. A revised blueprint for the Government Center laid claim to the venerable Sears Crescent building on the edge of what would be the new City Hall plaza. And that would never do.

Wild-eyed with indignation, Whitehill practically kicked Kane Simonian's door off its hinges at the BRA to demand an explanation for the mindless plunder of ancient turf. Not for the last time, Simonian said with gusto that the complainant should go see Ed Logue. Sears Crescent had dominated Cornhill Street, which was also the location of Yankee Boston's holy of holies—the office that once housed William Lloyd Garrison's antislavery paper, *The Liberator*. High-level meetings ensued between the stodgy past and the buttoned-down present to yield a rare old Boston "compromise"—nothing would change. Logue agreed that the Crescent rounded out the plaza, and that was that.

But across from City Hall plaza, another crescent-shaped building was in the works that would separate the courthouse complex behind it from City Hall. Three low-slung office and retail buildings were built in installments by Beacon Construction in red brick and granite to blend into a sprawling new Government Center. Center Plaza was one of the first innovative renewal works by Norman Leventhal, an MIT engineer who took a chance on introducing the only nongovernmental building in old Scollay Square. It went up on a shoestring in distinct parts, with each new barren segment carrying a plain sign of high promise: TO BE CONTINUED. His pièce de résistance took its place more than a decade later on the waterfront as the elegant Harbor Hotel.

Center Plaza was followed by a profusion of office towers in the financial district, as each depository tried to outdo the others with new digs—State Street Bank, Boston Safe Deposit and Trust Company, and then National Shawmut bank were three of the pioneers. The New England Telephone Company was not far behind with a new building, and for the first time in decades, two tall apartment towers were in the works for the reclaimed waterfront.

But even with Whitehill pacified, the final facet of Government Center was the most controversial. Collins and Logue decided to replace Franklin Floete's centerpiece with their own—a brand-new $30-million City Hall with a vast vista that would take up much of the once-squalid square. It made its mark right away—even as a model on a tabletop. The polarizing design was both hailed as a bold innovation and denounced as a ridiculous upside-down cake.

The schematic was the result of a competition to keep the architectural design out of the hands of a political firm that had given the most contributions to city politicians. Logue was against an esthetic vetting because it meant delay but the bankers around Collins wanted it and, not incidentally, so did the mayor.

Collins put a commission in place and put his trusted deputy, Henry Spagnoli, and several businessmen on it to bird-dog the process to make sure it stayed scandal-free, acting on the certain knowledge that a massive new public building would be a honey pot for graft in the Curley tradition, drawing a swarm of buzzing architects, brick-and-mortar companies, and contractors. The new mayor couldn't think of a worse way to start an administration than to wind up with a "ball game" building to house it. He only had to look up Beacon Street to see the trouble-plagued public parking garage being excavated underneath the Boston Common, a project that eventually led to the indictment of its unstable board chairman, who went on the lam just before being convicted of embezzlement.

Spagnoli said Collins was adamant about having City Hall be an odor-free zone in pungent Boston. The supposedly refined architectural world was as polluted as the more rough-hewn contractors' world, just as driven by the payola of political contributions and used to getting jobs without competitive bids. "I went to him a couple times," Spagnoli remembered. "I was just looking for advice and ideas. He shooed me away. 'Don't talk to me.' I mean he meant it."

After several months the field was cut to three architects, with each submitting a model of his vision for the anchor building of the New Boston. The winner was to be revealed by the mayor at a commemoration amid the grandeur of the Museum of Fine Arts. Spagnoli stood beside the mayor in his wheelchair at the edge of a table holding the winning—and sight unseen—model. It was discreetly draped before its public showing as the mayor pulled the cover off. He was horrified. He had gotten his pristine process, but he hated the result.

Collins pulled Spagnoli down beside him as if he were a chain on an old-fashioned toilet. "What's this?" he demanded in an urgent whisper. "I'm going to kill it right now. I'm going to kill this thing."

Spagnoli, just as horrified because he had become committed to the audacious new building by I. M. Pei, demurred with suppressed panic. "Give it a chance. Say it's interesting tonight. Kill it tomorrow."

For his part, Logue was watching the mayor closely from the other side of the table. He saw him blanch and could almost hear him thinking, *My God, what's that?* But Collins quickly recovered his public face and smiled tightly to his broader audience. The mayor pronounced the model "interesting" and the event historic.

The next day Spagnoli brought the mayor to the Museum of Science, where the City Hall Commission had commandeered a room as a workshop. It housed the early, low-tech version of a virtual tour, with large-scale mock-ups of the imposing interior.

Collins stayed noncommittal as he wheeled past the replicas, but Spagnoli sensed the mayor softening as he saw the immense ground-level lobby and how the council and the mayor's office were layered on top of a grand space. The top three floors were set aside for out-of-the-way administrative offices. Spagnoli pointed out how the council was sunken below auditorium seats so it would work under public view just as the Greeks had done, and touted the lobby's cathedral ceiling as befitting the Athens of America. "He took it in and was thinking about it this time. My final argument probably had more effect than the Romans and Greeks. I said, 'It's going to be controversial, but, good or bad, people will come to see it. It's so different it'll be a tourist attraction.' Which actually happened. He squinted at me and said 'Well, OK.' To me, it was the mark of a strong man with an open mind. You could talk to him."

The mayor was not alone with his reservations. The building's low, rambling structure, with the top floors honeycombed with small windows, reminded some of an Aztec fortress. The reviews were one or the other. Marvel or disaster. It was both praised as uniquely ungovernmental, no weak-kneed copy of "State Housedom," and trashed for looking like "the crate that Faneuil Hall came in." Like it or not, it took its heavy, squat place on the Boston horizon to permanently divided reviews, the signature building for a new square and a new beginning.

After it was clear that the Hynes carryovers were finally on their way to completion, Logue set out after his true quest—a modern metropolis with a revived neighborhood to complement a new center, a vision shared by his boss from lower Roxbury.

After he settled into his Beacon Hill home, Logue took extended walking tours of the city from West Cedar Street, where a brisk twenty-minute stroll took him to enclaves of sagging housing and flagging spirits, especially in nearby Charlestown. His diagnosis was that the old town needed a spark, a burst of enthusiasm and confidence that would come with rehabilitation of aging stock.

His no-small-plans-allowed philosophy was seconded by the mayor and his allies from the business community, who were getting what they wanted downtown and were well pleased at the prospect of salvaged neighborhoods on the outskirts of their new domain.

But the big plan to stir minds was so expansive that no one was sure what to make of it. In the fall of 1960, with significant progress in hand on the Pru and the Government Center, Mayor Collins announced a bold initiative for a $90-million development program that would put half of the city's population and a quarter of its land in Logue's locus.

Neither man was interested in rehashing John Hynes. Selling the good man short, they saw Hynes as an amateur in search of an overview, who went from one unrelated project to the next, clearing slums while chasing the Pru for a decade. They had an integrated plan in which all the parts would fit into an urban mosaic to transform a city.

There were to be ten discrete mini-plans implemented by a newly muscular BRA emboldened by a reconstituted "blighted area" development law that became the preamble to Ed Logue's mission statement. With more federal money than had ever been committed to one city, Logue zeroed in on the Irish strongholds of Charlestown and South Boston and minority neighborhoods in Roxbury and the South End. He also set his sights on mostly Irish Jamaica Plain, Italian East Boston, and student-heavy Fenway. The palliative press release was that this was a mandate to clear blight, fix public housing, and erect new schools. But there was also a growing unease in the neighborhoods that there had to be a bulldozer hiding amid the fine print of happy pronouncements.

But for the first half of the decade, neighborhood fears were subsumed by the welcoming tenor of press coverage that was driven by the hard facts of life in a city beset by a drab downtown and run-down neighborhoods. Redevelopment also had the impetus of publishers anxious to get going after hearing out business leaders who, after all, paid for all those retail advertisements. Assigning editors soon shared an interest in the benefits of a New Boston. Along the way, the crescendo of applause for downtown renewal overwhelmed mounting neighborhood protests concerning downplayed demolition plans.

The "good news" era was kicked off with a bylined article written by Mayor Collins in a special Sunday supplement that urged Boston to discard its "hoop skirt appearance" for the exuberance of renewal. He introduced his new prescription of "planning with people instead of for people" to ward off worries of West End debacles.

The sheer high energy of Logue's juggernaut subdued most opposition, though the unseduced became an exclusive club of diehards. The dissidents gravitated toward Bill Foley, a City Council member from South Boston who had become an implacable foe of renewal. Unlike many of the rabble-rousers, Foley had the intellectual stamina to stay with Logue and dissect his plans for weaknesses. At least for the first take. Foley's opening remarks were usually on target, but, as he elaborated, they tended to fall into overstated acrimony. Foley nearly always talked himself out of his main point.

At City Council meetings, the unflappable Logue's strategy was to patiently outwait Foley until the bile inevitably runneth over. One memorable encounter entered the Book of Lore. Logue was sitting behind one of two desks in the council chamber as Foley railed against him and his insensate agency. With Foley in full-throated denunciation, Logue calmly got up and, supporting himself on the two desks with the palms of his hands, began to swing his body slowly backward and forward as if he were killing time in a park. As Foley climbed the scale, Logue seemed to awaken from a reverie and returned to his chair. It took Foley ten minutes to come down from the outer edge of effrontery.

Foley's volatile temperament marginalized him as a political figure, and there were few impediments to Collins and Logue as they reached the halfway point in their joint tenure. Relatively quick success with the Pru and old Scollay made for an easy reelection run for John Collins. To go with a lowered tax rate and reduced budget, he had two big projects well under way and Ed Logue was just beginning his missionary work in the neighborhoods, finally free of someone else's plans.

While Collins rolled over the narrow candidacy of Gabriel Piemonte from the badly outnumbered Italian North End, his trouble-free reelection in 1963 had a portentous footnote. It also marked the emergence of Louise Day Hicks of South Boston, whose intense following made her the biggest vote-getter on the ballot in her reelection to the school committee. While Collins privately disparaged the heavyset Hicks as that "doughy" woman, she proved herself a formidable mayoral prospect by galvanizing the Irish wards with her strident rejection of charges that Boston's schools were segregated.

In that second-tier fight, there were flashes of intense white resentment of accommodations demanded by black leaders and the collateral threat of urban renewal to the "things as they are" culture in the neighborhoods. The sanctity of "our" schools became an article of faith.

Hicks's fiery voters became the political fault line that shook the ground under Collins and Logue. Collins may have won a resounding reelection in 1963 as well as finally obtaining a reliable majority of the City Council, but storm clouds were building in the in-close neighborhoods.

Despite the mayor's easy victory, "planning with people" was soon derided as empty sloganeering in three-deckers under siege. Even though the early protesters received scant attention in the press, they represented a mushrooming movement that would demand its day, as angry shouts against the tyranny of eminent domain evolved into a primal howl to stop integrated schools. The bloody resistance would shatter political careers and divide Boston as much as any Yankee-Irish clashes of yore. Banker Ephron Catlin and James Michael Curley had discreet differences of opinion compared to the ten-year war between the National Association for the Advancement of Colored People (NAACP) and the Boston School Committee.

CHAPTER **9**

I Am a Legend

ED LOGUE

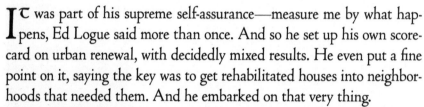

I<small>T</small> was part of his supreme self-assurance—measure me by what happens, Ed Logue said more than once. And so he set up his own scorecard on urban renewal, with decidedly mixed results. He even put a fine point on it, saying the key was to get rehabilitated houses into neighborhoods that needed them. And he embarked on that very thing.

His legendary equilibrium was rooted in his mastery of two worlds—the real one from a modest Irish Catholic household in Philadelphia, followed by seamless assimilation into the gentlemen's club at Yale. He came out a plump patrician man who remained boyishly handsome well into middle age. His blended background meant he could go either way in rough-and-tumble Boston. Charm 'em with glib patter or run 'em over with flyboy profanity. Or just drive Bill Foley crazy by pretending he wasn't in the room.

But by Ed Logue's own clear-eyed standard, he would fail. Despite notable success with the Pru, the Government Center, and waterfront revival, he seldom got what he wanted in the neighborhoods. In fact, he had to retreat from three of eight designated sections. Time and again, he settled for half a loaf.

But urban renewal was not just a numbers game and certainly not the only metric for Ed Logue. In Boston he pushed a reclamation project in a city on the brink, teetering on a tipping point that could have sent it sprawling into second-rate status for good. Logue stopped that. It was no small thing. Scollay Square did not persist as a perpetual embarrassment. Office towers did sprout in a once-moribund financial district. Slum-ridden neighborhoods of high crime and little hope got vital upgrades. Ed Logue stepped up to the plate at this critical time in the 1960s and saved downtown and fought gamely to inject a middle class in places in desperate need of amelioration.

But excessive gentrification became the rub, a long-running question of social justice that marred his legacy. Pulling in the well-to-do from the suburbs was clearly more important to him than renovating houses for people who lived in the neighborhoods. He seems to have tripped over his boundless ambition and expansive vision by taking on too much, too soon. His battle plan opened on too many fronts at once.

Even with a lot of things going for him—strong business support, his mastery of new federal funding, a pervasive sense that the time was right—Logue seemed to move precipitously. It was as if he knew he had a small window to do big things in Boston. Likely the two terms of John Collins. So he jumped on his main mission: neighborhood transformation.

He knew what he needed from the first day in a peevish town. Logue arrived as an urban consultant, but declined to take the top job at the Boston Redevelopment Authority until he was granted the most centralized planning and renewal powers ever given to a single executive in a large city. The only thing he took slowly was his reckoning of Boston's inner neighborhoods, taking them in by walking tours to get a feel for a tired old town. The upshot was a big-ticket plan for massive renewal—$90 million when a million was real money and the middle class made between $5,000 and $6,000 a year.

After serving as a decorated bombardier in Italy during World War II, Logue brought back a command presence to Yale Law School and began his career as a Philadelphia lawyer in 1948. But he left the law quickly and for good to work for Chester Bowles when he was Connecticut governor and then ambassador to India. He returned to the environs of his alma mater in the 1950s, taking over urban renewal in New Haven. He was quickly lauded there for doing more with less than anyone had ever done in a city its size.

Logue was always an action guy, impatient with those who nurtured grand plans with no political underpinning. To him, renewal was the art of the possible based on a blend of policy and politics. One without the other was nothing more than a blueprint stashed in a drawer.

To this end, his neighborhood start-ups were vital events and far more about political wiring than grassroots support. They were beachheads for the invasion to follow. His BRA became a mini–propaganda machine for each neighborhood that pushed "understandings" forged with local advocates who supposedly spoke for the whole. The strategy was aimed at getting the equivalent of a big election-day turnout and then proclaiming a mandate no matter how rigged the process or close the vote was. The dispositive public hearings were all one-time affairs where approval was deemed a final order. No second thoughts allowed.

But by his own criterion—that urban renewal rose or fell on extensive residential rehabilitation—his objectives went largely unfulfilled. In the Irish enclave of Charlestown he got about 10 percent of his opening bid for new housing. He was shut out in the largest Irish bastion, the politically volatile South Boston. He never even got started in East Boston and Jamaica Plain. He got one luxury apartment building out of Allston, but it took ten years and brought a barrel of bad publicity from rough evictions. He made out the best in the first project in a minority neighborhood near Roxbury's Franklin Park. But his later sortie into the South End, another increasingly minority section in transition, sowed a bitter harvest for decades to come.

His blanket promise that there would be no more West End obliterations needed careful parsing. What he meant was there would be partial rather than wholesale demolition. As he moved from one place to another, the razings were denied at first and then gradually acknowledged as they were obviously in the works. Demolitions were scaled back as part of a bluffing game to make communities grateful that only 20 percent of the project area was leveled. Throughout his eight-year reign, he was remarkably blasé about his last priority—the fate of displaced poor people. Like a general with the broad view, he saw the evicted as the grunts of the urban wars, the necessary price of progress.

Urban researcher John Mollenkopf, in his 1983 study of contemporaneous renewal projects in Boston and San Francisco, did a tally of the Logue era that drew some bottom lines from the clouds of construction dust. For every three housing units leveled, only a single new one took their place. And the equivalent of an entire neighborhood was displaced.

The figures: 9,718 low-income units demolished while only 3,504 new units were constructed. Of the total, 982 came with federal subsidies for low-income or elderly residents. About 22,000 low-income citizens of Boston were displaced and left to sort things out on their own.

After early success downtown, Logue wanted to make his lasting mark with a redo of tattered in-close neighborhoods. Beginning in 1962, Logue embarked on a slightly mad juggling act that had him and his staff fanning out across the city to sell renewal. The initial targets were four low-income locations with some of the worst housing stock— Charlestown, Allston, Washington Park in Roxbury, and the South End. They were out most weeknights on missionary "planning with people" visits, proselytizing with great effect in one place while getting shouted down with epithets in another.

The contrasting receptions were in relief in Washington Park and Charlestown. It was a happy collaboration when neighborhood leaders wanted it and civil war when they didn't. Blue-collar Charlestown didn't.

After Logue's progress downtown, his first move in neighborhood rehabilitation focused on a low-resistance, good precedent section of increasingly black Roxbury. Logue first turned to Washington Park, which had just ended a decade-long shift from 70 percent white to 70 percent black. In the 1950s, residential leaders had sought to get on the Boston Planning Board agenda to head off encroaching blight.

Washington Park had a proud history, with its residents changing from Brahmin to Jewish until middle-class blacks began moving in during the 1930s, jumping the hostile Irish section on its periphery. They settled on the slopes leading to the greenery of Franklin Park, which was part of Frederick Olmsted's renowned nineteenth-century Emerald Necklace around the city.

But the shifting demographics of the 1950s saw whites withdrawing from the lower-lying section of Washington Park as poorer blacks moved in. When Logue was ready to roll, the beleaguered black leadership ran into his arms. The BRA director found Washington Park had unique advantages that he hoped to transplant elsewhere—committed middle-class leadership that bought his entire rehabilitation package.

His first community allies were ideal: Otto and Muriel Snowden were a cosmopolitan couple who personified an endemic element that avidly sought to preserve residential character by housing renewal, new school construction, and street and park upgrades.

Washington Park was Logue's only gimme. It was a project-in-waiting, with a built-in collaborative constituency. It had a strong and amenable community council that had attracted a thousand residents to a pro-renewal hearing even before Logue arrived. It already had some committed funding and survey work in hand. Its mandated group actually wanted to increase the number of houses to be razed and residents to be relocated. The black leadership had been ignored so long in Boston that it was beyond malleable. Its offer of 60 percent relocation was such that Logue rejected it as irresponsible.

Yet it was the closest Logue would come to unequivocal victory. He accomplished more there than in the other ethnic neighborhoods. The BRA cleared 35 percent of the housing stock, far higher than Charlestown or the initially pliant South End.

But the renovated property with a patina of goodwill was also the first display of the BRA's real intent—to knock down substandard housing for the poor to provide upgrades for new residents with higher incomes. In Washington Park, city planners didn't even pretend—as they did elsewhere in profusion—that they would relocate those dislodged in the project area.

While all residents in need of relocation were poor enough to be eligible for public housing, no such project was planned for Washington Park. Even though the BRA had to know better, it blithely announced the normal public housing turnover could absorb 1,275 families cut loose by the Roxbury renewal. It was disingenuous at best to suggest that the deeply segregated world of 1960s public housing would accommodate large low-income black families in projects across the city. It became quickly apparent that only a token number of rehabilitated units would be available to the displaced, with rents exceeding what eight of every ten of them could afford.

For all its promise, Washington Park also exposed a persistent dilemma for city planners seeking upgrades in minority neighborhoods.

There would be new housing, but no new schools to finish off the improvement. To Logue's chagrin, the state racial imbalance law of 1965 required that schools have no more than 50 percent minority populations, which presented a mathematical impossibility for a 70-percent black neighborhood like Washington Park to get new schools that complied with the law. So rehabbed sections in minority neighborhoods were going forward without new schools, a prospect that became part of the rallying cry against development down the road in the South End.

Yet Washington Park was solid progress that left Logue more convinced than ever that his community strategy was sound, that if he got the right neighborhood leaders on board to spread the word, the BRA could put a fifth column in place and ram the projects home.

But he underestimated Charlestown. Logue didn't fool many on its Irish slopes, where renewal was introduced on a parallel track—some would say universe—when Washington Park was under way. It wasn't long before "planning with people" was seen as planning with the tanked; Charlestown would be Logue's toughest nut. It may have been a dump along Main Street from City Square to Sullivan Square, but the way residents there saw things, it was their dump and their town. Not even the priests Logue sent in could soften up the faithful.

Like Washington Park, Charlestown had noble roots that went back even further, all the way to the Puritans as a rigidly religious outpost that gradually became a small space too far off the beaten path. But the legacy of staunch independence and solidarity persisted as part of its traditional New England pedigree. As early as the colonial rebellion, it was more way station than redoubt. Its shores were where Paul Revere rowed on April 18, 1775, to jump on a horse to warn Lexington of the pending British attack. And it was through Charlestown that the beaten British soldiers withdrew to their Boston barracks.

Just as famine refugees had in the North End, the nineteenth-century Irish immigrants in Charlestown found their way to the worst housing along the waterfront amid the tumbling docks below Breed's and Bunker Hills, which were still part of the Puritan plutocracy. By the end of the Civil War, more than a third of Charlestown's population were Irish off the boat, most congregating along Warren Avenue, which became known, with little enthusiasm by the upscale natives on the heights, as "Dublin Row." At the turn of the century, Charlestown, abandoned by most of its forebears, had become the city's most Irish neighborhood. But even then, it was little more than a tramway for commerce and for suburban commuters, first by electrified trolley and then by the dreaded elevated railway.

Starting in 1901, the El began screeching out of the West End over the bridge to Charlestown's City Square and along Main Street and then to its real destination—the suburbs north of Boston. It was a quick and easy trip for downtown workers, but a curse to those who lived below the belching trains and had to coexist with its endless cycles of din and dirt. On the edges of town, the docks deteriorated and a drab existence of unreliable shipping employment took hold.

But by the early 1960s, most of the brick town houses on the heights were occupied by lace-curtain Irish, well after the last Yankees had decamped for the countryside. But the town remained a divided place, with the "top of the hillers" personified by William "Mother" Galvin and his seven daughters lording over valley dwellers like the McLaughlin brothers, all dockworkers turned loan sharks.

Up on the hill, Mother Gal was a reformed political brawler who became a more civilized president of the City Council and whose daughter Kathryn had married a future mayor, Kevin Hagan White. Down in the valley, townies thought the Galvins had put on airs. Around the same time, Georgie McLaughlin would start a deadly gang war at a drinking party on Salisbury Beach, New Hampshire, near the Maine border. He took exception to a comment made by another gangster's girlfriend by calling her a whore and spitting beer in her face. The isolated discord spread widely and madly, with most of the underworld forced to take sides. All three of the McLaughlin brothers would be gunned down during the Irish war of the 1960s, with a body count that approached forty. One victim was beheaded.

It was at this time and in this place that Ed Logue sailed into Charlestown's upstairs-and-downstairs society, knowing little more about it than what he saw in his walking tours of its slums—the worst he had ever seen in an urban setting. He began selling his vision of "better houses for better lives" to skeptical audiences of all stripes. They distrusted downtown anything, and could see the last BRA housing renovation over the bridge in the West End where Emerson Place was being occupied by outsiders.

Nevertheless, Logue thought there would be a smooth segue from Washington Park to Charlestown. Both were in obvious decline and had business support for broad renewal. Charlestown was the poster child for an upgrade. The stat sheet: It had acres of substandard housing that had lost about one third of its value since the Depression. It had been abandoned by more than half of its population. And unlike the West End, Logue was selling renovated homes and not cityscape towers.

On the surface, the politics seemed to bode well for a change. For starters, there was no Charlestown version of Bill Foley screaming about plunder in the City Council every Monday. In fact, there was an ostensible ambassador in play with the BRA board's chairman, Monsignor Francis Lally, who also served as pastor of St. Catherine's Church in Charlestown.

But even after the BRA drastically scaled back its opening bid on demolition from 90 percent of the homes to 11 percent, there was a rising tide of "townie" skepticism. They knew how worthless assurances had been in the West End on the other side of the Charles River just five years earlier.

Logue began most of the Charlestown meetings with an invocation that the West End was none of his doing, and was ancient history that should not be held against him. Despite growing headwinds, he gamely fought on for the kind of consensus he forged with businessmen about downtown renewal and community leaders in Washington Park. But there would be no middle ground pulling together for the commonweal in Sullivan Square. To the townies, Logue was just a smooth-talking version of Kane Simonian lying about the extent of demolition.

Charlestown was a tough sell. It had turned even more inward during the 1950s suburban exodus, and was more bound than ever by the ethnic and religious ties that streamed back generations. The natives called it "our town," and that status trumped everything, even being

Irish or Catholic. Better to be an Italian Protestant from Charlestown than an Italian Catholic from the North End. A local priest told MIT urban studies professor Langley Keyes that "Italians are wops when they don't live in Charlestown, but they are townies when they live here."

Logue found himself confronting the quintessential tribal place of Boston, captured at one community hearing with rare understatement when a townie simply announced his credentials like a boxer being weighed in. "I don't represent any organization here today," he said. "I just represent my family clan, which is ten sisters and brothers and their husbands and wives, 103 grandchildren and sixty great-grandchildren. This adds up to 185 that want to be recorded as against urban renewal." The sentiment was received with thunderous applause and became the basic argument—we stick together and we don't want it.

But if local opposition could dig in for round two, so could the bombardier Logue. There was no getting around the fact that it was to be a messy fight. Logue's staff redoubled its effort to sabotage fire-breathing opponents by isolating them as the *only* opposition and then dismissing them as extremist kooks.

And Logue wasn't whistling Dixie when he said, "For every sound truck that goes around spouting lies, we'll match it with three. And I'll even man one myself if I have to." He was very much a presence at the big-stakes showdown in March 1965 at the local armory on Bunker Hill.

His staff had arranged for their partisans to be lead-off speakers in favor of renewal, and to keep things on an even keel. But everyone there had their minds made up. One townie boiled over, denouncing the promise of federal and city funds for renovations. "I don't have to do it," he enjoined. "It's my home and that's what I'm fighting for. You can stick the money up your ass."

To keep the meeting out of the ditch, a vote was suddenly called for by a local priest. A single simple question was moved: Will all those in favor of renewal please stand? Among the avid counters was Edward Logue, standing on a tabletop scanning the crowd for yes votes, looking like George Patton on a hill in Tunisia. The proposition barely passed.

It had taken two years for Logue to settle for one tenth of what he wanted, wrenching neighborhood approval for demolition of 11 percent of housing stock in exchange for his negotiating with the state to get the El removed from Main Street. In a BRA report, Logue had lingering criticism for a "highly vocal minority" in Charlestown that he said obscured wider support for renewal. But he lost the numbers game badly and had other vocal minorities awaiting him. He couldn't wait.

Southie—the feisty fortress long synonymous with the best and worst of being Irish in Boston—proved a bridge too far for airman Logue.

The other BRA ventures into smaller Irish enclaves had little to show for themselves. But they were triumphant sorties compared with the howling rejection dealt Logue in resolute South Boston.

It wasn't as if Logue didn't have a case. In the beginning, his planners did an inventory of Southie and found that half of the housing was substandard and half of that needed to be torn down and reconstructed. In addition, nearly half of fourteen nineteenth-century school buildings were so dilapidated that they should be demolished.

But, in 1963, when it got to be a brass-tacks proposal with a hard figure of $30 million attached to it—a time when work was under way in Roxbury and fur was in the air in Charlestown and Allston—Southie dissension steamed toward open rebellion. It reached a fever pitch that made it clear insurgents would wage a house-by-house battle to reject outsider developers in search of a quick buck on hallowed ground.

A "no way, nohow" meeting in the fall of 1965 was of such solemn purpose that politicians were allowed to attend but not speak. No political grandstanding tolerated. An aroused audience of two thousand jammed into the Broadway Theater to roar approval for a panel of activists condemning BRA plan R-51 as "outright theft" and "community rape." The message was "We'll fix our own houses in our own way like we always have."

The pols were consigned to cameos, with the crowd giving one of its biggest ovations to Louise Day Hicks, the hometown chair of the school committee who was eyeing a run for mayor. But the crowd rallied most fervently to the red-hot rhetoric of Gerald Tetrault, a young teaching fellow at Boston University fresh from a long fight against the BRA on the other side of the city in Allston.

His rhetoric was Churchillian: "Fight, fight like hell. It's immoral to take land from one man and give it to a developer for profit. It's outright theft and should be punished by law instead of sanctioned by law."

It was as if the theater atmosphere carried the dissidents back to the days of silent pictures with wild cheers for pure-of-heart favorites and gravelly boos for dastardly villains. Logue and his planners were vilified as aliens in a hostile land. One of the citizen committee leaders summed up Southie's case: "We were born in South Boston, we grew up in Boston, and we raise our children here. These people come from Texas and New Haven and tell us how to live, and we don't want them."

But Bill Foley, a round-faced man with a classical education and an erratic temperament, was the perfect Southie foil to the urbane Logue. Foley's public speeches and private asides were a lively mix of Navy profanity and Latin aphorisms that made him the best informed and least predictable city councilor. His mismatched attire, usually a suit jacket with chino pants, reflected his eclectic interests—flying to skiing to sailing to military history, with some MacArthur in the mix but mostly Napoleon. But his mood could shift in seconds, even in the time it took him to move from one side of the council chamber to the other, a broad smile becoming a hangman's scowl by the time he reached his desk.

At council meetings, he usually arrived late, bursting noisily into the chamber, his arms waving above his head as he pranced his way to his chair, an Irish Zorba doing something akin to a step dance. Then he got down to the urgent business of denigrating the latest Logue surrogate sent to the council to say "give peace a chance."

While Foley's once-rising mayoral star had faded in the wake of his cutting jibes, there was no way Logue was going to beat him on his home turf. He was a thin-skinned Southie pol who nursed his bruises, but he could also get it right occasionally. He put his finger on the class issue that was at the core of Boston life and at the root of the renewed ethnic warfare that was to come over segregated schools.

Foley saw that behind the heavy condescension within Logue's BRA was an elitist disdain for undereducated working-class neighborhoods clinging to family and church. Logue, he said, wanted everyone to be middle class so they would be just like him. Foley couldn't think of a worse idea.

Even with a bombastic crowd behind him, Foley was more than dogged in his pursuit of Logue, as much obsessed as ruthless, turning on all in his path who weren't for lynching the BRA director. His jihad even came to include his benign if taciturn colleague from Southie, John E. Kerrigan, a former interim mayor long forgiven for running off with a showgirl to New York in the 1940s. Both were on a downward trajectory in the polls in 1965, with Foley getting a late boost by claiming the BRA still had a secret renewal plan for South Boston. Logue, of course, dismissed it as election-year scare tactics from the unscrupulous Bill Foley. Both were right.

The denouement occurred two years later as vintage Boston theater in the council chamber, with Foley refusing to accept a BRA retreat from Southie unless it was accompanied by a formal surrender, something Logue, a highly decorated World War II vet, found both laughable and superfluous.

By the start of 1967, the BRA's Southie project was indeed dead on arrival, but the most Logue would concede in his escalating exchange with Foley was that the plan lacked broad community support and the federal government had canceled it. Despite Foley's prodding, he refused to declare it null and void.

As was his wont, Foley pressed on for the white flag of abandonment, but was left to congratulate himself on lifting the "shadow of eviction" from 1,500 families in his district. Logue blithely called mass evictions a "fiction" of Foley's imagination, a gentle enough riposte but one that came at the end of a long afternoon of counterpunching. Foley became unhinged, shrieking a finale: "You're dead. You just haven't been buried yet—you're dead."

On that charming colloquy, planners quietly tossed in the towel without saying so. Like the North End and its vocal leadership and voting blocs, Southie was beyond the political pale for renewal. It finally received the "good letting alone" it accorded its own gangsters. Stopped cold in South Boston, the BRA also dropped its plans for other resisting

neighborhoods in East Boston and Jamaica Plain. Despite the grandiose rollout in 1960 for citywide rehabilitation, the BRA found itself restricted to the inner-circle neighborhoods with low-income residents and
little political clout.

Logue's last stand was in the disheveled South End. Along with the
slums of Charlestown, it had been designated as the other community
most in need of renewal when John Collins took over.

Built on a shored-up tidal flat in the mid-1800s, the South End had
a brief fling with the town's upper crust before it was abandoned by the
gentry in favor of the new town houses in the more recently filled-in Back
Bay, a section closer to downtown and ancestral Beacon Hill.

Its faded grandeur and precipitous decline was captured in John
Marquand's novel *The Late George Apley*. In the 1870s, George's father
had bellowed "Thunderation!" when he spotted a fellow in the neighborhood sitting on a stoop in shirtsleeves. Aghast at the slippage in public
decorum that surely presaged decline, the Apleys became the vanguard
of an exigent resettlement on Beacon Street. Shirtsleeves in public, along
with a sharply sagging market for oversized town houses, was enough to
start a wholesale evacuation of proper Bostonians. Unacceptable informal attire was the final straw for the Apleys during the "Great Panic"
recession of 1873.

It was all downhill from there. By the turn of the century there were
37,000 lodgers in the South End, making it the largest rooming-house
district in the country. Most of the tidy row houses with their steep
stoops and mansard roofs became boarding hostels, with many sinking
further into shantytown tenements. After the Yankee exodus, a cohesive
Irish settlement congregated around the Cathedral of the Holy Cross
on Washington Street and thrived for fifty years deep in the interior
section of the neighborhood. The church had become the seat of the
Boston Archdiocese in 1875 and was the center of gravity for a two-fisted
neighborhood that spilled over to Roxbury, with notable alumni including bare-knuckled world heavyweight champ John L. Sullivan, who
trained at O'Donnell's gym, and James Michael Curley, who delivered

groceries along teeming streets before turning to the roughest game of all—Boston politics.

After the Irish gave way to an influx of Russian Jews, the once grand South End was lost in a boiling cauldron of immigration. Until the twentieth century, its dominant groups followed the usual pattern of Yankees to Irish to Italian. But then things moved at warp speed with successive waves of newcomers, turning it into the most diverse neighborhood in Boston, an instant home to poor refugees from Lebanon, Greece, Syria, China, and Russia.

The South End also suffered a fate similar to Charlestown's when, at the turn of the century, it became a congested commuter corridor for downtown. It had two thoroughfares, two railroad lines, and, worst of all, the oppressive Boston Elevated Railway, which cast a pall of soot and darkness over everything along its route to Scollay Square. In a contemptuous slight by the Yankee authorities, the El overshadowed the Holy Cross Cathederal's grand portico while providing nary a stop in the South End.

Along with the city's core, the neighborhood slumped into a permanent torpor in the aftermath of the Great Depression. It was the hardest hit of the inner ring of neighborhoods from which even the poor began to flee. The South End accounted for about half of the city's 100,000 population decline during the 1950s.

By the time John Collins was elected, the sense of abandonment in the South End was palpable, and the new mayor put it on the top of the renewal list. Ed Logue saw it as an ambiguous place with a huge upside that might recapture its lost grandeur.

But by any measure, it topped the blight index, seen by city officials as the dysfunctional home of "5 percent of the city's population and 95 percent of its problems." The neighborhood had lost nearly half of its population between 1950 and 1960, and was in racial transition, with the white quotient falling from 74 percent to 60 percent. It had three times the number of low-income familes as the rest of the city. Whole streets of neglected homes began to fall apart as commerce dried up and skid row took hold, snaking along underneath the El that ran the length of fearsome Washington Street. It was the densest and poorest of all the neighborhoods.

But after limited success and outright defeats elsewhere, the South End loomed as a last foray for Ed Logue's legacy. It was a must-win, a red-lettered top priority that would have far-reaching consequences. It proved to be an exhausting final battle that took some of the fight out of the hard-nosed mayor and, if being a carpetbagger wasn't enough, finalized Logue's image as an elitist who was incompatible with elective office.

Like most renewal plans, the South End blueprint looked good on paper. It had support from some community leaders and contained many of the worst slums in Boston. It was a long-neglected place that deserved its standing at the core of Logue and Collins's opening agenda. And while the community benefits were stressed in the opening rollout, a collateral motivation was that a new neighborhood would be a short walk home for white-collar workers already populating the new Prudential Center.

As he set out, Logue had every reason to believe he could retain the twin advantages of support from community leaders with a stake in renewal and ineffective opposition from a diffuse poor population.

In 1965, with Washington Park well under way and Charlestown and Allston in quelled defiance, Logue began a stealth campaign in the South End of planning with "certain" people—middle-class leaders who wanted what he was selling.

But it all rested on a submerged fallacy, the inevitable discovery that the South End would be the same old story: housing for middle-class newcomers at the expense of displaced locals. Progress for sure. But at a certain cost to City Hall's credibility. As the hidden agenda had been sized up in South Boston, the South End's minority community began to see a charlatan bobbing behind burnished renewal plans to clear land reserved for outlanders.

When the plan inevitably fell short on housing for the indigenous, and promised schools were never built, some protesters turned militant and spilled into the angry streets as cynicism about the Vietnam War and urban racial discord began overrunning the second half of the 1960s. South End leaders such as Thomas Atkins and Ruth Batson and

Mel King began formulating plans to shift the fight to a more winnable arena—demonstrable segregation in Boston schools. After all, while the heavy-handed school committee members may have been defiant provocateurs, they had also been clumsy enough to leave their bigoted footprints all over their minutes. In fact, the renewal wars on three front lines—the South End, Charlestown, and South Boston—spawned the strategy and shock troops for the looming battle over forced busing that shattered city life a decade down the road. Except that the next time, the neighborhoods turned on each other instead of railing in unison against City Hall.

But before one urban battle begat another, the South End's unique immigrant blend of Greeks and Syrians and Italians and Jews and blacks slowly began to find one voice and some common ground to fight back against Logue's BRA. It would be steeply uphill.

Of all the bogus reassurances in all the neighborhoods, the South End plan was the most deceitful of them all. Behind closed doors at the BRA, the neighborhood was privately seen to be as irredeemably blighted as the old West End, blotted with street after street of dilapidated buildings that would simply have to go. According to MIT urban studies professor Langley Keyes, there was a consensus within the agency that it would have to do precisely the kind of property clearance that it was promising to avoid at community meetings.

Slowly the BRA began unveiling the same kind of scare statistics on crime and grime that the sociologist Herbert Gans had objected to in the earlier campaign to eradicate the West End—things like one third of the men being out of work, few households having cars, and an alarming neighborhood tuberculosis rate. While there was truth to it, it raised the question of whether the social malaise was sufficient to demolish acres of homes. Once more the circular argument was advanced that the unskilled and poor had to move because they were unskilled and poor.

In a verbatim flashback to the West End, assurances were made to the City Council that no locals would be forced out for want of adequate replacement housing. Nothing could have been further from the truth. The empty promises were intentional swerves to duck a fight at the beginning and keep the ball rolling toward a fait accompli.

While BRA officials spent hundreds of hours in local meetings, their actions were a strategic subterfuge rather than a community consultation. It was a highly targeted—and highly successful—public relations gambit. It built momentum to such an extent that shortly before the BRA was hooted off the stage at the Broadway Theater in South Boston in 1965, its elastic renovation "concept" for the South End was roundly endorsed at a public meeting. The stacked meeting scorecard was 130 supporting renewal and 20 against.

The spadework paid off quickly as Logue got to work on one of the largest neighborhood projects in the country. Announced in the spring of 1966, it called for rehabilitation of three thousand houses and construction of an equal number of new rental units, scattered public housing for three hundred families, five hundred units for the elderly, five new schools, and seven playgrounds.

Although the South End's sparse middle class had initially welcomed the upgrade, it eventually began to splinter, and some advocates joined longtime denizens when fear grew that there would be wholesale demolition.

The project's scope should not have been a surprise, yet it took a while for its true dimensions to sink in. As the magnitude became clear, there was a delayed reaction, first from blacks and Hispanics and then even from some original advocates. Ultimately the South End's protest spread elsewhere in the city. It was not long before the relentless Bill Foley chipped in, saying the project was the usual formula—new housing for the rich and displacement for ten to fifteen thousand poor people. "It's as simple as that," he said with surprising brevity.

Even given Foley's overheated rhetoric and penchant for wild swings, time would prove him more right than wrong. Precise bottom-line figures on renewal projects are notoriously hard to come by, but urban specialist John Mollenkopf's study that included the South End found that about 7,500 persons were displaced there, nearly all of them minorities or elderly white residents. While it was half Foley's maximum figure, it was still more than all the evictions in the West End. In addition, more than three times the entire landmass of the West End was leveled. Of

606 acres covered by the South End Urban Renewal Plan, Mollenkopf stated that 186 acres—or 30 percent of the total—were acquired and cleared by the BRA. Nearly half of the project's area was used for new housing, a quarter for commercial use, and the rest for infrastructure.

As advanced by the BRA and pushed hard by some middle-class homeowners, the renewal was presented as a selective and narrow upgrade. In fact, it was extensive, with about 5,215 units—or one in every four in the designated area—being destroyed. The renewal put about three thousand new units in the ground, but the clientele were nearly all newcomers. Ed Logue's true vision for the neighborhood, at least near the Pru Center in Back Bay, prevailed.

But the BRA paradox of mutually exclusive objectives—a new middle class for the South End, and a pledge to protect the interests of low-income residents there—played out for years. In a tumultuous marketplace, at times marked by open class warfare, boardinghouse tenants were evicted on block after block by suburban gentry restoring hostels into the original town houses. The resettlement was also rocked by a sustained crime wave by black teenagers that drove many new owners back to the suburbs. By the end of the 1960s, there was yet another renewal diaspora, with many minorities forced into Roxbury and North Dorchester.

While the reclamation work transformed parts of the down-and-out South End, the 2000 census data does not support the notion that a mostly middle-class neighborhood took hold. Indeed, the median income is barely above the city's norm, and its poverty rate has remained higher than the rest of Boston's. But while its interior streets have shuffled along, the South End's outer edge near Back Bay became what Ed Logue wanted—the largest urban setting for Victorian homes in America. The 2000 census data yield one telling statistic bearing out Logue's long-term plan of a yuppie village. The median monthly mortgage payment of $2,487 indicates the homeowners likely held downtown jobs providing substantial incomes.

But the South End seemed destined to be a half-baked project, a sporadic upgrade at best. Federal funding for new housing dried up, and construction lagged behind demolition. Once more, there were gap-toothed lots dotting evolving streets, and evicted tenants were left to drift on by.

Even Logue's own accounting at the end of his tenure had only moderate progress to report. There was renovation of high-end units and some earlier scheduled public housing. But there were no new schools or playgrounds or parks, and infrastructure work was way behind schedule. The one sure thing was that the number of low-rent units had been cut in half, falling from about fourteen thousand to seven thousand. Only five hundred locals were relocated, mostly to housing outside the South End, and just twenty-five local families got into rehabilitated units in their old neighborhood.

Logue may have flashed his true colors on the "process" in a retrospective conversation he had at the end of his tenure. Heading out of town, he told good-government maven Herbert Gleason, who had specialized in renewal issues for John Powers and become an integral part of Kevin White's administration: "You know, Herb, there's only one trouble with urban renewal—too goddamn much due process in it." A snide joke on himself.

Politically, the South End devolved into a messy draw, an untidy end for Logue's tenure. He had many wins in his eight years as czar, but most of them were in the beginning and downtown. He won a small pyrrhic victory in Allston, compromised in Charlestown, and gained an uncertain advantage in the South End. But the dissatisfaction there rumbled onward, exposing the calculated cynicism behind his planning with people.

The South End proved so intractable it may have taken the fight out of a very combative customer, Mayor John Collins. At least for running Boston. Early polls showed he would have a tough race for reelection in 1967, which was one reason why he ran for the US Senate in 1966. But he more than lost "his" city in the statewide Democratic primary. He got skunked in Boston, losing twenty-one of twenty-two wards.

Aide-de-camp Spagnoli, who had been campaign manager for the mayoral runs, took a backseat for the statewide race. But in the last two weeks before the election, he picked up negative reports from his political sources around the city. "I went to see the mayor and said we're in trouble in Boston. He said, 'It's too late, Henry. I can't change that now.' He always thought it was the Boston Irish thinking that the mayor had left them and would bring him down for it. He was right— there's nothing you can do about that." Critics have also noted that Collins may have outfoxed himself by "yo-yoing" the tax rate, dropping it 12 percent in the senatorial election year, but being forced to boost it back up by 16 percent in 1967. Some savvy Boston voters saw through it and held it against him.

Collins had peaked as a political figure, and Logue would take his blasé dynamism into the arena to finish the job that many felt was already overdone. Boston College historian Lawrence Kennedy, who has been a consultant for the BRA, called Logue's legacy "mixed," blaming some of it on his "top down" managerial style but much of it on the mounting disillusionment with government in general that came with Vietnam and then Watergate. Clearly, by the end of the Collins years, there was a wider angst in place than pockets of discontent over eminent-domain takings. The issues that had prompted tenants to tell Monsignor Francis Lally to shove it seemed quaint. Ultimately, the architects of the New Boston were rejected by the wizened residents of the old town.

After Collins left office, he became reactionary and somewhat bitter, resenting what he saw as the callow charisma of his successor Kevin White and his collection of Ivy League whiz kids. He also disdained the undisciplined leftward tilt of the McGovern Democrats, and the World War II veteran in him was appalled by draft-card-burning Vietnam protesters. It all pushed a rock-ribbed conservative so far right that he headed Democrats for Nixon when the president ran for reelection in 1972.

Although his administration had benefited mightily from the urban policies of Presidents Kennedy and Johnson, Collins always claimed he didn't forsake the Democratic Party. "It left me," he said, "and millions of others to follow their crazy policies of social engineering and abortion." One measure of his evolving ideology beyond the high emotions of Vietnam was his sharp reversal on transportation policy. Though he vowed as mayor in 1962 to stop the Southwest Expressway, which would have torn up parts of his old neighborhood, he did an about-face ten years later as president of the Greater Boston Chamber of Commerce, denouncing the "ecological extremism" of expressway foes. (The extremists came to include Republican governor Francis Sargent, who stopped the disruptive railway.)

Collins stayed in the game, but on the periphery. He practiced law, taught urban studies at MIT, and took leadership roles in business-oriented civic organizations. In the late 1970s he was a behind-the-scenes adviser in the one-term reign of pro-business conservative governor Edward King. But he always maintained his public equilibrium, an unwavering but polite public figure who remained tough as ever backstage. Reputation intact, he died at seventy-six in 1995.

A few years after Collins was out of office, Ed Logue paid homage to his old boss in a speech at the Massachusetts Historical Society: "Collins was tough. Schooled in Boston politics, he knew all of its ins and outs. In a remarkable way—the parallel with Franklin Roosevelt is striking—his crippling illness gave him a special strength, great determination, a unique perspective. . . . I don't think I saw anyone fool him. No one frightened him. No one was long in doubt about where he stood."

After his mayoral bid in 1967, Logue tried academia briefly, also at the urban affairs department at MIT. But, at forty-eight and full of energy and unfulfilled dreams, he found his next challenge in urban redevelopment in New York. That was even more challenging than his plan for Boston. He became the director of the Urban Development Corporation in 1968—but only after driving his usual tough-minded bargain. He got the autonomy he craved, and a broad mandate from a powerful, non-meddling boss, Governor Nelson Rockefeller. Most important, he could follow his "no small plans" rubric by focusing on low-income housing needs throughout an entire state, assured of financial support from the US Housing and Urban Development Agency and a state-backed bond commitment that rose to $2 billion.

Logue set out to build at least fifteen thousand subsidized units a year in places where private investment wouldn't go. In the beginning, Logue was authorized to bypass local zoning rules and begin construction even before contracts were executed. That proved to be an impatient efficiency that boomeranged when the Nixon administration cut back on federal funding and inflation surged in the early 1970s. Eventually the walls caved in on Logue's bold housing initiative. He fell far short of his housing-unit goal in New York, building but 33,000 in seven years—about one third of what he was after.

By 1975 half of Logue's projects were in financial trouble, with his development corporation paying the highest borrowing rates of any public agency in the country. It was a dramatic reversal of fortune, with Logue forced to resign, reputation tattered, his program contributing to the singular failure of publicly aided housing. Despite some solid low-income projects such as Roosevelt Island near Manhattan, the UDC went bankrupt and most of his housing goals went unmet.

But the indomitable Logue was back at it in a few years. He formed a consulting firm, but his final project, in the late 1970s—to build new housing in the scarred South Bronx, one of the saddest implacable symbols of urban decay in America—stumbled forward but was disbanded in 1985, long after it was moribund.

One of Logue's acolytes and successors, Stephen Coyle, recalled visiting him in the overwhelming decrepitude of the South Bronx at a time when federal funding had all but lapsed and the project there was clearly failing. Coyle caught the poignancy of the moment: "You had a sense of a promethean figure doing penance—the master builder surrounded by urban decay, with the federal government abandoning him."

Logue went back to academia and his consulting company, but he lacked the challenge he always sought of making hard decisions that made a difference. He eventually retired to Martha's Vineyard, where he died at seventy-eight in tranquil West Tisbury.

While his flame flickered with no streets to reconfigure or designs to impose, he never lost sight of his hard-fought standing on the Boston landscape. Well into retirement, he led a group tour to China, where each member was given a map with Chinese location names, accompanied by a companion legend giving English translations. When the guide asked whether everyone had a legend, Logue chortled, "I *am* a legend." And so he remains.

CHAPTER 10

Whither Boston

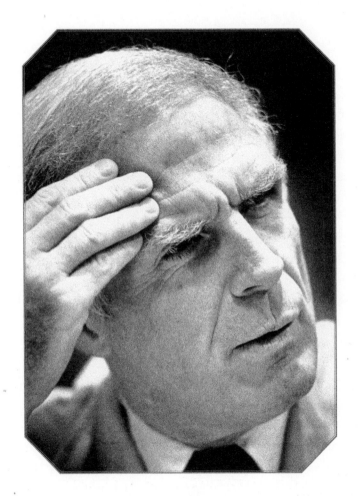

KEVIN WHITE

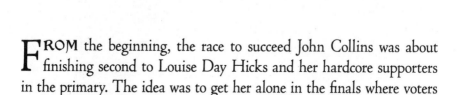

From the beginning, the race to succeed John Collins was about finishing second to Louise Day Hicks and her hardcore supporters in the primary. The idea was to get her alone in the finals where voters would be forced to decide if they *really* wanted a lightning-rod lady with an ugly message as mayor.

Ed Logue never saw himself as a long shot in all that, but that's because he liked his chances in anything. And why not? It had worked out for him in most things in Boston, and he wasn't running for mayor of Southie, where he was reviled. But he was in retail politics now, not just one-time-only community meetings to ram a renewal project home. It was an arena where his assets with the business community—Yalie, profanely patrician, even his carpetbagger perspective—counted for little. In fact, they began to cut sharply against him.

As the summer of 1967 ebbed, polls showed Logue splitting the Goo-Goo vote with Harvard blueblood and Rhodes scholar John Sears, a rare Republican who actually held elected office in Boston as a legislator—despite talking and living out of the nineteenth century. He was a descendant of John Winthrop, the first governor of the Massachusetts Bay Colony. He called his wife "Honey Sweetie" and they both sometimes wrinkled their noses at each other as endearments before their divorce in 1970. It became clear that Sears and Logue were cutting up the same vote to make way for an engaging newcomer, Kevin Hagan White, the Massachusetts secretary of state.

As the summer wore on, Logue also lost what he had always viewed as his ace in the hole, the backing of the *Globe*'s energetic editor-in-chief. Tom Winship liked Logue's brash style and had one of his wife's relatives and Vault prime mover Charles Coolidge working him over about how much Logue had done to save downtown. But the paper's political editor, the fast-moving and well-connected Robert Healy, pulled Winship in a different direction. Healy conceded the downtown bouquets for Logue, but argued that the politics didn't work. In a measure of how strongly the *Globe*'s leadership was determined to beat back Hicks and the racist image she meant for the city, Healy remembered a brass-tacks talk he had with Winship about who could best beat Louise. "The case against Logue was that he was an aloof carpetbagger who had kicked hell out of the neighborhoods. It was kinda preposterous. No one was sure about White, but he didn't have Logue's arrogance or baggage and he had the best chance against Hicks. It took a while for Tom to understand that."

With primary day nigh, Logue knew he had to stop White or it was over. In a late gamble, the Logue camp tried to pull a rabbit out of an old hat, getting an unknown—a man named Richard Iantosca of Jamaica Plain—to challenge the validity of White's nomination papers. Iantosca was a nobody who rocked the house.

In a congested field that had few issues beside Hicks reminding voters that they knew where she stood on segregation and with her nine rivals failing to gain traction with this or that, the preliminary campaign was jolted in early September by the charge of impropriety against White.

The arcane ballot battle took hold in a vacuum, propelled by the irony of White's singular public profile as Massachusetts' secretary of state. For most of the previous decade, one of his main jobs was to ensure that elections were aboveboard and signatures on nomination sheets were in order. He was being skunked in his own backyard.

It may have been a tempest in a teapot, but for twelve days it held center stage as a compelling mystery, the drama heightened by Iantosca's disappearance from his home and workplace. Yet it was deadly serious while it lasted, striking at White's stewardship as a political figure and raising questions about his competence that would persist. The stakes were clear: If three hundred names were ruled invalid, White was off the ballot.

The denouement, however, turned out to be fatal for Logue. As the public furor seemed headed to court and embarrassing depositions appeared likely for both Logue and Collins, they pulled the plug on the ruse, admitting that Iantosca had been acting at their behest. Logue always insisted that he was right before he was wrong, that his experts found that many of White's signatures were suspect. But he still had Iantosca, a man Logue didn't know and hadn't met, file a challenge with the city. The final impression was that you didn't want to play cards with Ed Logue.

Iantosca, who stayed in Boston for ten years after the challenge and later worked as a salesman for chemical engineering firms in Minnesota and Florida, recently elaborated. He called the incident his "fifteen minutes" but was blasé about the long-ago ruckus.

He said he filed the protest after his lawyer asked him to do a favor for a friend who also happened to be Logue's lawyer. Was he used by the Logue camp? He said, "Yes and no." It was "yes" in that he was doing someone else's bidding in a partisan skirmish, and "no" in that he genuinely believed there was forgery in White's nomination papers.

After he filed his challenge, Iantosca said he went on a long-scheduled two-week vacation to a New Hampshire cottage. While the story boiled over in the Boston press, Iantosca said two "political types" visited his father at the family's Pleasant Café in Roslindale. He claimed he never knew who they were, but later federal documents revealed that the pair were the most feared gangsters in Boston at the time—Stevie Flemmi and Frank Salemme. They got involved through an underworld figure connected to Theodore Anzalone, a North End confidant of White's who became assessing commissioner and endured in his inner circle for decades. Iantosca said the men told his father that the café's liquor license renewal was in jeopardy unless he told them where his son was. The father declined, but was so angry about the incident that he didn't speak to his son for a year.

Sideshow over, Hicks began lampooning Logue's outsider advantage, urging him to bag his carpets and take his expertise back to New Haven. She routinely dismissed him as "the Intruder" as she rolled to a resounding win in the preliminary. She took nearly 30 percent of the vote in the crowded field. White—with a vital boost from spoiler

Sears—sneaked into second place. It would be frumpy Louise and her diehards against dashing Kevin and his Ward 5 intelligentsia.

The final election dynamic shifted from the mixed legacy of urban renewal to embattled neighborhood schools. Hicks, as the you-know-where-I-stand chairwoman of the school committee, put race smack on the table—while denying it all the time. All her initiatives came in an anti-minority wrapping. She may have had the seething white neighborhoods in her corner, but the fretting establishment coalesced against her and the rancor she meant. It, too, knew where she stood. After the preliminary result, White got fast formal support from major political figures, including civil rights champion Senator Edward Kennedy, a Republican governor, John Volpe, and Beacon Hill gadfly John Sears. The *Boston Globe* abandoned its milquetoast policy and endorsed a mayoral candidate for the first time in its history.

The incendiary Hicks had galvanized two opposing constituencies— working-class white neighborhoods for her and a work-in-progress coalition for White—pro-business Brahmins, downtown Irish executives, and minorities.

The pivotal race was on, another turning point for the Irish electorate, which had come of age when Honey Fitz barely beat James Jackson Storrow in 1910 and when the next generation turned out Curley in 1949. This time it would be a more sharply defined old Irish versus new Irish story, with the polarities residing in fed-up Southie and two-toilet West Roxbury.

Louise Day Hicks was the pampered daughter of a banker and part-time judge in South Boston, a respected man who gave customers leeway beyond the end of the month. It was more than dollars and cents to Judge William Day, and his civic concern is memorialized in Day Boulevard, which runs along the water in South Boston. His daughter grew up in awe of him and struggled to get through law school to please him.

As a former teacher, she gravitated to the School Committee because it was community-centered, a way to give back. Her elocution-school manner of speaking evolved into her own stilted political style. No glad-handing for Louise. But her giving back was more about jobs than education. Shortly after the Irish took over City Hall with Fitzgerald's ascension, the populace had wrested the school system away from the Yankees. By the 1920s, the Irish had taken an iron hold on the school department and its ward-based school committee. From then to Louise, all but four members of the school committee were Irish.

Hicks was quickly immersed in a particularly Irish Catholic institution where patronage was the sine qua non of the operation. And the workplace was permeated with the kind of chauvinistic parochial-school rules under which most of the docile female teaching staff and a prissy male administration had been educated. By Hicks's time, the system had evolved into sort of a secular nunnery that doted on the rectory.

The mandate was the same throughout the system: take care of your own—superintendent to kindergarten teacher. For decades, it was easily the biggest employer of Sullivans and Murphys in the city. The committee's obsessive focus on hiring and firing turned it into a cutthroat employment agency. Custodians frequently made more than teachers, and the school nurses were paid nearly double the salary of those doing real work at Boston City Hospital. Its unpaid committee members depended on campaign fund-raisers to augment their personal income, usually from law practices.

The apparatus had evolved into an extortionate enterprise that preyed on teachers who had to ante up or be transferred or even fired. Committee members tended to stay put, as it wasn't much of a launching pad for higher office, the exception being Maurice Tobin, who progressed from the committee to mayor and then to governor. But mostly it got you to the City Council if you were lucky.

In the beginning, Hicks had no lofty ambition. Less than a decade after passing the bar and opening a small practice, she ran for the first time in 1961 as a reform candidate, pledging to take politics out of the committee, a naïve promise at best for someone taking her place in an inbred patronage haven. But she brought a genuine lace-curtain background to a hustler environment and seemed a natural to work with Goo-Goo Yankees to get some educational development on the Sullivan and Murphy agenda.

However, the autocratic trappings in a servile system quickly changed the lady out to please her father. *Noblesse oblige* became *semper fidelis.* When a Harvard professor, speaking at a seminar for teachers in Boston, made a caustic reference to the committee's stance on integration, the system's fine-tuned grapevine got word to Hicks of the indiscretion before the professor was finished speaking. She called him immediately to chide: If that's the way you feel, Boston will get by without your seminar.

The incident was prologue to her true calling. In January 1963 she was elected chairwoman and immediately confronted by documented charges of segregation in the Boston schools. The new chair was greeted with a report that thirteen of the city's schools were over 90 percent black and that eleven of those were chronically shortchanged in per-pupil costs—$228 versus $350 for the whole. The first time around, she assured black leaders that she understood and sympathized with the grievances, and that she was thinking about solutions.

Then the tenor changed and lines were drawn for good. In June 1963, President John Kennedy finally came down hard on the side of civil rights in the face of defiance by Alabama's governor, George Wallace, who opposed court-ordered integration from the steps of the state university. After months of redneck abuse of protesting Freedom Riders, Kennedy stopped worrying about alienating Southern congressional chairmen and became indignantly unequivocal, depicting the Alabama standoff as a national affront: "A moral issue as old as the scriptures and as clear as the American Constitution."

Among other reverberations, Alabama empowered long-suffering black parents in Boston. They rallied behind Ruth Batson, who, as chairwoman of the NAACP's education committee, served notice on the school committee. She, too, was unequivocal: "I know that the word *demand* is a word that is disliked by many public officials, but I am afraid that it is too late for pleading, begging, requesting, or even reasoning. . . . We then make this charge. There is segregation in fact in our Boston public school system." Unlike her lonely early battles for equity, Batson now had some numbers behind her, with the post–World War II black population in Boston reaching 104,000, or 16 percent of the whole, while the white population was reduced by nearly one third during the same period. By the early 1960s, Boston's black population had moved from a sliver to a stake.

Both sides took to their battle stations while Hicks tried to find the middle ground. Hicks worked with three prominent blacks, Paul Parks of the NAACP and Otto and Muriel Snowden of Freedom House, to devise a statement that would head off a school boycott by black students. The budding compromise blew up when Hicks concluded that the terms had been altered at the last minute to make it stronger than she agreed to—or than her base would allow. She angrily withdrew her support, and her final statement became a political credo: "I repeat what I have said time and again. We do not have segregation in the Boston schools."

After her dalliance with compromise, Hicks never wavered again. She stood firm with one emissary after another, including one from President Kennedy who dearly wanted to avoid nasty racial conflict in his backyard. Even a dangled judgeship offer made no difference. In the process, she found her issue—or, as J. Anthony Lukas put it in his book *Common Ground*, "It found her."

But as she rose to the forefront of a national white backlash, it was never clear whether Hicks was as hard-edged as her rhetoric, or merely transfixed when confronted by the furor she had generated. Did she just hold her ground no matter what? Or was she paralyzed by the events she had unleashed?

In June 1966, just five years after she had been elected and three after she had found her message, an ugly standoff at a black elementary school indicated that her steadfast demeanor rested on a little of both, that she operated with bullheaded vacillation. She demanded her place on the dais, but was not entirely sure what to do when she got there.

As she waited to speak at the Patrick T. Campbell Junior High School graduation, a Boston minister challenged her from the audience. Reverend Virgil Wood, Boston's fiery representative of the Southern Christian Leadership Conference, announced that "a foul enemy of ours had been brought into this place." Wood wended his way to the stage and asked the student assemblage, "If this were a synagogue, would you have invited Adolf Hitler?" Soon the students began chanting, "Get out! Get out!" But Hicks sat impassively between two policemen in her white gloves and matching dress and hat. Finally, Wood stood before her and spoke bluntly into her straight-ahead stare. "You are a trespasser here," he said. "Go home. I ask you to leave." Still she sat. It was not until students swamped the stage that Hicks consented to have police lead her out a side door.

Whether propelled by bravado or grit, Hicks led the pack for mayor in 1967, the race hers to lose. It seemed the perfect time to ride the building white backlash. The summer had been a storm of race riots in Newark and Detroit. Boston, too, had seemed on the brink, with lingering bad feelings after police had gruffly cleared out a sit-in at a Roxbury welfare office and set off a looting and arson spree along Blue Hill Avenue, the neighborhood's commercial thoroughfare. Hicks began to see black demonstrations as campaign ads for her.

But the rancor was double-edged, raising realistic fears that a Hicks election would light up the night sky and turn the city into armed camps. The left-leaning media demonized Hicks as the "Bull" Connor of the North while Kevin White made airy moderate statements to lock up the frightened black and liberal vote. His biggest asset was that Hicks scared voters. The home-stretch questions were, could Hicks expand her hard-core primary voter base? And could an inexperienced White hold an uneasy alliance together?

All the while, the storm swirled around the straight-ahead Hicks, a large woman with a singsong voice and a school-mom manner. The crux of the campaign became whether enough working-class whites would risk race riots to put her in the mayor's chair. Just how angry were they? Did they want her running the whole show, or just standing guard in the schoolhouse doorway?

But Hicks never saw her prospects as an either/or proposition. She thought that one would lead to the other, that being a guardian would make her mayor. Indeed, she linked them when she declared for mayor in May at a Boston hotel. Dressed in a peacock blue outfit and announcing somewhat inanely that "my chapeau is in the ring," she made no secret of her strategy. "I have guarded your children well," she said. "I will continue to defend the neighborhood school as long as I have a breath left in my body." The sacrosanct school around the corner was no longer just the embodiment of community values. Hicks meant a white school with no quota of black students dictated by meddlesome outsiders. It was a potent message in a hothouse atmosphere, but it was pretty much all she had. Hers would be a campaign short on specifics, starting with a slogan—"You Know Where I Stand"—that was a sly attempt to say it all while saying nothing.

Kevin Hagan White was bred for politics, with champion genes on both sides. His mother was a Hagan whose family were Irish immigrants that arrived in Nova Scotia during the famine, but didn't reach Massachusetts until several decades later. Her father, Henry, opened a shoe store downtown and rose to be president of the Chamber of Commerce and eventually was elected to the City Council as a Good Government Association candidate. A Novie Goo-Goo.

But Henry Hagan was not a natural. He was the other kind of Irishman, the reflective type who could be smugly judgmental and cold. He was a loner who was slow to compromise, but managed to make lasting alliances—surprisingly with a politician as pragmatic as Martin Lomasney—but he wearied of the City Council tumult and returned to his books and shoes.

In 1928 his daughter Patricia married the other kind of Boston pol, the gregarious son of a Galway brewer, a renowned athlete who played quarterback at the best jock school in town—Boston College. Where Patricia Hagan was subdued and dignified, Joe White was raucous and extroverted. He loved the game of politics as much as he loved sports, serving four terms in the house, four years in the state senate, fourteen years on the school committee, and a decade on the City Council, with one term as council president.

Joe White had once set his sights on being mayor, but settled into the second tier. And he always kept some money in his shoe to deal with electoral vicissitudes, holding a light-lifting political post in the state's department of public utilities for decades—his you-never-know job.

When he came of age, Kevin White looked down on city councilors as crass hacks, perhaps overly conscious of his bloodlines. His father, grandfather, and father-in-law—Mother Galvin—were all past presidents of the council. But it was his father who relished the process the most, priding himself in always doing well in the upper wards in the southern section of the city, where second- and third-generation Irish families had taken their place in the middle class.

Joe White was a storyteller and something of a performer, stopping just short of the stage Irishman who embarrassed his firstborn son. He enjoyed the endless round of banquets and parades and that political staple—Irish wakes. A pol to the core, it took him a half hour to make his way down a corridor in the State House or to navigate City Hall.

Patricia White thought it all rather unseemly, preferring to stay home in West Roxbury and read Tolstoy or Willa Cather. A former schoolteacher, she read European Catholic intellectuals such as Cardinal Newman and became an erudite Adlai Stevenson liberal. Kevin, as the oldest of her three boys, was her favorite. Joe smiled more on their second son, Terrence. Growing up, Kevin was a hell-raiser who clashed with his towering father, who, by the time the boys were teenagers, had become a heavy drinker. Joe did his hardest drinking outside of the house in deference to his abstemious wife, but alcohol made for combustible clashes with Kevin when Joe tumbled home unhappy with the world.

While Kevin gravitated toward his mother's refinement and intellectual bent, he retained some of his father's roguish charm. He blended them into a singular political figure—a moody, reflective man who could dominate the electorate when he cared to, the rare politician who could get away with a take-me-or-leave-me temperament. While his personal magnetism was a clear and early asset, Kevin also lacked the true intellectual firepower of his mother. Mildly dyslexic, he was a lackluster student with as much pretention as potential. He skated by in school, barely graduating from Tabor Academy. But, using his headmaster's connections, he took his broad smile to Williams College, one of the nation's elite schools. Again, he did not distinguish himself in college as a political science major but skated onward, using connections once again to get into what had become the best training ground for politics in town—Boston College Law School.

In 1956 he married into another political family—the Galvins of

Charlestown. William "Mother" Galvin had seven comely daughters, but he didn't get his moniker for his brood. It was from his days as a bartender and as a Realtor with his eye always out for a sale. When patrons overimbibed, he was the barkeep who cared, carrying them home to the front stoop. And when he got into politics, he had a waiting room on the second floor of his brick town house with straight-backed chairs where the faithful would sit until called in for a visit.

While all of his daughters were prized in the political world, ash-blond Kathryn might have been the most fetching. Kevin had her for good from the first smile. The same year she graduated from the Newton College of the Sacred Heart, she exchanged vows with the young lawyer Kevin White who had used family pull to become an assistant district attorney in Suffolk County.

Luck seemed to follow White around. A handsome and spoiled young man who had squeezed by at three prestigious schools, he would fall into a statewide office within four years of getting out of law school. And he had to be talked into it by his brother Terry. In 1960 the secretary of state Joseph Ward was leaving office to run for governor, and Terry saw it as time to strike. Patricia was against it, thinking mistakenly that Kevin was too refined for the political life and too shy for hustling votes on the hustings. Joe White didn't think his unfocused kid was up to it. But Terry persuaded everyone there was a power void at the lower ballot position, and they'd be derelict not to grab it at the nominating convention.

But once Joe White got in, he was all in. Senate President Johnny Powers, a year after losing to Collins for mayor, was chairman of the convention. Terry and Joe cornered him. If Kevin could come in second on a runoff ballot, would Powers support him? He shrugged, but didn't say no. With the top spots decided and the hall emptying out, Joe White and Mother Galvin prowled the floor, calling in chits from decades in politics.

After three ballots and fistfights with opponents who tried to get a quorum called in the dwindling auditorium, the hardcore delegates still standing proclaimed a mildly interested Kevin White as the Democratic candidate for secretary of state. He was so unknown that presidential candidate Jack Kennedy later introduced him at a rally as "Calvin Witt," but he was on the statewide ballot. White went on to claim the exalted title and mundane job of secretary of state, where he stayed long enough to get the seven-year itch in 1967.

White's major accomplishment was sponsoring the Corrupt Practices Act, which required candidates for statewide office to reveal their contributors and expenditures, a basic obligation that was still deeply resented by old-timers who preferred cash money and no records. Minimal as it was, it was enough at the State House to get White a dangerous reputation as a progressive.

In 1962 White made a high-risk choice with long-range implications when he backed Eddie McCormack against Ted Kennedy in the seismic race to succeed President Kennedy as US senator from Massachusetts. The clashing clans put everyone who was anyone on the spot. They were in the blue-moon dilemma all pols seek to avoid—publicly declaring who they are for in a big race, and living with the consequences.

Kevin sided with Eddie, a respected attorney general and fellow constitutional officer, partly out of a familial obligation to McCormack's uncle—then speaker of the US House. John McCormack had once helped Joe White. But it was less straightforward than that. White was nurturing a perceived slight. Ted had once asked him to drive his wife to a political event. ("What does he think I am? A driver?") About the same age as Ted, White saw him as a long-term rival, while Kennedy viewed White as strictly second-tier. And there it would stay until a final schism.

Kennedy crushed McCormack, who stayed viable enough to be soundly defeated for governor four years later. In the meantime, White treaded water and considered his options. He came to a destiny crossroads in 1966 when, tiring of the low-profile ceremonial outpost that mostly handled the paperwork for elections, he cast about for more challenging work. Governor was taken and attorney general seemed destined for Harvard Brahmin Elliot Richardson. But the tough lineup had another opening that was down the road a piece: the 1967 contest for mayor of Boston. And, as with Joe White's job at the DPU, Kevin would have a safety net. He could be defeated for mayor, but keep his hand in the game by retaining his jejune perch as secretary of state.

White was put off by the nuts-and-bolts work of being mayor—all the sewer contracts and snowplows of it. It wasn't grand enough, and his view of that never changed. And he dreaded the hobnobbing at wakes and banquets that his father thrived on. Despite his personal magnetism, political banter was something that White never got good at. All things considered, he'd rather go to the movies and wait for a decent shot at being governor.

But once again Terry got him to change his mind. The argument had legs—the mayor's office was a high-profile place in the turbulent sixties, where an ambitious pol could make his mark. And move up. Just look at John Lindsay in New York City, edging toward the national stage as a presidential hopeful. After a Come to Jesus meeting at a local golf course, Kevin White agreed to run for mayor, with his brother at his side as campaign manager. They banked on people being tired of the brittle efficiency of John Collins and the sure-fire standard refrain for the end of eight years of any mayor—time for a change. When Collins called it quits, the same was said of Ed Logue.

So, after another drama out of *Hamlet*, White was in—until something better came along. Even in the beginning, he wore his ambition on his sleeve, hinting broadly at his intentions. In one of the early meet-the-candidate profiles in the *Globe*, he was quoted as saying, "What makes a good secretary of state or governor is someone who wants to become president." Or a mayor who wants to be governor. Indeed, he said as much to a political reporter well before he formally announced his candidacy. In January 1967 the *Globe* reported that White was convinced he had a much better chance to become governor as a sitting mayor than as secretary of state because he could stay higher in the news and raise more money.

But, until then, there was the not-so-little matter of Louise Day Hicks.

She may have been a one-note candidate, but she stayed neck-and-neck with White while he ruminated about his options.

The subtext issue with Hicks was always whether she could handle the panoply of issues that challenged mayors. Her core didn't care, but the broader voting spectrum did.

In mid-October she complicated things for herself by making the mistake that everyone, especially the media, was waiting for. Pandering to her law-and-order constituency, she vowed to raise police and firemen's pay by one third without any idea of where the money would come from. It was an amateurish mistake under pressure that underscored why voters were leery of having her stand alone at the head of government.

As she got farther in over her head and announced that she would go to Washington, D.C., to get funding, *Globe* political editor Robert Healy went to work against her. Reflecting upper management's anxiety about a Hicks administration, Healy had back-channel discussions with Ted Kennedy about stopping Hicks's effort to get federal money. Years after the fact, he said Kennedy was keenly aware that Hicks getting a commitment for cash could be the margin of victory.

Through US House Speaker John McCormack of South Boston, Hicks had lined up a meeting with Arkansas senator John McClellan, who controlled a relevant law-enforcement subcommittee. Healy said Kennedy agreed to talk to his colleague about it. Was there an explicit understanding of what would be done? "No," Healy said, "There's never any specifics discussed on something like that. Ted said he'd talk to McClellan about it, and it sure looked like he did. One of his staffers later told me it happened. Anyway, she came home empty-handed, didn't she?"

Piling on, McClellan confirmed that he had a perfunctory meeting with Hicks as a courtesy to McCormack. The senator was as noncommittal as one politician can be about another. "I didn't recognize her," he told a reporter. "Honest to God, I didn't know who I was talking to."

But even Hicks's pay raise gaffe didn't produce the clear separation among voters that White's camp was hoping for. The race stayed tight.

White's fresh new face was obscured for ten days in October when the Red Sox took over the airwaves and the city's psyche in a closely played "Impossible Dream" World Series. The town shared the rush of a team going from dead last the year before to improbable pennant winners. But as election politics took a backseat to baseball, it was a momentum breaker for a newcomer wooing the undecided. When the election came slowly back into focus after yet another Red Sox defeat, White had trouble gaining traction, even with Hicks booting the pay-raise issue.

White's problems were compounded by an image issue of his own. By temperament and style, he was never a back-slapper. He was always better chatting with women than men. But he had begun to show the graver symptom of a career-long malady—hubris. If Hicks was one-note clumsy, White was elusively grandiose.

White was drawn to the big ideas of policy and away from the minutiae of campaigns and day-to-day government. He could be engrossed by urban policy in spurts and be spellbinding at small house parties, but he disliked working the streets asking for votes in Field Corner or along West Broadway.

After a chaotic preliminary race, with White's daily schedule in disarray, he was forced to move out of the orbit of his brother Terry and toward a brilliant political novice, Barney Frank, who was fresh from Harvard but already versed in the intricacies of policy and vote-chasing.

To this day there is debate among White aides on the merits of Terry White as campaign manager. Some say he was a sound long-range planner who was undone by an unmanageable candidate. Others portray him as the problem. But all agree that Frank brought coherence as the "outsider" White would listen to. The fast-talking and quick-thinking Frank put the candidate in the right place at the right time, saying the right things. The chasm between Terry and Barney only grew wider, with Terry's camp thinking Kevin was losing touch with core voters—the middle-class guy who would look up to the flash and dash of White—as long as he didn't get too big for his britches. The Ivy League side started calling Terry "Raoul" after the brooding brother of Fidel Castro.

Frank not only organized the home stretch, but he also could handle Kevin. And Herb Gleason, who went on to be White's top lawyer for eleven years as corporation counsel, was glad of it. "There would be house parties arranged," he said, "and no one would show up. There were supposed to be campaign workers with signs at certain locations and they wouldn't show up. The headquarters were always scrambling to keep up with that. Barney was a godsend. He got the trains running on time with his super energy and eighteen-hour days. He kept Kevin where he was supposed to be."

Gleason disputed that White went high-hat without Terry keeping him down to earth with middle-class voters. "Kevin stood a better chance of getting the middle class with Barney than with Terry. I think the results bear that out." He was barely correct. It was a split decision, with outer wards for White and the Curley wards for Hicks. The deciding swing vote emerged from the high-income enclaves of Back Bay and Beacon Hill in combination with the minority neighborhoods of Roxbury and Mattapan.

While some polls gave White a comfortable lead, his top aides remained skeptical of that reckoning. They knew Hicks had a hidden vote, and that Irish voters in the high wards were lying when they said they were undecided. Too late in the game for that. Said Gleason, "I never trusted the lead. Hicks had been so identified with bigotry by then that people were less willing to say they were for her. I just remember being constantly anxious." Indeed, the final election cut both ways in nearly equal portions, with White eking out a narrow advantage, winning by 12,249 votes out of the 192,673 cast.

But a win's a win. After the election, when everyone took time off to clear their heads, White attended to one last important task. He persuaded Frank to forgo academia and become his chief of staff. Barney stayed behind his messy desk and worked up a chart on every job the new mayor could appoint, listing three or four candidates for each slot. A rested White worked his way through it as his administration was about to take charge. With huge input from Frank, he filled key posts with Harvard-affiliated candidates, bringing in Hale Champion to run redevelopment, Sam Merrick to deal with labor relations, Bill Cowin as a speechwriter, and Dave Davis to run city finances. They may have been wonks with no roots in the community, but they were also savvy operators who knew the ropes.

In the end, Terry White was outflanked. In a final indignity after the election, his inability to deliver jobs to his supporters took the legs out from under him. On the inaugural eve, he called his brother to inform him he would not be coming to the gala. Kevin White wept at the realization that his administration would begin with a breach in his family.

For her part, Hicks slipped slowly into obscurity. She ran for mayor again, was a single termer in Congress, joined the City Council, and then fully retreated to a one-day-a-week sinecure at the Boston Retirement Board. Her livelihood focus shifted from politics to her family's real-estate investments in Back Bay.

But she stayed to the decade's bitter end on segregation, more obdurate than ever. Her strident positions put her in lockstep with John Kerrigan, a loutish and lecherous race-baiter who got the last spot on the Boston school committee in 1967 as Hicks left. For a while, Kerrigan became the pockmarked face of the anti-busing movement in the desegregation fight to come, drowning out the moderates who correctly saw the threat of busing to quality education in Boston and the unfair trauma it would cause children carted into hostile territory in both directions. The moderates were after less busing, while Kerrigan just said no to virtually everything. It wasn't long before the outlandish Kerrigan disgraced himself for good by publicly denigrating a black television reporter. He outdid himself by offering the man a banana, then mimicking a monkey's crouch and scratching his armpits, ending his pantomime by proclaiming the reporter a "generation away from swinging in the trees."

The boorish Kerrigan was a trap for Hicks. Even given her better impulses, she was stuck with him. While she never stooped to his demagoguery and always stayed the prim lady from City Point, her abiding axis with him is what the record shows.

In the mayoral-campaign aftermath, she always did what she could to deflect and delay the state board of education as it tried to implement a plan to balance Boston's schools. By 1971 the system was as segregated as Selma. Two thirds of the black students were in schools at least 70 percent black, and eight of every ten white students were in schools at least 80 percent white. Over nearly a decade, where minor accommodation could have gone a long way, Hicks's intransigence made a dramatic disruptive court order to fix discrimination inevitable.

Colin Diver's career closely tracked the erratic meteor that was Kevin White. In the first term, Diver's trajectory took him from being a newly minted Harvard lawyer out to save Boston from racial discord and urban decay to a dejected burnout trapped in the crossfire between black neighborhoods that demanded too much and white ones that were against everything.

As chronicled in Lukas's *Common Ground,* Diver started out marching happily behind the new mayor, who seemed committed. Until he didn't. Diver was suddenly caught up in the riptide when quicksilver Kevin tacked to the right to maneuver around strong headwinds. Over three years Diver watched White backslide from commitments to black neighborhoods on housing, and even from some Beacon Hill admirers, when the piqued mayor concluded both had deserted him in 1970 when he lost an election for the job he really wanted, Massachusetts governor.

At the end of the first term, Diver observed White's continuing metamorphosis with dismay as the mayor set out to reinvent himself for a rematch with Hicks in 1971. Stung by the derogatory sobriquet "Mayor Black" given him because of policies favorable to minorities, he did a U-turn to pacify rambunctious Irish and Italian neighborhoods. And ran over Colin Diver.

But, in the beginning, like most people first exposed to White's charm offensive, Diver was enticed by the youthful mayor's exuberance and rhetoric. In April 1968, barely three months in office, White was deep on the speaker's list at the annual Harvard Law Review banquet in the opulent and arched surroundings of the Harvard Club's central hall on campus. It brimmed with firepower from Congress, Wall Street, and the legal profession.

White followed a former dean of the law school and an undersecretary of state. But his brief remarks came days after the assassination of Martin Luther King, and he shook the rafters with a call to action. "I bring tonight the conviction that if we are somehow to escape destruction," he said, "we must accept without reservation the proposition that the plight of the black man is the greatest single crisis in America today— the axis around which every other problem revolves." White put himself foursquare behind integration, and pledged an effort approaching Lincoln's "above all else" devotion to the Union to promote a single society based on parity between whites and blacks. "This is our commitment in

Boston. I need your assistance. I hope there are those here among you, among the very best young lawyers America has produced, some who will choose to join us in this commitment."

The room rose as one in a standing ovation, and Diver was spellbound by the power of the words and the eloquence of the new mayor, deciding then and there that he shared the vision and wanted to work for this charismatic man who was about to reshape his city. Later that night he talked of nothing else with a classmate who, like Diver, had already signed on with a white-shoe law firm in Washington, D.C. But Diver's heart wasn't in it. When the classmate argued the speech wasn't a clear-cut recruitment by White, Diver had a clipped answer. "Let's find out." He was in Barney Frank's office the next Monday.

Despite his sweeping oratory at Harvard, White was nonplussed that someone would take him literally and sign up, that someone in his audience would take his words more seriously than he himself did. It may have been just another political speech to White, but Diver seized on it, utterly determined to grapple with what he saw as America's greatest challenge—forging a just society. When he got vague answers from a besieged Barney Frank, he called another Harvard contact in the administration and asked if he needed an assistant. Sam Merrick did, and Diver was at his side two months later.

For all his attraction to grand ideas, Kevin White had never sifted through them in a systematic way to forge a defined ideology. He had been floating around in the vague prestige of being secretary of state and hadn't quite figured out what extraordinary thing it was that he would do with himself. Colin Diver, a decade younger, knew what he wanted the minute he heard it.

Gifted but undisciplined, White followed his itinerant intellect to a dual track of governance. In the beginning he roared down the ideological trail blazed by the incandescent Barney Frank because it had the noble purpose of reducing racial tension and, just as important, offered the political advantage of attracting suburban votes for governor.

By the time White had taken office, neighborhood renewal had run its uneven course and the new priority was problem-solving for neighborhoods in distress. White could photo-op his coat-over-the-shoulder with the best of them, and even play basketball for a John Lindsay minute with city kids. He thought in television images and talked in vivid if elliptical metaphors, and his first starring role was as an urban fighter who played to two audiences. He would be an inner-city tough guy in Dorchester and the gutsy Last Liberal in Newton.

But after a peripatetic rollout, it began to backfire in white neighborhoods. He had run too far in one direction. The bad reviews reached a crescendo through one of the major initiatives of the opening days, an outreach program known as "Little City Halls," which operated out of ten fifty-foot trailers across the city to bridge the gap with any alienated voters. But they were hardly just dispensers of goodies and goodwill. They were also the mayor's "eyes and ears" in the neighborhoods. Each manager was given standard marching orders by the mayor. They were not to rush into his office to say their area was on fire, but rather to tell him if it was *going* to catch fire. Their message about the building blowback on programs for blacks was "There's heavy smoke out there, boss."

White found that fighting off "outsiders" played well wherever he went in the city. Resisting airport expansion in East Boston's backyard and a runaway federal highway in Jamaica Plain were slam-dunks—even when the city didn't fully succeed. At least the mayor tried.

But it was a different story entirely when white neighborhoods were asked to pitch in to help the mayor fulfill pledges to the black community. The eminently sensible "Infill" housing program defined the dilemma. It was designed to scatter one thousand units of prefabricated housing on vacant lots owned by the city, and provide quick and cheap housing that sidestepped crime-plagued high-rise projects that scarred the terrain. It seemed a win-win that promised affordable housing without stacking hundreds of poor people on top of one another.

Yet Infill ran into a ferocious barrier—the Irish mind-set. It held that minority programs must be restricted to *their* neighborhoods. Never in *mine*. It wasn't so much racist—though there was some of that—as it was ethnocentric. It was a worldview that resembled the closed society the Irish had encountered in Beacon Hill when they arrived in the mid-nineteenth century. In both neighborhoods, good relations started with a medieval understanding that everyone had a proper place and stayed there.

The strong aversion to Infill housing became a watershed moment for Kevin White's political ambitions in a segregated city. It was a hot-button item in white neighborhoods that saw it as a slippery slope toward full-scale integration. The old-line Irish sections—Charlestown, West Roxbury, and Dorchester—spurned the program in quick succession. There was progress only in black areas, and even then most units went unoccupied.

Colin Diver struggled to pull it together for the greater good, but succumbed to the larger issues that enveloped low-income housing for minorities in Boston. He was buffeted by the extremes of white prejudice and black entitlement that devoured good intentions. No matter how minuscule and tentative the initiatives, racial equality didn't stand much of a chance against tribe and turf.

The two distinct facets of Kevin White—the sleeves-rolled-up mayor doing battle for downtrodden neighborhoods and the smoothly elegant proponent of integration at the Harvard Club—began to clash rather than collaborate. While he threw open City Hall's doors to women and minorities, really for the first time, he also became increasingly frustrated when his actions resulted in only more demands and little gratitude. Kevin always needed the love.

After less than three years on the job, he had his eye firmly on the exit. In the summer of 1970—as White's planning for the governor's race moved into full swing—he hosted an informal meeting at his Beacon Hill town house with a handful of top aides to resuscitate Infill. It was the kind of technical discussion that tested White's notoriously short attention span, and as the talk veered into HUD subsidies and FHA financing, the distracted mayor drifted to the other side of the room and launched into a loud and rambling telephone conversation with his political buddies about gubernatorial strategy.

With a sinking realization, Diver understood from across the room that not only was the mayor tired of Infill but he also didn't care much about running Boston anymore. "My God," he recalled in an interview with Tony Lukas, "we've lost him. . . . All he can think about is that damn governor's race!"

But White was as doomed as his Infill program.

He barely survived an internecine primary with two strong Democrats in September to face formidable incumbent governor Francis Sargent. In mid-October, the rigors of the campaign put White in the hospital with a perforated ulcer. But he bounced back strongly in the contest's sole debate, though it was so late in the game his performance didn't have time to percolate within the electorate. Both men had winning smiles, but White was the more relaxed and polished performer. Yet the governor still connected with one solid roundhouse, dismissing the mayor with the unkindest cut of all, aimed straight at suburbia—Kevin White may seem a cut above, but he's really just another "Boston pol."

While it was not the skunking that John Collins suffered four years earlier in his Senate race, Boston voters again humbled a sitting mayor trying to use the job as a stepping-stone. White's effort to move up evaporated in the early returns from Boston. He ended up losing his city by seventeen thousand votes and was wounded by the returns from his own Ward 5 on Beacon Hill and his ancestral home in West Roxbury. Sargent carried both by two-to-one margins. The city vote left White in the desperate position of hoping to make up the difference from the suburban vote he had been wooing since he became mayor. But Sargent was, after all, a Brahmin from the leafy-horsey town of Dover, and he ruled in the Route 128 belt, winning statewide by 150,000 votes. Almost a landslide.

And yet it had not been a quixotic lost-cause run for Kevin White. At times it seemed a toss-up. Outside the city, his poll ratings had been very high, nearly equal to Sargent's. But even given that, the bottom line was fatal—suburban voters thought they were both doing such a good job that they should just stay put.

As well, White leaned too heavily on house polls that consistently put him closer to Sargent than he ever was. They always had the mayor in the game and running behind, always within striking distance of four to five points. As it turned out, Sargent's own polls had consistently put him ahead of White by twelve to seventeen points. The ultimate poll crashed down on City Hall on Election Day. Sargent won by twelve points, a 56–44 percent shellacking. It was a bitter, humiliating defeat for a sitting mayor of Boston to lose even his home precincts to a suburban Yankee.

The defeat gnawed at White, who was given to scapegoating and funks. He felt let down by some of his staff, forgetting that his top people were doing double duty for several months, and by his original supporters who got so much of his attention—upscale neighbors and minorities awash in new programs. He went into one of his surly tailspins, telling aides testily that he was done with being mayor.

The ending was all the worse because White had convinced himself that he was going to win, that he would somehow pull it out. Sometime in October, he and Sargent had agreed that win, lose, or draw, they'd have a private lunch after the election. It was tough to get up for, but it was White's idea and he was stuck with it. They had it in a private room at Pier 4 on the waterfront, drivers waiting outside. Sargent was gracious, but White returned to City Hall in a mood most foul, and began pacing about like King Lear. He said again and again, how could I lose so badly in my own town to a Republican from Dover? And again and again, I'm done. *No mas.*

His aides began to peel off, happy that the disconsolate White was heading off on a ten-day vacation to Puerto Rico. But his press secretary, Frank Tivnan, stayed behind to urge the mayor to observe the old maxim of never making major decisions when you're down. Tivnan also gingerly gave him some food for thought for reelection in 1971. "I think our polls were very bad," Tivnan said. "Before you make any decision, we should hire a first-rate professional pollster and get some real good numbers. Not only about horse races but about issues, profiles, what people don't like, what we should do, a thoughtful strategic memo." White angrily brushed him off. But around midnight, he called Tivnan to say he'd been thinking about what he had said. "Check it out and do it while I'm gone."

Tivnan hit the jackpot on his first call—the top political aide to John Lindsay, whom White admired and emulated. Tivnan asked for the names of three or four of Lindsay's best pollsters, but was told you only need one—our go-to guy is Tully Plesser. He was as conservative as Lindsay was liberal and was not just a political pollster but someone who did a lot of corporate research. Plesser worked with Tivnan on a questionnaire and had it in the field within days. The results were in when a somewhat rejuvenated mayor returned. He met Plesser for the first time at the Parkman House to go over what had been wrought.

Based mostly on kitchen-table interviews, the poll was a rich document that probed for attitudes and not just voting preferences. Plesser told White that if the election was held that week he'd get trounced by Hicks or City Councilor Joseph Timilty. But the key finding was that the dissatisfaction was reversible, that people were disappointed rather than angry. The pollster said a new start was possible in the middle ground, the high wards where Irish voters had gone for Sargent. Plesser said they had had high hopes for White, but that he was now seen as a weak mayor across the board—on police, crime, and cleaning the streets and parks. In short, a guy who caved to minority and pressure groups.

Tivnan remembers Plesser stressing that if the mayor legitimately toughened up with concrete policies and governance and not only imagery, he could turn it around. The two key words were *consistent* and *tough*. Tivnan said it took an outsider to convince White that he needed to alter the way he thought about running the city.

One of the ironic by-products of the new approach was that, at a time when White had despaired of ever gaining national status, he put himself on the map as a reinvigorated mayor. In running for reelection, the next best thing became being a major player in the national conference of mayors. He joined John Lindsay of New York, Tommy D'Allessandro of Baltimore, and Carl Stokes of Cleveland in holding a series of highly effective dog-and-pony shows around the country. They clamored for revenue sharing from the Nixon administration to deal with the latest version of the urban crisis. The CBS program *60 Minutes* did a segment on the conference, and White ate up the national limelight. And he found himself not wanting in comparisons with other prominent politicians.

So, after the gubernatorial debacle and the existential crisis that followed, a funny thing happened. White started to like being mayor. If he had not run for governor, he would have gone his desultory way through the last half of his first term and probably been defeated for reelection. But after Plesser laid out the strategy and time line, the mayor saw his mission more clearly. He became an energized candidate lashed to a new theme—a tough mayor for tough times.

Much of the redo came from a stream of new ads stressing how White raised hell with landlords and shredded airport expansion plans. But his political instincts were also percolating. His liberal team lost its captain when Barney Frank left to return to Harvard and then on to a long career in elected office. White gravitated back to the comfortable old-shoe group that had been with him in the beginning, notably the steadfast and clever Ed Sullivan, a former teacher who had worked with White at the secretary of state's office; Larry Quealy, who knew the Irish turf; and Tivnan, who massaged the message.

White not only talked tough on crime and taxes, but he also began to backpedal on civil rights and the alphabetized lineup of minority programs, with his most dramatic reversal coming when he fired a black tenant advocate from the board of the Boston Housing Authority. The 1968 appointment of Doris Bunte, who lived in the troubled Orchard Park project, had signaled a shift toward citizen participation. Her dismissal was for insubordination, but the fight was really about patronage jobs and the political benefit of appeasing angry white voters. When her independent agenda was deemed disloyalty at City Hall, White barged into Frank's office, demanding to know who this Doris Bunte woman was, and why she wasn't doing what she was told. Frank told the mayor that when she was appointed, "I told you about her and you said 'yah, yah.'" The fuming mayor quickly converted that into Kevinspeak. White said, "You've been around here long enough to know 'yah, yah' means 'no, no,'" and was out the door. While removing Bunte served a dual purpose of pacifying an irate mayor and reconnecting White to mutinous neighborhoods, it eventually cost him his new policy guy, Colin Diver, who thought the Bunte firing was White at his petulant worst. But there were high fives elsewhere in City Hall.*

Looking back after a second career in academia as a law school dean

---

*After a long and bruising hearing at the City Council, Bunte was dismissed after

and college president, Diver said the clashing perspectives were inevitable and somehow productive. "I defined the world as a place full of urban problems: 'Let's go find ways to solve them.' But a career politician like Kevin defined the world as political power: 'How do I get more of it?' It's true we weren't on the same page at times, but they often overlapped. Kevin really did love the city even if it ultimately didn't offer him enough."

Despite all the reverse field running to head off Hicks and neutralize tinderbox neighborhoods, White's rematch election was decidedly anticlimactic. When he was having his troubles in the Irish neighborhoods, Hicks was on television with a rare burst of candor, saying with her sly smile that the mayor's chair was there for the taking. But as the campaign got under way and White got his feet back under him, Hicks traveled her plodding road of low-key small house parties that had her preaching to the choir. There was no plan to break out from her core voters because she and her advisers were convinced her voters were the majority. Her strategy was to tend her flock and then drop last-minute attack leaflets around town.

After the gubernatorial defeat just a year before, there was initial concern in White's camp that he might not even make it back to the final runoff against Hicks. But the mayor rode incumbency and Hicks's passivity to the top of the primary election in September. He then rolled to one of the bigger mayoral wins in the twentieth century—62 percent to 38. The wards that deserted him for governor—especially his home precincts in Beacon Hill and West Roxbury—were back in the fold.

In the long run, the most significant vote in 1971 was the respectable third-place finish by dogged city councilor Joseph Timilty, a former Marine who thought White's support was soft and the mayor a prima donna. He came away from the first contest convinced he could take White if he got him alone in a final. Hey, he thought, Hicks's vote isn't going anyplace, and I've got some of my own.

---

what critics called a show trial. She was reinstated by court order in 1972—well after the mayoral election.

After his easy victory over Hicks, White didn't give Timilty much thought, though he worried a bit about the effect of Timilty's good looks in future contests. On a gut level, elections remained beauty pageants to Kevin White, contests that turned on who had the best jib in the water.

But he put aside his thwarted ambitions and hurt feelings and went about the humdrum business of governance in 1972. Until lightning struck like a summer storm on a humid July afternoon.

Kevin White was suddenly a why-not thought to the team around George McGovern's surprising presidential insurgency. At the Miami convention, top aides were scrambling to pick a vice-presidential nominee. Two pie-in-the-sky prospects, Senators Walter Mondale and Ted Kennedy, had already said no. But White had picked up steam as a "realistic" second-tier choice who could balance the tickets as an urban Catholic with labor ties from New England—and, as important, someone who would take the job.

For a while, it seemed another against-the-odds serendipity in White's charmed political life. The crosscurrents had been against him. He had supported the early favorite, Maine senator Ed Muskie, who had flamed out by shedding a tear about a minor aspersion on his wife's character. And White was alienated from the Massachusetts convention contingent loaded with McGovern delegates. Making his selection all the more remarkable was that he had met McGovern only once. The mayor even spurned going to Miami as an event that had nothing in it for him.

And at first blush it appeared that Ted Kennedy, who had veto power over any nominee in his backyard and a tender relationship with the mayor, could live with Kevin White. He called White to give him a heads-up that he was on the short list and, since they were both a few miles apart at their Cape Cod summer houses, quickly followed up the call with an offer to fly him down to Miami on his plane.

With time running short and White's staff rushing madly to provide background biographies for campaign officials and the national press, McGovern called White at 1:40 p.m. at his Monument Beach cottage.

After finding they were simpatico on ending Vietnam and the urban crisis, White quickly agreed to be the running mate. After he hung up, White was exultant, but his wife, Kathryn, put her hand to her mouth and said, "Oh Lord, Lord, Lord."

As momentum began to take over, seasoned campaign manager Frank Mankiewicz called a time-out to double-check their flanks. He wanted to know, has this really been cleared with Ted? Mankiewicz urged McGovern to talk directly with Kennedy again to make sure the senator from Massachusetts was all right with the prospect of another Boston Irish Catholic achieving national prominence.

The second conversation was brief, with Kennedy tersely telling McGovern that White was okay by him. Mankiewicz pressed McGovern on what was actually said. "Okay, if that's the way you want it." Mankiewicz heard dissonance. "That means 'no,' George." To make sure, McGovern made another call to Kennedy, who made plain his growing reservations. In a matter of hours, Kennedy went from offering White a plane ride to Miami to telling McGovern he could not campaign for a ticket that had White on it. At 4:05, McGovern talked to the deflated mayor for a final time, apologizing but shutting the door. "For reasons that I can't explain to you—and may never be able to explain to you— I've just offered the vice-president nomination to Tom Eagleton."

The end of a heady day was sudden and crushing rejection. Kathryn White wept softly that night, and the mayor, moody on his best day, stared disconsolately out to sea, brooding bad thoughts about Teddy Kennedy.

White's problem with Kennedy was a decade old, back to when they were both starting out. After White had been secretary of state for a couple years, the state house had several ambitious statewide officeholders vying to move up. White saw them all, including himself, queued up on the runway with the Kennedys operating the airport. White decided that the only way around the logjam was to support Eddie McCormack in 1962. White thought the McCormacks would be more political help for him down the road. But he didn't account for the fabled Kennedy memory.

In the aftermath of rejection, the White camp struggled to figure out what had happened so late in the game. It heard immediately that there was a rebellion by big-name liberals in the Massachusetts delegation like John Kenneth Galbraith and Boston College Law School dean Robert Drinan, who were viewed as purists still miffed about the firing of Doris Bunte. But no one thought that that small mutiny was enough by itself.

Ultimately, White's inner circle concluded that Kennedy, right from the start, had little enthusiasm for putting a home guy on the national ticket. They thought he was on autopilot in the morning, but that his disenchantment grew during the day as the implications became clearer. He saw that the mayor's ascent would create a rival Boston pol for the bigger stage. And when it came to rivals, the Kennedys were Corleones.

Several months after the Kennedy Kibosh, Mark Shields, a journalist who would later work on White campaigns, had dinner with the mayor on Beacon Hill at White's neighborhood hangout, the Charles Restaurant. They went at fickle fate this way and that and sighed. Shields's final take: "Teddy's a selfish bastard."

But after all the gnashing of teeth and cries of treachery, White surprised him with a dead cold look of pragmatism, a Corleone stare of his own. "I would have done the same thing to him if I had the chance."

But the cascade of bad news also brought with it a propitious event that allowed White to rebound quickly, and gave him his groove back. The night he limped back to town from his lost weekend, he was confronted by rioting in the South End. And that was just the beginning of a long night that showcased the mayor at his charismatic best. It also convinced him—and some of his staff—that he had the stuff to get back to the national stage on his own steam.

The head-spinning turnabout began when he got an emergency call that the police were struggling to contain street fighting that had escalated to firebombed stores and widespread looting. White toured the area at dusk and won over street kids at the Cathedral Housing Project, and the tumult seemed to recede. White then faced another explosive problem: the Rolling Stones, finishing an American tour, were scheduled for an evening performance at Boston Garden, but bad weather had diverted their flight to Rhode Island whereupon Mick Jagger and Keith Richards got themselves promptly arrested for jousting with a local policeman.

At the Garden, the restless crowd, fifteen thousand strong, was edging toward a riot itself. White took center stage to talk to the throng as if it was his pal, explaining that he had just bailed out the Stones for them but confiding also that trouble had erupted anew in the South End, with two cruisers overturned, and that he had to send police doing crowd control at the Garden to deal with the street violence. ·

He laid it out for them with hyperbolic flair: "But now I need you to do something for me. As I stand here talking, half of my city is in flames. . . . I want you to do me a favor. Just cool it, will you? Cool it for me. Cool it for the city. And after the concert ends, just go home." The half-stoned audience roared its approval and did as directed. They just went home. There wasn't a single arrest at the Garden that night.

It was a virtuoso performance, a magical connection with what could have been an unruly mob. It was White at his best—smooth, poised, persuasive. The tour de force was also a reminder of his magnetic persona for young liberal aides who had all struggled at times with his intemperate downside. For a while, White even thought that McGovern would have to turn to him again after Eagleton's mental health issues forced him from the ticket.

But it was over. Journalist Mark Shields saw it as a fatal game changer for a gifted politician who would have thrived at the national level. Just think, Shields mused, about how it would have been for White if he had run for vice president that year. He'd have been the sole survivor in a stark landscape looking forward to 1976. George McGovern vanquished in a rout. Nixon and Agnew banished. George Wallace and Curtis LeMay consigned to their stone age. Sargent Shriver who? Jimmy Carter barely under way in Georgia.

"Kevin would have emerged as the positive story in 1972 and stood apart as a national figure on the move. The press would have liked him as an appealing guy, an interesting guy, an established guy. He would have won high marks for having gone through a tough one with McGovern. But with none of the blame for what happened."

He may have been deflated, but White had the bug for good,

buoyed by his beauty-pageant view of politics, seeing himself as some-one who could walk the runway with anyone. Who was the competition? Flat Walter Mondale, chatterbox Hubert Humphrey, irascible Ed Muskie, stolid Henry Jackson. Jimmy Carter, peanut farmer/governor who talked singsong. Whose jib flashed like his? No one's. But was that enough? White always thought that good looks and crowd appeal was enough. He began looking past the nitty gritty requirements of the job he had. And why no one had ever gone directly from being a mayor to the presidency.

But even before the Nixon landslide, in September 1972, White traveled to Woodstock, England, with Harvard professor Sam Huntington and his wife, Nancy, to plot a presidential campaign for 1976, blithely looking past the 1975 mayoral election. After his psyche healed, he formed an exploratory group of close advisers. The obvious obstacle was Ted Kennedy's long shadow and longer memory. If Kennedy got in, the nomination was his. But there were less-evident hurdles along the primrose path of high ambition. Like the omnipresent drag of being an urban mayor in troubled times. And a Marine named Joe.

Chapter 11

Maybe Not Wendell from Worcester

Judge W. Arthur Garrity

F OR nearly two years, Kevin White had watched it through a glass, darkly.

He first thought he could lay off segregated education on the school committee whose maladroit malevolence had created the mess in the first place. But its leadership simply saw criticism as a political advantage with aggrieved white parents. It made their day.

The mayor then thought he could delay it in court as a way to kick the can down the road. But his legal advisers slowly convinced him that the law was definitely against the discriminatory status quo. Finally his famous instincts told him he was dealing with a loser that he couldn't finesse. Once trouble tumbled out of the schools and into the streets, it would become *his* problem for all to see. He was in for it.

He began preparing for the busing that he once promised would never come to Boston while he was mayor. He leaned on Robert Schwartz, a liberal adviser on education policy and a former principal at an avant-garde school on the West Coast. Schwartz's assignment was nearly impossible: find the mayor some small middle ground in the chasm between the irate NAACP and Southie rabble-rousers. The fissure in the city also divided White's own staff, with his old guard leaning toward accommodating anti-busers and the young Turks toward bowing to the power of law and the intrinsic equity behind integration.

The mayor's ruminations, which roamed from the existential to the metaphysical, brought him to the realization that he was not just dealing with unequal treatment of the races in city schools. He concluded there was a momentous disconnect between Bostonians and the suburbs that put rational solutions beyond his control. That there was something as irreconcilable between city and suburb as the differences between white and black students at South Boston High School. The sentiment was seconded by the psychiatrist and author Robert Coles, who, as an early critic of the crippling class factor, said that wealthy suburbanites and their children should not be exempted from the city tumult. He told a *Globe* columnist that "busing should not be imposed like this on working-class people exclusively. It should cross these lines and people in the suburbs should share it."

But while the mayor chafed under the unequal burdens at work, he was also looking for political cover, working his instinctive way toward a safe position that went beyond just reiterating that the looming catastrophe was not his fault.

In the spring of 1974 he didn't have a lot of running room, so he turned to his best format, small groups in neighborhood homes, going into semi-hostile territory, except incendiary Southie, for some of his inimitable tutorials. He used morning coffee klatches to prepare anxious voters for the worst. His pitch was twofold, delivered in his theatrical blend of brio and candor. Message number one was "the law is the law and civil strife hurts us all." And, second, "I'm with ya but there's not much I can do for ya." He was after points for trying.

By this time Kevin White knew litigation was winding down that made massive busing inevitable in his city. What he didn't quite grasp was what having Judge Wendell Arthur Garrity in charge would mean.

The McGarritys hailed from County Sligo and shortened the name to Garrity after three immigrating brothers landed in a puritanical New Hamphire town, seeking refuge from the wrong side of another failed uprising, the Irish rebellion of 1848. At midcentury, Milford was the personification of the Granite State, with a booming quarry and a rigid society based on temperance and abolitionism. The brothers plied their ancient stonecutting craft and joined a growing Irish quarter that had settled around a cotton factory in an austere Yankee town. Two local heroes were William Lloyd Garrison and Wendell Phillips, who received stirring greetings when they visited from Boston. It appears that the Garritys adopted a sharply different perspective on slavery from that of most urban Irish immigrants, who intensely resented what they saw as Yankee coddling at their expense.

Hence, down the line, there would be two Wendell Arthur Garritys with replicated educations and Yankee sympathies.

Even with his abolitionist leanings, Charles Garrity pulled up stakes for Massachusetts in a huff when he bumped hard into local animus against "papists." He was a cooper who wanted to own a farm, but found when he won a land auction that no deed would be transferred because of an anti-Catholic state law. Federal Judge W. Arthur Garrity's grandfather had to make his barrels and then build many three-deckers in Worcester, including a big one for his own family on Vernon Hill, another growing Irish commune.

Two of Charles Garrity's sons became lawyers, mostly at the behest of their bookish mother, Margaret. Wendell Senior went across town to Holy Cross College and then to Harvard Law School, becoming one of the first Worcester Irish to get into the then-Yankee bastion. He set up a diverse local practice that he proudly averred didn't depend only on Catholic referrals. Wendell's wife, Mary Kennedy, grew up as part of the servant staff of a well-to-do and benign merchant family to whom she remained loyal all her life. She had no patience for traditional Irish disparagements of the ruling class. And before it was fashionable, Wendell senior was one of a smattering of Irish who belonged to the local NAACP.

For all their emulation of refined Protestantism, the Garritys remained devout Catholics to their toes, solidified by the demands and virtues of the spartan regime of the day at Holy Cross. Even when Wendell the younger was there, it was monastic in its daily demands of early mass and a strict dress code, and it was intellectually onerous in the Jesuit emphasis on classical languages and an armada of philosophy and theology courses. The king of kings was Saint Thomas Aquinas of the tight syllogism and the natural rights of man reposing not in law books but in the deity. The notion of natural justice yielding self-evident rights propelled American revolutionists, abolitionists, and, at times, W. Arthur Garrity.

A century after his forebears landed in the middle of a quarry town in New Hampshire, Garrity married Barbara Anne Mullins, an elementary school teacher who had graduated from Regis, a women's college with some cachet. Her monogram was BAM, so she became known as Bambi, another Yankeeism. Arthur clerked for a federal judge and was an assistant US attorney before starting a law partnership with colleagues. The young couple moved into an apartment in wooded Wellesley in the early 1950s, and never left its environs. He joined the Boston Bar Association, favored by Brahmins over the Massachusetts bar, which was dominated by the Irish. For the suburban Garritys, Saint Patrick's Day became something of a dilemma. If they hadn't quite forgotten where they came from, they were horrified by the boozy, ragtag parade that bumbled down Broadway in Southie.

The Garritys greatly favored the urbane Irish way trailblazed by the Kennedys, exemplified in the preference for fast asides over gauche guffaws. Arthur had a hand in Jack's 1952 senatorial victory over Henry Cabot Lodge Jr., but moved toward the inner circle in 1958 when Jack already had his eye on a presidential run two years hence. It was a jam-packed election cycle, with Kennedy doing double duty by seeking an emphatic Massachusetts win to keep his electability unchallenged, but also moving around the country to campaign for colleagues who could be helpful in 1960. With Kennedy out of state half the time between the primary and the final election, the super-organized Garrity became the master scheduler, once getting Jack to fifteen stump speeches in fifteen communities in a single day. Kennedy got both his landslide and presidential chits for next time.

But Garrity moved up the Kennedy bench when he brought his logistical dexterity to the Wisconsin primary in 1960, a race Kennedy almost conceded to his main Democratic rival, Hubert Humphrey, who was nearly as popular there as in his own neighboring state of Minnesota. In typical Kennedy fashion, once they committed, it was whole hog, flooding the state with friends, relatives, and celebrities. But staid Arthur Garrity was at the helm, and his fastidious hard work carried the day, with Kennedy taking two thirds of the delegates.

Among other things, the important primary victory put W. Arthur on top of the list for US attorney in Massachusetts after Kennedy's narrow election in 1960. But it was not to be a seamless transition for a streamlined man averse to muss. He was to replace an impeccable Brahmin, Elliott Richardson, a rising Republican star who was in hot pursuit of Massachusetts officials, including the baronial Turnpike Authority chairman William Callahan, for taking kickbacks from highway contractors.*

The Kennedys rushed Garrity through the US Senate so quickly that Richardson was soon yelping that a cover-up had been orchestrated by Bobby's Department of Justice to spare the administration a scandal in the home ward. And, by implication, that Garrity was a Kennedy hack put in place to sweep the investigation under the rug. While it did seem for a while that Garrity had sidetracked the cases, it was just another example of his way of doing things in his good time. Ultimately he obtained indictments against nearly all of the contractors named by Richardson, with half of them convicted.

By the end of his five-year tenure, Garrity's efficient probity had him on track to be the president of an institution as Yankee as the Athenaeum or the Trinity Church—the Boston Bar Association. But then something far grander came up—a federal judgeship, though with another Kennedy twist. An old Boston war horse greatly favored by the president's father, Joe, wanted to jump from the gamey Boston Municipal Court to the highest federal bench in New England. When the *Globe* revealed that Francis Xavier Morrissey had counterfeit credentials, the nomination fell apart in humiliating withdrawal in 1965. The disinfectant became the unchallenged rectitude of a gaunt, bald, bespectacled lawyer who also knew how to work a precinct.

As a judge, Garrity was all of that. He proved to be excessively polite, exceedingly hardworking, and exacting to the point of religious fervor. Dispassionate in demeanor, he was fiery in dealing with cases about drugs or pornography. He tended to hold clients against lawyers, telling one in a smut case that it was "because of lawyers like you" that soci-

---

*One of the lustrous gems of Massachusetts lore was produced by Richardson's long grand jury battle to examine the contents of a safe deep inside Callahan's inner sanctum. It yielded hundreds of copies of Richardson's 1939 drunken driving record and little else.

ety was being regularly sullied. One criminal lawyer complained to the author J. Anthony Lukas that Garrity was a puritanical control freak and that his detachment covered a "boiling cauldron of prejudices, biases, notions of how people ought to behave. Like all puritans, he has a pathological fear of losing control. Drugs and pornography represent loss of control and that's why they have to be punished so severely."

While he was known for carefully sifting through all the facts and reading every piece of paper submitted, Garrity also tended to see things through a narrow lens. After he drew the Boston desegregation case by lottery in 1972, he saw it immediately as a simple matter of race, looking past the deep hurt and context of Caucasian class rivalries. Indeed, he saw it literally as a black-and-white matter. When Garrity drew the Boston case, a Jewish colleague was relieved that he didn't get the case. He told a friend that you needed to be Irish Catholic to handle this one.

But maybe not one named Wendell who came from Worcester.

Tbe strongholds against busing on the eve of Garrity's 1974 ruling were manned by battle-scarred veterans of earlier class warfare with Ed Logue's urban renewal efforts in Charlestown and South Boston and Logan Airport's predatory expansion in East Boston. They had become savvy street protesters who had survived existential threats to their way of life. At first they saw the new peril as simply more elitism from outsiders telling them how they should live their lives. They had been there before and thought they could handle it. Or at least cut it down to size.

The persistent tension of the busing antagonisms was deep-seated white resentment about what they saw as the exalted status given black protesters by the media. They viewed militant blacks and their occasional allies, the Vietnam protesters who had burned flags and flouted conventional mores, as un-American. Hicks had long derided indecorous agitators as leaders of the "filthy speech movement." Her adherents seethed when the press seemed to grant their opponents martyrdom while portraying their own side as racist, when all they wanted was for no harm to come to their children or their schools. Stereotypes on both sides framed the debate and ruled the day. Black Power and the Silent Majority were heading for a showdown.

Although the dispersal of black students was eventually going to be citywide and was met by several pockets of rabid resistance in Hyde Park and West Roxbury, the clearinghouse was South Boston. Besides being the first big target, that neighborhood's disproportionate impact came from being able to back down Ed Logue and from having hard-nosed leadership that moderate factions lacked. Southie was monolithic in resistance, brooking no dissent. With rules long understood, the slightest deviation led to excommunication.

The strategy was to surround an ivory-tower judge with an unyielding ruckus, exacting a political toll that usually worked. The message was secondary to the noise level. In addition to decibels, there was the Boston political culture in which all things seemed as negotiable as parking tickets. With enough pressure, Garrity would have to come around. At one rally, one woman misread the power connections so badly that she demanded to know why the governor didn't just fire the judge.

Busing had become the perfect Irish fight, another in the endless series of irresistible lost causes. As columnist Jimmy Breslin wrote of anti-busers: "They were doomed before they started. Therefore they can be expected to fight on."

But they had the wrong guy in W. Arthur. He seemed galvanized and even vindicated by the clamor. But what he saw as rectitude seeped into inflexibility. He seemed blinded at times by the power of his findings, believing the ham-handed discrimination he uncovered on the record justified any rectifying solution he came up with. Determined to move forward quickly, he adopted a busing plan devised by a state board of education that had been squabbling with the Boston School Committee for a decade over its foot-dragging on the Racial Imbalance Act.

Its roadmap, later partly disowned by its principal architect, seemed punitive in pairing Southie and Roxbury, as if saying to obstructionists like Hicks and Kerrigan, "How do you like *them* apples?" And for all his fastidious analysis and careful reflection, Garrity ended up using somebody else's plan that had been forged in the heat of battle. He may not have even read it from beginning to end.

While spending fourteen months meticulously documenting intentional segregation by the committee in the prior decade, Garrity gave perfunctory attention to the momentous political and strategic implications of a busing plan rooted in swapping segments of high schools in Roxbury and South Boston. It was a breathtaking notion, both myopic and misguided.

The busing battle lines were first loosely drawn when the 1965 Imbalance Law was devised by mostly suburban liberals in the legislature, making Massachusetts the only state to mandate adjustments to schools with more than 50 percent white students, a requirement that singled out Boston and the western Massachusetts city of Springfield.

In the capital city, the law was immediately viewed as the second incarnation of the tyranny imposed decades earlier by rural Protestants in the "Boston bills" that restricted Irish Catholic control over dispensing liquor licenses and picking police commissioners. The newly imposed "balance" bill's transportation requirements became known by the equivalent of a guttural profanity—forced busing.

But, after nearly a decade of waltzing with the dilatory state board, the school committee detected a newly assertive hardliner coming its way. Charles Leslie Glenn may have had a carpenter grandfather in Northern Ireland, but, as a Harvard grad and son of an Episcopal priest, he was seen as more "them" than "us." In fact, he was an Episcopal priest himself, and a doctrinaire liberal who walked the walk. He had led black student boycotts in Boston and lived in an integrated community in Jamaica Plain. Privately he was appalled by what he saw as rank Southie bigotry. And now, as the head of the Bureau of Equal Educational Opportunity, he turned a steely eye on South Boston as he began mixing and matching the student assignments into a high-stakes algorithm.

All the elements had converged in a test case in 1971 that made a new school in Dorchester the site for the showdown. The mixed neighborhood had become mostly black, but the state law mandated that there be a fifty-fifty racial mix at Lee Elementary School, which had been built with 25 percent state funds. In an election-year decision, the committee had gone along on a 3–2 vote with the Lee quotas in order to get state money released to the city and help avoid a tax rate increase. Proponents had made a strong case that Lee School was the time and place for some integration. But after the assignments went out to white households, it all hit the fan.

Hicks, who was serving in the US Congress but politicking hard for her second run for mayor that fall, stoked the opposition at a jammed Dorchester neighborhood meeting, hitting high notes on resisting the new assignments that were to be implemented in days. "Should we be forced to send our children into an area where we know that harm can come to them? I say no, a thousand times no." Her speech not only received foot-stomping applause, but put the ball back in the school committee's court.

While Lee was supposed to be balanced at about five hundred whites and five hundred blacks, the first two days of school saw only 149 whites show up. The thousand noes landed squarely on the slouched shoulders of committeeman John Craven, no one's idea of a profile in courage. His vote had made the difference in August, and he was hooted and hissed when he appeared at the overflowing meeting in September, which was so crowded it had to be moved out of school committee headquarters to an auditorium.

Craven quickly switched his vote to nullify the new plan, and things tumbled back to the status quo. He blamed the school department for misleading him by saying that no forced busing would be necessary for the Lee School and, taking the sanctifying oath once again in abject circumstances, announced that he always had and always would oppose forced busing. In a word game, Craven was misleading about being misled. The department hadn't lied to him because, in fact, no busing was required for any of the assigned students, who all lived within the mandated walkable distance to the school. But, face saved, Craven was swept out of the hall on a crescendo of cheers, and Hicks proclaimed the reversal a win for participatory democracy. It was short-lived for Craven, who, having changed his vote while in the midst of running for the City Council, was soundly defeated.

But the Lee School revision was a battle won that signaled a war lost. It gave busing opponents a false sense of bravado and invincibility, a communal sense based on the idea that a corner had been turned on the bumpy busing roadway. For all the high fives, turning around a school committee vote would mean nothing in a federal court. And court was where the larger issue would be settled.

Two companion court actions combined to diminish the echo of a thousand noes. The state froze $200 million in new construction for Boston schools and withheld $14 million in scheduled aid. The committee, never lacking chutzpah, sued for the money, prompting the fired-up state board to countersue, demanding that the board abide by the balance law. The dispute headed toward penultimate battle in the state's Supreme Judicial Court, and would become part of the record in Arthur Garrity's court.

In addition, black parents in Dorchester, smarting over the Lee School reversal, sought out lawyers to deal with what they saw as the latest indignity to go with decades of discrimination. They started with pro bono lawyers who had Deep South civil rights experience and who got them to other lawyers that led them to their ideal man—J. Harold "Nick" Flannery. He had worked for the Justice Department's civil rights division under presidents Kennedy and Johnson, a veteran of dozens of Mississippi desegregation cases. Flannery, who had recently moved home to take the job as deputy director of the Center for Law and Education at Harvard, had been following events and evolving law and told a friend that Boston was a "sitting duck" for a segregation suit.

While the state board pressed its case for implementation of the balance act with Charles Glenn's "quota" maps in hand, Nick Flannery was working in federal court on a different but complementary "segregative intent" track with the NAACP. After reviewing fifty-three plaintiffs from several black families, the lead litigant became Tallulah Morgan, a twenty-four-year-old mother of three children in Boston schools. She would be paired in history with school committee chairman James Hennigan.

Within two years, in October 1973, the Massachusetts Supreme Judicial Court ordered the school committee to implement the state's busing plan for the fall of 1974. And in federal court, Arthur Garrity, having drawn the *Morgan v. Hennigan* desegregation case in 1972, was poring over school committee minutes that yielded egregious evidence of discrimination. He found that school assignments funneled black grammar school students into largely black high schools and whites from their grammar schools to largely white high schools. The committee had devised a dual system in which parental accommodation was a one-way street—whites could escape mostly black schools, whereas blacks were trapped in place.

The white escape routes evolved from a jury-rigged scheme in which portable classrooms were welded onto jammed white schools so that whites could be assigned there instead of going to underutilized black schools nearby. In one of several similar instances, Garrity cited how the school committee had bought a closed Catholic school in the white Roslindale neighborhood and bused only black students to it, directly past a white school with empty seats. While Garrity had been criticized for holding his decision too long, it appeared that besides being diligent, he was strategic, waiting for the state decision to be announced first so his edict would be part of a one-two punch that would promote community acceptance.

Despite the evidence, the "never" attitude of anti-busers was such that the opponents thought they were winning. They had moved from the Lee School reversal to the even headier triumph in May 1974 when their clamorous objections turned around a governor. Facing a tough reelection fight that fall, Governor Francis Sargent tried to split the difference by tinkering with the Racial Imbalance Act. While he once again vetoed the legislature's repeal of the act, he stunned his liberal supporters by offering his own substitute plan. Sargent proposed supplanting the act with a voluntary busing program rather than a mandatory one. The clear intent was to implement a one-way system that bused black children to magnet schools on the city's periphery that were supposed to offer a qualitative difference—but never did.

Louise Day Hicks gushed that the plan was vindication, and an air of unreality descended on Irish neighborhoods who saw the Lee School turn totally black and a governor pushed over to their side. They began believing the crisis was over. No buses would dare roll their way now.

On the first day of summer in 1974, Wendell Arthur Garrity, the fastidious judge of strong intellect and brittle temperament, stepped out of the shadows of his cloistered courtroom in Post Office Square and dropped a cluster bomb on a sleepy city lulled by the status quo. Without equivocation, he ruled there had been rank discrimination and mandated busing to end segregation in the city schools. Nothing was ever the same in Boston.

His irrefutable finding was that the Boston School Committee had intentionally segregated the schools, shortchanging black families at every turn with such matter-of-fact malice that it put the discriminatory decisions in its minutes. But his solution, taken at face value from plans drawn up by an overrun bureaucrat at the Massachusetts Department of Education, turned the city on its ear, prompting a sustained furor that shocked the ascetic jurist, who was used to deferential compliance. The virulence left him blinking resolutely at the waves of outraged protest. Yet he never wavered. To a fault.

With the law and findings on his side, Garrity decided that the only way to break the hold of discrimination was to go to extremes and conduct the "root and branch" extirpation advocated by the plaintiffs. He ordered the whole draconian nine yards. He agreed with a notion unthinkable in white neighborhoods—that racial balancing should take place in the black high school in Roxbury and in the citadel of white resistance at South Boston High.

Kevin White knew it was double trouble, both for the city and for his national ambitions for higher office in 1976. His last stratagem was to appeal to Boston's better self, playing the stern statesman while shunting the responsibility to the overwhelmed school department. He hoped a sudden summer storm would blow itself out. But his meteorological readings missed both the intensity and endurance of the black cloud that settled over the city. Before long, he was dealing with class warfare. He thought it would be over in weeks but it lasted years.

One eminent lawyer put the issue in perspective at the outset. Harvard Law professor Louis Jaffe, who was involved as a consultant in the parallel state litigation about busing to achieve balanced schools, sought to inject the real world into the proceedings by warning of massive

Southie resistance and dire things to come if no adjustments were made. But Jaffe's argument was paid no mind.

His was the first of several red flags ignored by the single-minded Garrity. He had immersed himself in the prerogatives outlined in a succession of US Supreme Court decisions in the late 1960s that struck down statutory Jim Crow segregation in the South and established the principles for heading northward. But common sense sometimes got lost in the conflating precedents.

While the seminal *Brown* decision in 1954 struck down blatant school segregation in the South, it did not even address the kind of wink-and-nod segregation practiced in Boston. Indeed, *Brown* lay dormant for years until the assault on separate and unequal school systems picked up steam in the 1960s. Even at that, initial efforts to attack the more subtle racism in Northern school systems failed. Courts weren't buying the plaintiffs' argument that the Constitution's equal-protection clause not only required an end to segregation but also conferred a right to an integrated education. Plaintiffs' suits in Gary, Indiana, and in Cincinnati and Kansas City were rejected by appeals courts and ultimately by the Supreme Court. By the mid-1960s it seemed that the courts were abiding de facto segregation, leaving in place the evolved double systems for white and black that existed in cities like Boston, hidden behind the rationale of evolved housing patterns.

But then plaintiff lawyers took a different tack, focusing instead on the intentional harm done by school boards that gerrymandered districts and selectively transferred students. Courts began accepting the legal action inherent in evasive tactics that thwarted the clear intent of *Brown* to stop segregation.

Successive federal cases piggybacked one another at the end of the 1960s. First the "freedom of choice" system of separate and unequal schools in the South fell. The next step toward Boston was a decision giving judges the right to impose busing of students as a remedy.

Garrity's task was made easier and clearer by a Supreme Court decision made at about the same time the NAACP filed suit in his court in 1972. It allowed judges to examine student assignment practices to ferret out "segregative intent." The NAACP's suit no longer had to rest on

Southern-style de jure discrimination through unconstitutional laws on the books. It could prevail by demonstrating between-the-lines de facto segregation, Boston style. In truth, the city was a lawyer's field day, offering de jure evidence with policy set out in minutes, and de facto from its practice of busing black students past underutilized white schools to overcrowded black ones.

In June 1974, with less than three months to go before school was to open, Garrity found the system intentionally segregated and ordered the school committee to implement a plan already devised by the Massachusetts Board of Education, a plan that Garrity and his consultants would tinker with for nearly two decades. For Garrity, his unfolding decision would mean death threats and deputy marshals standing guard at his Wellesley home. A man whose idea of an expletive was "criminy" had to barricade himself inside his suburban bungalow on weekends while caravans of cars from South Boston drove by, their occupants shouting and chanting obscenities at him.

But still the spartan man in the spectacles never flinched, self-assured that he had it figured out. He had read the law, had studied the maps, and had sprung a radical solution on a town used to jeremiads about balancing schools but no action.

Not this time. Suddenly the outlandish was the law of the land. Black students to South Boston and whites to Roxbury. This September. Ready or not.

At about the same time, the best hope for an equitable solution to segregated schools—the kind of shared societal burden espoused by the erudite and thoughtful Robert Coles—was shot down by a backtracking US Supreme Court. In a Detroit case, it overturned a lower court's decision mandating metropolitan busing that had set off a conflagration in the suburbs. The court ruled that because cities themselves caused the segregation, only they could solve it by balancing their own student populations.

It also meant that Boston was one of the few cities with enough white students in its system—60 percent—to have busing make a difference in getting to a balanced composition. Indeed, Detroit, with its white school population of about 20 percent, was one of the prime examples of why busing could never achieve what proponents wanted—integrated configurations. The net result was that desegregation would be an entirely urban affair and pit low-income whites and blacks against each other for the same paltry piece of pie.

In Boston they would fight over the right to go to lousy schools. At the dawn of busing, South Boston High sent 30 percent of its graduates on to higher education, and the predominantly black Dorchester High sent 28 percent. They were equal-opportunity dead ends.

But even as the Detroit case ruled out the most equitable solution, all the legal precedents enveloped Boston. They made W. Arthur Garrity omnipotent. He saw the evolved law as a perfect mosaic and began his full-steam-ahead plan for realigning the racial makeup of Boston schools. And as the protests burst all over the cityscape—and even had some liberals urging reductions in the size and age of students to be bused— Garrity's response was to begin planning even more extensive busing of students into alien turf.

As the senior senator from Massachusetts, Ted Kennedy was steeped in his family's history of pushing civil rights in the Deep South against the worst of racist America. He clearly viewed resistance in Boston as wrong-headed and small-minded.

But while he had seen the benefits of standing tall in the South, as brothers Jack and Bobby did in Alabama, he misread the magnitude of the anger and sense of betrayal in South Boston and Charlestown, the two Irish Catholic neighborhoods that would bear the brunt of the busing upheaval. If he saw the protesters as bigots, they began to see him as a Garrity apologist who lived away from the fray, in Hyannisport.

Shortly before the buses were to roll in September, a clamorous group from Southie, named ROAR (Restore Our Alienated Rights) and led by Louise Day Hicks, gathered to chant anti-busing slogans and sundry calumnies outside the federal office building downtown. Suddenly on the scene, Ted Kennedy was catnip for catcalls.

The escalating protest next to the JFK Federal Building was the first clear sign that Garrity's order would be a house afire. It turned combustible when Kennedy, who had agreed to meet with a small ROAR delegation in his office, was entering the JFK Building and saw a podium among the rambunctious crowd. Startling his aides, he impetuously headed into the crowd to address a rally in no mood for lectures about moderation or good citizenship.

At first the crowd curtly turned its back on him, but then suddenly surged around him. Within moments Kennedy was a live target for the bitter frustration that had built up in the fleeting weeks between Garrity's order and the opening of school. Eggs and tomatoes filled the air, spattering on Kennedy's coat. One woman punched him square on the shoulder. Then there were vicious, personal taunts about the accident at Chappaquiddick, his alcoholic wife, Joan, and shrill questions about why he didn't bus his own children.

Kennedy was quickly in a physical struggle to get clear of the rostrum and into his office building. He broke into a trot and then a jog as the crowd became a hounding mob. It pressed Kennedy against a huge glass doorway until a man-sized section of it shattered. The sharp noise was the only thing that slowed down the horde as a badly shaken Kennedy was able to retreat to his office on the twenty-fourth floor. A half hour later, when Kennedy talked to reporters in his office, his hands shook as he held a coffee cup, and his voice was still tremulous.

But for some in the crowd, there was a scene of rough justice. A South Boston woman, who later fled to the suburbs, said the incident was overdue. "It's about time the politicians felt the anger of the people," she said. "We've been good for too long. They'd pat us on the heads, and we'd go home. No more."

It was war out there.

One of the casualties was the "better selves" strategy of Mayor White. Before the ugly Kennedy incident, White had planned a series of low-key appeals to reason. His advisers felt his earlier virtuoso television appeal for calm was being squandered as the Kennedy rally put blood in the water for good. The planned peace overture was held hostage to the television image of a desperate Kennedy darting through the crowd. It was a vision that motivated both sides. For the anti-busers, it was "Look at him run"; for the NAACP, it was "He stood up for us."

Garrity's order had put White in the one place he abhorred—all alone, without political cover. But the dilemma it presented was his fate as Boston mayor in the 1970s—how do you retain progressive cards and liberal support without alienating blue-collar Irish? As was his wont, the mayor personalized his plight with one of his visceral metaphors. "I'm a demolition expert trying to defuse a bomb," he said. "If I make an error, I will become a paraplegic, both politically and otherwise."

Behind the scenes, he reached out to his old adversary, Louise Day Hicks. He needed a covert ally in Southie, and with her career on wane as a city councilor, she needed the mayor's clout to stock her shrinking political machine with city jobs. White hooked her up with their mutual friend, veteran troubleshooter Larry Quealy. In a secret truce, she agreed to support White's agenda before the council, alert him to trouble from anti-busers, and keep ROAR neutral when White stood for reelection the next year against Joe Timilty.

Even with the backdrop specter of Kennedy's dash for safety, White was cautiously optimistic about keeping the lid on as school opened.

Desegregation was deafening. To get up the hill to South Boston High, the buses had to race their engines, and the racket rattled the nearby three-deckers. The buses arrived in the tight formation requested by police, and parked in a snug line in front of the school. The police took positions on the sidewalk side of the buses, and the protesters on the street side. The crowd was armed with insults and eggs and beer cans. Fists and two-by-fours slammed against the arriving buses filled with black teenagers. There were chants of "Go home niggers." The bus doors slid open and terrified black students darted out.

Judge Garrity, who monitored the first day from his chamber, decided everything had gone well, with thousands of students bused to new schools. The *Boston Globe*, which had editorialized in favor of the plan, reported that school opened peacefully.

The first day's success or failure was in the eye of the beholder. Attendance was a problem from the beginning, and by the end of the school year the system had lost ten thousand students for good. On day one, 29 percent of the students did not show up. Nowhere was the attrition more obvious than in Southie. The high school had a projected enrollment of

1,300 students, but only 56 blacks and 68 whites entered its cavernous halls. At Roxbury High, only 235 of 900 assigned students showed up, nearly all of them black.

At the end of the school day in South Boston, the high school buses got out quickly and safely, but those carrying younger black children home from the nearby Gavin Middle School were bombarded by crowds that had gathered along Day Boulevard. Cans, eggs, bottles, and rocks flew at the buses. In all, eighteen buses had shattered windows or dented sides. Nine students were injured, mostly by flying glass. The youngsters were terrified by the sudden thumps and crashes and the sea of angry faces along the route, some of them children as young as themselves and some grandmothers with gray hair and twisted faces.

Yet city officials proclaimed it a satisfactory day—except in what was designated an "isolated section of the city." At a press conference, Mayor White allowed that security was going to be increased somewhat, but left unsaid that the police presence in South Boston would be quadrupled.

But it was too little, too late for horrified black parents who demanded a meeting with the mayor. One told community liaison Paul Parks, "We're tired of goddam South Boston living above the law and we want to tell him that." White reluctantly agreed to a session at the Freedom Foundation in Roxbury later that night, a meeting that shattered the mayor's wan hope that desegregation might be at least manageable if not peaceful. White arrived with some aides, but Otto Snowden told him that he would be the only white person permitted into the jammed auditorium.

The mayor opened by reiterating his earlier pledge of beefed-up security. But that fell flat. The angry crowd reached its apex when a distraught mother reminded the mayor of his televised promise that the children's safety was guaranteed. "I believed in you," she yelled, "and you let me down." The crowd exploded in a noisy condemnation of broken promises. The mayor yelled hoarsely above the crowd to give him another chance, breaking into a sweat at the thought of earlier positive neighborhood meetings being stamped out by permanent acrimony. Tomorrow, White pleaded, tomorrow will be different. There will be new rules in place, he said, and the children will be safe. White walked off to a smattering of applause and headed to a side door. He was ashen when he clambered into a waiting car. "Wow!" he kept saying. "I could have been slaughtered." Badly shaken, he was dumbstruck that he had already proclaimed the first day a success.

It only got worse, with the first public safety crisis buffeting City Hall the weekend after school opened. It started as a rumor that members of a gang in South Boston, dominated by notorious racist and killer James "Whitey" Bulger, were handing out guns to teenagers, and that they would be part of a protest march scheduled for Monday. Through an aide with national law-enforcement connections, White turned to the FBI in Boston, who began knocking on wise guys' doors to let them know they were being watched. And White worked through Majority Leader Thomas "Tip" O'Neill, who came from nearby Cambridge, to advise President Gerald Ford that federal troops might be necessary.

White also reached out to Garrity to coordinate planning for going forward. But the mayor's legitimate concern about public safety was rebuffed in the first of several icy interactions with Garrity, who viewed *ex parte* contacts with his robed self as wildly out of bounds. When a White aide called the judge at home so the mayor could brief him on the latest dire development, Garrity's wife relayed a message that the judge viewed the call itself as inappropriate and even contemptuous. Contemptuous! White was stunned. He was dealing with the president of the United States and the director of the FBI about the prospect of gunfire in his city and this local judge was telling him to get in line and file a motion.

City Hall was left stumbling around to discern Garrity's view: Could it be that the judge saw the situation as he set the policy and, without consultation, the mayor had to take it from there? White hit the roof at the thought, ranting to aides, "That stupid son of a bitch. That arrogant ass. He issues his damn order, then retires to his suburban estate and refuses to talk with the only guy who can make it work." In the paranoid Boston world of race and politics, it made the mayor wonder if the judge's Kennedy connections were in play.

White banned the march scheduled for Monday and put a massive police presence in South Boston to deal with roving bands of men and teenagers. There were a score of arrests and several injuries, but no shooting. As the week went on, another attempt to reach Garrity on public safety issues received an even sharper rebuke. The intermediary for the mayor was told the city should save it for open court.

Days later Garrity underscored his arm's-length position by making the mayor a formal party to the case. While the ivory-tower Garrity allowed that he hadn't anticipated the resistance's intensity, he still refused to take special measures to uphold public safety. He seemed to be saying to the mayor, "This deal is hard all over, so stop whining and learn to work with the school department hacks." The mayor, scrambling to get more police boots on the ground, bellowed to his staff about the obtuse judge, an arm-waving denunciation that included the ego-driven nub of it: "What the hell does he think? He's bigger than the mayor of this city?"

But September's snippy discord at the top was nothing compared to conditions on the ground. South Boston High was a daily battleground. Racial tension escalated quickly, and there were constant fist fights between black and white students all the time, mostly in the cafeteria. The headmaster was knocked to the floor during one brawl. After spaghetti flew regularly from one side of the lunch room to the other, a permanent police squad of ten was dispatched there. Fifteen more were deployed throughout the school's four floors.

On the surrounding streets, Boston's shock troops, the Tactical Patrol Force (TPF), bore the brunt of parental ire whenever there was a notable ruckus inside. Their ranks around the school were bolstered to three hundred. While many of the officers had strong Southie ties, they were soon viewed as traitors to the turf.

The bad feelings peaked on October 4—boycott day. Nearly ten thousand protesters—one third of Southie's population—marched down Broadway. The tone was defiant, and the sentiment was captured by State Senator William Bulger, a younger brother of the head of the Irish gang. "This is no time for the faint of heart," he exhorted. "The enemy can go straight to hell." As the crowd surged by the TPF contingent blocking the G Street access to the high school, bottles and stones and tirades streamed around them.

A couple of nights later, someone threw a brick through the window of a TPF cruiser and three officers chased the vandal to the front door of the Rabbit Inn, a drinking man's establishment. The bar emptied and about thirty men swarmed the police, who had to retreat. Payback was swift. The following night there was a planned assault, an out-of-control police riot based on a phony provocation. After the TPF invaded the bar, ten persons were treated at Boston City Hospital and the Rabbit Inn was as thoroughly trashed as at an Old West saloon brawl. The damage included smashed liquor bottles, overturned booths, cascaded cigarette and pinball machines, and a shattered jukebox.

Publicly, White criticized the lack of professionalism, but also made an impromptu visit to the TPF brigade at its staging area at the Bayside Mall, where it assembled each day outside of Southie to wait for word of trouble. White motioned the officers around him and confided, "The next time you guys go into the Rabbit Inn, just make sure you do twice the damage but in half the time." The men roared their approval. But bitterness lingered in Southie.

Within days of the intramural mayhem at the Rabbit Inn, the most indelible of all the violent events stained the strewn landscape. It was just short of a Mississippi lynching.

While ROAR always maintained that South Boston was not intolerant of blacks and only opposed sending its children outside its boundaries, what happened on October 7, 1974, precluded any benign interpretation of how aggrieved young men of South Boston felt about blacks on their turf.

André Yvon Jean-Louis had no idea he was taking his life in his hands when he stopped his green Dodge at a red light at the intersection of Old Colony Avenue and Dorchester Street. The Haitian janitor was on his way to pick up his wife after work, but he had just strayed into the hot zone of Boston's racial strife.

For nearly a month, the intersection had been a makeshift demonstration ground, with the crowd varying in size and intensity each day. But this day's gathering of one hundred was larger than usual, chewing on the lingering fallout of the recent violence at the Rabbit Inn. The mood was ugly when someone spotted Jean-Louis at the light.

Just the sight of a black man at the light turned the grousing crowd into a howling mob that surrounded his car and began to rock it. He frantically locked the doors, but the hooligans smashed all the windows. The door was pulled open and he was hauled into the street, where one man began punching him in the face as others held him.

Nearby, two motorcycle policemen, in the area on bus escort assignment, saw the mob and drove straight into it. The first officer to get through the crowd dismounted to pull the man punching Jean-Louis away, but then the officer was jumped from all sides and thrown on the ground. The other officer retreated, repeatedly yelling "Mayday" into his radio. The mob bore down on Jean-Louis and the fallen policeman and beat and kicked them both. One of the attackers then thought twice and pulled the black man clear of the scrum, freeing a panicked Jean-Louis to run up Dorchester Street. "Get that nigger!" someone shouted, and the race for Jean-Louis's life was on. Several men were able to run ahead of him and then head back toward him, punching the Haitian as he made his desperate way forward. He was trapped anew.

In desperate flight, he darted off the sidewalk and tried to vault a short wrought-iron fence onto a porch, hoping to break down a door to escape. But the numbers made it useless. He clung to the railing, but a man wielding a hockey stick beat his hands loose. Jean-Louis was once again on the pavement. A bearded youth kicked him in the groin.

Just as the crowd was about to resume what would surely have been a fatal beating, a responding patrolman, Robert Cunningham, ran toward the crowd, thinking, "He is going to be dead if I don't fire." He fired two warning shots in the air, and it worked. The mob stopped long enough for Cunningham to get to Jean-Louis. He and an accompanying sergeant lifted him to his feet and, guns drawn, backed away from the crowd to their crusier.

It was darkness at noon in Boston. In just one month, Ted Kennedy had been chased by a mob; the mayor had been berated at the Freedom House; the Rabbit Inn had been tossed; a Haitian had been beaten half to death; and scores had been injured inside South Boston High and on buses taking students home.

But the most feared event was yet to come—a serious injury to a white student by a black at South Boston High. On a December morning, the ambulance siren signaled that the inevitable had happened. In the fight at ten o'clock, Michael Faith was stabbed by a black youth. He was rushed to Boston City Hospital, where surgeons repaired punctures in his lungs and liver.

Word spread instantly throughout South Boston. In minutes, several hundred whites had gathered outside the school. The milling crowd expanded as white students poured out of the doors after the incident. Left inside the fortress school were 125 black students and teachers and administrators. In a contagion of spreading anxiety, fearful black parents gathered at the Bayside Mall about two miles away.

By eleven o'clock, Louise Day Hicks had arrived with a delegation of white mothers. She and Senator Bulger entered the school to talk to the headmaster and a police official. Bulger carried a bullhorn with him, but after they exited the building, he handed it off to Hicks, leaving crowd control to her. She didn't know it, but it was her farewell speech.

She was pale and without makeup when she spoke to the crowd. Though she had defused angry gatherings over the years, she'd never faced anything like the enraged one outside South Boston High that day. "You and I love South Boston and have lived here all our lives," she told them. "We have a very serious situation here. There's been an assault on one of our boys . . . my only concern is for you . . . There's only one thing I'm asking of you today. I want you to let the black children go back to Roxbury."

"No!" was the roared answer. And then: "Send 'em back to Africa! Bus 'em back to Africa!"

Again she pleaded with them. "Do it for me. . . . I'm asking you because I've been with you all the way. Please help me." "No!" was the loud and final answer. Finally a burly man boomed her swan song: "Shut up, Louise." It was an announcement that her "people" were deserting her. Blanched, bullhorn lowered, she was the one who had to go home.

After police and bus officials finessed a backdoor exit for black students, the mob slowly dispersed. But all sides knew that a knife attack on a white student had abrogated the more refined "unshared burden" argument against forced busing. Philosophy was for debates; blood in a school corridor was for the ramparts. Even moderates emphatically put safety first. The Michael Faith stabbing meant that busing would indeed not be for the faint of heart.

While Garrity was imperiously inflexible and officials were stuck with his hand-me-down state plan for busing students, he never figured out how to handle the renegades on the school committee who routinely flouted his authority. The judge kept ordering the committee to provide his court with an expanded busing plan for Phase Two in 1975 that would include the new hot spot of Charlestown. But the board buried it in broken promises. Then the Faith stabbing gave the board majority— John Kerrigan, Paul Ellison, and John McDonough—the political cover it needed. They felt they had the license to submit a sham desegregation busing plan that lacked a scintilla of specifics. And, more important, they figured that the judge would be afraid to jail them for contempt in an explosive atmosphere that would make them martyrs.

And they were right. Garrity held a contempt hearing to sternly discuss the vacuous school committee plan, but then blinked on incarceration. The upshot was that Kerrigan was able to leave federal court with his trademark smirk on his face.

Yet if Garrity had the gumption to call the committee's bluff on refusing to produce a sensible plan by putting Kerrigan and his crew in jail for contempt, it could well have cost the chairman his lawyer's license and meal ticket. It might have made Kerrigan a fleeting folk hero, but jail would have shut him down hard—and forced him to commit to something concrete and not just play to the crowd.

The frustrating dealings with the recalcitrant board left Garrity more isolated than ever. Ultimately he concluded he would have to plan Phase Two on his own, with a couple of consultants who didn't know the local history or terrain. He expanded his search for expertise, but going forward it would mostly be the three of them poring over maps and school data on a tabletop, deciding the fate of families all over Boston by sending white students hither and yon in a disruptive numbers game.

Garrity was far tougher with the White administration, which had to be responsive to a broader audience, when it began intimating that it planned to shutter South Boston High for the year. The police reported there were rumors of black and white students compiling "hit lists" after the Faith stabbing. They raised closure with beleaguered school superintendent William Leary, who was open to it. But Garrity was livid about the notion. At a hearing on the issue, the judge made it clear he thought he was being maneuvered into fixing something that local authorities had broken. Ensuring safe education was their job, not his.

Between the lines, he told the mayor's lawyers that White had let South Boston boil over and now expected the court to get him off the hook. It was another example of each man thinking the other was ducking his basic responsibilities. As White saw it, Garrity had caused a public safety calamity in his city and then refused to provide federal marshals to help restore order. As Garrity saw it, White was grandstanding to embarrass him and make him the fall guy for political problems heading into an election year.

But no blinking this time. To Garrity, closing the school would mean he had failed. So, after an extended Christmas break, South Boston High would stay open, trapped in a standoff, a sad symbol of disintegrating education, lodged between a mayor who saw most things as negotiable and a judge who saw most things as immutable. With attendance a fraction of its enrollment, the high school lumbered on through the rest of the year, with police escorts up the hill and down the hill.

White became dismayed as the crisis extended into 1975. It evolved into an unprecedented political event for the adroit mayor—everyone had their asses covered except him.

On one bad day, after a long discussion with his staff about whether to criticize President Ford for his intrusive stand against busing in Boston, the mayor found himself winging it before microphones without having resolved in his own mind how to chide Ford but not appear to abandon white parents. After making a hash of what he had to say about the president, his frustration with Garrity got the best of him at the press conference. He left the impression he would barely obey the law and might not support the Phase Two busing plan for the next school year. Confusion reigned. He ended up satisfying no one and struggled to get back on track for days. But he knew what the maelstrom had done to him. For the moment, he lamented that he was "George Wallace with a striped tie."

The internal debate, according to press aide Frank Tivnan, reflected continuing concern about White's national profile. He couldn't be George Wallace for a flickering minute. Backtracking on busing, Tivnan said, "would not help his national ambitions. And he had not let go of those. He may have pulled his hand back from the fire once in a while, but by and large he was really out there consistently saying busing is the law of the land."

Hfter the dust had settled a bit in the new year, even Garrity saw the need for some fresh views and outside input as he went about devising Phase Two. In early February 1975 he appointed a panel of four masters to help him. It was led by Eddie McCormack, the former attorney general and, more important for this assignment, a onetime city councilor from South Boston. The mission offered a conundrum—how best to expand the plan, which had only involved 40 percent of the school population in this first tumultuous year, but also attract moderates drowned out in the cacophony. For nearly two months the panel mapped a less confrontational plan for the second year while Garrity held his own counsel in his chamber.

All the while, Garrity had his own ideas for the second year and had assembled his own team led by a strong-willed integrationist, Robert Dentler, the dean of Boston University's School of Education, who had worked on desegregation plans in other cities, and his black associate dean at BU, Marvin Scott. The third member of the inside team was the judge's only link to the street, Martin Walsh, the regional director of the US Justice Department's Community Relations Service. The Dentler group retained great influence with Garrity for a dispositive decade.

The planning for the second year came down to a test of wills between Dentler and McCormack. The former attorney general had the political skills, but Dentler had an unfair advantage: Judge Garrity's ear. McCormack juggled two constituencies, the court and public opinion. He wanted to reduce the number of students bused, and spread them among more schools. Above all, he wanted to disengage the combustible

South Boston High from a high school in Roxbury. His plan was to amplify the voices of moderation that had been silenced by the bomb throwers.

The masters' plan covered the entire city except for East Boston, dividing it into nine school districts. Each wedge of the pie included black neighborhoods toward the narrow center, and white communities toward the more expansive outer rim. Whites would be bused toward the interior and blacks toward the periphery. Each student had the right to attend a school within his own district. However, the student could also opt for one of thirty-two citywide magnet schools offering special programs with enrollment ratios dictated by the system at large: 50 percent white, 35 percent black, 15 percent other minority. But district schools would be allowed to reflect the racial composition of the district itself. The percentage of white students would fluctuate widely—ranging from 80 percent at West Roxbury High to 25 percent at Dorchester's Jeremiah E. Burke School. But the biggest change was eliminating busing between South Boston and Roxbury by melding younger students from both neighborhoods to more neutral ground in Dorchester.

The plan got mostly good reviews as a balanced program that offered significant racial integration while giving white parents the hope for some neighborhood autonomy. It was supported by the *Globe* and the *Herald* and in stage whispers by White and Governor Michael Dukakis.

But the extremists on both sides didn't like it. Pixie Palladino, new to the school committee from East Boston, called it "rotten" because it still had busing. But the most influential "no" vote came from the NAACP's Thomas Atkins, a former city councilor and mayoral candidate, who urged a formulaic adherence to strict racial balancing. In April the plaintiffs filed a brief asking the court to redraw district lines in the masters' plan so that no school would be allowed to be more than 65 percent white or black. The revision would be the end of Eddie McCormack's considered view of the city. McCormack saw pressure building on Garrity to bus even more students and to keep Southie and Roxbury together.

McCormack's fears became reality on May 10, 1975. Garrity required a more uniform racial ratio across the city. He abolished the Burke High School district because it was too black, and kept the first-year combatants from South Boston and Roxbury at indefinite loggerheads. It was cautious and by the numbers, but Arthur Garrity's second-year plan ended any hope that moderates could play a meaningful role in the most momentous social issue of a generation. The judge directed even more busing and a new set of assignments that transferred many white students to a new school for the second year in a row.

The moment lost, Mayor White got off the fence, proclaiming himself "bitterly disappointed." Ed McCormack felt so betrayed that he couldn't bear to read the morning papers after Garrity's decision.

Working closely with Garrity, Dentler rewrote the masters' report stoking the extremes, making the day for the rabid anti-busers and encouraging some NAACP leaders to go to the bitter end. While it's unclear whether the masters' plan would have had a dramatic effect, what's certain is that the last chance for moderation was lost, a realization that became a chill wind.

Amid the finger-pointing and unexpected criticism, Garrity did some background politicking on his own, holding off-the-record talks with the *Globe*'s political editor, Robert Healy. Healy said they met a few times for lunch on a park bench near the waterfront, and, except for their mutual admiration of the Kennedys, it's hard to imagine a meeting of two more disparate Irishmen. On one end was Bodacious Bob, who could get away with wearing a navy blue beret with a World War II trench coat, more than an accouterment given his thirty-five combat missions over Germany as a bomber navigator. He roared with pleasure when once told he looked like a French spy. On the other end was austere Arthur, deadly serious and all business in a black suit, hands folded in his lap.

Healy was an old-school character who bridged the anything-goes *Front Page* era and ducks-in-a-row Watergate coverage. He started as a copy boy, a head start doubtless aided by his father's being a union official in the mailing room. After returning from World War II, he became a street reporter who phoned in his stories to rewrite. But he became a savvy force at political conventions and on the campaign trail. His finest hour was covering the assassination of Bobby Kennedy. He was not far behind the candidate when he was shot down in the kitchen of the

Ambassador Hotel in Los Angeles. Healy stayed up for two days, filing fact-packed stories for every edition. He was also a colorful font of old Irish sayings of dismissal. The harmlessly inept had hard noggins where you could "hang the wash between their ears." But worse still were the hopeless who didn't know it, pompous lost souls who "couldn't find their ass with either hand." He had a shrug for those who thought he crossed the line backstage as he chased a column that pushed the *Globe*'s agenda. And so he sat with the judge on a side street near the revived waterfront.

"Arthur would bring an apple," laughed Healy, who was known for copious expense accounts. "He never went too high off the hog." He said he heard from Garrity after he wrote a column carrying a message from White that the judge should adopt the masters' prescription. He said Garrity was frustrated because he believed his hands were tied when it came to modifying the state's racial-balance-law quotas requiring that no school be more than 50 percent white. That's why, Healy said, Garrity couldn't accept a plan that included a district that was 80 percent white. Yet, in the end, given the numbers, Garrity accepted districts that were not fifty-fifty.

Healy said Garrity was clearly protective about a decision that he saw as a national path forward. "He was very conscious of that. It just wasn't enforcing a local law. It was a precedent to guard."

But the ultimate extent of the Phase Two busing had its own aftermath, with the numbers disputed for a decade. Anthony Lukas contended in *Common Ground* that the busing requirement of 14,900 students, as mandated by the masters' plan, was upped by Garrity to 25,000. Dentler countered that Lukas's starting figure for the masters was short 4,000 students bused to magnet schools on the city's outskirts. Ronald Formisano, a historian who wrote a scholarly book about busing fifteen years after the firestorm, noted that the magnet-school students went there by choice and were not mandated commuters. In any event, he said, there was a 25 percent increase in those bused in the second year.

Long after the uproar subsided, Charles Glenn, the original architect for the state, rued the way his plan had played out. He decreed his plan a flop that was compounded by Garrity's bigger flop. In an article, he criticized the judge and his experts for not revising his work, but rather following the "same fatal process" that disrupted students' lives for a second year in a row. Students became hostages who were used to balance one school in the first year, only to be moved to balance yet another school in the next.

The severe dislocation left many parents demoralized, and spurred "white flight." The masters' plan could have held white students in place. Some claim it could have boosted the enrollment by ten thousand. But the student population of sixty thousand at the end of the first year—a one-third reduction—put enrollment on a steady decline.

In the wake of Garrity's Phase Two plan, many families were like distraught bystanders after a collision at a dangerous intersection. But there was nobody to call an ambulance. A "Boston mother" of six wrote Garrity after the new assignments were out in 1975. She related an *Alice in Wonderland* experience about her two youngest children. In Phase One they were assigned to a new school, even though the neighborhood school they were attending was 51 percent white. The new one was only 25 percent white and a place where her third-grader was harassed. After the first year she had hoped they could return to the neighborhood school that was a five-minute walk from her house. But no. They were scheduled for yet another school and a much longer bus ride. Her message to the judge conveyed the sad struggle of sensible people: We're law-abiding citizens, but we will never send our children to their third school in two years. "We will never allow our children to be used again in this social experiment."

It would be in the cold-comfort category, but the architect of the first year's plan wound up agreeing with much of that sentiment. Charles Glenn said he grew to recognize the value of parental choice as a factor in student assignments but conceded that the very word—"choice"—was off-putting in the beginning because of the bad connotation it carried from Southern school systems. Freedom of choice there was a forbidding technicality—black students had the theoretical right to transfer to better white schools but everyone knew better than to even try.

Glenn's major hope for Phase Two was that it adopt the student assignments of the first year. At a courthouse meeting, he pled his case to Dentler by asking him to leapfrog Phase One districts and focus on new turf. But Dentler would have none of it.

Glenn recalled: "He said to me—and I'll never forget it—'I can produce a better plan than you with both hands tied behind my back.' A rather arrogant statement, I thought." Glenn added that Dentler's reassignments in the second year were "just a terrible mistake. It meant more chaos at a difficult time." In a dramatic turn from his starting point, Glenn said that parental buy-ins on assignments became a crucial element in other desegregation plans he worked on in Massachusetts. After he left in 1991, he went on to teach at Boston University, where he wrote several scholarly works about international education and, like Dentler before him, served as Dean of the School of Education.

But Garrity's stamp on Phase Two revisions meant more mayhem on the relentless road to an antithetical result—a minority school system far more segregated than the one it was supposed to fix. It also accelerated "white flight" and put Boston farther down the road to a have-and-have-not society in which blacks and Asians and Hispanics live on the outskirts while white professionals live and work downtown.

As school was about to open, Mayor White held a briefing on the second year of busing with new school superintendent Marion Fahey, a naïve pawn of the school committee. Aides noticed White scribbling feverishly on a yellow legal pad as Fahey gave her singsong best hope for the next round of busing. One of them looked at the page after the meeting. It was covered with one phrase: "Holy shit."

By the time the buses rolled into South Boston, Tom Winship had been the catalytic editor of the *Boston Globe* for a decade, a job he inherited from his father. In ten years his high spirits had pulled the paper out of its torpor and made it the dominant media voice in town, coming out early and strong for civil rights and against the Vietnam War and bringing in new talent that fueled a run of Pulitzer prizes.

Busing to fix racial imbalance didn't just seem the reasonable solution to him. It was a moral imperative. He saw it as righting a wrong, and embraced it as a tough stance against the twisted priorities and faces he saw in the Irish neighborhoods. In an early 1967 article, writing as editor-in-chief, he pulled no punches, strongly endorsing Ed Logue's massive urban renewal program, viewing the "new Boston" as part of a better deal for city blacks. He noted that de facto segregation had "blighted" the school system and that the racial balance law offered the best way forward. His list of unfinished business in the new era included giving a "far better break to the Negro community. . . . Black power? Yes, in a constructive sense."

Tom Winship was an unabashed liberal who loved his role as a power broker in town, playing favorites in elections with abandon, viewing the role as a contact sport and one of his cherished prerogatives. Some of it seeped into the news columns. While there was usually a method to his madness, he could be mercurial and undisciplined, traits that chafed on buttoned-down William O. Taylor when he became publisher in 1978, but endeared him to reporters. His personal touch was legendary, frequently beginning conversations with "Having fun yet?" and papering the city room with "tiger" notes for good work, as in "Way to go, tiger." The ultimate accolade for a story was to have it deemed a "pissah." While the paper's old guard found him disingenuous and patronizing, he openly indulged smart young reporters, once driving to New Hampshire to bail one out who had been busted for pot. A perfect Pied Piper for the sixties and seventies, he turned an engaging Eisenhower smile toward young people. It extended to his own family; at a big gathering at his Vermont farm, he would rouse slumbering nieces and nephews at dawn in the barrackslike attic by standing at the top of the stairs, dripping from his shower with a towel barely around him, and cracking a buggy whip over them, shouting navy exclamations about pulling up their socks and greeting the day.

Globe staffers could always tell when he was in the building. There was a nearly electrical charge in the air near his office. A garrulous eccentric who reveled in it, he was straw hats come the first of May, red suspenders over striped shirts, and seersucker suits out of season. He was a story-idea machine, some wildly off the mark but others dead on, all pulled from his running notebook, an eclectic bible that he tended daily. While he gushed regularly about the promise of Boston, he stayed put in a leafy spread in Lincoln with a horse barn out back. On the train to work, he read the papers like a monkey eats a banana, tearing out stories and throwing the carcass over his shoulder. An irate commuter once bagged the detritus and mailed it to the publisher, saying this happened every day.

When the wretched behavior of the school board intersected with Garrity's powerful findings, the result morphed into a mandate for Winship. For him, that was all you needed to know. The purposeful segregation was there on the public record, with blacks getting the short end of the stick on books, buildings, and teachers. He knew some of the long-suffering NAACP litigants, and detested the school board demagogues. Since he controlled both the editorial page and news coverage, he put the *Globe* foursquare behind the court order.

There were disagreements with political editor Healy, who saw the underlying class issue in the South Boston resistance. "Tom and I disagreed about how strong we should be in favor of busing," Healy said. "Tom swallowed the thing whole. The more the better. Because of my background of growing up in Roslindale and working at the South Postal Annex in Boston at Christmas as a young guy and being in the army, I knew the brick throwers saw it as first the schools and then their jobs at the post office." But Healy kept his reservations inside the building and never put them in a column.

Winship was undeterred even as he began to understand the tough job ahead. He knew he was dealing with an epic story that needed more than just saturation coverage with the usual lineup of reporters. Busing required stronger editorial control and maybe a fresh eye from outside. That person turned out to be Robert Phelps of the *New York Times*.

It became clear that busing turmoil would be an exigent test for the *Boston Globe* with the newspaper of record trying to hold the lonely middle ground while business leaders and leading academics stayed unequivocally on the sidelines.

The freewheeling Winship's sympathies had been reflected in the tone of the *Globe*'s coverage of the Vietnam War and civil rights and the counterculture and feminist movement. But busing was different, and he seemed to sense it. It was the ultimate local story, and so volatile that only rigorous neutrality and warts-and-all reporting would protect the paper's credibility. Winship and Healy had been a great team for forging a writer's haven where good reporters were given leeway. Phelps had the tricky job of preserving that environment but making it more an editor's paper with clearly understood standards of objectivity.

In the run-up to September, the pull and tug began. Black ministers, who held sway in the publisher's office and with Winship, were imploring the paper to drop the balance standard to focus exclusively on intransigence. The paper's president, John I. Taylor, had already essentially promised them that it would accentuate the positive and downplay violence as a way to avert further trouble. In short order, South Boston leaders concluded the paper was siding with blacks—again—and boycotts of the paper were planned and then ominously followed by rifle shots into the front and back of the newspaper's plant.

The man of the moment was Phelps, who had recently been hired from the *New York Times*, where he was known for his high standards and strong pencil. But he had run afoul of the *Times*'s oppressive executive editor, Abe Rosenthal, and was dead-ended after the *Times*'s early failure to chase the Watergate scandal hard enough. An editor's editor, he had made a near religion of objectivity and sought to tighten up the too "loose" *Globe*. He adopted *New York Times*–style "story" editors to better organize and control the news spilling out of the multifaceted desegregation battle.

There was some controversy about the opening-day coverage being too soft for proclaiming the advent of busing as "generally peaceful," but the violence in South Boston was included in a comprehensive mix of stories. Later there was some debate about whether the real news of the first day was that nearly all schools opened without incident or that there was massive resistance at one.

But, in the eye of the storm for months, Phelps's commitment to even-handed journalism helped win the *Globe* a Pulitzer for its busing coverage in 1975. His eye and hand were evident in an extraordinary 150,000-word special section at year's end that recapitulated the good, the bad, and the ugly of desegregation in Boston.

The daily violence at South Boston High—two miles from the

paper's plant—spilled over to the *Globe*, which had major highways at its front and back. Nightriders put bullet holes in windows on both sides, most noticeably in the *Globe's* lobby and in the large glass façade in front of its presses. It got so dangerous that the police put sharpshooters on the paper's roof. But throughout, the *Globe's* leadership stuck by Judge Garrity and, less firmly, with the political machinations of Kevin White.

While the editor and the mayor shared many traits, especially short attention spans, Winship grew impatient with White's finger-to-the-wind approach to the issue. Indifferent to the politics, Winship urged the mayor to be more unequivocal about integration's goals.

But White had become the *Globe's* devil it knew. For all his political gyrations, White had slain the Louise Day Hicks dragon and brought in an all-star administration of Ivy League urban planners. Yet there was an uneasy undercurrent in the mayor-editor dealings during busing as White sought political cover and Winship nudged him toward unambiguous commitments. It didn't help when a story was published about Winship being the most powerful man in Boston.

But, in the final analysis, White became the *Globe's* guy for beating back Hicks and doing a respectable job during the busing maelstrom. Winship came to believe the city needed White and his team, especially when he looked at alternatives.

Winship saw White's likely opponent in 1975—state senator Joseph Timilty—as an earnest but lowbrow guy who lacked White's panache. Timilty felt the *Globe* saw him as four bad things: Irish. Catholic. Marine. Dorchester. That overlooked the fact the paper was put out largely by Irish Catholics. But there's no question that white wine and Williams College carried more weight with Winship than Budweiser and Parris Island.

Remarkably, for all the turmoil of busing, White was in the best political shape of his tenure as he entered the 1975 election year. He was still detested by the shrinking Hicks voter base, but across the city, residents didn't seem to hold busing against him. It was not his doing, it was a court order, and the mayor had done what he could to keep Boston from imploding.

In February he got the results from another secret poll by Tully

Plesser. In marked contrast with 1971, when he was seen as a weak and unfocused leader, he was now viewed as strong and in charge. He had held the city together, and respondents even commented on the dramatic change. Mayor Black was dead.

In a horse race with Timilty, White was ahead by seventeen points. But Plesser's presentation at the Parkman House came with a caveat. He told the mayor and his top advisers that the huge lead put the mayor on a pedestal. The other side, he said, will have the same numbers and conclude they have to knock White off his lofty perch. Plesser's advice: Be prepared for a dirty campaign.

That turned out to be an understatement.

CHAPTER 12

Halloween Massacre

JOSEPH TIMILTY

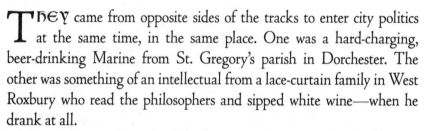

T<small>HE</small>Y came from opposite sides of the tracks to enter city politics at the same time, in the same place. One was a hard-charging, beer-drinking Marine from St. Gregory's parish in Dorchester. The other was something of an intellectual from a lace-curtain family in West Roxbury who read the philosophers and sipped white wine—when he drank at all.

In 1968, Mayor Kevin White and City Councilor Joseph Timilty arrived on the scene as Boston was shifting gears and catching its breath after a decade of fractious urban renewal. The city had lurched forward to break free of the retrograde Curley regime, but the ethnic neighborhoods were badly estranged from the frigid City Hall of John Collins, still fearful of the wrecking balls and evictions that came with someone else's idea of progress.

Timilty and White came together as the city was moving from one phase to another. They started out in the disheveled old City Hall on School Street that was overrun by clutter and folklore and, within weeks, began packing boxes to move one block to the controversial new building that had reclaimed the southeast quadrant from battered old Scollay Square, the new cornerstone of Government Center.

The two men sized each other up as ambitious pols do, probing for strengths and weaknesses. White didn't think Timilty was smart enough. Timilty doubted that White was tough enough. Both had a point.

The first conflict came quickly. Timilty said it stemmed from old-fashioned patronage, with White breaking a commitment to help a Timilty neighbor in Dorchester become a deputy fire chief. It was never discussed, but it rankled.

From then on, Timilty was looking for a fight. He got one over next to nothing, a chance conversation that blew sky-high. It happened on a sunny spring day as Timilty was headed into old City Hall and White was hanging out of one of the upper windows, gesturing and laughing in his histrionic way with someone on the street below.

Timilty yelled up to the mayor, "They invented air conditioning so guys like you wouldn't fall out of buildings." And then conciliation. "The police did a good job yesterday" in dealing with minority protesters during an angry demonstration about whether a South End site should be a parking lot or a housing project—the first skirmish at what became "Tent City."

White looked down with a slowly formed smile of little warmth. "Come up here, you. Let's have a talk."

It would be their first and last real chat. It roared downhill immediately when Timilty asked White if he was willing to put his first major initiative—the Little City Hall program—under civil service. They wrangled over whether the program was designed to allay neighborhood concerns or provide White with foot soldiers in a reelection campaign.

Timilty pressed the point, and White flared. "You don't understand, do you? This is a new day and everyone understands that but you. I've got cardinals and bank presidents lining up to kiss my ass, and I have to listen to you."

Timilty said, "OK, here's what we do on this new day. You resubmit all your programs to the council and we start from scratch."

White was on his feet yelling now. "Cardinals. Bank presidents. And you."

Both men glared as a stream of White's aides came into the inner office. A secretary reminded the mayor of his next appointment, and Timilty left without saying good-bye. But there was a spring in his step. First blood.

fast-forward seven years. A lot had happened. Mayor Black. A gubernatorial rout. Some ballast. Hicks again. The veep debacle. Busing. White had toughened up. Timilty had become a state senator with a broader view.

The one thing that had not changed was their mutual disdain. Faker Kevin. Dumbbell Joe. They had no interaction, traveling in different social circles and avoiding each other at political events to the point of back-door exits. Except for one time in what an aide to White still calls the elevator ride from hell.

The mayor and his aide were at the Sheraton in the Back Bay following a political event when the elevator door opened to Timilty and his wife, Elaine. Everyone stared daggers, and the foursome rode down in stony silence for an endless minute before bounding off in different directions. Not a word spoken. "I was soaking wet by the time we got to the lobby," said the assistant.

It should have been over before it began, with a poised incumbent mayor of national stature reigning supreme and coasting on a big lead and a ton of money. In the election of 1975, Kevin H. White should have cruised through the countryside like Sherman rolling over token opposition from Georgia to the Carolinas.

But *au contraire*.

It became a vicious brawl that ended White's hope for running for president, a mud fight reminiscent of when Curley blackmailed Fitzgerald out of the race in 1914. It still stands out as the Last Good Fight in Boston, a clawing, writhing battle that became deeply personal, a time of fear and loathing that left seasoned political pros exhausted and scarred. Issues were obliterated by charges that White presided over a corrupt regime and that Timilty was beholden to bookies and former police commanders with underworld connections.

After a slow start, the campaign became a succession of minor scandals that morphed into a charged environment that put White badly off his game. A year after Watergate had driven a corrupt president from office, there was a growing sense that White was unraveling and hiding out in his rose garden. The election became a perfect storm that combined an angry electorate fed up with high taxes and broken liberal programs and yet more busing and Vietnam ignominy. As well: a post-Watergate media consumed by "gotcha" stories in a hothouse atmosphere.

In the beginning, it was the *Boston Globe* tilting strongly toward

White and dominating the media market. But, soon enough and in an unprecedented way, Boston television heated up with critical stories about the mayor, and in the end, the *Herald* tanked for Timilty so flagrantly it probably hurt him.

City Hall became a bunker, and Frank Tivnan, the boyish-looking mix of candor and guile who was White's press secretary, remembers it with a shudder. "Seventy-five was so fucking bad, just a bloodbath. From our perspective there was a media onslaught by Channels 4, 7, and the *Herald*. It took us by surprise because Kevin had worked the media so well for so long. But we had TV guys charging around like they were prosecutors and one lurid headline in the *Herald* after another. Those three, in our eyes, couldn't have been any worse. There were all for Timilty and had personal reasons and power plays and axes to grind behind them."

From his perspective, the *Globe*'s support was lost in the maddening din, almost drowned out completely when the shelling began in the final days. "When rockets fill the air and the sky is red," Tivnan said, "the *Globe* loses its clout. Its reasoned approach doesn't get the attention and influence it usually does in a calm environment. When you've got two TV stations and the *Herald* reinforcing each other every day, it overwhelms just about everything."

And while City Hall saw the *Globe* as the lonely voice of reason, Timilty and his staff saw it as an unprincipled harlot who distorted stories to protect "their guy." In their view, the *Herald* may have gone too far at times, but TV had it straight.

The election of '75 was the culmination of the class warfare that began when Honey Fitz narrowly defeated arch-Yankee James Jackson Storrow, except this time it was an internecine Irish affair between blue-collar neighborhoods and downtown lace-curtain ones. Collins versus Powers times ten. With not much irony, Joe Timilty still insists it wasn't an all-Irish battlefield because "Kevin White isn't Irish. He's Beacon Hill."

One of Timilty's young bright lights, assistant campaign director Sydney Hanlon, who went on to be district court judge in Dorchester, said the campaign was suffused by class distinctions. The question underlying the election was whether real neighborhoods could survive without one of their own at the helm. And, most broadly, whether Boston could retain its middle class.

"The town was class driven," she said. "It was more about class than even busing. The liberals looked down their nose at anyone who said the word 'neighborhood' or talked 'white flight.' It was tough to take because these were people who sent their kids to private school and were lecturing parents on the need to send their children on dangerous trips across town to balance the schools. And it was these people who were writing Joe Timilty off as a racist without a leg to stand on."

The other view—perhaps the "haves" perspective distinctly not shared in Dorchester and Southie—was that Timilty was right, to his detriment, about White being more Beacon Hill than Irish. The mayor was seen as a charmer with vision who, with his knack for attracting talent, was on his way to turning the endlessly polarized old town into a world-class city. In this view, White's forward-looking agenda outclassed Timilty's instinct for fighting the tired old battles that nobody cared about anymore in a city turning less Irish by the day. If White was an elitist, then, well, that was all right with them.

Looking back, Mark Shields, a political commentator who worked as a consultant for White in the '75 campaign, said the mayor's élan was all the more visible because the Timilty camp had a vision deficit. The way he saw it, Timilty supporters were not "for" something as much as they were just "Down with Kevin."

"That's not a plan," Shields said. "The organizing principle was their antipathy for Kevin rather than some great competing view of where they wanted to take the city."

That said, White could get carried away with his style advantage and get downright snide. Like when he dismissed Timilty as "ignorance disguised in an attractive appearance." Strong exception noted, Timilty was not unhappy playing Everyman. "Just because I didn't go to Amherst or Smith or wherever the hell he came out of," Timlity said, "doesn't mean I don't have the experience. There are a whole lot more of people like me than like him."

"People like me" came out of the rough-and-tumble of Dorchester, where Timilty was an outstanding athlete, a former Marine, a small businessman who drove his own truck, working as driver and manager for a family linen service that was a relentless six a.m.-to-six p.m. routine, including Saturdays and every holiday except Christmas and New Year's Day. In high school, he lettered in football, hockey, and baseball, then he went to Providence College for less than a semester before joining the Marines. His brother Walter remembered him as a tough street fighter as a kid, "a big guy for his age—a pretty tough guy growing up." Joe did three years in the Marines and considered making it a career until it was clear his father was seriously ill and the family business needed him at the helm. He came home in 1960.

Timilty was a neighborhood jock who also had a strong political pedigree. His uncle and namesake had been a police commissioner and one-time candidate for mayor who was the son of turn-of-the-century senator Diamond Jim Timilty. Joe's grandfather started off in the city yards, but ended up with a construction company that did very well under Curley.

His uncle was a confidant of Joseph Kennedy, the founding father of the clan. Both Ted and Bob Kennedy occasionally stayed with Uncle Joe while they were students at Milton Academy. Young Joe worked for Ted in the 1962 campaign, just as Kevin White was with Eddie McCormack. In 1961 he married Elaine Benson, a South Boston woman he had known since grade school.

He got into politics for one reason—to be mayor of Boston. He showed his tenacity by running unsuccessfully for the City Council twice before winning in 1967, the year White was elected. Timilty finished third for mayor in 1971, and came away from the election thinking he could take White if he got him alone in a final. In the aftermath, he felt he needed a higher profile and a change of scenery from the dilatory, backbiting council. He moved on to the state senate in 1972 by beating the redoubtable if aging Michael Paul Feeney in a special election, and he always said that Feeney would have beaten him in his prime.

He and Elaine had five sons and two daughters, with the oldest son a Marine and the youngest son holding a doctorate in the classics. Two followed him into politics. Elaine's perspective on politics was to make sure it didn't mean her children were brought up by babysitters.

As a senator, Timilty was increasingly seen as a progressive, the right-wing Marine softening and moving to the center, especially with a crucial vote against capital punishment at the State House. Elaine saw a difference as he headed into his axle-breaking confrontation with Kevin White: "He's mellower and has a broader scope."

Not that he was laid back on the stump. Timilty might get beaten, but he was never outworked. He thrived on the menial stuff that drove White crazy—pressing the flesh at subway stops in the morning and running ragged doing fund-raisers and house parties at night. He wasn't as sophisticated or beguiling as White could be, but Timilty was comfortable and casual with voters who were usually taken with his rugged looks and impeccable head-to-toe appearance. At a minimum, he could do two things White wouldn't—talk baseball over a beer.

But there was an elusive quality to Timilty, a military close-to-the-vest manner. His top press aide, Ed Jesser, said, "You know Joe and you don't know Joe. He can shut down. But you knew his basic qualities and that's what kept everyone loyal to him. He is decent and indefatigable. He had this boundless energy. During the campaign, we'd all go to a café in Roslindale Square at ten at night. He'd have three quick beers and then he'd be gone. And he'd be the first guy in the next morning.

"He never wanted any information longer than two pages. There was just so much that he was willing to keep track of. He hated clutter. He had three aides at the State House and a nothing office. He just needed a place to keep warm so he could run for mayor. What I remember most is how he always kept moving. Even when he was at home with his family. He ate his meals standing up, moving between the table and the refrigerator and the refrigerator and the cabinets, picking up this and picking up that."

After a slow start, the 1975 campaign began with a sudden thump in mid-April when White was blindsided by an investigative story in the *Globe* that his fire commissioner, James Kelly, had been strong-arming the rank and file for cash contributions to the mayor in a pony-up-for-promotions scheme.

It was a public-relations disaster that dimmed the progressive halo around White and gave Timilty the opening to start chanting "faker" at the mayor.

The response from the White camp was bungled. At first both Kelly and White denied fund-raising was even taking place. Kelly: "We're only interested in saving people's lives." But the commissioner quickly back-tracked when reporters confronted him with copies of his fund-raising letters to firemen. He then said well, OK, but no arm-twisting. A few miles away at City Hall, White first said there was no fund-raising at all, and then that he wasn't sure. After the interview, when he learned that Kelly had come clean, an agitated mayor called one of the reporters at home to insist he had been truly in the dark about a long-standing shakedown on his behalf in the fire department. "I'm telling you the truth," he said. "Do you believe me? I need you to believe me. Say it with me—I believe you, Kevin."

An investigation by the state attorney general knocked the mayor off his white steed, leaving him paralyzed for weeks by the likelihood that Kelly and some aides would be indicted and that he might be impli-cated in a pay-to-play conspiracy. Kelly was indicted before the primary, but acquitted after the election was over. White, however, never got his legs fully under him as the race unfolded.

It was a searing lesson in the vicissitudes of politics. In three short years, White had rebounded from the McGovern disappointment to emerge stronger for the unforgiving furies of busing, only to take a tumble that left his reformer status in doubt and vulnerable to a man he detested. It took him weeks to recover.

Paul Goodrich, Timilty's campaign manager, said that corruption was not his camp's original focus. As it began, he thought the Timilty narrative was going to be "aloof Kevin" being too uppity for a job that "man of the people Joe" was dying to do. But he said the sudden fire department scandal got at how complacent White had become and how far he really was from his clean-cut image. It became the opening they were waiting for.

At the end of April, Timilty declared his candidacy with a fore-shadowing of what would be his major issue—a climate of corruption at City Hall.

White's media advisers saw it as an immediate dilemma, leaving them to wrestle with a media in gunslinger mode. The problem, said press aide Ralph Whitehead, was that there never was a concrete charge that could be rebutted. Instead, he said they were enveloped by an atmospheric catchphrase, "a climate of corruption," that would build on itself with each new charge, no matter how threadbare.

Whitehead, a Chicago journalist turned professor at UMass–Amherst, cut his teeth on politics in the torrid campaign of 1975. He was chosen as press secretary for the campaign to keep election media separate from City Hall. It was sort of a summer job for the laid-back Whitehead, who wasn't looking to catch on with the White administration. He had a good job but wanted political education from the trenches. And that he got. Years later, he still views the campaign as a dangerous time for journalism when inexperienced reporters with little supervision jumped headlong into the muckraking pool. Whitehead remembers it vividly for the wretched excesses of post-Watergate fervor. While he saw the fever subside as the years went by, he retains his Rule of '75: "Muck expands indefinitely to occupy the available rakes."

Timilty's press aide has a different perspective, focusing on the journalistic exposé that stuck. Ed Jesser wryly acknowledged that the firefighter scandal was "our nuclear weapon. It was clear that these noblest of creatures, the friendly local firemen, were forced to give money to evil ward bosses to be promoted. From that point on, we were able to keep the pressure on White, and he did not respond well to it. We could chart the progress in our polls over the spring and summer. We'd inch up and White would inch down. And we could move faster on things. White was weighted down by having to defend his policy record. Joe had only a voting record to defend, and nearly all of it was good for Boston."

But even with the scandal serendipity, Timilty was badly outgunned in resources and tested political operatives. White's charm may have evaporated for a while, but his political team was still the best ever assembled for a city election. Curtis Wilkie, new to Boston out of Mississippi but the *Globe*'s main reporter on the election, who went on to cover eight presidential campaigns, said White's 1975 staff had the most talent under one roof he ever saw. "They were real smart and real hard-nosed," Wilkie said. "They all went on to do very well in the political trenches."

Despite the advantages of a flummoxed White and a compelling campaign theme, Timilty was still up against it. He had no money, no name recognition, little press, and a hostile *Globe* because of political editor Robert Healy constantly pushing White in his column.

And despite some considerable strengths, Timilty's inner circle was a green team overmatched by White's pros, a committed group that still didn't know what it didn't know. Besides pollster Pat Caddell, who had worked for Dukakis and would rise to national prominence with Jimmy Carter, and strategist David Garth of New York, they were mostly political junkies, several of them lefties who'd cut their teeth working for McGovern. According to Jesser, the big intangible asset his team had was Timilty himself: a tough Marine with a great-looking family who was a lot smarter than he got credit for. "He knew the issues. And he was the hardest worker you ever saw. He really wanted that job and it showed. Joe had pockets of people around the city who would kill for him."

As Timilty's unit felt its way along, White's people, after the fire department disaster, didn't make a major mistake the rest of the way. But they struggled with one huge deficiency beyond their control—a candidate without two feet on the ground. The mayor would disappear for days, and they had to make excuses for him not campaigning while having no idea where he was. Most seasoned pols would be miffed by media criticism, then fake it, even laugh it off. But White brooded, stewing in black Irish juice.

It took months for White to discuss the ramifications of the fire department fund-raising, finally telling the *Globe*'s Wilkie in a rambling seventy-five-minute interview, as he moved continuously from chair to chair in his office "like a restless cat," that the charges had "a psychological effect on everyone around here," and that "there's been some damage to me at least inwardly."

But that was too defensive for his advisers, who pushed him to go on the offensive in mid-August with what had been a whispering background campaign among selected reporters that Timilty had mob associates. In a *Globe* interview, White directly assailed Timilty's ties with bookies Donald Killeen, who had been murdered in gangland fashion in 1972, and Bernie McGarry, who had died of natural causes in 1974. The mayor backed into it by saying his friends were of a higher caliber than Timilty's. "I've never associated with some elements in this town. . . . Joe Timilty and I don't associate with the same type of people. And they are the measure of the man."

Timilty welcomed the innuendo as an attack that wouldn't stand up and would make White look bad. While Timilty knew both Killeen and McGarry casually, he had nothing to do with their businesses, and the low blow made the lordly White seem the grubby pol. Timilty's answer, in effect, was damn straight we don't like the same people.

At the time, Timilty conceded but downplayed a relationship with McGarry, who was a friend of his father's, and Killeen, who was the dominant bookmaker in Southie until his assassination. Years later, he made no bones about it. "Donald Killeen was a friend of mine. When he put up Timilty signs in South Boston, they stayed put up. I enjoyed his company. But I certainly didn't get involved in any of Donald's business. So, I knew it couldn't amount to any real damage. Plus, I finally had White getting into the fray. I thought we could mix it up and I could win on that one. When it came down to it, all they could say was I knew a bookie who got killed years earlier. And I could scream dirty pool."

While the evolving campaign became unremittingly tense, the bookie issue was one of the few that offered some comic relief. Timilty was scheduled to speak at a Polish club in Dorchester on a Friday night when the campaign got word that a bookie was working the crowd at the bar and posing as a potentially embarrassing encounter for Timilty, who would shake hands with anyone who had a pulse.

Assistant campaign director Hanlon—who had worked in the McGovern campaign while at Brown University, and in Dukakis's winning gubernatorial effort in 1974 while at Harvard Law School— decided she would head off trouble at the Polish club.

So there she was, twenty-five years old, barely five feet tall, but hands on hips, working her way down the bar, demanding to know from each male patron if he was a bookie, and if he was, would he please leave before the press showed up. "Who's the bookie who's going to get Joe Timilty in trouble tonight?" she asked, one by one. One of the men silently got up and left by the back door. Mission accomplished.

But there was a second, more ominous part of the character assault that seeped into the media—that Timilty was close to deposed police commanders with purported underworld ties who would return to power if Timilty was elected. It was in the same vague innuendo category as the bookies—Timilty did know a superintendent who had financial ties to a tow-truck company he supervised, and another who had mob associates. Both commanders' names were found on a bookie payoff list that led to their sudden transfers followed by quiet retirements. But Timilty had only had cursory contact with them as a city councilor on public safety issues and neither was active in his campaign. Given their baggage, it's inconceivable that either would have been rehired if Timilty was elected. Yet their shadowy reputation would reemerge as a sudden melodrama in the final days.

To keep it alive, White began including his 1972 hiring of a Mr. Clean outsider as police commissioner as part of his litany of accomplishments. In addition to the city economy being in decent shape and a stable tax rate for four years, he talked about how he revamped a police department that had been stung by a payoff scandal with bookies. In his second term, White had hired a chief from St. Louis who cleaned house. Robert DiGrazia had brought his big frame and good looks from the Midwest and soon had the highest favorability rating of any public figure in the city. But could he keep his boots clean when it got muddy in Boston?

As the summer was ending, White's tentative reentry into retail politics was receiving mixed reviews, even inside his camp. His advisers devised a high-risk strategy to take him off the streets after several fumbling public appearances at political events. It had gotten so bad that White was seen pulling up to a rally, scanning the scene, and—not liking it— roaring off, leaving aides to ad lib an excuse for the missing mayor.

The new tactic was to have White be AWOL but for the commonweal. About two weeks before school opened for Phase Two of busing in September, White announced he was stopping his campaign to plan a smooth beginning of the academic year. The hiatus would not only eliminate missteps, but would also mean Timilty would be left to flail away on the stump by himself. All the while, White would be mayoral on television every night with police and Governor Dukakis assuring parents that students would be safe this time around.

Even White was of two minds about the double-down bet: If busing went well, he'd be off the dreaded stump and ducking all the other issues. But, as the mayor asked rhetorically, what if busing goes poorly and "eats me up"?

The strategy slowly backfired as TV images shifted from White's reassuring firmness to club-wielding cops wading into yards of irate parents as rock-throwing youngsters circled behind them. What started well for White ended up to Timilty's advantage, with undecided voters moving his way, especially moderate anti-busers.

And Timilty didn't have to do any grandstanding to please the Hicks vote, winning kudos in the media for not playing the race card by calling for resistance on the street or by a school boycott. Hicks, by then a firm if secret ally of White's, trotted out her Tweedledum-Tweedledee dismissal of the race, indicating there was no substantive difference between the two candidates as part of a sly artifice to help White by keeping her voters at home.

The closest Timilty got to making political use of the renewed busing turmoil was a television ad with three of his sons in front of a neighborhood school where he reaffirmed his opposition to the court's remedy, but then emphasized his commitment to safe passage for children. It was not even close to the red meat that the diehards—and most of his staff—were demanding. His campaign mantra focused on Boston's deteriorating lifestyle—that it had the nation's highest cost of living, an unemployment rate second only to Detroit's, and the third highest level of violent crime of major cities.

Looking back, Timilty said it was tempting to go with pollster Caddell's advice to give an aggressive speech urging resistance that could have delivered a jump of eight points in the polls—or just about all the undecided vote. But that went against Timilty's gut, and he thought his more calibrated stance was good enough. "I had a strong position on busing," he said. "I thought it was wrongheaded. It was devastating to the city as a whole. There were no winners out of that mess. Black kids get a better education? No. School more balanced? They're worse.

"But back then I was constantly preoccupied by what a minefield it had become. You had kids riding around in buses and people throwing rocks at the windows. Say the wrong thing and some kids would pay for it. It was a heavy responsibility. In some ways, it was easy for me. I had three of my own kids on those buses. But I was stuck in place and could not really capitalize on what should have been a bigger advantage for me. And White's people knew it. I could not say what I really wanted to say because I was afraid some kids would pay for it. 'Stop the madness' was what I wanted to say. 'It's not gonna work.' But it would have promoted violent resistance and it was out, just out.

"And it was tough. Every day I had my best people saying to me, 'Say something different. Stop the buses. Boycott the schools. Keep the kids home. Block the buses. We all know how you feel about it. So do something.' I'd say, 'No, no, and no. It's a bad time and I'm not about to make it worse.'"

But busing was a problem for White as well. He lost his bet that being mayoral on television would get a restrained school opening. The vehemence was dialed down slightly from year one, but the video was still something out of the French Revolution, with insurgents charging through the streets of South Boston and Charlestown and battling with cops wearing face masks and body shields. If it wasn't quite bedlam, the electorate seemed to have grasped that the mayor was hiding behind the two thousand cops needed to maintain a fragile peace in a city under guard.

What's more, it was clear that White was going to have to change his ways if he was going to win. Even late in August, White was still the aloof loner who ducked a commitment for a "safe" Back Bay house party to go to the movies by himself. He began to realize that not pressing the flesh was reaching the street as indifference and that behaving like a "Boston pol" might not be so bad for someone wanting a third term as mayor.

It turned around somewhat for White when a small success paid a large dividend. Press secretary Tivnan recalled that the bunker period for the mayor had led to a house divided at City Hall. "Most saw the need to get him back circulating, but some said, 'No, wait, he's not in a good place and let's ride it out and he'll come around.' My advice was 'Let us set up mayoral events and you go act mayoral.' But he did not buy it for the longest time.

"But, finally, we had a breakthrough on a hot summer night. The city was selling surplus property—a pretty mundane thing, but the events were popular and drew crowds. It was in Brighton and tied in with some community event. Kevin was reluctant, did not do it willingly, but once he got there, his whole personality changed. He had a great night. From that point on, we could get him out to neighborhood events."

After the schools simmered down a bit, White acknowledged his busing strategy had been a bust. He returned to active campaigning a few days before the preliminary election, but, still shaky, adamantly refused a television debate with Timilty. In a *Globe* interview after he resumed formal campaigning, White revealed a siege mentality. "That place [City Hall]," he said, "is a pressure cooker and the slats [top aides] were going out from under me. I was lashing out at the press in particular, maybe perceiving ghosts and goblins that weren't there. I saw a potential run on the corporation." His growing fear was he'd be washed up at forty-six with no job and no prospect except a law-office life that would drive him crazy in twenty minutes.

At that time, Timilty felt himself gaining ground that was verified by his polls and the rare indecision he saw in the White camp. Timilty sensed something tentative in the other camp. It was also around the time that his aides obtained a leaked memo that urged White to "tarnish" Timilty. "They realized they could not win with White just being Kevin White," Timilty recalled. "It became clear he was finished on that basis. His so-called charm had run its course. So they decided, Kevin, here's what you have to do—you have to go after Timilty. As the race tightened, they had to muck me up."

White got a temporary boost from a *Globe* poll two days before the primary that gave him better than a two-to-one lead, 52 percent to

25 percent. But it was a fleeting mirage when the winning margin turned out to be less than half of the twenty-seven-point forecast. Even White's campaign manager said that "we gave more credibility to the *Globe* poll than we should have."

The 54.2-to-43.2-percent finish was nearly all good news for Timilty. He clearly benefited from an anti-busing backlash, especially in South Boston and Hyde Park, but the light turnout—38.6 percent, the second lowest preliminary in twenty years—meant many anti-busers stayed home. White allowed that "statistically we won, but psychologically we got cut up a little in the last rounds."

What the results really meant was that the mayor was in a dogfight and that the resounding bump from a big victory, so necessary for his national ambitions, was in ashes. His hopes for a long-shot place on the 1976 ticket were slipping away in slow motion. He told the *Herald*, "This has been the toughest year of my life. . . . It's been the most difficult year in the last thirty years to be mayor of this city. We've got the police out there going into crowds with horses and dogs."

But then White caught a huge break that he had nothing to do with. The final six weeks of the campaign were effectively cut in half by baseball. The Red Sox became the only story in a baseball-mad town when the team got into a hard-fought World Series. For three weeks the Big Red Machine from Cincinnati, with Hall of Fame players such as Johnny Bench and Joe Morgan, were all that voters and the media cared about. After the second game, White was only too happy to bask in reflected glory in his seat behind the dugout. "The town's heart was at the ball park," said the mayor. "The whole town is caught up with it. This town is entitled to have all this enthusiasm and euphoria over the Red Sox after all it has gone through." But he was talking about himself.

Even though the town was awash in baseball, the sports analogy for the final stretch belonged to football. White adopted the "ball control" offense of the old Green Bay Packers, with the mayor moving steadily down the field with short runs and safe slant passes. And he could dictate the pace despite Timilty's prodding for a debate and issuing papers on neighborhoods, crime, and city taxes. With two and a half weeks to go—and the Red Sox still playing—Timilty needed a jolt, either a racial incident to underscore busing's bleak trap one more time or a new corruption charge to get White out into the open field.

And he got one.

It came to Joe Timilty directly, who kept it away from most of his staff except for his evil twin, Robert Caulfield, a media maven who was connected all over town and whose high energy had him holding the toughest job in television for years—news director at Boston stations. He hated Kevin White about something personal that no one ever quite figured out. On the wagon, Caulfield still chain-smoked his way across the city's watering holes every night, massaging contacts and dropping dimes.

Timilty said he brought Caulfield a game-changer who was delivered from an unlikely source—Yankee developer Gerald Blakeley. Timilty said Blakeley was affronted by what White had done to him and other real-estate moguls when he ran for governor five years earlier. White had convened a fund-raising breakfast at the Ritz in May 1970. Among the score of "invited" guests was Blakeley, who was also the owner of the hotel itself, but whose major business was running the Cabot, Cabot & Forbes realty firm. White was accompanied by two aides who could cause developers maximum trouble—the assessing and building commissioners.

Timilty said Blakeley remembered well that Timilty had helped him with the development of the 60 State Street building when he was a city councilor, and that White had been difficult. Timilty said what bothered Blakeley the most was the shakedown aura of the five-year-old Ritz breakfast. "Yankees don't like to be held up," Timilty said.

Blakeley backed Timilty for mayor with a donation that was deemed apostasy by White. Timilty: "Blakeley contributed to me and then the shit hit the fan for him. He was seen as a traitor by White. But he is how I learned about the breakfast and I passed it along to Caulfield."

In turn, Caulfield handed it off to a vaguely disreputable television reporter, Jack Kelly, who rushed it on the air without running it by any of the principals. The story was promptly denounced as shoddy journalism as all the moguls ran for cover. But it became the story that refused to die, partly because Caulfield had adopted it as a personal mission. And because White couldn't keep his story straight.

The more that came out, the worse it got. White first said the breakfast never happened. Then that it did happen, but he wasn't there. Then that he was there, but had nothing to do with any fund-raising. With Caulfield stoking the flames, the rest of the Timilty camp simply got out of the way.

As the Ritz story unfolded, Timilty campaign manager Goodrich said it was hard to figure if it was all sinking in. "It was a complicated story to tell. But did it help us? Sure it did. It put the White camp into a permanent retreat."

Somehow, what started as a one-day story—a five-year-old incident with all parties denying all—caught hold. White singlehandedly turned it into a thunderclap by repeatedly lying about it and getting caught by documentation. The event that didn't happen had a recorded guest list and a Ritz breakfast tab of $282.20 that was paid by City Hall.

But at first blush, when White's aides thought they had all the developers in buttoned-down denial, the mayor issued a blanket denial that would stick like flypaper. To wit: "The meeting never even occurred. I couldn't be more emphatic." And words to eat: "If I'm lying, I don't deserve to be mayor."

Both sides would claim the Ritz story had become a smear tactic. Timilty cried foul at stories intimating that the underworld had a role in getting the story on television. White fumed about continuing stories with unnamed sources saying developers were shaken down. But Timilty had the facts on his side. And the Ritz firestorm revealed the fissures within the police department itself, with the hierarchy siding with White but the rank and file pulling for Timilty.

The day after the World Series, which had ended with another dispiriting Red Sox defeat, the two candidates finally had their only debate. But it was a low-wattage affair on the radio at ten in the morning. White did a lot of deflecting and complaining about "dirty" politics, but generally held off an overly pugnacious Timilty. The most telling exchange happened after the debate as the candidate headed to the door with Timilty still swinging and White still patronizing.

On the way out, White bade Timilty a sarcastic farewell: "Joseph, thank you." Timilty: "Why not have a ninety-minute TV debate? What are you afraid of?" White: "Your articulateness." When Timilty pressed him again for the TV debate, White said, "Oh, Joe."

Less than a week from the final election, a *Globe* editorial chided White for not being more forthcoming about the Ritz, but turned that into a compliment for his not being accused of taking the illegal contributions for personal use. Despite the facts at hand, it concluded with a career award: "Kevin White has been one of the best mayors this city has had."

But if the *Globe* was way out front for White, it was subdued compared to the *Herald*'s tanking for Timilty in the last two weeks. Between the lines, the hand of former mayor John Collins and his long-standing animus for White was visible as the paper ran recycled Timilty position papers and front-page editorials and weak "exposés." One of them had a former state secretary of elder affairs contending that White's workers made unauthorized use of his name in a letter to senior citizens in Allston-Brighton. Kirk O'Donnell, White's astute young campaign manager, felt that the weak story meant the mayor's campaign had finally turned the corner. Even high-level Timilty aides were ambivalent about a page-one endorsement from Collins, feeling it was a backward tug from a mayor who had alienated the neighborhoods Timilty was courting.

But the real difference in the race was the Halloween massacre of 1975.

for weeks, Bob Caulfield had been telling Timilty that it would get rough at the end, and it would be personal and it would come from DiGrazia, who was about the only political figure in town with any stature as the campaign slouched to the finish line. Since Timilty was a two-term city councilor and new state senator who had filed only a handful of bills, there was virtually no track record to attack. So it would have to be aspersions about his background and character.

Timilty remembers it as if it were yesterday.

Two nights before Halloween, he and some campaign aides were at a big media event at an Italian restaurant in the Back Bay, hosted by a television broadcasters' association. Timilty's group was milling around outside on Dartmouth Street as DiGrazia and his retinue made a noisy exit. Timilty recalled that "they had had a couple drinks and were smirking as they headed for their cars. I couldn't resist a comment as they passed by. I said to DiGrazia, 'There isn't a good cop here if they put all of you guys together.' And DiGrazia said, 'You won't be so happy tomorrow. You won't be so smart tomorrow.' "

What the police commissioner meant was a press conference he would hold the next morning that put him in the fray with another recycled assertion of impropriety. This time it was that Timilty was under the influence of deposed cops who wanted back in. But the new twist was that the charge came from the highly regarded top cop.

Timilty: "It was complete nonsense. But it stopped our momentum. Bang. The polls showed it. You could feel it."

On the day before Halloween, the *Globe*'s Curtis Wilkie was assigned to a police headquarters press conference at eleven a.m. He was none too happy about it, even before he got the details. He recalled thinking, "I don't cover the police department. I had never even talked to DiGrazia before. I scratched my head and went to my city room pod with seven other people, one of them being [*Globe* columnist Michael] Barnicle. So I was grousing about having to go see DiGrazia and what the fuck is this about? Barnicle laughed and said that he had just left the police department and saw one of White's political guys, Mark Shields, there. So the bulb went off in my head about what was going on—that there was a political background."

Earlier that morning at City Hall, it was press secretary Frank Tivnan who was none too happy. He had been bigfooted by Shields, who was looking over Tivnan's shoulder as he wrote copy that DiGrazia was to deliver. The scriptwriting was the last in a series of tense meetings held that morning, discussions that Tivnan said "were not a good portrait of government in action. Tensions were very high. We knew we were slipping very badly in the polls. And we knew a hostile media would play up something good for Timilty and downplay anything good for

White. Unless—*unless*—what we said was so powerful that they could not ignore it. There was a feeling that, with all the mudslinging in both directions, neither Timilty nor White had any credibility left. The only guy left standing with credibility was the police commissioner. The notion was pushed by Mark Shields, and it became his production. He was all over the planning and plotting of it that day."

While Tivnan chafed at Shields's aggressive style, he had agreed with White's gut instinct in October, when the race was tightening by the day, that his team needed someone from outside with political savvy, someone not swimming in all the day-to-day details, who could take a big-picture look at the landscape. That became Shields, a shrewd political operative with local ties who was brought in from Washington, D.C. The onetime altar boy from Weymouth was a full-steam-ahead ex-Marine who played rough. He had worked on the presidential campaigns of Robert Kennedy and Edmund Muskie, and would go on to write a column for the *Washington Post* and then find his niche as an amiable, quick-witted commentator for public television.

Years later, Shields shrugs and says of course he turned to a "white knight" with sky-high favorable ratings when everybody else was out of juice. "His numbers were astounding, they were something like seventy-five (favorable) to twelve. We wanted to turn it into a DiGrazia versus Timilty race. We wanted it to be a referendum on DiGrazia instead of Kevin. The way we framed it was DiGrazia would leave town if Timilty won. The question was, do you want to keep him as Top Cop or not? Some may say it was inappropriate for the commissioner to get into the fray at that stage, but it shouldn't have come as any surprise. He was Kevin's guy."

It proved to be a controversial master stroke. Tivnan said the dividends were immediate and that White's staff felt the same shift that scared the Timilty camp. "The DiGrazia thing was very important for us," he said. "It gave us a leg up at a time we were hurting badly. It stopped them from driving across the goal line and allowed us to head in the other direction. The mayor became a better candidate after DiGrazia. He was dog-tired and sick of it all, yet more clear-eyed. It picked him up."

But what got lost in the weary celebration was this—was it true?

DiGrazia's entry into the race put a new face on recycled charges. But this time they came from the tall persona and reformer rectitude of the commissioner. The mayor's handlers were after an image as much as a message and they got one in a telegenic, self-assured DiGrazia. Depending on the point of view, he was either dynamic or smarmy.

The first salvo was a full media push. The *Globe* story, published on Halloween, was nuanced and noted that DiGrazia had waded into the final days of a torrid race and that he acknowledged meeting that day with Shields. But most of the other media treated it as a bulletin from Olympus.

The message, originally floated during the summer, was as elusive as ever: Timilty had been "influenced" by cops forced out of office by DiGrazia. But the commissioner would neither name names nor elaborate on any connections between bad cops and Timilty. He simply made the charge, but offered no proof. In fact he had none, as that would have required two things he didn't have—clear-cut evidence that certain cops were dirty and, just as important, that they were involved with the Timilty campaign.

Instead he wrapped himself in his own flag, quickly shifting away from the purported conspiracy into whether his reform agenda was now in jeopardy. He said it was "obvious" his reappointment had become a campaign issue, even though it had never gotten big play and Timilty had recently said he would retain DiGrazia at least until his term expired in 1977.

DiGrazia posed his own straw-man question: Could the public get Timilty *and* DiGrazia? "There is no way those people [deposed commanders] would allow him to retain me in this position," the commissioner said. "If he's elected, I'm gone." And his reform measures would "go no further."

And the last-minute offensive had a second installment. It came the following day in a WBZ radio and television report and in the *Globe*. It was yet another "investigation" from White's agent in the police department, traffic-cop-cum-superintendent John Doyle. But this time DiGrazia let himself be the conduit for a contention by Doyle that organized crime had played a role in getting the Ritz story on the air as part of an effort to defeat White. Lost in all the innuendo was that even if it was true, it had nothing to do with Timilty.

While DiGrazia did little more than put his imprimatur on Doyle's report, it gave unsubstantiated allegations from an unnamed police informant much more altitude than they warranted. The *Globe* story contained excerpts from the Doyle report that contended Jimmy Martorano of the Winter Hill Gang put one of the developers at the Ritz fund-raiser together with Jack Kelly of Channel 7. In an interview, Kelly, who broadcast the initial report, confirmed he knew Martorano, but said it was part of his beat to know wise guys.*

While the *Herald* jumped in to decry the McCarthy-style tactics by DiGrazia, the Timilty camp feared a mortal wound.

Sidney Hanlon: "Everyone was worried about it right away, and it really did have a dire effect, even with the no names and innuendoes and all that. People were not as cynical then and DiGrazia was this big appealing authority figure. And Boston was not Los Angeles with its history of corrupt cops. I think enough people wondered—could this be true? It was a bad question at the end and it hurt."

Paul Goodrich: "Our polls showed us in a dead heat at 47–47 and with a clear edge in the six percent undecideds, who were all leaning our way, going against a two-term incumbent. At that point, who's undecided about Kevin White? So we were taking them five to two. If we stayed on course, we would have won by about two percent. DiGrazia stopped the rush our way. He gave voters a reason to rethink Timilty. A serious person was raising some serious questions, and there was no time for answers."

At the end of a long, tense election night, White won by taking just about all the undecideds. His margin of victory was the tightest of any

---

* In fact, Kelly knew underworld characters all too well. Just three years later, he was massacred with four others at a Mob restaurant while playing cards. It was raided by masked men looking for cash and cocaine who opened fire when one of them was recognized.

race since the adoption of the 1951 Plan A electoral system of September preliminary and November final. The tally was White with 81,187 votes, or 52 percent, versus 73,659, or 48 percent, for Timilty.

Timilty's concession came after a five-minute standing ovation. He began congratulating Kevin White, but was interrupted by shouts of "No, no!" and "Recount!" As solace for everyone, he said, "Like the Red Sox we took the battle to the last half of the ninth in the seventh game."

White had won the Italian vote in East Boston and the North End, the liberal vote in Back Bay and Beacon Hill, the black vote in Roxbury and Mattapan; he had eked out a transition neighborhood in Jamaica Plain and was strong with the elderly in Allston-Brighton.

White told the *Globe* on election night, "I thought I was gone. I really did. No bullshit. I thought it was gone. Oh yeah . . . it was the whole thing: busing, time for a change, everything." In the immediate aftermath, the mayor sat sullenly on his meager victory and fumed anew about media mistreatment. He entered the hospital for exhaustion after it was over.

Timilty spent the day after working off the tension in the best way he knew how—a ferocious game of handball at the YMCA. In interviews, he said politics was not about getting knocked down but about getting back up, but when the questions stopped, he looked off blankly into the mid-distance as if to see what had happened.

Decades later, his jaw sets hard when he talks of 1975, about his unshakable belief that DiGrazia and the *Globe* stopped him in the "red zone" as he was about to score. He noted in passing that DiGrazia got his comeuppance when, having sought reappointment through a smear, he got fired by White anyway. "I thought DiGrazia was stronger than that, but he wasn't. Hey, they deserved each other."

But it's the *Globe* that sticks in his craw. The way he sees it, politics is supposed to be a rough game, but a newspaper is supposed to play it down the middle. He said the *Globe*'s editorial page failed on two fronts: it never pulled all the evidence of malfeasance together into an overall assessment of White's tenure, and it took no position on a television debate. "When's the last time that a major media outlet did not scream for a debate in a hotly contested race?"

Timilty and the *Globe*'s Healy agree on little about 1975, but have the same bottom lines for vastly different reasons. Healy still takes some pride in being part of a winning strategy that reelected White. "There's no question that DiGrazia and *Globe* support tipped the scales," Healy said. "And it worked because it was true—the bookies were all over Timilty."

Asked why there were no stories done that named names for such an explosive charge, Healy said the bookies gave cash and left no fingerprints. "What I had from a guy who ran a gas station and made book in Hyde Park was that big-time bookies were pouring money to Timilty to get friendly cops back running the show. It was all unreported money, so how do you do a story? But it was real."

While street reporters were resigned to Healy having the discretion to write pro-White columns, they resented his intermittent intervention in the daily coverage. But the intense conflicts at the *Globe* were simply a microcosm of the deep divisions within the electorate.

Even after twenty-five years of covering presidential campaigns, Wilkie never again saw anything like the raw schism of Boston in 1975. "It was haves and have-nots," he said. "Clearly, the *Globe* was allied with the haves. I think the Taylors [the *Globe*'s publishing family] were far more comfortable with Kevin than with Joe. . . . And Kevin was a *Globe* pet from the beginning because he beat Louise and weaned the *Globe* off the fence on the editorial page. They realized they had to stand for something. And that they had all been in it together."

Wilkie said he had no private preference about who won. He admired both men—Timilty for not playing the race card that would have surely got him elected, and White for holding the city together during busing and assembling a remarkable staff. But by the end, he was stunned by White's fragile state of mind.

His most vivid recollection was a wild ride he took with the mayor on the Saturday before the election. White was a notoriously bad driver who got caught up in his animated stories and talked directly to passengers, ignoring the road ahead—in this case the narrow and winding Jamaicaway. Wilkie held on for dear life during several near collisions. He said that White was so agitated and talking in such a torrent that he was nearly foaming at the mouth. "[White] really seemed to be cracking up at the idea he might lose and kept calling his predicament 'a run on the corporation,' a hostile takeover from within."

Looking backward from Florida retirement, Bob DiGrazia copped a rueful but careful plea to political expediency in 1975. He got used, and he knows it.

Regarding the Ritz story, he said, "The information came from John Doyle, who was the superintendent of organized crime. As things developed later, it was a report thrown together at the urging of the mayor's office. As for documentation, there was very little, if any." Was it fair? "In retrospect, probably not."

He said he had been "foolish" to rely on others for information on both the press conference about deposed commanders and then the Ritz. He said his press conference statement had been prepared by Shields and that, to his regret, he "fell in line" with City Hall.

"I think what happened was they knew that if I said something, people trusted me. And so, yeah, I was foolish to trust them." He remembered being conflicted when he was summoned to the mayor's suite on election night, where White told him that his press conference had made the difference. He said he didn't know what to say to that. "It was, oh, I don't know, insulting."

DiGrazia said that the high impact of his standing quickly worked against him with Kevin White. He said the mayor soon viewed him as a political threat, and that, after the election, White played a murky political game with him, trying to gauge whether DiGrazia had an electoral glint in his eye.

"I never got the word directly that I would not be reappointed [for a five-year term]," DiGrazia said. "White came to me and said he was not going to run four years hence, and that he was going to put all his political power behind me so I could run for mayor. Would I like that? I told him I wasn't interested in anything political. It was political enough where I was ... yeah, it was a test to see if I was interested, so he could get rid of me if I was." He must have hestitated too long in answering whether he would "like that." Writing on the wall, he took his high favorability numbers with him to a chief's job in Maryland, some nine months after White's reelection.

If he had it to do over again, what would he change? "I would have been less trusting of my employees . . . yes, John Doyle."

And of what the mayor's office directed you to do? "Right."

While he has mixed feelings about Boston, his tenure there was a high-water mark in his career. He went on to be chief in Montgomery County, Maryland, where he got embroiled in a protracted standoff with the police union that made him a lightning rod in negotiations, and the discord eventually did him in. He left in 1978, after only two years in office, and became a law-enforcement consultant. But he clearly missed running his own department and maybe even the byzantine byways of Boston politics. He moved to Florida in the early 1990s.

Kevin White was never quite the same after 1975. He ended up furious with the media he had massaged masterfully for fifteen years. And that changed his whole approach to politics. An iron fist instead of the winning smile. Dick Daley, not John Lindsay. Going into the election, he knew his fresh face had some miles on it. But hounded at every turn? He never got over how the media turned on him. When the election ended, he was deeply chagrined that it had been so close, and determined never to be so vulnerable again. He would be feared, not loved. And some admirers who watched the transition called 1975 the demarcation between "good Kevin" and "bad Kevin."

CHAPTER 13

Losing Ground

The Busing Decade

Following white flight and an immigrant influx, the percentage of very poor families in Boston tripled between 1970 and 1980. Despite a population drop, the rate of those falling into low-income levels far outpaced the rest of the country.

1970 FAMILY INCOMES

	51,168,599 families	142,019 families
Income Levels	**U.S. Percentages**	**Boston Percentages**
Below $1,000	2.5	2.8
1,000–1,999	3.4	2.8
2,000–2,999	4.4	4.9
TOTAL	10.3%	10.5%

1980 FAMILY INCOMES

	59,190,133 families	117,832 families
Income Levels	**U.S. Percentages**	**Boston Percentages**
Below $5,000	7.3	12.8
5,000–7,499	6.2	8.9
7,500–9,999	6.9	8.6
TOTAL	20.4%	30.3%

Source: Boston Redevelopment Authority

B USING bombardments.
Garrity tyranny.
Timilty-White class warfare.

What was *wrought?*

There were two enduring whirlwinds in a traumatized city: the downward spiral of the schools and the socioeconomic reverberations of white flight.

After the 1975 election, White washed his hands of the schools for good, and education was ceded to W. Arthur Garrity and his technocrats.

Students became strangers in a strange land in neighborhoods that turned their backs. No more Southie-Eastie football rivalry or a multitude of other communal connections. Most high schools became minority islands adrift in white bastions that no longer cared. A decade after the cataclysm, people in South Boston called their high school the "federal school." One alum who played football there reminisced mordantly about what had been lost. "It's an empty building on a hill now," he said with a sigh.

In Southie, Charlestown, and West Roxbury, schoolhouses became orphans plagued by soaring dropout rates and plummeting test scores. Despite extensive and costly renovations and curriculum revisions mandated by a federal court's micromanagement, Boston students have remained uniformly inferior in achievement tests and college boards when compared to statewide averages. The SAT gap has actually worsened over time, and the system's high school dropout rate of 25 percent has steadily remained twice that of the state's average.

The two whirlwinds gained momentum simultaneously. The tumultuous schools situation begat migration that diminished neighborhoods. One third of the families with children left town, marooning the shrinking blue-collar enclaves left behind. By 1980 the city had 42,000 fewer school-age children than ten years earlier. The long-established sociological demarcation between the college-educated with downtown jobs and lower-middle-class families became even more pronounced. Many of the lower-income households slipped into poverty.

On the streets where working people lived, life lost a step and pretty much stayed that way no matter who was mayor. Post-busing Boston moved toward a have-and-have-not society where, for the first time, the proportion of really poor families greatly exceeded that in the country as a whole. At the end of the busing decade, the proportion of Bostonians subsisting at the bottom of the family income brackets had tripled, going from about 10 percent of families to 30 percent. Census data showed that the sudden surge of poor families at the end of the 1970s persisted into the new millennium. Most recently, the Boston Foundation, the city's oldest philanthropy, discovered poverty deepening dramatically among minority children, a reflection of the overall trend of rich and poor income extremes. As of 2009, the foundation found that the top 5 percent of wage earners held 25 percent of the city's income while the bottom 20 percent accounted for 2.2 percent.

Taken together, school desegregation and the tyrannical tenor of public affairs damaged the essence of community—that strongly held views counted for something and would be heard.

And what *of White and Timilty?*

Although the old antagonists stayed in elected office for eight more years after their epic clash, neither prospered. Timilty's voters migrated, and White devised his Chicago-style invincibility machine for a job that left him cold. Even though liberals and blacks made the difference for him in the tightest race in a generation, he never quite forgave them for letting it get so close.

Like White, Joe Timilty left office in 1984, retiring from the senate to become a real-estate developer. In one of the intertwining ironies of their public lives, White escaped relentless pursuit by the US attorney's office over his dubious fund-raising, while Timilty was ensnared in a political prosecution over a minor violation of banking laws. But that's where it stopped being minor; Joe the patriot was shipped out to a federal penitentiary. The only time White ever called Timilty was to commiserate with him about getting "screwed" in court. Timilty was convicted on a single count of bank fraud, but still headed off to a minimum-security prison in Pennsylvania.

The end of Kevin White's reign was like watching an aging ballplayer lumbering around third base with the catcher already holding the ball. He didn't even slide to make it look good. The mayor of singular style and grace who willed the city to elite status played out the string with studied nonchalance.

He served two final terms, making adroit use of what is usually political suicide—aloofness from the average voter. But instead of being turned out as uppity, he was adopted as a moody iconoclast, classically advertising himself as "a loner in love with his city." It was a perfect fit that bonded his panache with the body politic.

The working-class exodus over busing helped the mayor. The anti-busing crowd was never his cup of tea. The migration cost Timilty any chance he had of catching White. After nearly losing to Timilty, White rolled over him in 1979, using his new obsession with machine politics to make strong inroads in the ever-negotiable South Boston, once hostile territory. Meanwhile, Timilty lost much of his base in the outer Irish wards that were turning over.

The election of 1979 featured an astute tactic by White, who began an early negative advertising campaign that painted Timilty as a waffling senator who voted on both sides of issues. While there were few examples, Timilty still underestimated the campaign's impact, and it hurt him. Like the nebulous "climate of corruption" charge that enveloped White in 1975, Joe the Waffler was a sobriquet that stuck in 1979. The campaign also saw the return of the old Kevin, who was relaxed and engaging in his public appearances, never more so than when he hosted an afternoon event on City Plaza with Ray Charles. When the crowd seemed distracted, White said OK, let's try this—I'll play the piano and Ray will run for mayor.

While he had stumbled badly in the election of 1975, he finished strong, becoming the iron-fisted master of City Hall. In the wake of the chaos of busing and the departure of ethnic white families with children, White conquered a depleted playing field. He held his liberal-elderly-black coalition together, but expanded it by seducing Southie with patronage politics. The proposition in South Boston became "busing got us nothing but grief, so let's go with a winner with jobs to give." By 1979 White had finally done what his father and brother urged in the beginning—cater to a blue-collar base and do it out of a centralized City Hall, orchestrating precinct captains. As in Chicago, services for votes. No vote, no fixed pothole. But the mayoral election of 1979 was the be-all and end-all. After it was over, policy was put on autopilot, with White absent from City Hall for weeks at a time.

He faded at the end, but White will be remembered as a stylish presence who became the perfect ambassador and advocate for making Boston a world-class city. And for making its residents, at least those living downtown, feel that way about it. He was also tough enough to hold the city together during busing, even if he couldn't do the same for himself the next year.

Jack Connors, an advertising executive who became one of Boston's most successful businessmen, was with White for most of his tenure, massaging the image of a mercurial mayor. Where others saw weakness, Connors saw strength. He's convinced White's moody hubris was just what Boston needed and liked. "He was attracted only to the big ideas," Connors said, "and that helped him get 'his' city in place. He was always tinkering with his redesign for the city and if he didn't always get it right, he had it heading in the right direction."

Other mayors, he said, gravitated to the day to day minutiae, running to photo ops and funerals. "Kevin hated that stuff. He was unembarrassed to be above all that. He was more about royalty than mayoralty. What kept him going was forever adjusting a grand plan for Boston."

Connors said White, for all his grandiose notions and entitlements, could be self-deprecating about running his city. Connors remembered a small thing that had White laughing at his limitations. One spring day, the mayor looked out his majestic window overlooking Faneuil Hall and saw how straggly the center strip on Congress Street had become. He called the DPW and told them to spruce it up. That became a cement truck. "We stood at his window watching the truck pouring concrete into the middle of the street. Order flowers. Get cement. It made Kevin's day."

But city finances were no laughing matter. White was deadly serious about protecting the city tax rate that was the measure of every mayor. And he took bold action at two pivotal points to keep bills under control for property owners.

The best metric for activist Kevin White is his first decade, when he took dramatic action at the beginning and end to shore up the city's treasury.

In a brilliant power play by a rookie who hadn't taken office yet, the mayor-elect forced the legislature to fund a major change in policy in 1967 that shifted the burden of public welfare from the municipalities to the state. His wedge was that the speaker of the Massachusetts house wanted his old job—secretary of state. White said he would not relinquish it until the tax increases to pay for the state takeover were passed. Legislative leaders fumed at the hauteur, but passed the bill in four days so all the succession dominoes could fall in place. The boon for all cities and towns also meant $9.80 came off the Boston tax rate. A home run to start the game.

A decade later White took care of Boston homeowners once again, a policy change that equaled the welfare coup. He championed a complex plan for tax relief that achieved a simple objective—allowing municipalities to tax residential property at a lower rate than commercial buildings. It required getting approval through a statewide referendum authorizing tax "classification," and developers immediately sued to prevent Boston from using city funds to promote the 1978 petition. It was a contentious issue that went to the US Supreme Court, no less. But by the time the full bench ruled against Boston, the referendum had been overwhelmingly approved. Today, the commercial property tax rate is about three times the residential.

While he was capricious about development, seldom staying inter-ested enough to get to the finish line when there were the inevitable complications, there was one that held him to the end. In fact, he put his personal stamp on it. As only he could, he made it *his*.

The sole renovation that endured on the mayor's scattergun agenda was the one he took personally. It had bugged him from the first day he peered out his massive office window overlooking historic Dock Square. As far as the eye could see were the ruins of a legendary but bygone mercantile era.

While Ed Logue had revived the waterfront, the final piece of that sprawling project was at once the most promising and problematic—what to do with the once-grand Quincy Market building with its impos-ing porticos that had been overrun by the detritus of antiquated supply and demand.

It was named after Josiah Quincy, Boston's second mayor, who had begun the first urban renewal in the 1820s. He cleared out the ram-shackle strip between the Faneuil Hall of Revolutionary War fame and the waterfront by building an elongated marketplace for tradesmen and farmers. But history repeated itself with a vengeance when the area re-verted to disarray in the twentieth century. The surrounding narrow streets were marred by disheveled warehouses that overshadowed the dingy market building—and fortuitously spoiled Kevin White's view.

The idea for making the area a downtown shopping mall to attract tourists with shops and restaurants began to percolate as White began his second term in 1972. It was a disorienting year for the mayor who struggled for equilibrium after nearly making it to the McGovern ticket. Gradually, he saw political advantage in renovation. A revived Faneuil Hall area would help make Boston a vibrant city suffused in history that would draw people from across the country. And they would learn that White had made it all possible.

After White got over his post-McGovern blues and began his quix-otic pursuit of the presidency, his fabled instincts kicked in on the political benefits of having a showcase at his backdoor to symbolize his Boston. He first listened to Benjamin Thompson, a Cambridge architect of great imagination, who saw the space as one of the first urban malls. Thompson was named to a team of developers while the BRA moved forward with federal preservation funds, stripping down gunked-up granite buildings in a messy, disruptive reclamation that took several years.

Thompson eventually found a kindred partner who shared his vision of a downtown mecca for tourists. James Rouse of Maryland was a dynamic pioneer of the 1950s suburban mall. But he also saw the reverse trend in all its potential. As their blueprint jelled into a bold idea, their "walkway to the sea" from City Hall to the harbor had the mayor enthralled.

White had to win reelection one more time to see the renovation through. Quincy Market also got a name change with its makeover, becoming known as the more historic Faneuil Market. After a boffo opening in 1976, the crowds never abated, ever drawn to authenticity and gastronomy. The market received instant acceptance and an annual gate that surpassed that of Disneyland—12 million visitors came year after year. The Collins era saw government remade in Scollay Square, but the new Faneuil Market drew an admiring crowd from across the country. Every day.

In his time, nearly forty new office buildings were put in place as well as a dozen new hotels, most notably Copley Place, which combined retail space with a Westin and a Marriott across from the Trinity Church in Back Bay. But nothing pleased White more than Faneuil Hall. "The Prudential Center is Hynes," he once told a reporter. "Center Plaza and City Hall belong to John Collins. But Faneuil Hall," he said, pausing to bang his chest hard, "Faneuil Hall is mine!"

Ultimately—and it didn't take much pushing, given his background and predilections—White went decidedly high-hat. Enough of the busing rabble and unwinnable neighborhood housing spats. He shrank his purview to City Hall events and downtown development. His world-class city was more for tourists than for residents. He associated mostly with business leaders and bankers and architects, and did a flurry of meet-and-greets with diplomats and dignitaries in his regal reclusion at the Parkman House. His last term reflected the new realities of the post-busing Boston of surging poverty rates and more low-income families. As the economy slipped into recession, there was a final paradoxical frenzy of office building that White fostered. As downtown prospered, the mayor laid off nearly four thousand city workers, a sure sign that he was done with elected politics.

The last part of White's tenure was afflicted with long-term incumbent's disease and incessant warfare with an ambitious US attorney after his scalp. The skirmish consumed much of the last term and was pushed to the hilt by the formidable William Weld, a federal prosecutor on his way to being governor. Weld waged a Captain Ahab pursuit that included convicting a score of midlevel officials for kickbacks and bribery within City Hall. But it always fell short of the wily mayor and his close inner circle of savvy loyalists.

But if White's circuitous fund-raising wasn't a crime, it was a public relations disaster. The timing couldn't have been worse. It came at one of the lowest points in the city's modern economic history. In 1980 the Brookings Institution gave Boston the lowest ranking of 154 cities measured by an urban travail index. Yet White stayed inured to it all, both politically and personally. Perhaps a loner out of love with his city, he was partly insulated by the magnificent paradox of Boston, a benefit largely of his doing—the city's downtown stayed a vibrant attraction even in a down economy. But that was hardly mitigation in the hard-bitten neighborhoods that found themselves at the bottom of the distress indicia of unemployment, violent crime, and poverty. When White took office for his final term, his city was ranked below Detroit, Newark, and Oakland on the grid of grief.

Despite the economic tailspin and high anxiety in the neighborhoods, White's final agenda was about legacy and retirement. He plotted a soft landing for his afterlife, and his policy initiatives centered on what even aides called his "edifice complex." Like many modern mayors, White wanted to leave spiffy downtown buildings behind him, seducing posterity with the tall wonder of it all.

Even a resounding final reelection in 1979 had done little to stimulate his fragile attention span. Within a year his new machine began to fray under a mayor who knew he would never use it again.

Bloom long off the rose, White ogled the exit sign. His last term seemed as much about feathering nests as about devising policy. He had seen John Hynes and, to a lesser extent, John Collins scuffle along in retirement without a sinecure, and Kevin White required a deluxe 401k plan. Even before the final inauguration, he forged alliances with two of the city's dominant backstage powerhouses—John Silber and Edward McCormack.

Silber, the hard-driving president of Boston University, had the higher profile of the pair. He had embarked on a decade of expansion at both ends of his sprawling campus on the west side of the city, and needed the mayor's intercession.

The other forceful figure was McCormack, the former attorney general who had been a key ally of the mayor during busing. He had begun building his own sub-rosa real estate empire of office buildings, condominiums, and hotels during White's reign. His stealthy pathway to projects also required a friend in high places.

In the final years, McCormack obtained pieces of ten approved projects, a success rate so astonishing that it was likened to batting .800 in the major leagues. In a race to the finish line, he sealed six lucrative deals in 1983, White's last year in office. At the end, he had accumulated partnerships with a gross value to him of $41 million. Five years after the last White administration, McCormack had cashed out of three office buildings and a project option for an estimated gross income of $12 million.

While developers were keenly aware that McCormack was White's confidant, it apparently was not reciprocal. People close to White say the mayor became bitter that McCormack proved to be an elusive ally after the mayor left office. In a rambling 1989 interview with the *Globe* about McCormack's personal building boom, White was asked about his role in the good fortune. "Let me just say if McCormack got these things, I could care less. I'm out now. My head is elsewhere . . . Hey, Ed McCormack isn't even interesting, for Chrissake. . . . I'm being facetious and don't print this, but if Ed McCormack offered me half of his projects, I'd have a perfect right to them."

John Silber proved more reliable. After several actions by the city helped BU expansion, White moved from City Hall in 1984 to the Commonwealth Avenue campus, where he became a popular professor of politics. And on munificent terms. It wasn't well known at the time, but White obtained a fifteen-year contract to teach a once-a-week seminar for $125,000 a year. Plus a driver, a car, and a BU suite on renovated Bay State Road. The package was worth an estimated $3 million. White's former press secretary, George Regan, said the contract was necessary "in case Silber got hit by a bus."

The City Hall–BU connection was a soft song in three-part harmony.

The first stanza wafted in from the State House as White began his last term. Kevin Harrington, a former senate president and lobbyist extraordinaire, brought Silber and White together to mull their similar interests and future synergy. While White wasn't an active player in a real estate deal that got BU a cut rate on public property in Boston, one of White's minions gave it cover with a questionable appraisal.

The state transfer of the National Guard Armory on Commonwealth Avenue to BU in 1982 involved a late-night power play and a cluster of legislative leaders. It seemed to have something for everybody, including a fee for Harrington. While three official appraisals put the armory's value at between $4.6 and $8.5 million, one of White's former BRA directors, Robert Kenney, pegged it at $1.75 million. The state sold it for $2.5 million.

The second deal with a sudden end began in 1981. The city reversed itself after appearing to side with neighborhood protests over BU dormitory sprawl. It seemed to drive a hard bargain with the university by requiring sixty days' notice before property could be converted for student use in Audubon Circle on the edge of Back Bay. But the conversion of thirteen buildings into 137 rental units was quickly cleared by the city's board of appeals. And that was just the beginning. Before it was over, hundreds of student units were acquired outside an established boundary set by the city and university. The acerbic postscript from one neighborhood activist: "There is no housing policy. It's all ad-hoc decisions by the mayor. If the mayor had lunch with Silber, it's done. What are two blocks—after lunch."

White completed the BU trifecta as he was leaving office, orchestrating a sizable donation to the school by the John Hancock Mutual Life Insurance Company. In a tightly timed sequence, White allowed the company to renege on an earlier agreement to tear down one of its buildings near Copley Square and build a park. But with a hitch. Hancock could keep its building as long as it gave BU $4.7 million for a new science center. In bang-bang transactions, the mayor arranged a zoning change to protect the building just before the company made the gift.

While BU was White's Easy Street retirement, he did not escape the bumpy ride that nearly all subordinates encountered with the prickly Silber. When the BU president decided to run for governor in 1990, White assembled his old A-team of advisers to help Silber get organized. But Regan remembered the gathering at Silber's office racing downhill when Silber "carried on" too long about some minor adverse publicity. Regan said another White aide finally told Silber he was missing the point of the meeting. "Kevin was deeply embarrassed and somewhat estranged after that," Regan said. "Their interactions were the only things Kevin couldn't get out of."

But if White couldn't have his cake and eat it, too, at BU, he held hard to his contract until it ended in 1999.

All said and done, White's most enduring stamp was an insouciance that left it to voters to stick by the moody loner. Or not. The take-it-or-leave-it bargain seemed to be that as White went about making Boston a world-class city, he was entitled to extravagant accoutrements. And he always benefited from being a perfect fit in a tuxedo.

The last word on Kevin White goes to his daughter Patricia, who twice ran unsuccessfully for City Council and came to view her interest in politics as more genetic than nurtured. Talking about her father's famously tempestuous career, she told *Globe* political reporter Brian Mooney that her father carried it all on his sleeve. The inside view was pretty much the same as the public's. "Mercurial, petulant, larger than life. All the words that were used to describe him, he brought them all home with him." White died January 27, 2012, at eighty-two after a decade-long struggle with Alzheimer's disease.

Joe Timilty, who so carefully, even nobly, kept busing from becoming a conflagration, became one of its biggest losers. He lost his Irish vote when white families fled Boston, mostly for the South Shore. While the exodus was a continuation of a trend that had started in the 1950s, it was done at an increased rate during the turbulent 1970s.

The white flight that Timilty tried to stem eventually enveloped his own family. In 1980, when his three oldest sons were to be transferred again to help "balance" inner-city schools, his wife, Elaine, did a brass-tacks review. Sitting at a kitchen table covered with maps, like Rommel under a desert tent, she looked up and said "enough." Her seven children's education would not be disrupted yet again by a mindless numbers game in a failed experiment. The Timiltys moved from the mixed neighborhood on the Dorchester/Mattapan line to suburban Canton.

Timilty's specialty at the State House was urban housing. He enjoyed the life and work of being a pol, but while he had a niche in the senate, he was never going to be part of its leadership. When he ran for mayor he had clashed with William Bulger, the senator from South Boston, who had insisted on being the sole spokemen for the city's delegation on busing. Timilty averred that he had his own views and, after all, he was the guy running for mayor. There was also some Dorchester and Southie chafing. Bulger, who supported White in 1975, went on to be senate president three years later. Dead-ended, Timilty got out of the game he loved in order to become a real-estate developer the same year Kevin White went to BU.

In the boom years of the mid-1980s, Timilty renovated several Boston schools into condo buildings, but at decade's end in a fading market, he fell in with some sketchy characters in a troubled East Boston project.

When the units weren't selling, Timilty turned to "native" brokers in the closed Italian neighborhood. They turned out to be fast-and-loose players who moved the units by attracting customers with a no-money-down sales pitch. In turn, they deceived banks that provided the mortgages without revealing that the buyers had used hidden second mortgages for the down payments. When the economy soured and banks later foreclosed on some of the units, it found there was less equity in them than the sales documents showed.

In retrospect, it appears the real problem with the second-mortgage issue was that national banks, complicit or scammed, were exposed to lawsuits by stockholders claiming incompetence and deceit. Bankers with clout turned to the FBI to shift the blame to the street level. Timilty was at the end of one of many chain reactions. It led to a political prosecution, with an acting US attorney chasing a permanent appointment and Timilty presenting a high-visibility scalp.

Compared to the later subprime mortgage scandal, the second-mortgage gambit beneath condo sales at a converted gumball factory in East Boston was quaintly transparent.

Yet, in the early 1990s, a handful of second-mortgage sales were enough to send Timilty to jail. With the brokers getting probation or negligible time in exchange for testimony against him, Timilty had a grim choice—become a snitch or go to jail. In a confusing time, he was sure of just one thing—no way I'm rolling. He went to trial and was sentenced to six months.

Outgunned from the start, Timilty neither flinched nor complained.

His fight started in earnest with his arrest in 1991. He had tried to surrender voluntarily, but piqued prosecutors refused the offer because Timilty wouldn't plead guilty to a charge that carried an eighteen-month sentence. Instead, the FBI knocked on his suburban door at five thirty in the morning and asked that Timilty come with them immediately. Timilty made them wait in the driveway while he showered and dressed in one of his best suits. When he got in the backseat, the sleepy agent at the wheel asked Timilty the best way to get to Boston. Timilty: "You decided to do it this way so I can be paraded in front of the media looking like shit. You figure out how to get to your own office." They rode to town in stony silence.

And what *of blue-collar Boston?*

Against Kevin White's glittering skyline, Boston became a fetching city of downtown commerce and renovated town houses in Beacon Hill and multimillion-dollar condos in Back Bay and parts of the reclaimed South End.

But it was a dazzling veneer that obscured daily reality in an increasingly have-and-have-not place. On many streets where working people resided, life was stuck in neutral. Today fewer blue-collar families live in

Boston, and they have less inflation-adjusted income than before busing began. Those left behind in the bottom stratum now must send their children to a failed school system that has two thirds of its former enrollment. The minority ratio in city schools has gone from 40 percent in 1974 to 89 percent today. The family poverty rate has escalated since busing tore up the landscape. The voter turnout is half what it was when Kevin White started out. More than ever, politics is an insider's game, tightly controlled by City Hall workers and their families and friends who dominate elections to protect incumbents and their own jobs. In the decades since Timilty almost toppled White, turning out an incumbent mayor has become just about impossible.

The root of today's disparate Boston is migratory. While there are several factors behind the shifting demographics, most are on the edges of one dispositive trend: young poor in, and aging middle-income out.

The gradual exodus at midcentury evolved into a cataclysm for the city. It began as part of a national trend in older cities in the 1950s, when urban residents left dilapidated homes for newer and more easily financed suburban digs, and, later the same decade, for higher paying jobs. In both cases they were driven by the prospect of a brighter future.

But the second wave in the 1970s was entirely different. Many émigrés resembled the famine Irish of more than a century earlier, who didn't want to go, but felt they had no choice. If it wasn't the existential threat of starvation, it was still dire. They fled chaos in the schoolyards and the altered makeup of once-cohesive neighborhoods. By decade's end, one of every four white residents, mostly ethnic Catholics, had departed. In broad terms, the exchange was 130,000 older Irish and Italians heading out, and about 50,000 younger Hispanics and Caribbean blacks moving in. The starkest stat at decades's end: 42,000 fewer school-age children than when the decade began, and 40 percent fewer youngsters under age five. Families with children had packed up and left.

There was none of the bright-eyed departures of the 1950s, when opportunity beckoned. The metaphor for the 1970s departure was the last helicopter out of Saigon, with refugees hanging from the rope ladder over the anguish of those on rooftops. With police regularly hitting irate residents with batons around schoolhouses, busing became Boston's

Vietnam. The brother-against-brother civil warfare softened a bit over the years and a warmer nostalgia crept back when expats came home for reunions in Southie and Charlestown. But there was an emergency-evacuation feel to it while it was going strong: U-haul trailers peeling off toward the expressway and out of town.

Although defenders of the Garrity agenda roundly discounted white flight as a polemical overstatement of long-established population trends, an analysis of the 1970s migration found a marked increase over the 1960s. When measured as a percentage of the population, the proportion of those departing in the busing era is 60 percent higher. They called the court's bluff. In effect they said "If you continue the mind-boggling transfers of white students, we'll leave." It continued, and they did.

The first time around, in the 1950s, the emigrants were also mostly whites who left areas with the poorest housing stock—Charlestown, South Boston, the North End, the South End, and Roxbury. The Irish neighborhood with the best housing—Dorchester—remained stable. And the outer-ring neighborhoods of Roslindale and West Roxbury and Hyde Park actually increased in population.

But in the 1970s, Dorchester and the white part of Mattapan emptied out, accounting for the lion's share of the total. One of the most dramatic racial shifts occurred in the outer neighborhood of Hyde Park, which saw a huge influx of blacks from nearby Mattapan to take the homes vacated by whites. The local high school was just behind Southie and Charlestown in terms of strife. The busing trauma also impacted Roxbury, the black center of the city that suffered similarly to South Boston during the uproar. Both ends of Garrity's bus route lost about 20 percent of their populations.

The job picture also changed dramatically after busing. There was a huge shift to services and professional jobs, and away from blue-collar work in factories and trades. Next to service industries, which were dominated by health-care and clerical business jobs, was the rise in high-end positions in finance, insurance, and real estate. Of these, the surge is most noticeable in the securities industry, which increased sevenfold in thirty years, from about 6,000 in 1970 to 42,000 by the millennium.

But the fallout from the busing era on the working poor and middle class is seen most clearly in the decennial census data on family income. Before the 1970s, Boston's share of lower, middle, and upper income levels closely tracked national allocations. At the end of the 1960s, there was actually a small but hopeful blip in the middle where incomes slightly exceeded the rest of the country in families earning between $5,000 and $10,000 a year.

But then came the 1980 measurement, and it described a socioeconomic tsunami, a harbinger of the income extremes that frame Boston today. According to an analysis of US Census Department data by the Boston Redevelopment Authority, the end of the busing decade saw a fundamental reordering of income distribution across the board. Buffeted by a deep recession, even the high end sagged briefly.

Yet it was the surge in poor families that is most striking. Boston didn't just lose ground in the 1970s. It was overrun. The percentage of poor families—the three lower brackets for those making $10,000 or less—was off the charts. In 1980 one of every five families lived on $7,500 a year or less.

By decade's end, there were strong gusts of change that rocked Boston's working families and put them behind the eight ball for good: white flight; disproportionate unemployment; Hispanic and Caribbean immigration; a jump in subsidized housing. All these conspired to swell the ranks of very poor families while the middle class fled the bad schools and a depressed job market.

The disparity between Boston's share of very low income families and national percentages persisted over the next two decades. The city's later income gains on the high end only made matters worse for working families. The money moved upward from the middle. In 1990 the notable shift was the comparative increase in the percentage of those comfortable families who earned between $55,000 and $150,000. Hardly a tide lifting all boats. Compared with national data, the trend had hardened into obdurate facts of life by 2008—excessive percentages of low income families by a wide margin, well behind in the middle range, and one third above for those making $150,000 or more.

Politically, the shifting demographics and suddenly altered income picture immediately contributed to the demise of the busing demagogues.

The old warhorses of busing had overpromised and lost much of their rabid constituency. Almost overnight, they became has-beens who stood for the bad old days. Their vote had left town, and most of the newcomers didn't go to the polls.

Boston was well on its way to becoming a city of chasms between professionals in finance and medicine living in the Back Bay, Beacon Hill, and the South End, and the rest of the workforce living in the depleted ethnic neighborhoods.

The dichotomy was seen most vividly in the schools. A decade after the buses were bombarded and white Catholics fled, socioeconomic metrics told the sad tale of those left behind. By 1985 nine of every ten students were from families with incomes low enough to be eligible for free or subsidized lunch. About two thirds of the families made do with $15,000 or less—about half of the median for the city as a whole. Indeed, the family poverty rate in the busing decade jumped nearly 50 percent, going from 11.3 percent of the populace to 16.7 percent.

While the city became dramatically richer and poorer and sagged in the middle, the schools lost nearly all their diversity. Middle-class students evaporated. And as the school population became destitute, black parents began having second thoughts about the revamped system. A 1982 *Globe* poll found that a vast majority favored the old, if abused, open enrollment program over court assignments. And the quotient favoring court-ordered busing had fallen precipitously from half in 1974 to 14 percent. Even some of the original plaintiffs in the Garrity case favored the "choice" demanded so stridently by ROAR a few years earlier. It seemed the food wasn't so hot once everyone got seated at the table.

Looking back over busing's toll, former Boston Teachers Union president and mayoral candidate Edward Doherty said, "We've lost a lot of political support for public education in this city. We've lost, to a very large extent, a middle-class constituency for public schools, middle class of all races."

And what *of the anti-busing movement?*

The anti-busers, who had risen with fist-shaking ferocity, exited with a grumpy whimper. They avowed "never," but buses still proliferated, jamming the city's streets every morning and afternoon. While the protest vote didn't dissolve, it was no longer willing to underwrite a lamentation going nowhere. The once-dominant movement collapsed almost overnight.

Yet the sentiment endured and even went national. In the 1976 presidential election, Boston voted for a crippled George Wallace, still stumping in a wheelchair after an assassination attempt, giving him its top spot at 29 percent. (Wallace finished third in the statewide vote that went to conservative Democrat Henry "Scoop" Jackson of Washington State.) The angry Boston vote shifted toward sending state and congressional Democrats a message about taxes and Vietnam and desegregation. It was a pivotal part of the boiling pot that turned out liberal Governor Michael Dukakis in the 1978 Democratic primary. The incumbent governor was beaten in the city by more than twenty thousand votes, losing 58 percent to 42 percent.

But locally it became more discerning as voters cast about for new ideas and faces. The year after Boston voted for George Wallace for president, it rejected Louise Day Hicks. The off-year election ushered in a far-reaching realignment, none more significant than the end of Hicks. She had topped the City Council ticket in 1975, but finished just out of the money in the tenth spot only two years later.

The election of 1977 also marked the unceremonious dumping of the bilious John Kerrigan, who had moved to the council six years earlier. His demise was hastened by revelations that he had kept a concubine on his staff. The first black man was elected to the school committee in place of the implacable Pixie Palladino, who was barely defeated. But out was out.

And it saw the rise of Ray.

The standout athlete from sports-mad Southie moved from the legislature to the council in a strong second-place finish. Raymond Flynn supplanted Hicks as a political figure in the town, and began a long-running rivalry with the only other power over the Broadway Bridge—Billy Bulger. Moving up in the state senate, Bulger was dismissive of a jock who never read the classics like his good self. The top-gun enmity got so bad that they eventually refused to sing Irish songs together. The most

Bulger was ever willing to give Flynn was that he could "read the wind like a wolf."

Flynn applied his athlete's endurance to his pursuit of the mayor's chair as if he were filling a lane on a fast break. He shrewdly set his own course, separate from the anti-busing crazies. Fervently against busing, he still managed to become the monotonic voice of reason. In 1975, with an opportunistic bent that would become his hallmark, he jumped the anti-busers' line when they thought they had an ally in President Gerald Ford, who had condemned Garrity's busing decision as part of the country-club Republican faux sympathy with blue-collar voters brimming with racial resentment. The ROAR crowd planned to send a delegation to the Rose Garden to extract concessions, only to look up and see Flynn on television as he exited the White House to a press conference where he overstated what the president would do for South Boston.

And what *of the beleaguered schools?*

Busing became a war with no winners. Garrity's decision was repeatedly upheld but universally reviled. ROAR lost at every turn, unless you count the voting-with-your-feet of white flight. Which did nothing for those left behind as the schools became twice as imbalanced. The stigma of the marooned emerged as the metastasizing low-income composition of the student body.

Busing's early epitaph was posted in its first year at the entrance of South Boston High. It was a mundane list of high danger, with the things not allowed inside including baseball bats, hockey sticks, umbrellas, karate sticks, pipes, brass knuckles, screwdrivers, wrenches, hammers, chains, whips, rope, combs, picks, rattails, scissors, nail files, and hat pins.

In the final analysis, all the well-intended curriculum innovations and renovated buildings imposed by Garrity and his advisers counted for little with the schools' increasingly low-income constituency.

And while it became part of the self-fulfilling prophecy of the vociferously departed, resegregation in the 1980s became as inexorable as forced busing had been a decade earlier.

Another part of the same circular prophecy of doomed schools was the end of community involvement. When the surrounding communities, which had clung so intensely to the neighborhood schools, realized the protests were for naught, residents relinquished their hold with the disgusted fury of the spurned. Even moderates treated reconstituted schools as abandoned property. It was education's version of vandalism's broken-window syndrome that propelled urban crime.

The social scientist Ronald Formisano has written that opponents made it abundantly clear that "lost" schools were not salvageable, and so "eventually, they would not be worth having—at least as examples of successful desegregation—because not enough whites stayed to create racial balance."

From the outset, the major impediment to viable schools was the steady stream of revised student assignments dispensed by the judge's faceless masters of the universe—Dentler and Scott. For families, it was like jumping on and off a wheel of fortune. Neither parents nor students had a sense of educational continuity, especially in the first stormy years.

Garrity's advisers also succumbed to dangerous wishful thinking when they dismissed the prospect of white flight. After two years of busing, and the dramatic shift of students to parochial schools and relocations to the South Shore, with some teenagers even sent to relatives in Florida and Ohio, Dentler denied that white flight had even occurred. He had the sun out in a thunderstorm.

And yet, for a while, he had some scholarly support which held that busing had a negligible effect on well-established migration patterns. But by decade's end, studies found that Boston comported with what happened in other cities beset by busing—the first year saw the largest of a strong resettlement. And unlike the steady seepage of the 1950s, the busing exodus happened nearly overnight, in one mayoral term. By the 1980s even Dentler and Scott conceded the profound displacement by admitting they had downplayed the "high velocity" of the first-year exits. It seems they knew about it all along.

One academic, who once had agreed with mandatory assignments and minimized the impact of white flight, came to a different conclusion as the exodus played out. Boston University sociologist Christine Rossell revised her view that compulsory busing had the force of a moral imperative. As the population shift became as clear as blood on a sidewalk, her second thought was that a voluntary plan might have been more effective. Unsurprisingly, Judge Garrity gave no quarter, insisting to the end that the white-flight criticism was a myth perpetuated by militants. His final I'd-do-it-all-again decree was like insisting an earthquake hadn't happened.*

Despite the heavy expenditures mandated by Garrity to change the School Department ethos and expand opportunity for black students and faculty, the Boston schools have not prospered by some standard measurements. While the judge got so deeply into the line items that he even ordered the number of basketballs each school would have, the dropout rate has persisted and achievement test scores have lagged behind the rest of the state.

Today, the system's downward trajectory is as traceable as a crash on Wall Street.

SAT (Scholastic Achievement Test) scores. Surprisingly, the Boston SAT scores compared better with the state when busing first began than after Garrity had run the system for more than a decade. The gap between Boston and statewide averages widened continuously until it plateaued in the last decade at a steady unfavorable rate, according to Boston school system data.

In 1977, just after the imposition of Phase One and Phase Two reassignments, the city/state gap was actually smaller than ten years later, when the differential settled into permanent deficiency. Shortly after busing began, the verbal mean score for the system was 12 percent behind the state's average, while the math mean lagged by 10 percent. The better early showing is likely explained by the low participation rate—only one

---

* Ultimately, a compromise was devised that tipped over much of the Garrity prescription. The city was divided into three zones in which fifty-fifty plans were adopted for elementary and middle schools. Each classroom set aside half of the seats for neighborhood students, who could walk up to a mile and a half to school, and the rest went to anyone in the city who wanted to go there. Siblings got preference, but racial makeup was not even a factor. There have been cries of politics in the designations to the good schools near home, but it has a much different tenor than the uproar over assignments to dangerous schools across town.

of every five Boston students took the test. Even with the added benefit of self-selecting college-bound students, the verbal mean was starkly low: 381 (out of 800). In fact, one of every five scored below 300. The gap with the state widened as the number of Boston test-takers increased.

In 1986, about the time that desegregation had run its bumpy course, the SAT picture had worsened. Despite an infusion of building renovations and curriculum changes, the verbal gap with the state had nearly doubled, to 23 percent. The math had worsened but not doubled. Among the worst performers were Garrity's original target areas in Southie and Roxbury, places chosen to break the strongest resistance to desegregation. South Boston High's mean verbal score was 284, and math was 380. And the mean scores at Madison Park, one of the successor schools to Roxbury High, were 278 verbal and 316 math.

In the first decade of the new millennium, the gap remained uniformly unfavorable, with math scores a steady 15 percent behind the state, mostly in the 440s, and verbal scores that were typically 19 percent behind, mostly in the low 430s.

Dropout rates. While Boston has improved from the disastrous level of 40 percent in busing's early years, it has settled into a disproportionate 25-percent rate for a four-year high school class. According to State Education Department data, the typical senior withdrawal percentage since 1994 has been twice that of the state average, roughly 7.5 percent to 3.5 percent. The lower high school grades had similarly disparate dropout rates.

MCAS Achievement tests. Less than a decade after Garrity formally relinquished control of the system in 1990, Boston stumbled badly when the new state achievement tests were first required. Over the last decade, however, Boston public-school students have gained some ground in the percentage passing the "proficiency" test, but have made no progress in reducing the high percentage who fail and, expanding the low percentage who excel.

Despite Boston's steady advantage in per capita student expenditures, most recently $17,000 a pupil versus a statewide average of $12,000, the city's students remained far behind those from across the state who got high rankings, and far ahead among test-takers who failed.

The standardized tests, known as the Massachusetts Comprehensive Assessment System (MCAS), are designed to meet the requirements of the Education Reform Law of 1993 that set out to measure performance in English, math, science, and history, and to instill public accountability.

After a five-year trial period, the tests counted for real in 1998 when the mandatory MCAS were used for "promoting" fourth-, eighth-, and tenth-graders.

For the first MCAS decade, 1998 to 2009, the Boston results were consistently unfavorable at both ends of the spectrum for excellence and failure. According to data from the Massachusetts Department of Elementary and Secondary Education, the tests for math and English show statewide students consistently had twice the percentage in the high-attainment category. And the converse was true for those who flunked— twice the percentage of Boston students failed than did statewide pupils.

Over the decade, however, Boston made strides in the middle ground of passing the proficiency test for promotion. After the first year when scores were uniformly disastrous across the state, school systems began to teach to the tests, and dramatic improvement was made. Boston was among the lowest in proficiency and had nowhere to go but up. In the first year, the percentage of statewide students deemed "proficient" was twice that of city pupils. In contrast, the most recent tests found that Boston had gained ground in the proficiency category, with the percentage of statewide students passing the test only one-fourth higher than Boston.

A 2003 *Globe* study found, however, that the Boston "survivors"— those deemed faithful students who consistently attended class year after year until graduation—had pass rates comparable to the typical Massachusetts pupil. It concluded that truancy and chronic stops and starts were more harmful to performance than deficient instruction.

But by most measures, Boston has become a minority system of relatively low achievement perhaps marginally better than other similar urban schools, but still not good. Throwing money at the city's schools during the Garrity decade and a half only served to make Boston the question instead of the answer. Why did it go so badly? Again, the Vietnam analogy seems apt, and not just the guerrilla warfare. Busing pitted low-income blacks and whites against each other *while* college-educated, higher-income families sat it out with suburban "deferments."

The only real hope for parity in dealing with desegregation crashed in Detroit when the US Supreme Court ruled metropolitan busing plans out of bounds in the 1974 *Milliken v. Bradley* case. When a federal judge required suburban districts to help the city integrate by taking black students, it led to a firestorm that burned all the way to Washington. The *Milliken* case principles as enumerated by the court made the proposition crystal clear—the inner-city poor would balance their own schools, if it was to be done at all. Garrity had actually pondered a metro plan, but put it aside after Detroit. As a result, it is fact and not populist rant that South Boston, Charlestown, and Roxbury carried nearly the entire desegregation burden while the surrounding suburbs stayed serenely exempt.

Ronald Formisano put the process into a single sentence: the lower classes did the desegregating, the middle class did the fleeing, and the affluent sat it out.

The disdainful dumping of the busing furor on the urban poor had enormous political ramifications. It was the beginning of Reagan Democrats and what Formisano called "the most powerful solvent" that washed away the original New Deal coalition of academics and unions. While desegregation was a hard sell just about everywhere, the schism in Boston was etched in stone. By the mid-1980s, a Harvard survey of the racial mix in desegregated schools found Boston had the steepest decline of white students of any major city—not entirely surprising, because it had a 60-percent quotient to begin with.

But by 2000 resegregation was rampant throughout the Northeast. White students in the region typically attended schools that were 80 percent white. Black students at majority white schools were down to 13 percent. In a pyrrhic victory, minority students have inner-city schools mostly to themselves. A national study in 2010 found Boston among the most segregated urban school systems for Latinos and blacks in the United States. These are the casualty figures at the end of a thirty-five-year war of attrition.

Busing's most unwavering foe, William Bulger of South Boston, president of the senate and then the University of Massachusetts, seldom gives a talk on any subject that doesn't eventually berate the blind support given a gross injustice. For him, it has always been an obdurate power play by the financially secure.

"You couldn't have done it in a place where people had a checkbook to get out from under," he said decades after the buses first rolled. "I think the proponents had such contempt for us that they thought we had no choice, that we were trapped.

"Being an unaffected proponent of forced busing of other people's children—whether you're a newspaper, a judge, or a social planner—means never having to say you're sorry."

CHAPTER 14

Still Broke

RAY FLYNN

WHEN Ray Flynn talks about his father, his eyes widen and he blinks hard and says suddenly that his dad was too small for the work he did, a frail stevedore who broke his health working the docks for his family of five sons. Clearing his throat, he accounts for his own big frame as an inheritance from his mother's father, Michael Kirby, who was six foot four and worked the waterfront in Ireland before emigrating to South Boston in 1913 with his brood. Flynn's maternal grandparents were from Clonakilty in West Cork, a hotbed of resistance to British rule and hometown of one of Ireland's great martyrs, Michael Collins. Flynn says his great-grandfather, John Collins, was a friend and a distant cousin of the legendary rebel who led the insurrection but was assassinated during the vicious civil war that followed when Ireland was partitioned and the Union Jack still flew over Ulster. Mike Kirby lived with the Flynns on Sixth Street and kept up with the politics back home on Saturday mornings when he took a trolley to Dudley Square to read every last word in the Irish papers that arrived in bundles at a store there. Then he'd shoot the breeze on the sidewalk with other immigrants about the Ould Sod. Ray Flynn said Big Mike had two immutable emblems in his world—the Holy Name Society pin on his scally can and framed photographs of General Michael Collins.

Flynn pauses pensively at the kaleidoscopic history in his genes, and then he brightens at the thought of stories about Lillian Kirby of Cork stock and Stephen Flynn out of Galway, who were born to hard lives in South Boston that he says built character and loyalty. They were raised a couple streets apart, and Flynn said his father's early journey was set to the lyrics of "Southie Is My Home Town," that he was literally "born down on A Street and raised on B Street." His mother was the last of ten children and the only one born in the United States. But while the memories are warmly nostalgic, it's as if time had passed his parents by, stranding them in menial jobs of an earlier era—cleaning offices and working the docks. By the Second World War, most Irish had moved on to city jobs or the post office or schools or hospitals. Even Flynn himself had a childhood that was much more Honey Fitzgerald's North End than Kevin White's West Roxbury. He acknowledges all that before shrugging it off. "That's the way it was here," he says simply. "Same with Cathy's [his wife's] parents. Her father worked the docks and her mother was a domestic."

Their parents had the jobs of the early immigrants because that was all they knew and all they had. But unlike those perilous times in the nineteenth century, there was a small safety net in place—and the Flynns needed every stitch of it in the late 1940s when the father came down with tuberculosis. Steve Flynn was sick for five years, spending two of them in a hospital in Mattapan, where the condition could be chronic but not incurable. Flynn dates the hospital stay to 1948 when he was nine years old and selling afternoon newspapers by running back and forth between day games at Fenway Park and Braves Field. Everybody pitched in, but the family was on welfare while the father was in the hospital. "He made it back," said the second oldest son with a wan smile.

Flynn remembered well a kindness in that difficult time, all the more remarkable to him because it came from another tribe in another part of town. There was a new medicine that cost the outlandish sum of eighty-five dollars, which his mother had tracked down to a doctor's office, even though she was unsure how to pay for it. A Jewish doctor on Beacon Street gave it to her for next to nothing.

But if there was struggle, there was also fun on a shoestring. Flynn has a high regard for the long ago, and it animated him as he recalled the solidarity behind annual outings when he was barely in grade school and the extravagant enticements were root beer and picnic baskets. His parents were part of a roustabout excursion group that headed out of town on a summer Sunday. Many of the men worked in the "wool houses" along Summer Street near South Station, sweatshops that refined the raw product from Australia during the 1930s and 1940s when Boston was the center of the wool trade in the United States.

The workers were given use of a wool truck for a weekend, and they drove it to Southie, where neighborhood women took the sides off and scrubbed the filthy, scarred wooden slats until you could eat off them. Then they packed the truck's open wagon with chicken dishes and beef stew and barrels of beer. Early on Sunday, they headed off for Norumbega Park in Newton for a picnic with a schoolyard of kids and a fiddler and accordion player for sing-alongs on the way. The first stop was eight-o'clock Mass at the Mission Church in Roxbury, where about a hundred strong piled in and out of the church. Flynn remembered the collegial teamwork, with everyone having a job and seeing it through. Once there, the boys played baseball, the women tended to the picnic blankets, and the men played cards. "There was love for each other," he said of the trip and the neighborhood it came from. "Nothing today compares to it. There was no politics or gamesmanship. If there was a need, a crisis, everyone was there with support."

And at the center was the church. People lived in parishes rather than precincts, and the Catholic calendar set the agenda and the rhythms of daily life. Even as a young kid, Flynn went to Mass most mornings. Looking back, he attributes his storied high energy to the survival regimen of a struggling household with five sons and an ill father. The boys were all up early for church and newspaper routes and delivering grocery bundles on Saturdays.

And then there was the young Ray Flynn's raison d'être—basketball. A born athlete who could do it all, basketball was his game from the start; besides being really good at it, it was something he could do alone and practice until dark. He played it seven or eight hours a day for years, insinuating himself into games over his head all around the city, including Roxbury. At twelve the gym rat even wheedled his way into Boston Garden as a Celtics' ballboy, scurrying after loose balls during warmups and then shooting around after the game until janitors threw him out. He got used to starting when other people were still in bed. "I had to do that," he said. "Just survival."

The hardscrabble and the hoops netted him the last basketball scholarship given at Providence College in 1959, one he almost didn't get because the coach wasn't completely sold on the competition Flynn faced in high school. He nearly flunked out in his freshman year, but then turned a corner and went on to be an academic All American on an outstanding team. He was the MVP in 1963 at the National Invitational Tournament, then the best in the country. He also found his formative political philosophy with a Dominican priest named Charles Quirk, who taught economics with a special emphasis on social justice. He introduced Flynn to the core of his political beliefs through the stilted language of a nineteenth-century papal encyclical, *Rerum Novarum*, that he said Quirk brought to life. After the wreckage of the industrial age, Pope Leo XIII called for an end to sweatshops and child labor, and for a decent wage and sanitary conditions for workers. Flynn calls it "the most important encyclical of all time. It roots all my politics. It wasn't Democrat and Republican politics ... it was social and economic justice and it formed the basis for my political philosophy centered on workers and the needy." He also pondered the writings of the Catholic social workers and authors Dorothy Day and Michael Harrington.

After graduating, he was the last player cut from the Celtics in 1964 when his sweet shot wasn't quite enough to keep a white six-footer on a championship team dominated by Bill Russell. He says Red Auerbach let him down just right. A year later, somewhat bereft, he took a job as a probation officer and threw himself into youth counseling and coaching, the next best thing to playing. He had his eye on politics when he found himself hat-in-hand with bureaucrats to get programs and equipment for city kids. He wanted to call his own shots and made his move in 1970, a year of cascading change in South Boston. He was elected to Bill Bulger's house seat after Bulger declared for Joe Moakley's senate seat. Moakley set off the chain reaction by announcing for congress after the legendary speaker of the house, John McCormack, resigned one step ahead of the sheriff. Louise Day Hicks beat Moakley in that race, but he bested her the next time. After the static sixties, there was a sudden realignment and Flynn was in the thick of it, the first in a series of Flynn seizing his moments. He became a mover instead of a petitioner, a youth worker who went where the action was.

Flynn's next move had to wait for the end of the short-lived anti-busing era in November 1976. He nearly topped the ticket for City Council in the year that Hicks was defeated. The next stop for Ray Flynn was mayor of Boston once Kevin White had left the scene.

In part, Flynn would be viable for mayor because voters were tired of busing and he never exploited it as the departed demagogues had. While he never wavered in his opposition, he instinctively understood he had to offer more than just another rant. The Johnny one note of it was a song of oblivion. While his agenda was always self-serving, he also stayed resolutely committed to fairness for *all* the neighborhoods. With some posturing, he catered to busing's interracial victims—the economically stressed families in both South Boston and Roxbury who bore the brunt of the disruption and strife.

From the outset, he combined a fierce loyalty to working families like his own with relentless self-promotion. After a while, the paradox of Ray—the mix of social worker and huckster—began to hurt him with the media as the publicity hound overshadowed the neighborhood activist.

But, from the beginning, Flynn had two assets the rest of the field lacked—rapport with teenagers who respected him as an athlete and as a rare commodity in an insular town. He wasn't xenophobic. He was on the front lines during busing, but always preached nonviolence where others winked at it. Looking back, he said, "The most politically disadvantageous place to be was there at the high school. But nonetheless."

He was every bit as unyielding as Louise Day Hicks or Bill Bulger, but seemed to see the shortcomings of street protests more clearly. He argued in vain that busing was an unconstitutional usurpation of power from lawmakers. But eventually his opposition to violence led to tentative rapport with beleaguered blacks on the other side. In one small but telling example of his independence, he was the only white political figure to go to the funeral of a black teenager killed by a white policeman in 1980. And he refused to sign on to the Southie leadership's clumsy "declaration of clarification" that said Roxbury was a fine community full of dangerous people.

He acknowledged that he flew solo on busing, but disputed that his different route was a political tactic. For starters, it drew intense flak, and, what's more, his sympathy was squarely with the resistance and its leaders. "I never wanted to put any of them down," he said. "I had a lot of respect and admiration for them." Yet his nuanced approach left him open to attacks from whites for being too soft and from blacks for having it both ways. But it still left him in a better place—on a small patch of middle ground.

And then there was the basketball advantage. He called it a different perspective.

"Well, they had their upbringing," he said of other anti-busing leaders. "I had a very different upbringing. I was the first white kid to play for an all-black, semi-pro basketball team in Boston. I'd be in a car with nine black guys and we'd be going to New Jersey, the Catskills, the Pocono Mountains. I'd go anywhere. I'd hitchhike to Harlem to play with all black players. . . . They asked Dillinger why he robbed banks, and he said, 'That's where the money is.' They asked why Ray Flynn is in Roxbury all the time, and it's where all the great athletes were. I was at the Roxbury Boys Club more than I was at the South Boston Boys Club."

Today, Flynn still walks a tightrope around the busing protests, but agrees that a lot of pols made a lot of empty promises as things unraveled. He said the pledges to stop busing were "colossal mistakes."

Instead, at the busing meetings, he'd say hold on, " 'you can't say that,' and people would start booing me. I was on the outs with those kind of statements. . . . It wasn't good politics at the time, but what it established was respect" for what was possible.

Flynn had to bide his time for six years as Kevin White petered out. If nothing else, he had a contrast to offer—a working stiff who knew the streets.

And he was a dog for work. After White finally stopped toying with the electorate in May 1983, Flynn had to overtake the candidate who was given the best chance of succeeding the mayor. At the outset, David Finnegan was favored because he was the most like White. The irony is that while Finnegan was a theatrical presence on any stage, he had his own impressive up-from-the-bootstraps narrative from a large Dorchester family. He worked full time while going to college and law school, and became a self-made lawyer known for flamboyant oratory. But the thing that cut against his populist background over the summer was a campaign chest stocked by businessmen and developers.

While Finnegan had a commanding early lead, he was attempting the tricky maneuver of jumping from the school committee to City Hall. And he had his hands full, keeping ahead of the relentless Flynn. The preliminary became the last tight Boston election of the twentieth century.

In the summer of 1983, when Finnegan slipped out of town for weekends on the Cape, Flynn pressed the flesh at a score of backyard barbecues. And while he and Finnegan were sparring, Mel King, a black activist whose battles with City Hall went back to the New York Streets project begun by Mayor Hynes, was coming up strong on the outside lane.

All of which made for a crowded, capable field, maybe the best in a generation. It was rounded out by progressive Suffolk County sheriff Dennis Kearney and voluble city councilor Lawrence DiCara. All were up to the job, but Flynn owned the distinct advantage of a cyclical staple in Boston politics—he especially wasn't like the guy who went before him. One of the best things he had was that he was no Kevin White, no Mayor Deluxe. Just as White wasn't the cold John Collins. Who in turn hadn't been the bland John Hynes. Who was particularly not the outsized and despotic James Michael Curley.

Flynn's humble Southie roots were a throwback that traveled beyond even the bleak Roxbury origins of Collins and Hynes. He was a townie in the Martin Lomasney and Honey Fitzgerald mold. Flynn's parents were from another era, and he was a Catholic who wore it on his sleeve. The question became, could his Southie appeal sell citywide? Despite its heavy voting and political fervor, South Boston never had the numbers to put one of its own in the mayor's seat. Flynn was aiming to be the first outlier from the isolated and internecine peninsula who didn't get himself branded as too extreme for high office, like the brilliant but crazed Bill Foley or the too-cute-by-half Louise Day Hicks.

If he was a plodder, Flynn moved in sure, straight lines. No zigzags or the Hamlet-like agonizing of Kevin White. What you saw was pretty much what you got. He was a worker, not a philosopher. But if he was earnest and plain-spoken, he was also opportunistic and hard-nosed, with an athelete's instinct for winning. If he got you down, you stayed down.

When Flynn declared for mayor in the spring, with White still half in and half out of the race, Finnegan was the frontrunner at 19 percent. But Flynn was within striking distance at 14 percent. Yet he set the tone for a high-risk and high-octane campaign by making his announcement in front of one of Southie's most plagued projects. The imagery seemed awry, putting him in the wrong place at the wrong time. But it was exactly what Flynn was after—smack in front of the most neglected place in the city, with a strong neighborhood guy looking straight into the camera, telling voters how determined he was to do something about it. He recalled the setting: "All poor welfare families. Most of the buildings were abandoned. Broken bottles, drugs. On one side of the street a firehouse had been closed. Across the street, the police station—Station 6—had been closed by [tax cutting] Proposition 2½. Up the street was a drug haven."

How did that become the right place at the right time? "Well, David Finnegan had come up with a great slogan—'It's Finnegan or Him Again.' He was the alternative to Kevin White. But White goes and Finnegan becomes Kevin White. People start to say, 'Look, if we want a change, why do we want Him Again?' But then there's this guy who announces in front of a project. That's change, isn't it? I didn't know if I could win or not, but I was going to roll the dice. I didn't care. I was going to run my campaign and the hell with it."

By Labor Day, the race had sorted itself out leaving three tightly bunched contenders: the unremitting Flynn; King, the tough-minded former state rep who had a solid base but faced long odds as a black candidate; and Finnegan, who still had the best chance of being the next mayor.

Given the alignment, it was clear that whichever Irish pol got into a final with King and his narrow base would surely win. The Labor Day question was "Will it be Flynn or Finnegan?"

Going in, Finnegan had the edge. The second youngest of eight children, Finnegan came from a political family. His barrister brother John had been chairman of the House Ways and Means Committee, the powerful committee that decided how much money legislation would get, and then was state auditor for six years. His father had been minority leader in the state senate until he crossed Cardinal William O'Connell in 1935 over some minor church entitlement and was defeated by a well-financed opponent.

Finnegan grew up in a house that required taking a position and defending it at the supper table. But it was a tight-budget household that was bereft early with the death from leukemia of his mother at age fifty-two. He got some financial aid to attend Stonehill College, a small Catholic school twenty miles from Boston, where he majored in philosophy, viewing it as the founding discipline for all the liberal arts. Frequently, Finnegan thumbed his way to school down Route 138 from Dorchester to North Easton and, hatless and ruddy raw on a winter day, made his way to class in a flimsy warmup jacket with hands jammed in his pockets. But he had a commanding presence at any forum, and that got him elected president of his class three times.

Less than a decade after law school, Finnegan was elected to the school committee in busing's second year. It was not hard for him to stand out there. He appeared polished at the podium, and his time at the committee was notable for his calm approach to busing debates and efforts to keep the committee out of the day-to-day administration of school matters. His brief against the court order was that it was unworkable policy rather than racially objectionable. He stayed scrupulously away from the ramparts and never planned to stay long.

After he earned some next-time points from a dead-last-place race for mayor in 1979—always framed as the Timilty-White rematch—he kept a high profile by doing a large-audience radio talk show on WBZ, one of Boston's premier stations. He was a small celebrity by the time he ran for mayor in 1983, but he had geared his early campaign as a contest against Kevin White, who, true to form, kept everyone hanging on his whim until his exit in late May. With five months until the primary, the "Finnegan or Him Again" signs were artifacts.

Finnegan lost his target when White withdrew, and he was immediately set upon by Flynn, who tried to get the race down to him and the front-runner. He stoked the electorate's vague reservations about

Finnegan into a slow-building image problem. Were his chronic late ar-
rivals at forums a sign that he was aloof like Kevin White? Did he think
he was better than us? Was he beholden to downtown interests?

With Flynn working his barbecue ground game all summer, it
was suddenly Labor Day and six weeks to go to the mid-October primary—moved back from the usual September date to give the city
time to reconfigure gerrymandered council districts to comply with a
one-man-one-vote federal court order. Flynn had pulled even in the polls,
and Finnegan found himself in the fading front-runner's dilemma—how
to do something aggressive and dramatic without seeming desperate.
With little choice, he went on the attack to bring the fight to Flynn and
to change the subject from his being bankrolled by developers.

Finnegan came up with what seemed to be a game-changer. Flynn's
campaign had dropped off flyers with different messages for different
neighborhoods. There was a brochure for white Dorchester and another
one for black Dorchester. Each featured pictures of activists with Flynn,
with one group white and the other black. The white brochure made
no mention of Flynn's support for equal rights for minorities, which was
prominently mentioned in the black version. Finnegan portrayed Flynn
as a busing extremist using an expedient if not outright racist strategy.

Flynn went into scrambling retreat. His campaign manager took the
blame, saying it was a thoughtless oversight and a mistake. Flynn ordered distribution of the flyers halted—and then let it all simmer for a
couple of days.

But in seizing the advantage, Finnegan went too far by saying that
the flyers were "designed to racially polarize our city." Flynn had always
been foursquare against busing, but had no history of being racist. In
fact, he was just the opposite and that was widely known.

The flyer issue faded with a shrug in white neighborhoods. Flynn
stopped apologizing and said "so what?" And he pounced on Finnegan
for calling him a racist, knowing he could get wide support in post-busing
Boston against any candidate trying to make the campaign about race.
Again.

Finnegan tamped things down by using a less aggressive criticism—

flip-flopping. Ray Flynn might not have been a racist, but he was a finger-to-the-wind pragmatist. It was an unremarkable charge, but nevertheless one that led to a memorable street debate that decided the election.

It began ten days before the October 18 primary that everyone knew would decide who would be mayor. Finnegan dropped his own racially uniform brochure on 150,000 doorsteps. "It's Saturday morning. Do you know where Ray Flynn is?" was the provocative lead-in to Flynn being on both sides of capital punishment; the Equal Rights Amendment; the recently defeated conservative governor, Edward J. King; and the recently elected president, Ronald Reagan.

But Flynn sidestepped the charges, contending it was personal growth on the issues and disputing everything else. He said he had de-cided against the death penalty after a long discussion with his wife, and had endorsed the ERA after mulling the issue for years. And he said he was always for King and Reagan and had as much evidence for his posi-tions as Finnegan had otherwise.

With the two playing word games down to the final weekend—ignoring the three other mainstream candidates as if they weren't there—the bad feeling spilled over at an impromptu television debate on the vast brick plaza in front of City Hall. This time the context was a Finnegan radio ad that likened Flynn to a chameleon. Flynn was in his City Hall office when one of his daughters phoned him about the latest salvo. He didn't know what it meant, and after a staffer explained the disparaging connotations, Flynn learned Finnegan was on the plaza doing television interviews, and bounded out the door to stick his nose in.

The television reporter was only too happy to broaden the forum to include Flynn and let it top the six-o'clock news. Things seemed to explode in Flynn's face from the first exchange. Throughout, Flynn was wild-eyed and boorish, shouting over Finnegan at every turn in a series of non sequiturs, chanting that the building behind them—City Hall—was not for sale, a not-so-veiled reference to Finnegan's support from developers.

The colloquy's intensity took nearly everyone by surprise as about one hundred aides and followers looked on helplessly. Finnegan kept his trademark cool, but, as things played out, it was the passion from the fiery neighborhood guy that scored the most points. Somehow he got the best of the exchanges. Finnegan: "Ray, when you're finished yelling at me, I'd be glad to respond." Flynn: "I'm not yelling at you, David.... You called me a lizard."

After the sudden shootout was over, Peter Meade, a seasoned politico who had worked for Kevin White but signed on with Finnegan, shook his candidate's hand, telling him, "Congratulations, I think you just won the election." And so it seemed. Flynn had boiled over, but the beleaguered neighborhoods were looking for a champion rather than a smooth dude after Garrity's tyranny and Kevin White's hibernation.

Flynn reminisced that it was all instinctive, that he was in a fight and he just slugged it out. "A lot of people thought I lost ... A lot of people had their heads between their legs that night." He said that he'd had to ask an aide what a chameleon was, and had been told it was an animal that changed colors to suit its environment. "I says, 'Like a lizard?' He says, 'Yah.'" Flynn took those as fighting words and charged out of the building to confront Finnegan with his aspersion and to raise what was percolating as a winner for Flynn—his strong support for "linkage" payments that required developers to pay the city to underwrite affordable housing and job-training programs. "I wanted to get a whack in about linkage because that ... really resonated, almost a defining issue.... David got caught on the wrong side of that. So I said the building behind us is not for sale. It was very political, but anyways that's what we do. And now you're calling me a lizard."

In the aftermath, Flynn was a man alone. All his aides thought he'd lost—even his wife, Cathy, who defines blind loyalty. He called her for her take. She hesitated and said, "Ray, you didn't come off very well. I don't know much about politics, but it didn't look very good."

So, troubled but undaunted, Flynn set off to finish the day of politicking. First stop was a Dorchester VFW Post full of union guys who let out a yelp when Flynn walked up to the bar. The place was rocking for him, and there was a standing ovation. Flynn was pleased if puzzled. "They just loved it," Flynn said. "I said, 'What the hell is going on here?'"

Flynn knew it was turning his way by his next stop, the nearby Eire

Pub. It was clear his voters were responding to his roundhouses instead of his playing it safe and programmed. The pub owner told him, "'In all my years of following Boston politics, we finally have an Irishman to stand up and fight for our values.' I said 'Tommy, what are you talking about—this bogus debate we had tonight?'"

Decades later, Flynn is still uncertain why his shooting-from-the-hip was so successful. "If I was getting paid as a political consultant," he said, "you'd a fired me. Because I didn't see it coming. Even to this day, I don't understand it."

The debate's ripples put a passionate neighborhood firebrand over the top. Flynn came in first, finishing 270 votes ahead of Mel King, the black candidate who had peaked. Finnegan finished four points behind Flynn (and King)—a fatal third.

The 167,000 voter turnout shattered all previous preliminary elections, and left Flynn in the catbird seat. Barring a major misstep, it appeared that King had maxed out, with no prospect of expanding his vote in what was then mostly white Boston. Going into the final election, the councilor from Southie would have his 48,000 votes, most of Finnegan's 41,000, and the distant runners-up total of 15,000.

For the onetime favorite, the seven-thousand-vote chasm was Dave Finnegan's swan song in politics. He'd taken his lean frame and composed demeanor to the trial courts and then to the arcanum of automobile insurance in Massachusetts, helping to turn a once-obscure company on the Rhode Island border into the dominant home and car carrier in the commonwealth. He'd traveled a long, lucrative way from the crooning master of ceremonies at St. Ann's CYO variety shows.

In the November final, all the cordial interactions between Flynn and King and the mutual themes of unity had little impact on core constituencies. When the ballots were in, Boston followed racial patterns to census-count certitude. Flynn rode a nearly monolithic white vote to a crushing two-to-one victory. In just one example, a West Roxbury precinct voted 1,061–54 for Flynn. About the only sharp difference during the many joint appearances of the two candidates helped Flynn in the Irish neighborhoods—King's insistence that Flynn should acknowledge that the plight of poor blacks was a more intractable social problem than that of poor whites. Flynn's position was poor's poor and we'll address both equally.

But both candidates knew the high stakes and walked on eggshells in the weeks leading up to the final to avoid a racial incident that could shatter the fragile harmony. Looking back, Flynn said, "Mel and I liked each other. We both wanted to win, but there were no cheap shots. There was no conversation about it, but neither one of us would do anything to damage the friendship or mutual respect."

However, he said there were some efforts to promote confrontation. He recalled one with relish. Flynn was invited to a forum in Roxbury to discuss civil rights, and he sniffed it out right away as a setup, knowing it would be packed with partisans anxious to jam him up over segregated schools. But he figured out a swerve, remembering that it was Mel King's birthday. On the way to the meeting, he picked up an oversized cupcake with a single candle on it.

"I walk into this room with not a single Ray Flynn voter in it and they were going to hit me about busing. Before we start I say, 'Excuse me, but before we start what I know will be a very lively professional discussion of the issues.' (What I really was saying was I know I'm not getting a vote out of this joint but I'm here anyway.) I said I had a presentation I wanted to make—they made the mistake of giving me the floor—a cake for Mel. I started telling them how well I knew Mel King and how we played basketball in the South End. I knew his brother, too. . . . We could have ended the meeting right then." As King looked on with a tight knowing smile, a filibustering Flynn never gave up the floor.

Reflecting on the big picture, Flynn said his view was simple—how you campaign dictates how you govern. "If it had been a contentious campaign, I wouldn't have been able to bring the city together. I was able to do that because of Mel King as much as anybody else."

On election night, the two men stressed the harmony and mutual respect. Throughout, they shared similar stances on housing and poverty and unemployment. King visited Flynn's campaign hotel and congratulated his rival for "waging a decent and hardworking campaign that does honor to Boston's neighborhoods and to the people who have for too long been ignored or repressed."

For his part, Flynn took a backhanded swipe at White's absenteeism and remote governance with his usual dash of hyperbole, promising the most accessible, hardworking, and dedicated administration "in the city's history."

If the struggling Irish neighborhoods had one of their own back in the mayor's chair, it was only the most obvious change in a city in transition. Mel King's rainbow coalition simply didn't have the votes in 1983, but it signaled a demographic shift that, while lacking political clout, began reshaping old ethnic neighborhoods. It wasn't the cohesive surge of ballot power of Honey Fitzgerald's day, yet it altered city life. In a short period there were 100,000 residents who spoke a foreign language at home. On one level, it simply meant there was a bigger bloc of low-voting immigrants than before. On another, neighborhoods were being transformed.

East Boston, once solidly Italian, was on the way toward a Hispanic majority. The Irish phalanx in Dorchester gave way to a mini-cultural revolution, with streets shifting to Asian décor while Haitians and other Caribbean immigrants clustered in colorful enclaves. The old Irish churches offered masses in Vietnamese and Creole. Change came as a polyglot din along Dorchester Avenue.

As always, Boston was a house divided, but one that Ray Flynn was ideally suited to straddle, at least for a while. His inaugural was the self-conscious opposite of the black-tie, invitation-only haute cuisine of Kevin White. Ray threw a block party, an open-door ball for thousands. And after it was over, the new mayor ran off to a fire scene at the recently opened Westin Hotel at Copley Plaza.

But the renewed energy wasn't just a manic mayor chasing fires. He kept his promises about diversity at City Hall, something begun in earnest under Kevin White. He would go on to nearly double the rate of new hires for minorities and raise it 20 percent for women. The city's expanded ethnic range was reflected in the appointment of minorities to substantive department-head jobs that included the housing authority and election commission as well as the treasurer, auditor, and purchasing agent.

Policy aside, Flynn's abiding trademark remained crazy energy, dashing around town doing mundane things that Kevin White would laugh at. He spent most of his time out of his office. He showed up at three-alarm fires and murder scenes. He rode shotgun in a snowplow during major storms. More than once, he led people out of burning buildings. He even helped end a hostage standoff, charging into the house in Dorchester with police. He set the tone for his tenure in the campaign when he was the only candidate to appear at all seventy-eight candidate nights, ranging from packed ward committee events to one in Dorchester with five people. Flynn saw it as showing voters that he cared about things that concerned them. And it had the collateral benefit of free publicity. Many of his forays were photo ops with advance notice to city desks.

But the final part of his outreach strategy was something that went beyond the constituent connections he claimed it was—late-night beer drinking with working men in barrooms. When it became an issue, his answer was that it never interfered with his work and he was always able to be up and out by seven a.m. for a ten-mile run. But it dogged him throughout his political life and was put in neon at the outset when Kevin White publicly proclaimed him a "boozer."

But all was high hopes and clear sailing as the Ray Flynn Years got under way. He embraced rather than ran away from his humble roots, always on the lookout for symbolic homage to hardships of earlier generations. And if it settled a score, all the better.

Flynn cited his mother's callused knees to jab Yankee Boston even before he got in office. Summoned to Franklin Street in 1983 for his first meeting at the relocated "Vault," the new mayor said he was met at the door by the board's chairman, who lapsed into the logistic formalities of Yankee small talk by explaining where the meeting would take place. A beaming Flynn cut him short, saying he knew the building's layout because his mother had once worked there. Flynn said the chairman asked, "Your mother? Was she a secretary up here, or a vice president?"

Flynn laughed as he reconstructed the exchange of clashing worlds: "I says no, but one of the greatest days in her life was she came home and said she just got a big promotion. I says, 'Ma, that's great. What are you doin'?' She says, 'I got moved from the fifteenth floor to the seventeenth floor,' which was the executive office. 'It's all rugs there so we won't have to spend the whole night on our knees.'"

Flynn demurred: "I didn't do it to embarrass them, but I wanted to let them know where I was coming from. They weren't dealing with Henry Cabot Lodges down here . . . the people of Boston were [lined up] behind me."

But his awareness about the need for future diplomacy didn't keep him from repeatedly telling the story at other Vault meetings. Former aides joked that it happened so often that one Vault member was overheard whispering, "Oh no, not the cleaning lady story again."

In fact, he struck a blow for his sainted mother on the slightest pretext. After his first reelection, he canceled an inaugural ball scheduled at the Copley Plaza Hotel because the management had ordered—and then quickly rescinded after union protests—that cleaning women use rags rather than long-handled mops to scrub room corners. The issue rose and fell while Flynn was on a post-election vacation, but when he returned and was confronted by capitulation, he still attacked, a bugle blaring for Lillian's two decades of cleaning office floors on her knees. Indeed, it had irresistible symmetry, a back-to-the-future moment that reverted to the first Curley administration, when the mayor, mindful of his mother's years on all fours on the obdurate marble floor of the cardinal's church in the South End, ordered that City Hall cleaning women be issued long-handled mops. When Flynn found himself smiling too long at the memory, he added, "I wasn't looking to make a big deal out of it."*

Besides its empathetic tone and lack of pretension, the Flynn administration seized on the perfect issue for a new agenda—payments from

---

* Lillian was Southie to the core and knew all the street life scuttlebutt. One day, Flynn's BRA director Stephen Coyle, whose family had moved from Southie to Waltham, was with the mayor when someone tapped him on the shoulder. It was Lillian. "You got an uncle Alabama?" she asked. "Well, yes," said Coyle diplomatically, "he's my cousin but some know him that way." "You know how he got his name?" she continued. "I think there's more than one version," Coyle hedged. No, she said, just one. "Your uncle was in a bar when two men beside him were dragged out by a gang. Then they said to him, 'You with them?' Your uncle said, 'Nope, I'm from Alabama.'" Today, Coyle laughs that he wasn't about to argue with his new boss's mother about anything. But he allows: "It's a lot better story than my cousin being stationed in Mobile during the war."

lord high developers to benefit low-income families in need of affordable housing.

"Linkage" was not invented by Ray Flynn, but it's doubtful anyone made more of it. The idea was to have developers of new buildings pay a per-square-foot fee to the city, which would use the funds for affordable housing and job training. It became a rare total victory that took a couple of years to get in place, with strong resistance from the real estate community and even opposition from South Boston city councilor James Kelly, who said it was the work of the socialists around Flynn.

Not only had the Boston policy originated late in the developer-friendly White administration, but the notion was nearly ten years old, apparently emerging in San Francisco as a formulaic requirement that builders of office towers also construct a set amount of affordable housing units.

Flynn had pushed it hard as a councilor and candidate, but by the time he adopted it as a signature policy as mayor, there were programs in a dozen cities. Once it finally emerged from the City Council, Flynn was able to put his money where his mouth was by getting downtown to pay something back to the neighborhoods. He was also able to hand it off to an ideal architect in Steve Coyle, the new head of the redevelopment authority. And two decades after the West End facelift began, linkage saw the return of Jerry Rappaport, who led the opposition.

In his first year, Flynn had refined his plan to include a 17-percent increase over White's rate and that it be paid in about half the time. Plus, the increased fee went toward his top priority—the nation's first linkage-financed job training program.

In his first term, some elements of resurgence came together. Flynn grins boyishly when he ticks off the fast start. "It was like when I was playing basketball—I always knew where the net was, even when my back was to it. The city was coming out of a deep hole, there were layoffs. We had a deficit of $42 million handed us . . . [but] we cut every department and in eighteen months we had a balanced budget. We were able to push the new Boston Garden through, and finish the Navy Yard development in Charlestown. And put a $170-million addition onto Boston City [hospital]. We had the beginning of the Big Dig and the harbor cleanup. So things got moving and we got all our linkage conditions in place, despite obstacles."

The linkage system had to overcome political battles in the council, with Rappaport working behind the scenes, and to survive a challenge in the state's highest court over an increase in the fee and a reduction in the time period for payment. The legal contention that ultimately failed was that linkage was a tax by another name. The final schedule called for developers to pay six dollars a square foot for projects over 100,000 square feet, with about 80 percent for affordable housing and the rest for job training. The payments for downtown projects were due over a seven-year period, and over a twelve-year period for outlying neighborhoods.

The beefed-up program nearly doubled the amount of money developers would have contributed to the city's neighborhoods. There were some power plays and self-aggrandizement by high-handed neighborhood groups who received some of the money. But the results were on the ledger for all to see. The Housing and Neighborhood Jobs Trust fund dispensed $35.2 million to fifty-five projects accounting for 3,600 units, nearly all of them in the affordable category. Flynn caught the wave out of the mid-1980s with the inestimable Coyle at the helm. The first term had the biggest building spurt in city history—$6.8 billion in projects created fourteen thousand construction jobs in each year. One shining example was the renovation of the Charlestown Navy Yard, an innovative amalgam of affordable and market housing and high-tech and commercial office space.

Wind at his back, Flynn sailed into easy reelection in 1987, with one looming problem met head-on. It was clear in the months before the election that there was a pressing problem with segregation in the city's housing projects. The US Housing and Urban Development agency notified the city that the discriminatory pattern in waiting lists for "white only" projects had to be rectified—or else. Flynn took the bull by the horns and announced he was going to take action even before he faced the electorate for the second time. It would cost him Southie's two wards as he rolled to a 67-percent victory.

He began his second term by signing a consent decree with HUD that pledged to rectify decades of segregation. While the problem was clear in the 1970s, no one had the stomach for a double dose of desegregation while busing was under way. It was put off to another day that arrived in 1988. The case was made with the mere showing of a handful of documents—the racial composition of the waiting lists. About 80 percent of the sixteen thousand families awaiting entry were minorities. Once that was unclogged, there was a surge of blacks and Hispanics in the nearly all-white projects in Southie and Charlestown and East Boston. Flynn's sales pitch raised the specter of Garrity redux. "I believe Boston has seen enough of court receiverships," he said at the time. "We do not want to lose the right to control our own future."

Against a backdrop of the irrefutable math, Flynn talked straight at a post-inaugural meeting of five hundred people at St. Monica's Church. The audience didn't care about the arithmetic and was unmoved by the mayor's promise that no project resident, especially the elderly, would be displaced by the new fair-housing policy.

He was even tougher two months later, telling another hostile Southie crowd of five hundred that "I'm not going to come here tonight to tell you what you want to hear, knowing it is not acceptable to HUD."

By the end of his second term, the nearly all-white population in Southie projects had decreased from 80 percent to 70 percent Caucasian. Across the city, the reconfigured racial mix was 54 percent minority and 46 percent white. It was not painless, but vituperative resistance was neither widespread nor long-running. Most of the racial incidents occurred in South Boston. But the scope was contained. Overall, twenty of thirty-three verified incidents took place at the Old Colony, McCormack, and West Broadway projects, while some six hundred people of color had moved in.

"It was one of the best things I ever did," Flynn said. "It was simple at one level—the law requires it, and if we don't do it, we lose money. But I had to go before the people and tell them. I was up front about it. 'You won't like this, but it has to be done.' I talked to the judge who had the case in federal court, Joe Tauro, good guy, who said, 'If you come to terms I'll support you.' It could have been more national theater about Boston and racism, but I said I'd integrate voluntarily and the court stood by me.

"There was a certain vocal element, sure. I was harassed. 'Nigger lover' and all that. But it never turned real bad in Southie. There was a lot of social work involved."

Most of Ray Flynn's enduring political difficulties stemmed from his stubborn loyalty to a boyhood friend, Francis "Mickey" Roache, a long-time police officer who had specialized in racial relations to good reviews before being named commissioner in 1985.

Roache was fair-minded but calamitous as an administrator, and his department was soon rudderless and then dysfunctional as its detectives ran amok. It was clear from the get-go that he was a good guy in over his head.

Mickey went back to the Southie playing fields with Ray, and that was an impeccable credential in 1985. They were jogging buddies who conducted business on long runs. Roache was vintage Southie, even coming from the kind of good lad/bad lad household where brothers wind up on the opposite sides of the law. One of Mickey's brothers was crippled after being shot in an underworld beef.

But Roache was a central-casting model for the role of rugged, lean commissioner, a benevolent man who listened to a fault. And a good cop until he got Peter Principled. A managerial disaster, he was immunized as Ray's guy—until he started to bring them both down. The first crisis came after a long stretch of racial coexistence, but it pulled the rug from under its two most committed exponents—Roache and Flynn.

The beginning of the end for Mickey occurred on a Monday night at eight thirty when a 911 call came in from a husband saying he and his wife had been shot near a black neighborhood. A CBS production company had been given access to the calls as part of a special on urban crime. The producers had stumbled into one of Boston's seminal moments. It would be nearly as powerful as the image of busing bigotry captured by the prize-winning photograph of a South Boston hoodlum spearing a black man with a pole carrying a billowing American flag. Public housing integration was child's play compared to what happened next.

On October 23, 1989, the emergency line carried the fading voice of a badly wounded Charles Stuart, a young husband who had just left a birthing class with his wife at Brigham and Women's Hospital. He called the state police on his car phone and said he and his wife had been shot near the hospital, but he passed out from blood loss within minutes, despite repeated pleas by the dispatcher to "stay with me, Chuck." Police cruisers were able to locate the couple because the car phone line remained open and the dispatcher had the good sense to have cruisers in the area turn their sirens off and on one at a time. The loudest siren was closest to the scene, and soon police were at the blood-spattered car. The tape was national news, and the pressure was intense for a fast arrest for what appeared to be the murder of a pregnant white woman by a black man. The suburban nightmare.

The thirty-year-old wife, Carol DiMaiti Stuart, was killed by a shot to the head and Charles was shot in the stomach. They had been married four years and she was seven months pregnant. They met while she was working as a waitress and he as a cook at a restaurant in Revere, a largely Italian redoubt with a Mafia contingent a few miles north of Boston. But soon they were on an upward path, living in rustic Reading on the North Shore. Carol was a tax lawyer and Charles was manager of a high-end furrier on Boston's Newbury Street. The twenty-nine-year-old, darkly handsome man was straddling the two worlds of the scruffy town of Revere, where he grew up, and the upscale clientele at the Kakas fur store.

From his hospital bed, Charles Stuart told police that a black man had hijacked their car at an intersection near the hospital and forced them to drive to a deserted side street on the outskirts of the adjacent and crime-plagued Mission Hill. Police said Stuart told them that the shooting started suddenly after the agitated assailant concluded Stuart was "five-oh"—street slang for police. Perhaps it was the car phone that made the attacker think cop. Stuart said the assailant was a thin, five-foot-ten-inch African-American man in his late twenties or early thirties who wore a black baseball cap and running suit, and talked in a raspy voice.

With the mayor and the media breathing down the police department's neck, the hunt for a black killer became a police rampage through the Mission Hill housing project. Fast-moving detectives jammed up any and all black males with violent records, and squeezed informants until idle talk by teenagers pointed them toward a convicted felon named William Bennett, who had armed robbery but not murder in his background. But police suspected him anyway.

For the first month, Stuart was hospitalized, moving from critical condition to stable. But there were times while he was convalescing that he seemed oddly disconnected from the loss of his wife and prematurely born son, who had died within days of the attack.

But the severity of his wound backed up his story. Flynn immediately ordered "every available" officer to work the case. One measure of the near panic was that, on the day after the shooting, two dozen policemen converged on a house in Roxbury because someone saw a man carrying a gun. No one was held, not the least because the police had no ballistics to go on, and no murder weapon. It turned out that Matthew Stuart, one of Charles's brothers, had the gun.

When the initial police overkill subsided, the search for a black culprit was led by a small group of hard-nosed detectives who, seizing on braggadocio by teenagers about *bad* Willie Bennett, focused on the thirty-nine-year-old man. He was more a thief than a murderer, but he was deemed the one. He was a convicted felon who lived near the crime scene, and that was good enough. His name was leaked to the press as the key suspect.

Two months after the shooting, Stuart obligingly identified Bennett as "most like" the assailant in a police lineup. The rush to judgment was such that a source told the *Globe* that Bennett had confessed. He was about to be formally indicted in January 1990 when the case was turned on its head in stunning fashion, again playing out on national television.

Charles Stuart jumped off the Tobin Bridge.

The fur-coat salesman was a casual husband and stone-cold killer. He had assassinated his wife in a mad plan to get out of a deteriorating marriage. His grave wound had been a screw-up of what was intended to be a minor injury to lend credence to his tale about a black hijacker.

Stuart's younger brother Matthew, who was part of the murder plot and had disposed of the murder weapon, an obstruction of justice for which he would go to jail, buckled under the weight of watching an innocent man be railroaded for the murder of his sister-in-law. He began talking to police about the unthinkable—that Stuart had murdered his pregnant wife. The night before Bennett was expected to be indicted, Charles Stuart told Matthew that he knew the police were closing in on him. A feckless man too impatient for divorce had taken the path of least resistance for the last time.

The shock waves instantly shattered the political landscape. Among several reverberations, the suicide plunge showed how ready the Boston police were to browbeat an innocent black man to "clear" a red-hot case involving a white man and woman. It did collateral damage to Flynn's fragile unity theme of Boston coming together. Even Mel King moved into outright opposition, hosting an emergency meeting of black leaders at his house to press for a federal civil rights investigation of the police department.

And the unflappable US attorney, Wayne Budd, the first African-American to hold the office in Massachusetts, briefly bobbled the hot-potato case. While he issued a harsh report on the police tactics in the Stuart case, he was sharply criticized by civil rights specialists for not indicting marauding detectives.

While Budd didn't take action, it was not because he didn't see the case clearly. When he released his report, he pinpointed the key questions central to making a criminal civil rights case:

Did Boston police attempt to frame Bennett by coercing witnesses into providing false information?

Did they use false evidence against witnesses friendly to Bennett?

Did they falsify information to get search warrants?

Even as Budd concluded otherwise, his report indicated that Boston detectives had done all those things. The thorough report ended with a hollow thud—somebody should be fired. But that was a police matter.

Budd tossed the hot potato to Roache, who gave it to Internal Affairs, the renowned graveyard of misconduct complaints. Once there, the IAD ignored Budd's findings of witness intimidation and phony evidence. Its report simply found the police more credible than the witnesses, and that was that. The only measure taken was that the lead officer was disciplined for "inappropriate use of language."

Peter O'Malley was the homicide detective in charge of the investigation, and when one witness under duress volunteered to take a lie detector test, O'Malley said the only lie detector he used was "this guy sitting next to me"—Billy Dunn, a police officer notorious for his rough style in Mission Hill. The witness knew Dunn. He "hurt people."

Bennett's girlfriend, the mother of his daughter, was interrogated for hours in the back room of an apartment and berated repeatedly as a "stupid bitch" for associating with Bennett. She asked to be excused to go to the bathroom, but O'Malley refused, leaving her to wet herself.

The reaction of black leaders was swift and sometimes shrill. Flynn tried to defuse it with personal appeals, but the mistakes were multiple and the hurt too deep. Emotions ran high on both sides, with City Hall rallying to the police under siege.

The Stuart case became what Flynn had diligently sought to avoid— an incendiary black-white conflict. While he could spin most problems, drowning them in hyperbole and good intentions, he was stuck with the police overreaction that was due in part to his ordering all hands into the manhunt. It put him on the spot on his core issue of equal treatment for all races and classes.

In the aftermath of the Stuart case, one member of the NAACP said police and the mayor had "turned a community upside down with the virtual consent of an entire nation, violating every constitutional right of thousands of black males who were searched."

But the longer, more measured view came from Mel King, who was able to stand back a bit even when the rhetoric was boiling over. "I think people who are white in this city need to look deep down in themselves and examine where they came from on this. We all have to take a serious look at . . . the way we relate and treat each other."

But even a philosophical Mel King couldn't mitigate Mickey Roache, who seemed to sequester himself deeper in his office while his patron, the mayor, sidestepped nearly everything except his reelection in 1991. Although time took some sting out of the Stuart debacle, a basic trust with the African-American community got damaged along with the trampled crime scene.

The election of 1991 was a textbook version of the political maxim that you need someone to beat someone. Ed Doherty was not someone.

Despite Stuart and police disarray, two terms of surface progress in race relations and genuine improvement in blue-collar morale if not in pocketbooks were more than enough to propel Flynn to a historic victory. The problems bubbled but evaporated, no match for Flynn's campaign juggernaut. The mayor wanted a landslide to buff his national profile for a high-level job if a Democrat won back the White House the next year. Like most mayors, he had become restless dealing with the same obstinate problems that were exacerbated by a sudden recession that stopped Boston development in its tracks. Ray Flynn looking for a new job became the elephant in the room that no one wanted to talk about.

Reelection was never in doubt. A resounding mandate was the mission. Flynn was so ensconced that there was some concern in his camp that his only opponent would be a black activist who would have no chance of winning but could harp on the lack of real progress in race issues in Boston—a galling criticism with the mayor.

And then along came Edward Doherty. He was president of the Boston Teachers Union, which gave him just enough heft to get into the race. But the thing he lacked, which was so outlandish it hadn't happened in a final election for at least a half century, was having held elective office before. He'd had only one other campaign—a failed run for state representative two decades earlier. The only other distant contender was Reverend Graylan Ellis-Hagler, the founding pastor of the United Community Church in Roxbury.

It was the perfect lineup for the biggest victory margin in modern Boston mayoral history—75 percent. In the preliminary election, Flynn lost only 1 precinct, out of 252. It was in Ward 11, Precinct 1—the police-ransacked Mission Hill. In the final, Flynn got 'em all. It was Exhibit A in the case that an incumbent mayor of Boston with an intense, narrow base of city workers was impregnable.

Flynn's rout was abetted by Doherty, who, at one point, had to deny that he was a plant.

Even at that, the mayor didn't take anything for granted. He went at it with his usual speed—flat-out in his battered black station wagon, making ten campaign stops a day, giving stump spiels that were more pep talks than speeches, delivered in flat nasal perorations. There were no debates, pointed questions, new promises, television ads, or even coattails for friendly council candidates. As always, it was a solo act, a throwback to the old-time campaigns when small rallies and house parties were all there was. There were the usual complaints of Flynn grandstanding and abandoning candidates down the ballot.

The only question out of the landslide was how far it would take the mayor. What was next. Governor? Big national job? Or would he be just another Irish pol from South Boston who ran aground?

While flynn focused on his helter-skelter campaign, Mickey Roache rattled around in a parallel universe, relegated to the shadows of a City Hall in election mode.

Until the next broadside. In the wake of troubling questions raised by the Stuart case, the *Globe* dug into police methods and ethos in a 1991 series that showed the consequences of slapdash detective work. Boston lagged behind other major cities in arrests and prosecutions because police bungled the basics of crime detection, and supervisory oversight. The most glaring problem was the inability to make cases stand up in court, with murders pleaded down to manslaughter at a disproportionate rate.

The public-relations ripples forced a single-minded mayor to pull the station wagon over to the curb long enough to deal with the Mickey problem. He adopted the old ploy of throwing a PR problem to a blue-ribbon commission that would eventually issue palliative recommendations that were carefully placed on a shelf. In this case, it postponed any reckoning until Flynn was reelected.

But delay was about all Flynn accomplished by appointing the redoubtable Boston barrister James St. Clair to lead the inquiry. No figurehead, he. St. Clair undertook his assignment in May, and his commission presented its findings in January 1992—two months after Flynn's landslide.

St. Clair got the mayor's third term off to a rough start. Flynn received much more than he bargained for—a truly independent commission that called for Mickey's head and hoisted the mayor on his own petard. The report still rankles Flynn loyalists, who feel St. Clair exceeded his mandate and fell prey to Roache's enemies within the command staff.

In any event, St. Clair validated the *Globe*'s report and backed Flynn into a corner by calling for Roache's removal and a citizen review board as an antidote to a hapless internal affairs division that had been especially ineffective in dealing with police abuses in the Stuart case.

Indeed, the series cited ham-fisted crime-scene work in the Stuart case that compounded the original rush to judgment. Even if Bennett was the culprit, the crime scene was so bruised that it was just about certain that none of the physical evidence would have stood up. And to make matters worse, search warrants in the case had been falsified as the investigation blundered on.

When Flynn came in from the campaign trail to deal with more police blues, his hasty blue-ribbon fix turned out to be one of the worst political decisions of his career. He turned to one of the lions of the Massachusetts bar in St. Clair, a rainmaker in the white-shoe law firm of Hale & Door, whose distinguished career included representing Richard Nixon during Watergate.

It's unclear what Flynn thought St. Clair was going to do to defuse public dismay with inept police leadership and rogue cops. But it couldn't have been what he got. Which was a scathing 150-page report alleging severe mismanagement in virtually every facet of police work and a conclusion that Roache was totally ineffectual as a leader.

And, after word had leaked about how critical the report was going to be, Flynn didn't do himself any favors when he packed St. Clair's press conference with hecklers. It was a rowdy crowd when St. Clair and six other commission members began presenting their recommendations to catcalls. It was all put in further relief by the panel's aplomb. The protesters didn't just lose; they looked bad losing.

With his inaugural in bad juxtaposition with the St. Clair commission, the mayor's limelight dimmed to gray. He was backed into doing something he'd said he'd never do—bring in a strong number-two man to headquarters to restore order in the house and to put the police imbroglio behind him. On a cold day in February 1992, he brought back to Boston the ascendant William Bratton, a former Boston cop who, at forty-five, had already been chief of three major departments. Bratton had "heir apparent" written all over him and wanted to be number two as much as Nelson Rockefeller had wanted to be vice president.

Bratton came home from a tour as chief of the New York City transit authority. And headquarters went from media-shy to media hound. While a permanent frost developed between Bratton and Roache at police headquarters, it was off Ray Flynn's screen. The mayor began moving on the national stage, looking for his own landing spot.

After sitting on the 1992 presidential primary fence for perhaps too long, dallying with dark horse Tom Harkin of Iowa and then with the ambivalent Mario Cuomo and even with Ross Perot, Flynn became a dedicated disciple of Bill Clinton in the home stretch. He was a latecomer, but tried to make up for it with a head-down basketball sprint for a new president of the United States. Flynn logged thirty-seven straight days on the campaign trail, a more committed than charismatic stumper in stolid search of blue-collar Reagan Democrats in a dozen states.

Combined with the campaign whirlwind, the mayor thought he could parlay his showcase job as president of the National Conference of Mayors to head the US Housing and Urban Development agency or the Department of Labor. But they weren't a good fit for a guy who hated time behind any desk. He was in the running for ambassador to Ireland for a while, but that fell to someone with a bigger chit.

Even with all the back-channel static, Flynn never acknowledged he had tired of being mayor. It was heresy to suggest it then or now. Decades later, his answer is the same—he loved the job every minute he had it. Yet, for a year, he could be seen clinging to his perch while in a crouch to fly away. For he had to know this: no one much cares what an ex-mayor has to say about anything—unless it's Collins grousing about White the prima donna, or Kevin calling Ray a boozer.

It was an especially fretful time for Flynn, because he had no soft chair waiting for him in academia as White and Collins did. Nor a law practice or an insurance agency. And definitely not the corporate boards that greeted Yankee mayors after their noblesse-oblige service. Flynn had been a parole officer and a substitute teacher before beginning a quarter century of elected office. He was a paratrooper who liked being surrounded a lot more than being back at headquarters looking at maps. He needed some prestige for his stout ego, and some steady income for a family of six children. It was a tall order that had him scuffling and his administration somewhat adrift.

Even Thomas O'Connor, the gentle dean of Boston historians and a native of South Boston, described Flynn's job search as a "frantic and, at times, almost paranoid" endeavor. He wrote that the looming void was "frightening" to a robust man still in his early fifties.

Finally, three months after Clinton took office in 1993, Flynn took what he could get: the ambassadorship to the Vatican. He chewed on whether it was grand enough in title and remuneration. He liked the idea that he would be an Irishman in what had been a Boston Brahmin job, following Henry Cabot Lodge Jr., who served under President Nixon, and Charles Francis Adams under President Hoover. But even after he said yes on Saint Patrick's Day, he went back and forth to Washington seeking a larger budget and a bigger diplomatic role. Even after Ray announced his ascension at the Gates of Heaven Church with his wife and children, no one was quite sure he would go until he got on the plane. That took three more months.

It made for a busy June in Boston. Roache finally quit, and Bratton was fully in. Flynn moved to Rome and immediately began thinking about running for governor. But it all brought some cover for Roache, who was able to step down and announce for mayor on the same day. With Flynn's slow-motion exit, the special election to succeed him had already drawn a large field, with Roache jumping in last. Roache said he'd had a grand time as police commissioner, but he listed his service with the joyless precision of a prison sentence. Eight years, four months, and twenty-four days. He would finish seventh in a field of eight for mayor. But he rebounded the next cycle to top the City Council at-large slate for four terms in a row before settling snugly into the obscurity of being Suffolk County registrar of deeds.

And Thomas Menino, Flynn's ally on the City Council, had received a big boost when Flynn informed him of his impending departure and urged Menino to maneuver into the council president's slot, which would make him acting mayor when Flynn left—and give him the enormous advantage of an almost-incumbent in the fall election. Menino would become an enduring institution in his own right.

Before Flynn left, almost as a reflex he threw a last elbow at his would-be successors by extending Bratton's tenure to a full four-year term—much to the dismay of the contenders, who wanted a sixty-day appointment so they could get their own man in place if elected. But it made little difference, as it was to be a short term for the driven Bratton. Within five months he returned to New York City as police commissioner under the newly elected Rudy Giuliani. They coexisted to national plaudits until the mayor thought Bratton was getting too much credit for the dramatically falling crime rate. Bratton's last high-profile beat was commissioner in Los Angeles.

As for Ray, there would be one last reminder that race was always lurking beneath the Boston terrain. In May 1993, after hearing of trouble brewing at South Boston High, he raced to the school in time to see a déjà-vu race riot tumbling outside, with two hundred whites and blacks having at it in the schoolyard. Flynn got hit in the neck with a rock, and though he was treated and released from a hospital that day, it would leave him with a pinched neck nerve that required treatment on and off for years. It was an omen as he headed off to Rome that his Boston chapter was not completed and that there would be painful problems to pull him back in.

In another portent, Flynn was only in Rome a matter of months before there were trial balloons about him running for governor in November 1994. It was a telling sign that things were less than ethereal in Vatican City. The restless mayor chafed under the State Department's strictures on Flynn's freewheeling notion of personal diplomacy. And after a decade of calling all the shots, Flynn found out he had bean-counting bureaucrats as his boss. His plan to return in March to be in several Saint Patrick's Day parades—and stoke his political plans—was summarily overruled by the State Department as blatant politicking on duty.

His protocol peccadillo and outlandish plan to begin a gubernatorial campaign while ambassador were ominous signs of things to come. Flynn would soon be commuting home to deal with financial disarray, both personal and political. It seemed his long-standing campaign treasurer was a thief.

The story burst forth in the spring of 1994 when Flynn's exchequer, Douglas deRusha, stood accused of embezzling more than $500,000 while the distracted mayor gave him carte blanche as he bustled about running the city. It left the ambassador trying to do damage control from a continent away.

There was a blizzard of cross-charges about Flynn being in on it and running a slush fund while mayor and ambassador—allegations that never held up. While he was never charged with a crime, the bottom lines were all bad for the new ambassador. His seat-of-the-pants modus operandi had left him at the mercy of a hustler who clipped $500,000 in campaign funds, mostly to buy a Beacon Hill condo for himself and live the good life.

And that wasn't the worst of it. The state investigation found that one of Flynn's closest advisers, who oversaw city development and was deeply involved in raising campaign funds while holding vague authority over Flynn's personal expenses, was on the take. Joseph Fisher had taken a total of $50,000 in free renovations for homes in South Boston and Plymouth from a city contractor and for accepting a substantial cut-rate price for a family wedding reception.

When the tumult wound down, Fisher went to federal prison and Ray Flynn had to pay the state $10,000 for making personal use of $12,500 in campaign funds that included a family vacation to Disney World. Investigators looked hardest at how Flynn could pay tuitions for six children, and found he was barely able to swing it by refinancing his modest Southie home three times. And the embarrassing brouhaha cost

Flynn $600,000 in legal fees, which came from his heavily audited and nearly depleted campaign chest. The final word on his finances was pejorative but not criminal. State Attorney General L. Scott Harshbarger proclaimed it a "mess."

After some heat had left the deRusha fiasco, Flynn told the *Globe* it was a good idea at the time and he took a stab at mitigating the fact that he got snookered. DeRusha, he said, "had time to volunteer, knew finances, knew bookkeeping. I mean, hey, the price was right. I mean, we couldn't afford anyone else anyways." But a fox had been put in charge of the henhouse.

Flynn was always underestimated and nobody's fool, but he went against the evidence when he refused to accept that he had peaked as mayor of Boston, a job that meshed perfectly with his rambunctious nature. After a year abroad, his plans for governor were in ashes and his diplomatic career in early eclipse. When he first arrived in Rome, he thought he would have a broad cachet as a roving spokesman for Catholicism, but he was kept on a short leash by the State Department and the White House.

The bad fit took a worse turn when a tipsy Ray, home on liberty in 1997 and still talking about running for governor a year later, had several glasses of wine in the North End before bumping into *Globe* political reporter Walter Robinson, who was known for not taking prisoners. It was a fateful encounter.

Robinson began working a story linking Flynn's long-standing reputation for taking a drink and poor reviews as ambassador. Working with a reporter who went to Rome and another in Washington, Robinson's detailed report about a pub-crawling envoy and diplomatic waif sparked sustained protests about Catholic-bashing and character assassination.

The criticism persisted despite some undisputed accounts of Flynn having been seen intoxicated in public around Boston and getting mixed reviews at best on his stay at the Vatican. There was ample evidence that Flynn had grown indifferent to the paper-shuffling and demitasse aspects of the job, and had turned a deaf ear at a refined listening post where discretion and protocol were prized above all. He was at the office so little in the last months of a four-year stint that he had to call an aide one night to get the building's entry code. And Flynn's outspoken style and petulant pronouncements on political subjects drew two State Department reprimands.

In addition, the story's history of Flynn's public drinking wasn't much contested. But the accounts attributed to clergymen about pub crawls in Rome were vehemently denied by the priests themselves, who said they were misquoted and dismayed. *Globe* editors backed away from that portion of the story, and there was a sense in the political world that the report went too far. A segment sympathetic to Flynn was aired on *60 Minutes*. Robinson's rejoinder was that Flynn's history was fair game and highly relevant because he was considering a gubernatorial run.

The story remains bitterly resented by Flynn loyalists, who see it as another example of elitist disparagement and an unfair capstone to a career that should be celebrated for its high attainment. James Vrabel, a former Flynn aide, said it has become the last word on Flynn's reputation, over-shadowing myriad examples of a resuscitated city. "Who else ever got followed out of town to an ambassadorship?" he asked with narrowing eyes.

After he resigned as ambassador, Flynn wasn't seeking vindication so much as redemption. His run for governor in 1998, with little money or staff, soon fell apart. Months later, Joseph P. Kennedy II decided to bow out of the congressional district that included a slice of Boston, prompting a stampede of succession by nine candidates, including Flynn. The mayor became an early favorite because of his high name recognition. But his prospects faltered after all the other candidates formed a chorus about Ray's strident opposition to abortion.

It came down to an eerie last stand by a desperate ex-mayor in the final hours, as dusk fell on a rain-swept bus station in Roxbury. There he stood on a street corner hollering at passing cars and buses to give him a vote because of what he'd done for them. He was the only white candidate who could have campaigned in Dudley Square, but he was whistling past the graveyard.

Brian Mooney, a *Globe* columnist, was there with him. He wrote that "it was a striking tableau: Ray Flynn, coatless, his open collar white dress shirt clinging to his skin from the drenching rain, prowling a . . .

traffic island, imploring African-American and Latino motorists to help him. 'I need your vote,' he roared."

Mooney asked him what he would do if he lost. "We'll figure that out later. No contingency plans."

Today, Flynn lives in the only house he's ever owned in Southie, the one he bought for $11,000 in 1968. It's white, wood framed, crammed, a little beat up. But it gets good sun on a dead-end street a few blocks from the L Street bathhouse. He laments that the street has lost some long-time neighbors, one of them to foreclosure and two to condo conversions. It has brought an unwelcome surge in population and traffic. The street is a private way, so there was a time when every house had a permanent parking space in front of it. But now there are too many cars for too few spaces.

He's wistful about the days when there were seventeen kids on the street from Irish, Polish, and Italian families, and then about how fast it all changed. "Girls playing jump rope, boys playing stickball. No cars, so it's safe. But boom, three condos in one buildings; three in another, four across the street. I hurt my leg and couldn't park my car down the street, and so we've been fighting about that. Forty-something years in front of my house, but they don't care about that. No Saint Patrick's Day parties. No baby carriages. All you see is Volvos."

While one mayor for ten years has had to gimp and grouse his way home for want of parking, it's not entirely fanciful to imagine Kevin White cordoning off lower Mount Vernon Street to assure smooth egress to his Beacon Hill town house. And it's a fact that only a few hundred yards away from White's home, US senator John Kerry had an inconvenient hydrant moved from in front of his town house in Louisburg Square.

Flynn laughs it off as the way it is in Boston's endless tale of two cities. He reflected on his life and career one wintry morning in his tight, sunlit living room, so true to his roots that he's sitting on them.

"I'm full circle," he said with a grin. "I started with a bunch of kids and a lousy car and a little money in the bank. Now I've got a bunch of kids, a lousy car, and no money in the bank." But no regrets about the things he did for working families out of a beat-up black station wagon.

Epilogue

THE GREENWAY

THE Boston of the twenty-first century has an entirely different premise from the bustling Yankee harbor and environs of 160 years ago, where the Fitzgeralds and the Curleys and the Kennedys and so many Irish immigrant families found themselves trying to make sense of their hostile new home and struggling slowly forward to dominance.

After a half century of subjugation, the Boston of the Puritans became a battleground: entrenched Yankee versus combative Irishman, with all other parties reduced to supporting roles. But these second-generation Irish weren't tenant farmers tugging on their forelocks at the landlord's stoop; they were Americans now, and they meant to claim their full share in its glittering promise: jobs, education, religious tolerance.

The Irish ruled Boston for nearly a century, first grabbing their fair share and then some with Honey Fitzgerald, after being as shut out as any Alabama sharecropper.

Then happily enduring the brash avarice of James Michael Curley while thinking they were getting even.

Then unhappily finding themselves on the brink of bankruptcy amid decrepitude before righting themselves with John Hynes.

Then lurching forward for better and worse with the rough renewal of John Collins and Ed Logue.

Finally, a brief seduction by the flash and dash of Kevin White before busing forced many to the suburbs, a wrenching period when embittered neighborhoods felt overlooked and exploited.

By the time they got the quintessential neighborhood mayor in Ray Flynn, the Hibernian house was emptying out and turning a different hue. But as Curley had been mayor of the down and out, Flynn was mayor of the working poor.

Today, Ray Flynn, who may be the last mayoral mick, sits somewhat glumly among the spreading gentry in his native land, his street a Volvo parking lot. He mulls the irony that his post-busing policies made city life as attractive for upper-income newcomers as for thousands of low-income families he placed in affordable homes paid for with linkage money. But if yuppies have been lured to his safer streets and refurbished parks, so be it. His faded blueprint has been used for improvements now taken for granted.

The new landscape is in the firm purview of Flynn's successor, Thomas Menino, once a tireless councilor who has become mayor for life, heading toward twenty years after turning back a succession of Irish challengers. His gruff demeanor, mumbling speech, and instinctive intelligence are reminiscent of Chicago's Richard Daley. He's a shrewd neighborhood product who goes dawn to dusk, operating with political antennae that zero in on simmering problems before they become big, bad ones. But he's also a famously petty patriarch, prone to ego-driven fights with developers who think they're bigger deals than he is. Yet an indomitable mayor is somehow less relevant in today's Boston.

The shifting demographics and socioeconomic disparities have left Menino omnipotent and yet less influential. His policies and decisions affect a shrinking segment of the population. The high earners send their children to private schools and are unconcerned about implacable dropout rates and chronically inferior test scores. If they bother voting, they gravitate to Menino as a known quantity they seldom have to deal with. At the other end of the spectrum, low-income families are trapped by the bad circumstances of crime and ethnic confinement, and seldom vote. The mayor has become electorate-proof, operating behind the firewall of city workers and friends and relatives who comprise about 60 percent of the mayoral vote. Menino entered his fifth term in 2009 after his closest election in nearly two decades—and still won by eight percentage points. A contested rout is now a tight race.

One measure of the bare-bones mayoral electorate is that the hottest race in decades drew one third fewer voters in Boston than a special election to replace the late Ted Kennedy did just two months later. Two relative unknowns, Scott Brown and Martha Coakley, drew 153,000 voters on a sleeting day in January 2010. The big Boston turnout was part of the shocking end of the Kennedy era, with its straight bloodlines back to Honey Fitz. But nostalgia was out and the underestimated Brown was in, a Republican elected in part to vote against Kennedy's signature issue of health-care reform.

Boston bucked the suburban dissatisfaction to vote Democratic, but it was the broader national questions that stoked the city electorate, marked by a heavier-than-usual turnout in downtown wards.

As major elections settle into decided history, blue-collar Boston continues to bob along just above the waterline, bumping occasionally into the conundrum of the cityscape, the what's-*not*-there in their daily life. They appear as elusive dissatisfactions that pop up as a glaring incident and then recede back into a broken status quo.

After all the grief and money, where are the good, safe neighborhood high schools?

How is it that firefighters in one of the most expensive and inefficient departments in the country get huge raises for agreeing to long-overdue drug testing? How does that happen *after* one drunk firefighter and a coked-up one die in a mishandled fire?

Why does the police department have scores of officers whose salaries exceed those of the mayor and governor through overtime abuses? How does that happen year after year?

And why does the fifteen-acre Rose Kennedy Greenway Park above the $22-billion Big Dig remain barren? Lost for years in a clash of city and state jurisdictions, the grass gets cut, but none of the promised public-purpose buildings are in place along its edges.

Big things stay unfixed as the city struggles with a budget dominated by long-term obligations to its main constituency—municipal workers and their benefits and pensions.

And yet.

Downtown is indeed Kevin White's world-class city, a glimmer first discerned by John Hynes and pushed toward grandeur by Ed Logue. Its old Brahmin neighborhoods have uniformly held their value.

The population shift in the last decade produced a good news paradox for Boston stability and diversity. Even as Hispanic immigration exploded, the white population stayed steady.

Boston continued the millennium trend of becoming a "minority majority" city when the white population dropped below 50 percent in 2000 for the first time in its history. The 2010 census saw that decline from 49.5 percent to 47 percent.

But the number of Caucasians remained essentially unchanged at about 290,000.

The debatable premise at mid-decade was that Boston would lose population and that white flight would continue.

Just the opposite occurred.

Boston gained 4.7 percent or 28,000 new Hispanic or Asian residents. It was the first time in 130 years that the city grew faster than the state of Massachusetts as a whole.

And with an assist from the Great Recession's negative effect on job mobility, the number of whites remained unchanged—the first time that happened since 1950, or just before the migration to the suburbs began.

It remains unclear whether the new demographics augur a minority mayor in the near future. Despite the Hispanic surge moving its share of Boston from 14.4 percent to 17.5 percent for a total of 108,000, taking City Hall looks like a distant prospect. The hard facts: Whites still outnumber all the minority groups taken together. Incumbents, as Ray Flynn's and Tom Menino's track records attest, remain invincible. And boring down deeper into the Hispanic bloc finds the numbers soft— nearly one-third are below voting age. In contrast, only 8 percent of the white population is under eighteen.

One thing seems certain: The steady white migration is over. Building on Flynn's programs, Menino's obsessive concerns about city cleanliness and safety have lured empty-nesters and yuppies to downtown neighborhoods that view its restaurants, theaters, nightclubs, and sports venues such as Fenway Park and Boston Garden as an adult playground. That's unlikely to change.

And Boston is not alone in moving back to the future. A Brookings Institution review of fifty-nine American cities with populations of

300,000 or more found either an increase in the white population or a pronounced slowdown of the outward-bound. While it's no panacea for urban ills, city planners say the ethnic equipoise ensures an income mix that promotes livability.

Even the infamous Big Dig has finally paid some dividends.

Its history is not unlike that of Curley's Boston. It tore up the terrain amid corruption, incompetence, and skullduggery where the sticker price was hidden until a governor got himself elected in 1998.

It's apt that the most expensive construction project in American history was hatched in Boston. It was an interminable cost-plus contract that seemed beset by Curley as angry poltergeist. Indeed, it was reminiscent of the larded Quabbin Reservoir contracts in the 1930s that provided Boston's water supply. Yet the aqueduct system has stood the test of time. The Big Dig contract ran longer, going for fifteen years with a final cost now exceeding $22 billion with interest, the most ever for a domestic project. It hasn't been pretty to watch, or even vaguely efficient or economical. Money was poured over problems, and the state overseers were leagues over their heads.

But when it finally got done, after the relentless clouds of dust and a tragic ceiling collapse and leaky tunnels and a fallow topside, the city was mended. The Big Dig is still an epithet. An orphaned triumph. The wonder is that it works at all. But in fact it's a magnificent upgrade, with commuter traffic zipping along underground and a trip to the airport now taking ten minutes instead of at least an hour.

The Greenway, still brimming with promise, has already reunited downtown with the North End. The Big Dig unclogged city streets and, most of all, tore down the moldy green Central Artery that had severed the city from the waterfront and put an entire neighborhood in exile. The artery was a physical and psychological barrier that replicated the bold line the Yankees drew around downtown and Beacon Hill a century earlier.

Even after downtown renewal, many North End denizens never ventured across the ominous highway's dank corridor to the nearby Faneuil Marketplace. Like the forlorn Irish immigrants of the mid-nineteenth century, the later wave of Italians turned their backs on the city and looked steadfastly out to sea. It became the perfect home turf for the local Mafia.

While the North End eventually prospered from federal prosecutions of crime lords and steady gentrification born of its location, it has recently rejoined the city in a way South Boston never will.

Hanover Street, the boulevard that bisects the neighborhood and Boston history, has seen it all and come full circle. The new North End is Ed Logue's kind of town. The renovations are now on rooftops, and the most Italian thing about it is the increasingly pricey restaurants on Hanover Street. Gone most are the children and pile-driving of the Big Dig. There used to be five thousand youngsters. Now there are seven hundred.

Despite the tumult of steady gentrification and the pulsating and seemingly endless construction noise along its edge, it has held its population at a steady twelve thousand. The other constants have been two distinct trends—a rise in family income and a decline in Italian ancestry. Between 1980 and 2000, while South Boston and Charlestown stayed vastly Irish, the Italian quotient in the North End plummeted from well over half to less than a third. The median household income has gone from $15,000 a year to nearly $60,000, held down at that by older Italians in elderly housing projects. It was still about 50 percent higher than the city as a whole.

It's all bittersweet to the Italian natives, even as the DINKs (double income, no kids) do their level best to blend into the old Europe milieu that attracted them in the first place. And the natives are hardly bereft, having cashed in on the real estate boom and the steady supply of big spenders. Somehow it has been the easiest assimilation in Boston.

Mama Anna's Restaurant, at the tail end of Hanover Street, is a snapshot of Boston's new reality. For decades it subsisted in the heavy shadow of the Central Artery, only to be engulfed by Big Dig construction dust for fifteen years. But now it's back, with an expansive sidewalk café that edges easily into the new park.

Thus, Hanover Street. Home to Cotton Mather and Paul Revere

and Rose Kennedy. Once lined by merchant mansions that devolved into Irish tenements. A street where Thomas Fitzgerald hawked fish. And his son John talked everyone's ear off. And the Mafia came of age in a bloody shoot-out with Irish bootleggers. And blanketed for nearly two decades in Big Dig soot.

A promenade once more.

ACKNOWLEDGMENTS .

In the well-plowed field of Irish history, both here and there, the first acknowledgment is the homage due to all the historians who have provided context and insight for others to follow and build upon. It is a layered process that demands deference and gratitude. I've been daunted by several of the works that I've used and will give them each obeisance.

But there was no greater resource for me in the here and now than the energetic and knowledgeable Lisa Tuite, the head librarian at the *Boston Globe*. She was immense in fact-checking but even more so for her brainstorming on where to find material not readily at hand. She's a marvel of ingenuity and practical advice, as in "The clips don't go back that far; better write around it."

And for sheer knowledge of the depth and breadth of the Boston landscape, James Vrabel is the head of the class. He's enthralled by its history and has been a direct participant as an aide to Ray Flynn focusing on issues such as affordable housing, and then as in-house historian for the Boston Redevelopment Authority. He referred me to books to read, people to talk to, and places to find information. I also made use of his extraordinary chronological database that goes back centuries—a sort of time machine to navigate through the city's history. It can be sorted for geography, major figures, events, quotations, you name it. It's a companion to his book *When in Boston*, but it has ten times as much information. I'm especially grateful to him, along with BRA economist John Avault, for refining my understanding of the socioeconomic effects of the busing era on working-class families.

And to my editor at Crown Publishers, Sean Desmond, who brought me the outline of an idea that he nurtured with patience and perspicacity. Throughout what turned into a four-year project, he was upbeat and reassuring. His emphasis on clarity and readability was balanced by a willingness to let an author try different things and drill some dry holes. For better or worse, he gave me my head.

To Thomas Mulvoy, an esteemed colleague at the *Boston Globe* known for his passion for local history and for his strong, sure pencil. A former managing editor, he did me the honor of a "Mul Read" and caught a bushel of things, big and small.

And to the *Globe*'s premier political reporter, Brian Mooney, who has few peers when it comes to knowing the players and terrain throughout state and local government. He was a sounding board throughout my research and writing.

To Marty Nolan, one of the original Boston raconteurs, who was a force in Washington as a *Globe* columnist before he became editor of the paper's editorial page and then resumed political commentary from San Francisco. He's a quick and deft writer I've long admired and who was good enough to send me a hefty carton of books on Irish and Boston history from his personal library.

NOTES

Chapter 1, "Famine's Progeny"

It took me a while to get unclogged for the introductory chapter, getting some-what overrun by all the books on the famine in Ireland and the hostile half century that awaited immigrants in Boston. It was vital context for all that fol-lowed, but all that followed was my main focus. I wanted to give the formative decades their due but not get bogged down before getting to the political fig-ures. Then I correlated the unhappy fact that the leading cause of death of Irish fathers in Boston was industrial accidents with James Michael Curley's father dying on the job. And Fitzgerald's father arriving in the North End at the height of the Know Nothings' reign of terror to endure life in the first urban slum in America. So, the struggles of two "Das" helped show the way through the early history.

Books most instructive for the predation years in Boston included Thomas O'Connor's biography on John Fitzpatrick, the Bishop of Boston, who was a seminal figure as the Irish withstood the worst of the bigotry and deprivation: Thomas O'Connor, *Fitzpatrick's Boston, 1846–1866*.

As well: William V. Shannon's brilliant social history, *The American Irish: A Political and Social Portrait*; Oscar Handlin's *Boston's Immigrants, 1790–1880: A Study of Acculturation*; early immigrant tales in Alan Lupo's *Liberty's Chosen Home: The Politics of Violence in Boston*; and bits and parts from the early years of Doris Kearns Goodwin's work on the Fitzgeralds (*The Fitzgeralds and the Kennedys*) and Jack Beatty's biography of Curley (*The Rascal King*). Finally, John Mulkern's *The Know-Nothing Party in Massachusetts: The Rise and Fall of a People's Movement*. And information on my own family's immigration from Ireland dur-ing the famine was greatly augmented by Marie Daly, a dogged researcher at the New England Geneological Society in Boston.

Helpful books for "over there" are:

Edward Laxton's *The Famine Ships: The Irish Exodus to America*.
R. Dudley Edwards and T. Desmond Williams, eds., *The Great Famine*.
William Adams's *Ireland and Irish Emigration to the New World from 1815 to the Famine*.
Thomas Gallagher's *Paddy's Lament, Ireland, 1846–1847: Prelude to Hatred*.

Kerby A. Miller's *Emigrants and Exiles: Ireland and the Irish Exodus to North America.*

Robert Kee's, *Ireland: A History.*

Chapters 2, "Shawn A Boo," and 3, "The Good Shepherd" (Fitzgerald and Lomasney)

The Fitzgerald era is captured by Doris Kearns Goodwin's *The Fitzgeralds and the Kennedys: An American Saga.* Her book offers a comprehensive and readable treatment of lineage and lore. It's augmented by Thomas O'Connor, *The Boston Irish: A Political History;* John Henry Cutler's *Honey Fitz: Three Steps from the White House;* and Edward Kennedy's memoir *True Compass,* for boyhood recollections of Grandpa Fitzgerald. Background from this period also comes from a biography of James Jackson Storrow by Henry Greenleaf Pearson titled *Son of New England* and another Brahmin "contemporary," *The Late George Aply,* a novel by John P. Marquand. Useful books on Fitzgerald's mentor cum rival Martin Lomasney are Leslie Ainley's *Boston Mahatma,* and the tenor of the times from Joseph F. Dinneen's novel *Ward Eight* as well as news clips from the *Boston Globe* library.

Chapters 4, "Himself," and 5, "The Badger Game" (Curley and Coakley)

When it comes to James Michael Curley, there's Jack Beatty and everyone else. Beatty provides the authoritative work on the real and mythical Curley. His exhaustive research includes a review of sixty years' worth of relevant Boston newspaper stories. *The Rascal King: The Life and Times of James Michael Curley (1874–1958)* stands alone. Several other works lean heavily Curley's way. Books such as Joseph F. Dinneen's *Purple Shamrock, the Honorable James Michael Curley of Boston* and Curley's own autobiography, *I'd Do It Again, a Record of All My Uproarious Years,* live up to their titles, as does *Personal Incidents in over Forty Years with James Michael Curley* by Thomas Galvin. A more neutral and contextual book is *Campaigning with James Michael Curley* by Edmund B. Sullivan, Barry Mushlin, and Robert L. Colt. More recently, *James Michael Curley: A Short Biography,* a fond remembrance by William Bulger, a former president of the Massachusetts senate. Another laudatory history focusing on Curley's stewardship during the Depression is Charles Trout's *Boston, the Great Depression and the New Deal.* Also, in connection with Curley's successful legal action against a Boston publisher, several Massachusetts Supreme Judicial Court decisions on criminal libel were instructive along with *New York Times* articles on US

Supreme Court decisions refining the law on libel and commentary in the 1960s and 1970s. Lastly, an interview with Jack Beatty.

Curley's rival rogue, Daniel Coakley, is captured best as the featured eccentric in a marvelous anthology by Francis Russell. *The Knave of Boston and Other Ambiguous Massachusetts Characters* was supplemented by several extensive Massachusetts Supreme Judicial Court decisions in the 1920s on Coakley's disbarment and the court's removal of Nathan Tufts as Middlesex County district attorney and Joseph Pelletier as Suffolk County district attorney. As well, *Globe* news stories on Coakley's acquittal on related extortion charges and his later impeachment as a governor's councilor. Lastly, I drew from a collection of Coakley's radio rants in 1930 as transcribed and published by P. Edward Fardy of 60 Scollay Square, Boston.

Chapters 6, "Whispering Johnny," and 7, "All or Nothing" (Hynes and the West End)

As Jack Beatty dominated the Curley scene, so, too, does Thomas O'Connor capture the Hynes era. His book, *Building a New Boston, Politics and Urban Renewal, 1950–1970,* is a groundbreaking overview of the city's renewal struggle. Before him, no one had pulled it all together, leaving the history as scattered as an excavated corner of the West End. One important treatment of Hynes's first renewal foray in the West End is found in Herbert Gans's *Urban Villagers: Group and Class in the Life of Italian-Americans,* an updated version of his original research in the 1950s.

On the West End revenue issues, the administration of Mayor Thomas Menino provided access to archives of city records from the 1950s and 1960s. And the *Globe* library spooled up microfiche stories on the early days of urban renewal, especially the West End. One of the articles was the first story ever done by the *Globe*'s investigative team in 1970 on the gamey arrangement between the Boston Redevelopment Authority's board of directors and the operators of city-owned parking lots on the undeveloped portion of the Charles River parcels. Finally, interviews with Mayor Hynes's sons Richard and Jack, author Herbert Gans, developer Jerome Rappaport, and former BRA director Stephen Coyle.

Chapters 8, "Baby-Faced Assassin," and 9, "I Am a Legend" (Collins and Logue)

The administration of John Collins and his BRA director Edward Logue centered on urban renewal and, after it got rolling, the news coverage went from nearly nonexistent to a standard beat at all the Boston papers. There were scores of news stories on renewal in Roxbury, Charlestown, Allston, South End, and the failed effort in South Boston. In addition, there were three major decisions by the Massachusetts Supreme Judicial Court with helpful background on the Prudential Center development.

Collins began with one of the biggest upsets in Boston history but petered out with a shattering defeat, especially in Boston, when he tried to move up to the US Senate. All of his decisive actions—most of them in concert with Logue's renewal initiatives—were copiously chronicled and made available by the *Globe* library. Collins's deputy mayor, Henry Spagnoli, was a reservoir of anecdotes and commentary.

These books also provided insight into the politics of the era and the renewal process:

> Murray B. Levin's *The Alienated Voter: Politics in Boston;* Thomas
> O'Connor's *Boston Irish* and *Building a New Boston;* Langley
> Keyes's *The Rehabilitation Planning Game: A Study in the Diversity
> of Neighborhoods;* Alan Lupo, Frank Colcord, and Edmund P.
> Fowler's *Rites of Way: The Politics of Transportation in Boston and the
> U.S. City;* John Stainton's *Urban Renewal and Planning in Boston;*
> John H. Mollenkopf's *The Contested City;* Lawrence A. Kennedy's
> *Planning the City Upon a Hill, Boston Since 1630;* and the final
> report of renewal by Edward J. Logue, development administrator,
> Boston Redevelopment Authority.

Chapters 10, "Whither Boston"; 11, "Maybe Not Wendell from Worcester"; and 12, "Halloween Massacre" (White, Garrity, and Timilty)

The account of the election of 1967 is based largely on *Boston Globe* and *Boston Herald* news stories. Also I interviewed Richard Iantosca, Herbert Gleason, Frank Tivnan, George Regan, Colin Diver, and Mark Shields. Also helpful was material from Stuart E. Weisberg's *Barney Frank: The Story of America's Only Left-Handed, Gay, Jewish Congressman.* And I drew from a penetrating analysis of the Boston schools: Peter Schrag's *Village School Downtown: Politics and Education—A Boston Report.*

In addition to news stories, the busing saga is firmly in the purview of J. Anthony Lukas's masterwork, *Common Ground: A Turbulent Decade in the Lives of Three American Families.* This book was particularly useful in chronicling Colin Diver's journey through White's first term, Louise Day Hicks's encounter with the Reverend Virgil Wood, W. Arthur Garrity's family background and career, and White's meeting with black parents after the first day of busing in 1974. It was augmented by Alan Lupo's inside view of the White administration during the major busing decision in *Liberty's Chosen Home: The Politics of Violence in Boston*. Also I drew from the *Globe's* twenty-five-page special section in 1975 on the first year of busing, as well as a review of Judge W. Arthur Garrity's papers at the University of Massachusetts, Boston, and an interview with former *Globe* political editor Robert Healy.

Busing's aftermath relied in part on Ronald Formisano's *Boston Against Busing: Race, Class, and Ethnicity in the 1960s and 1970s* and Louis P. Masur's *The Soiling of Old Glory: The Story of a Photograph That Shocked America*. The footnote on Elliott Richardson's grand jury pursuit of the contents of William Callahan's safe is documented in *Man of the House: The Life and Political Memoir of Speaker Tip O'Neill* by Thomas P. O'Neill and William Novak. In addition, I conducted an interview with former Massachusetts Department of Education official and dean of Boston University's School of Education, Charles Glenn.

The election of 1975 account is based on news clips from the *Globe* and *Herald*, and from interviews with Robert DiGrazia, Paul Goodrich, Sydney Hanlon, Robert Healy, Edward Jesser, Joseph Timilty, Frank Tivnan, Curtis Wilkie, Mark Shields, and Ralph Whitehead. I also used material from old interviews with Kevin White from 1975 and 1989.

Chapter 13, "Losing Ground"

The updates on White and Timilty were based on *Globe* news stories and interviews with George Regan, Joseph Timilty, and Jack Connors. Again I consulted O'Connor's *Building a New Boston* regarding the Faneuil Marketplace development that Kevin White claims as his own. And George V. Higgins's *Style Versus Substance: Boston, Kevin White and the Politics of Illusion* was a useful resource.

For discussing the state of blue-collar Boston, I drew from *Globe* and *Herald* news stories, US Census data on Boston's population from 1950 to 2000, an analysis of census data on family income from 1970 to 1980 compiled by BRA economist John Avault, and anecdotes from Ronald Formisano's *Boston Against Busing*.

For assessing Boston schools I consulted *Globe* news stories about SAT scores comparing Boston and Massachusetts in 1977 and 1986 and a chart comparing city/state scores from 2000 to 2010. The State Department of Education provided information on city/state dropout rates and achievement test comparisons.

Chapter 14, "Still Broke" (Flynn)

My portrait of Flynn comes from *Globe* and *Herald* news stories; interviews with Raymond Flynn, Stephen Coyle, and James Vrabel; a City Hall report on Flynn's tenure; and finally, once more Thomas O'Connor's *The Boston Irish*.

Epilogue

The information here comes from the Boston Redevelopment Authority statistics on the North End and the 2010 census on Boston.

Index

NOTE: Page numbers in *italics* indicate photographs and illustrations.

97–98, 116–17, 118–19, 129, 161; early political experience, 120–21; family life, 119; and the Government Center, 175; and government reform, 130–31; legacy of, 370, 372–73; mayoral campaigns, 121–24, 124–27, 131–32, 135–36; and Powers, 162; and retirement, 315; and tax policy, 127–30; and urban renewal, 132–35, 136–38, 138–41, 149, 151; work style, 128–29, 130–31
Hynes, Marie, 119, 131
Hynes, Marion, 119
Hynes, Nancy, 119
Hynes, Richard, 119, 127, 140
Hynes, Thomas, 118

Iantosca, Richard, 211–12
immigrant and immigration. *See* demographic shifts; *specific ethnicities and nationalities*
industrialism, 17, 107–8
Infill housing program, 229–31
insurance industry, 130, 163
integration of schools, 183
Internal Affairs Department (IAD), 357–58, 361
Internal Revenue Service (IRS), 166
Irish immigrants and population, 2–23; and anti-immigrant sentiment, 13–17; and class politics, 10–13; and demographic shifts, 321, 375; and the Fitzgerald family, 6–7; and Hynes's mayoral campaign, 126; and Lomasney, 52; and the O'Neill family, 7–10; political legacy of, 370; and political power, 17–23; and the potato blight, 2–6; and race issues, 229; and White's election, 225
Italian immigrants and population: and Curley, 75; and demographic shifts, 33, 321, 375; and Hynes's mayoral campaign, 126; and organized crime, 375; and urban renewal, 134, 149, 181;

and West End redevelopment, 147; and the White/Timilty race, 303

Jackson, Henry "Scoop," 240, 325
Jaffe, Louis, 253
Jagger, Mick, 239
Jamaica Plain, 181, 188, 198, 303
Jean-Louis, André Yvon, 262–63
Jefferson Club, 37
Jeremiah E. Burke School, 268
Jesser, Ed, 286, 288–89
Jesuits, 244
Jewish immigrants and population, 33, 75, 126, 134, 149
Jim Crow segregation, 254
"Jobs for Micks" platform, 18
job training programs, 345, 351–52
John Hancock Mutual Life Insurance Company, 151, 317
Johnson, Lyndon, 205
judicial appointments, 111

Keany, Matthew, 31, 33
Kearney, Dennis, 340
Kelly, Jack, 296, 302, 302n
Kelly, James, 286–87, 296–97, 351
Kelly, John B., 95–96
Kennedy, Brownie, 106
Kennedy, Edward "Teddy": and Brown election, 372; and Fitzgerald, 45–46, 95–96; and mayoral campaigns, 213, 223; and presidential campaigns, 240; and school busing conflict, 256–57, 263; and Timilty, 285; and White, 221, 236–38
Kennedy, John Fitzgerald: and Bartolo, 167; and campaign techniques, 128; and civil rights, 215; and Curley, 96–97; and Fitzgerald, 45; and the Garritys, 245; and school busing conflict, 256–57; Senate election, 113; and urban policy, 205; and White, 220–21
Kennedy, Joseph Patrick, 43, 44–45, 246, 285

ABOUT THE AUTHOR

GERARD O'NEILL was editor of the *Boston Globe*'s investigative team for twenty-five years before retiring to teach journalism at Boston University. He was born in Boston and worked as a political reporter for the *Globe* at the State House and Boston City Hall. He started the New England and Health sections but spent most of his career in investigative work.

With *Globe* colleague Dick Lehr he coauthored *The Underboss: The Rise and Fall of a Mafia Family*, and *Black Mass: The Irish Mob, the FBI, and a Devil's Deal*.

He has won several regional and national reporting awards over the past three decades, including the Pulitzer; the prestigious Associated Press Managing Editors Award in 1977 and 1998; the Scripps Howard Public Service Award for a series on the Massachusetts judiciary; and the Loeb Award for business stories on a series about the Massachusetts pension board.

He was educated at Stonehill College and holds a master's degree in journalism from Boston University. He lives in Back Bay with his wife, Janet. He has two sons and two grandchildren.